THE PEOPLE'S GROCER

THE
PEOPLE'S
GROCER

John G. Schwegmann,

NEW ORLEANS, AND THE MAKING
OF THE MODERN RETAIL WORLD

DAVID CAPPELLO

neutral
ground
press

NEW ORLEANS, LOUISIANA

Neutral Ground Press
PO BOX 791432
New Orleans, LA 70179

First Printing, 2017

ISBN: 978-0-9982443-0-3
Library of Congress Catalog Number: 2016918950

Cappello, David
The people's grocer: John G. Schwegmann, New Orleans, and the making of the modern
retail world. Includes endnotes and index.
1. Schwegmann, John G. (Gerald), 1911-1995. 2. Biography. 3. Retail history.
4. Business history. 5. New Orleans, Louisiana—culture and politics.

Front cover image
Courtesy of Margie Schwegmann-Brown.
Photo credit: Frank B. Moore Photographers / Judy Held, granddaughter.
Front interior image
Pages ii–iii: View of the opening day of business at the Schwegmann's Gentilly
supermarket (November 25, 1957). Photo credit: The Charles L. Frank Studio Collection at
The Historic New Orleans Collection, acc. no. 1994.94.2.1663.
Image insert
Pages 1 (top left, bottom left), 2 (bottom), 3 (top left, top right), 7 (bottom), 9 (top), 10
(bottom): Courtesy of John F. Schwegmann.
Pages 1 (top right, bottom right), 3 (bottom), 4, 5, 6, 7 (top), 8, 9, 10 (top left, top right):
Courtesy of Margie Schwegmann-Brown.
Page 2 (top): Wikimedia Commons.
Pages 11–16: Used by permission of John F. Schwegmann / Margie Schwegmann-Brown.
Ads originally appeared in *New Orleans Times-Picayune* and *New Orleans States-Item*.

Cover and book design by Hilairie Schackai

Printed in Canada

1 3 5 7 9 10 8 6 4 2

neutral
ground
press

www.thepeoplesgrocer.com

Dedicated to all those who once lived the spirit of
"Makin' Groceries—Schwegmann Style"

Contents

Fortune's wheel turns faster than that of a mill, and those that yesterday were up on top today are down on the ground.

—SANCHO PANZA IN *DON QUIXOTE*, CERVANTES

What you leave behind is not what is engraved in stone monuments, but what is woven into the lives of others.

—PERICLES

Preface

THE CLOSEST I EVER CAME to a bona fide Elvis sighting occurred in a Schwegmann's parking lot on Annunciation Street. I swear, from out of nowhere, as I sat there waiting in the car, he suddenly appeared! Yes, it was the undead Presley himself, the former hip-swiveling honky-tonk heartthrob, the patron saint of blue-eyed soul, the King, leaning his now-robust frame against the front door of a worse-for-wear Ford Fairlane as he casually combed back his rockabilly locks. Shortly, a fading beauty in a skin-tight polyester outfit joined him—and off they drove into old New Orleans.

At that moment I was utterly struck with the Schwegmann mystique. Impassioned by this retail romanticism, I soon began to notice that Elvis and his lady friend were not the only celebrities who haunted the locally famous supermarkets. Indeed, each shopper in the entire cast of customers seemed to exude a certain star-quality—a charisma emanating from the genuine expression of deeply rooted and, by normal American standards, slightly exotic folkways. Basically, Schwegmann stores effused cultural authenticity, their matrons and patrons as "Naturally N'awlins" as you get.

All this took place during my first year in New Orleans. I had arrived here in spring 1995 from New York City, where I made my living as a business analyst. Attuned to the dynamics of markets, I immediately picked up on the unique character of the Schwegmann enterprise. But little did I know at the time that this business was on the verge of unraveling. I got a clue, though, in 1996 after reading confusing news reports about Schwegmann's troubles with recent acquisitions. Then by 1997, I knew for sure the end was near when the long-time independent grocery retailer sold itself to a leveraged buyout firm. Given much familiarity with similar circumstances, it was clear to me that gone forever would be its colorful character after surrendering to a junk-bond buccaneer.

Over the late 1990s, as I ever so slowly settled into the rhythms of the Crescent City, what became evident is that the same homogenizing forces that had already conquered many an American city were now attacking the unique cultural fabric of New Orleans. Not only did Schwegmann's bite the dust. The same fate befell K&B, a beloved local drugstore chain, along with a host of other culturally embedded retail institutions. With that realization, I heaved a sigh of regret for Schwegmann's and the rest, lamenting the loss of authenticity, and proceeded to mostly forget about it.

But out of the blue my romantic memories of Schwegmann's were rekindled during a millennial stint spent in central New York State. There I encountered the upscale wonders of Wegmans Food Markets. What a delicious contrast, I thought, between traditional and gentrified grocery store presentations. I filed away a semi-comical idea to write a book called *From Schwegmann's to Wegmans: A Study in Upward Mobility*. Little did I know then that an opportunity to write the first half of this retail epic would come knocking ten years later.

In early 2011, John Schackai—an architect, planner, preservationist, and multi-generational native of New Orleans—approached me with the idea to write a biography of John Schwegmann. He had been inspired by listening to an audiocassette interview of Schwegmann contained in the special collections archive of the city's downtown library. At first I remained ambivalent about actually writing a biography about such an obscure local retailer. But after much coaxing from an extremely enthusiastic Schackai, I ventured downtown to listen to the tape. I was hooked.

The interview of John G. Schwegmann, one of an expansive series conducted by Friends of the Cabildo Oral History Program, took place at his Airline store office in 1975, about a year and a half before he suffered a debilitating stroke. It is rambling, extremely revealing, and thoroughly charming. It served as a great starting point for a biography.

Yet the Cabildo tape was thin skin indeed and needed to be mightily fleshed out. Fortunately, I soon discovered two unpublished university manuscripts focusing on John Schwegmann. One was a master's thesis by Anthony J. Greco—now a distinguished professor of economics at the University of Louisiana at Lafayette—entitled "John Schwegmann and Fair Trade Laws," completed in 1971 and contained in the Earl K. Long Library at the University of New Orleans. The other document was a doctoral dissertation by Warren B. Nation entitled "A Study of Supermarket Growth and Its Economic Significance" (1957). While little can be found about the fate of Warren Nation, his enlightening dissertation devoted to supermarket history in general and the Schwegmann chain in particular lives on in Crimson Tide archives at the University of Alabama at Tuscaloosa. Both manuscripts contain opulent stores of retail information unearthed here for the first time. Together they present a revelation of the historical magnitude of the greatness of John G. Schwegmann—how he essentially invented the template for the modern retail world.

Nevertheless, uncovering these scholarly treasures still did not suffice to tell the whole story of this retail genius. More intricate and intimate details would have to be found. To this end I conducted interviews with John Gerald Schwegmann's son and heir, John Francis Schwegmann, and his daughter, Margie Schwegmann-Brown. Both were gracious, loquacious, and honest. Though humbled by their travails, both have remained understandably proud of their heritage.

Besides contributing rich insights into their father's life and character, John Francis and Margie each unexpectedly provided me with troves of indispensable documentation on the Schwegmann legacy. For his part, John F. allowed me access to a book called *Continuing the Tradition: A History of the Schwegmann Company, 1869-1994*—a limited-edition publication he commissioned in 1994 to commemorate the 125-year anniversary of the Schwegmann enterprise in New Orleans. (Distributed mostly to store employees, very few copies of the book still exist.) For her part, Margie surprised me by supplying oversized laminated copies of a series of intense reminiscences authored by her father covering the history of New Orleans, the Bywater, and the

Schwegmann family. This baroquely detailed series, of which I was totally unaware at the time, originally appeared in just three parts over late winter and spring of 1967. The laminated copies loaned me by Margie represented a greatly expanded version of this original effort. Entitled "Just Like Meeting an Old Friend," the fourteen-part series was published in weekly installments in both of New Orleans' major newspapers, the *Times-Picayune* and *States-Item*, over the spring and summer of 1978.

Combining all these sources presented a favorable dilemma. I finally had enough to go on to put together a respectable biography— but only from the standpoint of John's personal life and his business and political accomplishments. Left out would be the rich tapestry of extended family, friend, and associate remembrances of the great magnate, along with customer anecdotes about the cultural awesome-ness that made the supermarkets so popular. Reluctantly I decided to jettison these aspects of communal memory in favor of a focused narrative based on the life of a singularly gifted individual. My hope is to eventually expand the scope of this biography beyond its emphasis on John Schwegmann to include the infinitely entertaining and audaciously colorful stories of those who once shopped Schwegmann Brothers Giant Super Markets.

Writing this book has been a roller-coaster ride. While I feared getting the story wrong, it was great fun telling it anyway. A lack of published scholarship on the subject necessarily renders this biography a composite sketch put together from scratch, with inconsistencies and omissions on full display. Although I undoubtedly made mistakes and took a few undue narrative liberties in telling the tale of the Schwegmann legacy, I have endeavored to hew as close as possible to the truth. In drawing conclusions, however—well, that is another story. Is John Schwegmann in fact as prophetic and heroic as I claim him to be? Only time will tell.

1

VANISHING LEGACY
The Retail Genius from New Orleans

A s if struck by an earthquake it all came crashing down, the local supermarket empire built up so boldly and brilliantly over half a century now buried beneath an avalanche of financial detritus and legal recrimination. So ended the reign of Schwegmann Brothers Giant Super Markets, the legendary food store enterprise in New Orleans, Louisiana, in business from 1946 until its sudden, shocking demise in 1999. Mercifully, John Gerald Schwegmann, its founder and owner, was not around physically to witness the destruction, having passed away in 1995. Nonetheless, his abiding spirit has been forced to endure far worse—namely, the almost total erasure of his extraordinary legacy from the annals of American retail history.

While standard accounts of modern brick-and-mortar retailing abound in the names of such giants as Harry Cunningham (Kmart), Sol Price (Price Club/Costco), and of course the demigod himself, Sam Walton (Walmart), nearly in vain one searches these accounts for a mere mention of John Schwegmann. This is an extremely curious omission that begs for explanation. For John G. Schwegmann—by far the most creative innovator of the lot—essentially invented the template for the modern retail world. Furthermore, all the recognized giants, whether they acknowledge it or not, are beholden to John not only for his trailblazing concepts but, more importantly, for the courageous battles he fought on their behalf for a true consumer society based on discount pricing.

Such extravagant claims, of course, demand extraordinary proof. It is not enough simply to proclaim John Schwegmann the visionary prophet of the postwar retail order. Concrete evidence is required. Toward this end, consider a preliminary list of John's pioneering achievements. This fountain of innovation was the first U.S. retailer to build a prototype supercenter (1950) and a colossal-scale hypermarket (1957); first to implement a strategy of everyday low pricing (predating Walmart by decades); first to integrate garden centers and other full-scale specialty departments into a modern big-box matrix; among the first to field a successful food/drug combination store (complete with pharmacy); arguably the first independent retailer to locate the main parking lot in front of the store; and first with numerous other singular retail inventions in an astonishing array of areas ranging from architecture and store design to merchandising, store hours, and energy efficiency.[1]

But the innovations of this inspired retail genius went even deeper. His marketing strategy, for example—an approach replete with comical devices, idiosyncratic personal messaging, and blatant political advocacy—has never been equaled in terms of kooky appeal and unfettered freedom of expression. He also maintained an unshakeable loyalty to his hometown community, even against his own self-interest, well in advance of the "local economy" movement. This stubborn loyalty he expressed in numerous ways—from bond offerings aimed at his working-class customers to active participation in city and state politics and promotion of New Orleans history. It can be seen most clearly, however, in his refusal to expand his miniature empire outside the city he knew so well and loved.

Yet beyond his host of innovations, unparalleled marketing skills, and uncanny ability to anticipate trends decades in advance, what above all sets John Schwegmann apart from his retail giant peers is his fighting spirit. Such a spirit is seldom seen in any businessperson, retailer or otherwise, for whom the overwhelming tendency is to avoid controversy at all costs. Not so with John. At the risk of alienating his customers and the public at large, he routinely stood his ground, letting the chips fall where they may. In John Schwegmann's signature struggle against "fair trade" laws—a now-little-remembered slugfest over manufacturer price fixing—against all odds he emerged victorious, in the process inflicting a near-deathblow to this monstrous body of Depression-era acts and statutes. Not incidentally, with his 1951 Supreme Court victory over fair trade laws, John Schwegmann was instrumental in shifting the trajectory of the entire U.S. economic system in a more competitive free-enterprise direction.

Two primary sources fueled the fiery creativity, fierce local loyalty, and crusader zeal that drove John G. Schwegmann's heroic retail career. The first was the influence of his family, or more specifically his forebears. John's genealogical roots in the grocery store business could not have grown any deeper: his grandmother's enterprising brother established the first proper grocery store in New Orleans; his wayfarer grandfather opened a virtual chain of grocery stores back before there were chains; his "millionaire" uncle owned the leading grocery store in New Orleans' Third District; and his nose-to-the-grindstone father managed that store for nearly half a century. Clearly John had the food trade in his blood. So when the time came for him to open his own stores—including the first supermarket in the Crescent City—he brought to this task so much confidence in his judgment and abilities that he felt free to break new ground far beyond conventional bounds.

The second source fueling John's success was the influence of his hometown of New Orleans, and more particularly the working-class neighborhood where he was born and raised. Known mostly for its charming elegance and exotic excess, New Orleans has another side almost hidden from the tourist manuals, and even history books. This is the domain where the down-to-earth folkways of average people prevail over more elegant and excessive expressions. John Schwegmann came from such a place: a backwater downriver from the French Quarter set aside under American rule to house the city's labor pool.

Given the central importance of family and locality in the John Schwegmann story, both of these major influences are explored in depth in this book. Thus the life and times of significant forebears are chronicled, this in order to reveal how they helped form his moral core and business instincts. New Orleans is also a subject of prime interest, as this crazy city fundamentally shaped both his personality and vision.

Yet the true beauty of John's biography is that it stretches far beyond the confines of his family, city, personal experience, and professional accomplishment to encompass large swaths of business history that remain little told—and never within the context of the life of one particularly gifted individual. Thus this book is able to shed light on such neglected socioeconomic topics as the history of outdoor and public markets, the rise and fall of old-time corner grocery stores, the commercial vitality and small-town virtues of urban neighborhoods before the Great Depression, how real estate values suffered under the New Deal, the manner in which neo-populist politics influenced the rise of consumer society, the role of the "Golden Formula" in creating the modern mass market, and the hellacious story—now nearly erased—of the thirty-years' war over fair trade laws.

Regrettably, the collapse of John Schwegmann's supermarket empire is also related here. As will be seen, the very family and local ties that propelled his success also worked to sink him. Unresolved psychological problems eventually distracted and misled him, especially in regard to his misbegotten pursuit of politics, which turned John's later career trajectory topsy-turvy. More disheartening was an undying animus on the part of New Orleans' aristocratic establishment against this presumptuous upstart, this pompous people-power-promoting self-made millionaire from the wrong side of the tracks (literally). Of course, it did not help that he also earned enduring enmity from powerful national manufacturing entities that did not appreciate John's incessant attacks on their controlling interests. All these factors worked against John Schwegmann when it came time to honor his memory.

*   *   *

THERE IS NO MORE POTENT SYMBOL of the decay of John Gerald Schwegmann's legacy than the fate of the old corner store where he was born and raised. A two-story building located at the intersection of two streets named Piety and Burgundy (emphasis on the "gun"), this once proud crown jewel of the Schwegmann family was unceremoniously abandoned and left to rot after the catastrophe of Hurricane Katrina in August 2005. Fast-forward six years to the centennial anniversary of John's birth in August 2011 and, incredibly, the store was *still* in ruins, an island of dilapidation in a sea of gentrification. How this fetid state of affairs has been allowed to persist—indeed, as of this book's publication the old corner was still an ugly empty shell—remains a mystery. Surely the property should have been snapped up by now by some adventurous developer or savvy entrepreneur. After all, from a contemporary real estate perspective this old moldering building sits in a prime location, occupying valuable geographic terrain within a rich cultural milieu.

Physically, the property on which the store is sited is basically solid—a crucial consideration in an essentially liquid city. Built on relatively high ground just three blocks from a natural levee on the Mississippi River, this secure spot has not experienced significant flooding since Sauve's Crevasse way back in 1849.[2] Even Katrina did comparatively minimal damage here. More important than physical geography, though—for there are several other relatively well-protected areas within the city's undersea topography—a more elusive quality serves to increase the site's contemporary real estate appeal and enhance its speculative allure. For the old corner store is located right in the heart of what is now known as the Bywater, the cultural epicenter of the "new" (post-Katrina) New Orleans. It is no surprise that this hippest, most happening neighborhood in town has become an international magnet for what has been dubbed the "creative class." For with its utterly charming architecture and picturesque streetscapes, its easy proximity by foot or by bike to the French Quarter and Mississippi River, and the abundant opportunities it presents for interaction with the gnarly N'awlins' natives who continue to inhabit this Upper Ninth Ward neighborhood, the cultural flywheel that is the Bywater offers artistic and adventurous types the perfect setting in which to find the inspiration and authenticity they seek.

Given the virtues and values of this site, it is tempting to suspect some dark conspiracy, or maybe a malevolent curse, lurks behind the humiliating descent of this former Schwegmann family jewel into the blighted abyss. Yet indulging these suspicions would be to get too entangled in the symbol. For after all, this property has long been gone from the family stable, sold off decades ago. Most likely, the site simply suffers from insouciant neglect, its rot reflecting nothing more than the endless bickering of real estate brokers aimlessly dickering over the ultimate disposition of this prime location. Either way, however, whether caused by active malice or passive neglect, the wreckage of the old corner store perfectly mirrors the decay of the Schwegmann legacy—fading away now into the mists of never-remembered history.

What a shame for New Orleans if John G. Schwegmann were to be forgotten! This would be a tragedy of inexpressible magnitude, as lost to the city's posterity would be the valuable heritage of a fantastically successful native son, a man of genius and true character of the highest order—colorful, charismatic, eccentric—who in his very essence brashly and unabashedly embodied the creative culture and resilient spirit of this incomparable city. But even beyond New Orleans, a failure to revivify the Schwegmann legacy would represent a loss for the entire nation. For John was both a paragon of America's promise—achieving rags-to-riches success through hard work, ingenuity, and daring—and an archetype of its highest democratic ideals, displaying the patriotic courage to stand up and fight for what he believed was right. Finally, for reasons already made clear, business history itself would suffer immeasurably were this missing link's vital contributions to retail evolution allowed to disappear.

To begin to restore the Schwegmann legacy, return first to the old corner grocery store. Besides being home to three generations of the Schwegmann family, this store also served as a major Ninth Ward retail hub for roughly sixty years. Surely with such a record of community rootedness, the Schwegmann legacy cannot be properly appreciated without some understanding of the place that helped to shape it so profoundly. This is especially true in the case of John G. Schwegmann, who spent his entire formative years living in that section of the old Third District now called Bywater. Without doubt, the scrappy vitality of this peculiar neighborhood left a deep imprint on John, the virtually unknown titan of American retailing.

When New Orleans was founded in 1718, the sprawling area east of the city was mostly a rural wilderness of bayous and swamps.[3] It took a generation of intensive effort, including the building of a levee system in the 1740s, before this vast tract of ancient wetlands could be reclaimed for productive use. After being suitably drained and made available for planting, the primary cash crop grown was not cotton, tobacco, rice, or indigo, the most common staples of southern agriculture. Instead, in a bow to New Orleans' Caribbean geographical orientation and trade connections, sugar was the primary money crop planted here.

So if the old corner store had existed back in the 1750s, surrounding it would have been fields of sugarcane. Somewhere nearby a plantation house would have been located, one of a handful of such elegant edifices dotting the area east of the French Quarter along the Mississippi River. The owners of these plantations were well-connected Frenchmen, *ancien règime* aristocrats associated with the Company of the Indies. Their memories live on in such Bywater street names as Montegut, Clouet, and Lesseps.

Somehow these French sugar barons managed to retain their cultural and economic predominance over the eastern flank of the Crescent City throughout the period of Spanish ascendance, lasting from 1763 to 1803. This sweet deal came to an end, however, with the United States' takeover of New Orleans after the Louisiana Purchase of 1803. From the standpoint of anti-aristocratic, commercial-minded Americans, French holdings should be devoted to more lucrative pursuits than farming, and so the pressure was on to break up the plantations. With old aristocratic lands now up for democratic grabs, they were carved up and parceled out into tracts to be bought and sold in the city's rapidly expanding real estate market.

Here the convoluted geography of New Orleans comes into play, as Ninth Ward/Third District history only makes sense within the larger context of metropolitan development. The original settlement of New Orleans took place in what is now known as the French Quarter, also called the Vieux Carré ("Old Square"), located at the apex of the final northward thrust of the Mississippi River before it begins its serpentine descent southeast into the Gulf of Mexico. From this central location the city spread, following the river, in two askew directions: south and east. These contrary settlement movements resulted in the establishment of two new townships, or *faubourgs* ("false towns"), called St. Marie and Marigny, respectively.

In historical terms, Faubourg St. Marie came first, established in the late 1700s, followed somewhat later by Faubourg Marigny, formed in 1806. In geographical terms, referencing the Mississippi River's flow pattern, St. Marie was considered "upriver," while Marigny was considered "downriver."

In the historiography of New Orleans, most attention is focused on the French Quarter and upriver communities—including the American Sector (now called Downtown and the Warehouse District), Lafayette City (the Garden District), and Uptown. By contrast, downriver communities tend to be neglected. This is understandable. For what can possibly compete with the decadent glamour of the French Quarter or the glorious elegance of St. Charles Avenue? Certainly not the eastern downriver neighborhoods, marked out from the beginning to be the humble abode of the working class. Indeed, it is no accident that when New Orleans rancorously split up into three autonomous municipal districts in 1836—the French Quarter (First District), St. Mary (Second District), and Marigny (Third District)—Marigny was recorded as being the least affluent among them.

Notwithstanding its downscale reputation, or more likely because of it, the "Dirty Third" District continued to be flooded with working people, who spilled well beyond Marigny.[4] By the late 1830s this burgeoning eastward settlement was so vast it necessitated the creation of an altogether new municipal division called Faubourg Washington. This sprawling concatenation made up of six sold-off plantations stretched all the way from the end of Marigny past Holy Cross to the beginning of Chalmette.

AT THIS JUNCTURE IN THE NARRATIVE, the situation becomes downright confusing.[5] For in 1852—after sixteen years of a failed experiment in dysfunctional municipal governance—the three feuding faubourgs finally came together in the interest of facilitating expansion and furthering city prosperity. Along with the formation of a centralized government, a complex bureaucratic schematic was imposed over the city for purposes of efficient administration in such areas as voting, tax assessment, and property transactions. Officially gone was the charming old faubourg system. Replacing it was a more rationalized system, with the city now subdivided into a numbered grid of districts and wards.

In the current context, what is most relevant is how this administrative restructuring affected the eastern flank of the Crescent City. Well, considering that as of 1852 much of this eastward area was still unreclaimed swampland, city planners could do little more than throw up their hands and group sparse existing downriver communities together with vast tracts of "maybe-someday" real estate into an enormous mass of amorphous territory—an incoherent mess designated as the Third District (including Marigny) and the Ninth Ward (not including Marigny).

This gigantic eastern expanse of settlements and wetlands eventually came to include a multiplicity of distinct communities. Currently contained within the Third District, for example, are Marigny, St. Roch, Bywater, Seventh Ward, Holy Cross, Fairgrounds, Gentilly (with its numerous associated neighborhoods), and New Orleans East, among others. For its part, the Ninth Ward stretches all the way east from Press Street and Franklin Avenue to distant Lake Borgne, the wilderness of Bayou Sauvage, and the dividing line between Orleans and St. Bernard Parish. Just to add one more complication, in the 1920s, when the

Industrial Canal was built, the Ninth Ward was carved into "upper" and "lower" portions.

In considering the community diversity now represented by the Third District and Ninth Ward of New Orleans, it is little wonder that a difficult problem arises when attempting to recount the history of one particular neighborhood within this vast morass. This is the nomenclature problem. Although area inhabitants in the nineteenth and early twentieth centuries easily referred to themselves as residents of either the Third District or the Ninth Ward, this was before population expansion and intensive real estate development occurred. Since then, the once-easy references to numbered neighborhoods have been mostly drained of descriptive value.

So in a nutshell, this is the nomenclature problem: what does one call a distinct neighborhood that had no name back in the day but does now? After wrestling with this insoluble dilemma, a decision is taken here to employ contemporary terminology. Thus, at the inevitable cost of offending native sensibilities, the name "Bywater" is used throughout this book to describe the specific neighborhood where the Schwegmann legacy was nourished and flourished. This "reverse-anachronism" approach to the nomenclature problem—overlaying a new onto an old name—possesses one overriding virtue. It serves to pinpoint with exactitude the precise place under historical scrutiny, effectively differentiating this singular community from the cumbrous jumble of the Third District and Ninth Ward.

The decision to apply the name "Bywater" in retroactive fashion to describe the downriver community that developed immediately east of Marigny—a vibrant working-class neighborhood that arose in the early 1800s and reached an apogee of commercial splendor around the turn of the century—is a less than perfect solution to the nomenclature problem. Yet it fulfills its purpose if it enhances historical understanding and provides insight into New Orleans folk history, much of it still unknown—perhaps for want of a name. Meanwhile, a flexibility is preserved throughout this book to refer to the Bywater by its old-fashioned names, the Third District and Ninth (and Upper Ninth) Ward, whenever it fits the context.

*   *   *

IN ITS GEOGRAPHICAL LAYOUT, the Bywater resembles an elongated rectangle, its lengthwise-stretched checkerboard street grid pattern demarcated on the north by St. Claude Avenue and on the south by Chartres (inelegantly pronounced "charters") Street, with Press Street and Poland Avenue forming its western and eastern boundaries, respectively.[6] From its urban beginnings in the early nineteenth century, the Bywater has been devoted mainly to residential development, the original intention being to provide affordable housing for the swarm of laborers then opportunistically flocking to the richest city in the antebellum South. Yet even in its earliest adumbrations, a fair amount of manufacturing activity was scattered around the neighborhood. In the best-known example, the world's first steam-powered cotton pressing plant, built in 1831, was located on its western boundary.

Over its first roughly eighty years of urban existence, the Bywater experienced the entry of a dizzying succession of ethnic immigrants. First came a large surge of French-speaking Caribbean refugees fleeing Haiti (then called St. Domingue) in the wake of its 1804 revolution. Led by legendary general Touissant L'Overture, this Haitian uprising was roughly equivalent in shock value to Castro's Cuban revolution of modern times. In both cases, those who had prospered under the old system, not just wealthy landowners but also those who possessed advanced education or specialist skills, often chose to escape the political turmoil and head north for more amicable port cities in the United States. The process of Haitian immigration to New Orleans was somewhat drawn out, beginning with an initial rush between 1804 and 1809, and then tapering off, though continuing, through the 1820s.[7]

Ethnically, most of the Haitian refugees who managed to make it to New Orleans were Creoles—either of the French/Spanish variety or some European/African/Indigenous combination. Yet a significant proportion were *gens couleurs de libre*, or "free people of color," basically referring to liberated African slaves. Francophones all, the Haitian arrivistes naturally tended to cluster in the French-speaking downriver plantation lands, which were at the time in the initial stages of transformation from rural to urban space. Spilling eastward from Marigny and joining in with the residual population of previous inhabitants—including remnants of French families who remained after the plantations were broken up and a significant number of African Americans then still held in slavery—the immigrant Creoles and free people of the African diaspora wholeheartedly participated in this urbanization process.

Next to arrive in the Bywater were the Irish. While the first great rush of Irish immigrants to the United States occurred in 1846 in the wake of the Potato Famine, an earlier group came to New Orleans during the 1830s. Seeking economic opportunity, these precursor Irish immigrants certainly found plenty of employment in the Crescent City. For this was the heroic age of canal building, with work on the massive New Basin Canal commencing in 1832. Even more, as a thriving and expanding port city, New Orleans had lots of other jobs on offer—in levee building, construction, stevedoring, maintenance, sanitation, and domestic services.

This rosy picture of economic opportunity presented by New Orleans at the time enticed thousands of Irish to immigrate here, many of them clustering in the Bywater, the downriver zone set aside for the laboring classes. Once they got there, though, they found out the harsh truth: most of the jobs on offer were grueling, thankless tasks, both backbreaking and dangerous; and on top of that, the jobs paid a pittance. Even worse, the beleaguered, poverty-stricken Irish, often packed like sardines into "shotgun doubles," were at the mercy of horrible tropical and water-borne diseases, such as yellow fever, malaria, and cholera, that periodically plagued New Orleans, and against which they had no immunity. Nevertheless, somehow the Irish as a group persevered and left their indomitable mark on the Bywater, a neighborhood that has over time demonstrated great resilience.

Beginning in the late 1840s and lasting through the late 1850s, the first great surge of immigrants from Germany arrived in New Orleans. While a noticeable number of Germans had already come much earlier to the city—in the 1720s, right after its founding—this original influx was comparatively small and tended to scatter into the outlying "river parishes." In contrast, the tidal wave that poured into New Orleans more than a century later flooded the entire city with German immigrants.

This massive movement reflected a more general exodus from Germany to the United States that first took off in 1848. Many explanations are offered for the explosive migration at this time. One of the more understated is that those who left were fleeing an ill-conceived program of modernization. Be that as it may, Germans came to New Orleans in such numbers—both up to the Civil War and continuing for years thereafter—that in the half century between 1850 and 1900 they became the leading group of foreign speakers in New Orleans, displacing the French in the process. This tsunami of German newcomers dispersed to all parts of the city: upriver, downriver, and across the river. In parts of the Bywater, the infusion of working-class Germans was so great that the neighborhood came to be known informally as "Little Saxony." This is where the Schwegmann family settled.

For a full three decades following the Civil War, foreign immigration to the Bywater resumed, this time with a steady stream of South and East Europeans—Italians, Slavs, Jews, and other groups—expanding its population size and ethnic mix. By the end of the nineteenth century, however, this boisterous boom of newcomers was over, ended by immigration restrictions enacted at the top by the U.S. federal government. At that *fin de siècle* point, the neighborhood, no longer preoccupied with growth and assimilation, finally settled down to focus on making the most of what it already had in abundance—primarily a wealth of human resources. What followed can be described as the "Golden Age of the Bywater," a period lasting about a generation, from roughly 1890 to 1930, during which the neighborhood prospered like never before…or since.[8]

Certainly from a bourgeois perspective, these were the halcyon days. Quickly disappearing from the neighborhood scene at the time was a funky sort of antediluvian commerce plied outside in the streets by a motley army of roving salesmen pushing carts or driving mule-drawn wagons. Some peddled goods—fruits and vegetables; charcoal, wood, and kindling; brooms and mops—while others hawked services appropriate to the time, such as recycling rags, bones, and bottles; sharpening knives and scissors; sweeping chimneys; and repairing clothes poles and umbrellas. Rapidly rising to replace that old hurly-burly Bywater was the new hustle-bustle Bywater, which witnessed a fertile blossoming of modern stores and offices, places where a more respectable form of commerce was conducted inside.

To get a flavor of just how economically vibrant the Bywater was from the Gay Nineties through the Roaring Twenties, consider the cornucopia of shopping and recreational opportunities available at the time within just a few blocks of the old corner store on Piety and Burgundy. Specifically, within a radius encompassing four vertical blocks (Clouet to Desire) and six horizontal blocks (St. Claude to Chartres), there were three grocery stores, Eicke's, Martin's, and Schwegmann's; one licensed public meat market, Zengel's, which also housed associated butcher shops (Wagner's, Buckingham's, and Big George Flick's) and produce vendors (Chetta's and Vaccaro's); two bakeries, Sambring's and Fresch's; Pete Starker's candy store (which had a kite-building business on the side); Coyle's animal feed store; two ice houses, Ollie Taylor's and Uncle Jake's; two bars, Schwegmann's and the Bergeret Bar, which served oyster po-boys and other sandwiches in the back; Sambola's snack shop, which featured raw oysters and watermelon; Leonard's department store; Vaccaro's housewares; Sack's dry goods; Kircham's drugstore; LaLa's shoe store; and Tony Alonzo's barbershop. For entertainment there was the Piety Theater; and for swimming and boxing there was Wiltz's Gymnasium.

It should be emphasized that the superabundance of economic activity being described here was all taking place within a mere four-by-six block radius—and that numerous other stores and service venues were located just outside this matrix, all within fairly easy walking distance. Specifically, in a larger zone stretching west/east from Spain Street to Poland Avenue and north/south from St. Claude Avenue to the river there were two more public meat/seafood markets (Guillotte's at Macarty Square and St. Roch on St. Claude); at least one more grocery store (Votage's); three more drugstores (Livaudais, Roeling's, and Joe

Clesi's); a dairy (Hylett Wattingly); an ice cream parlor (Hosli's, which used real French vanilla beans); a restaurant/bar (Huerstel's, which claimed to have invented the frozen beer mug); two notions shops; a hardware store (Krantz's, where John Schwegmann Sr. liked to hang out around the pot-bellied stove with other neighborhood fellows); a shoe store (Pekovar's); two book stores (Siegfried's and Mumme's); a bike shop (located next door to Votage's and run by the grocery owner's son); and another barber shop (Parker's). To top it all off, in addition to the Piety Theater there were two other theaters in the vicinity (Hipp and Happyland), not to mention a dance hall (Pink's).

To fill out this picture of Bywater prosperity at the time, scattered amidst and on the edges of the plethora of retail and service businesses was an assortment of craftsmen and light manufacturers. Among others these included two tinsmiths (Hartenstein's and Hubbard's, both of whom came in handy for soldering stills), a blacksmith (Val Springer's), Dunbar's Molasses Factory, the Barataria Canning Co. (specializing in shrimp and other seafood), the Moss Factory (which re-stuffed mattresses), the Jackson Saw Mill, and Hubig's Pies.

As can be seen, the Golden Age of the Bywater came close to realizing what is basically the ideal of what is now called New Urbanism —a vision of small, easily traversable, self-sustaining neighborhoods integrated within larger metropolitan areas. Ironically, in other words, the primary place-making concept envisioned by suburban-alternative planners in our contemporary period is nothing new at all. Rather, it represents an attempt to recapture, with a green patina, what previously existed before. Indeed, it is difficult not to get the impression that the New Urbanists are simply nostalgic for what used to be and has since suffered a cruel death—a victim of larger, irrefragable, irresistible, irrefutable historical forces.

As BEFITS THE SPEED with which business is typically conducted in the subtropics, it was not until nearly a quarter century after its golden age that the Bywater neighborhood officially came into existence—with administrative boundaries drawn and a formal name bestowed only in 1947. How the Bywater actually acquired its moniker is a matter of some dispute. There are those who claim it was simply called after its telephone exchange. Others say it came from the winner of a contest sponsored by a newspaper. But however it happened, by the time it was officially named, the Bywater had long since ceased being a thriving, prosperous neighborhood. The ravages of the Great Depression and the deprivations of World War II had taken a severe toll here. And after suffering white flight during the early postwar years, which further laid waste to property values, the neighborhood sank relentlessly into a state of neglect and desuetude.

It took decades for the Bywater to recover. Indeed, only in the mid-1980s (some say slightly earlier) did the neighborhood begin its revival, a process still ongoing a generation later. Of course, by this time most of the Schwegmann family had long since moved on to greener pastures.

2

GRANDFATHER GARRET

Reckless Adventurer as Retail Entrepreneur

Though Germans were part of the North American melting pot from the beginning of colonial settlement, they remained a small proportion of the ethnic mix for over two centuries. Only in 1848, in the wake of drastic political upheavals back home, did a tidal wave of immigrants from Germany begin to flood the United States. About a decade later, hailing from the Osnabruck-Hanover region of northern Germany, several members of the Schwegmann family embarked on the same migratory journey to America. Alone among them—or so the official story goes—John Garret Schwegmann decided to settle in New Orleans.[1]

John Garret—who dropped the "John," went mostly by "Garret," but occasionally employed the name "George"—was atrocious at recordkeeping. He left no diaries, letters, or contracts to document his extensive business and real estate dealings. Consequently, his life must be pieced together mostly out of fuzzy family memories, stray official notices, and scattered property records. This is no easy task, as the family's timeline of events cannot be reconciled with the few objective sources that do exist. Indeed, to this day a mystery remains about a shadowy family member who played a part in Garret's real estate schemes—suggesting that he may not have been alone in New Orleans after all.

For now, though, the mystery will be held in abeyance while the standard family story is set forth. Bear in mind, however, that an alternate, and arguably more accurate, timeline of events is presented where appropriate.

BORN IN 1839, GARRET SCHWEGMANN arrived in the Crescent City around 1860. At the time, the allure of living in the richest, most wide-open city in the South must have been irresistible to such a handsome and adventurous young man seeking both excitement and opportunity. As things turned out, while he soon found plenty of excitement all right (although probably not in the way he anticipated), his opportunities were at first sorely limited.

Growing up in Germany, Garret had been trained as a cabinet-maker. But in his newly adopted city he could find no employment in this specialized trade. So he did what most immigrants were forced to do—namely, he humbled himself, hustled, and took whatever work he could get. In Garret's case, this turned out to be a job cleaning "privies," also known as "outhouses," which were regular features of homes in the days before municipal water systems. What his job involved was shoveling "you know what" out of residential cesspools into barrels, earning twenty-five cents per barrel filled. As Garret's grandson John wryly remarked over a century later, "This wasn't the best kind of perfume job you could get."[2]

Interrupting such drudgery, events soon took a dramatic turn. In 1861, just a year after his arrival in New Orleans, the South seceded from the North. Of course, being a fit young lad, Garret inevitably got caught up in what turned out to be the Civil War. In an interesting twist, however, he did not fight on the side of the Confederacy. Rather, he fought for the Union. Did Garret have a choice in this matter? Certainly the answer is fraught with controversy in the context of southern sensibilities. This is evidenced by how Schwegmann family memories continue to conflict on exactly what happened, with some family members insisting that Garret was drafted into the Yankee army, while others maintain that he enlisted. In considering this matter, it certainly seems possible that Garret's sympathies were with the North, given the general tendency of immigrants at the time to possess "anti-slavery propensities."[3] Yet regardless of whether he held these progressive leanings and acted on them, voluntarily joining the Union army, or was conscripted against his will into the accursed northern fighting force, the subsequent record is clear.

On August 29, 1862, shortly after Flag Officer David Farragut's successful naval bombardment of New Orleans and the takeover of the city by the vilified General Benjamin Butler, Garret Schwegmann entered the Yankee army. Serving with Union Army Company D of the Second Volunteer Regiment, Louisiana Infantry, Garret fought for two years without serious incident. But then on May 15, 1864, at Marksville, Louisiana, Garret suffered a severe wound in battle. A bullet struck his left cheek, the shot shattering his upper jaw and impairing his eyesight and hearing. While this injury—necessitating the removal of part of his jawbone and leaving his face slightly disfigured—left a strong residue of pain that afflicted him for years afterward, at least he survived. Garret was honorably discharged on September 11, 1865, and awarded a disability pension of $3 per month, with payout to commence January 15, 1868.[4]

After his convalescence and discharge from the army, Garret experienced better luck in finding employment than he had had previously. Indeed, in distinct contrast to his prewar experience, he ended up smelling like a rose. For he managed to land a position as a clerk at the premier grocery store in New Orleans at the time, a store owned by the Henke family. The Henkes were German immigrants from Gudenslowe-by-Minden, located in the Alsace-Lorraine border region near France.[5] Members of the family who ended up immigrating to New Orleans included two brothers, Ferdinand and Henry, and two sisters, Mary and Catherine. Yet they did not all come at once. First to arrive, sometime in the mid- to late 1850s, was the eldest brother, Ferdinand. To support himself, Ferdinand Henke went into the grocery business. His first "store" was an open-air stall in the French Market, located along the Mississippi waterfront at the edge of the French Quarter.

From a modern perspective, gazing through the refracted lens of nostalgic drawings, the old French Market of the antebellum years might appear charming and picturesque, an altogether quaint place to shop. In actuality, the retail environment there was abysmal by modern standards. For one thing, shopping for groceries at the French Market was no easy task. None of the goods being sold had fixed prices. This forced the retailer and customer to haggle over every single transaction, which was not a particularly congenial way of doing business, and certainly not a pathway to high-volume sales.[6] Moreover, shopping there was not at all convenient. Located outdoors and covered only by a pavilion, the French Market was open for just half a day: from five in the morning till noon. Worst of all, though, the place was deplorably filthy, plagued by dust, insects, and vermin.

Ferdinand Henke, bursting with ambition and imbued with a new vision of grocery retailing, chafed under these primitive conditions. So he made a bold move, setting up shop right across the street from the French Market in a proper retail store—an indoor building featuring actual walls, a ceiling, and windows. This new store, which he called by the Americanized name of Hank's Grocery, was innovative for the time. Fixed prices were established on all goods, and the store remained open for a full sixteen-hour day—from five in the morning to nine at night. Hank's Grocery was such a huge success that Ferdinand soon needed help in running it. So he sent for his brother back in Germany, enticing Henry to come to New Orleans by offering him an ownership stake in the business. Henry Henke duly arrived in 1866, all of fifteen years old, accompanied by his two sisters, Mary and Catherine.[7]

Henry Henke later went on to enjoy an illustrious career in the grocery business. In 1872, having fallen in love with a young lady from Houston, Texas, who refused to relocate to New Orleans, he sold his interest in Hank's to brother Ferdinand for $1,000, packed up two carloads of groceries, and moved out west to Houston. There he opened that city's first farmers' market, calling it "The New Orleans Store." Ten years later, in 1882, he partnered with C.G. Pillot to establish one of Houston's original grocery chains, Henke and Pillot (eventually acquired by Kroger).

SOON AFTER HE LEFT THE UNION ARMY, Garret strode into Hank's Grocery seeking employment. Apparently Ferdinand liked what he saw in this bright and charismatic Civil War veteran and offered him a position as a butter clerk. Garret must have been especially good with butter, or at least at "buttering up," because it soon became apparent that another Henke also liked what she saw in him, though not for mercantile reasons. This was newly arrived sister Mary. As it happened, Mary Henke and Garret Schwegmann soon began courting, eventually marrying on April 27, 1869, at Holy Trinity Church in the Bywater. Over the roughly fifteen years Garret and Mary subsequently spent together, the couple had five children: Garret Jr. (1870), Henry (1873), Mary (1876), Theresa (1879), and John (1883).

With a wife and budding family to support, Garret now followed a path commonly taken by American immigrants in the years after the Civil War: he opened up a grocery store. As the thinking went at the time, if you could somehow scrape up enough dough to do so, entering the grocery business was the way to go. The basic reasoning was twofold. First, by owning a grocery store, the family would at least have access to food. Second, the family would likely have a roof over its head, since almost all grocery stores at the time had living quarters attached either on top or behind the building.

Yet beyond these basic considerations, owning a grocery store seemed a great idea because it offered immigrant families a socio-economic platform, a stage they could potentially command to gain power in any number of ways: through making money, achieving prominence in the community, rising in class and social status, acquiring some degree of independence, or just basically achieving the American dream. Of course, as with all things that seem too good to be true, successfully owning and profitably operating even the smallest grocery store was a lot harder than it looked. As a result, even as myriad starry-eyed immigrant families perennially entered its ranks, the grocery store retail sector correspondingly experienced extensive annual shakeouts for decades after the Civil War.[8]

But here Garret was different. For in his own entry into the grocery business he held two huge advantages over the countless others who tried and failed to make a go of it—namely, he had previous experience and family connections. First, he already knew the basics of running a grocery store through his apprenticeship at Hank's Grocery. Arguably more important, he was supported and encouraged in his endeavor by the Henke family itself, then owners of one of the most prominent grocery stores in New Orleans. In all probability he had access to the credit lines and supply and distribution chains available to his new wife's family.

At this point in the narrative it is necessary to revisit the old corner store, used as a leitmotif in the first chapter of this book. Somehow the fiction has burrowed its way into New Orleans history—certainly facilitated by the flogging of this mythology by the family itself—that the store on Piety and Burgundy was established in 1869 as the original Schwegmann's grocery store. Yet this is a shibboleth, wrong on two counts. First, Garret's original store was not at this location. Second, he did not open the Piety and Burgundy store in 1869. For proof of these heretical statements, consider that the New Orleans Notarial Archive shows that the widow of a Mr. Theodore Lederer acquired the property in 1866—a property on a lot bounded by Piety, Love, Desire, and Craps streets—and she owned it until 1880. Only thereafter did Garret enter the picture.[9]

As to when and where the original Schwegmann's store actually did come into existence, the historical record is extremely unclear. According to one stray source, Garret opened his first store in 1866. But this early date conflicts with family accounts that he clerked at

Hank's Grocery through the late 1860s. The family's version of events would add credence, then, to one favored speculation that he opened his first store in 1869, the same year he married the boss's sister. But this first store was not located at Piety and Burgundy. Instead, according to the slim evidence available—a business listing for Schwegmann's appearing in a city directory in 1871—this original store was located on Dauphine near Port Street. A third speculation, however, places his first store at the corner of Dauphine and Enghein (colloquially pronounced "Engine," now known as Almonaster).[10]

Whatever the specific location of the first store, all available sources agree that it was a big hit. Indeed, according to Schwegmann legend, its profits were as high as $10,000—an astronomical sum by the standards of the early 1870s. If true, certainly this success could not have been accomplished by anyone who was lazy, foolish, clumsy, or crooked. On the contrary, Garret appears at this stage of the historical record to be the consummate hardworking, shrewd, competent, and honest entrepreneur. As his grandson John reminisced, he was "a faithful grocery merchant [who] always believed in giving people a bargain, giving them honest weight [and] good products"—this in stark contrast to many of Garret's contemporaries in the grocery business. It is likely that Garret's forthright approach to retailing best explains a refrain often used to describe a unique gift he possessed, namely that he had "a knack for making money."[11]

In light of the reputation he was building as a solid, dependable retail merchant, Garret's next career move was downright shocking. For he suddenly sold off his thriving first store, loaded up the family, and decamped out to California. When exactly he did this is unknown, but given subsequent events the move must have occurred sometime in the early 1870s. Why he did it, what impelled him to make such a daring move, remains shrouded in mystery.

Since available sources are uniformly silent on this question, and no family member seems to know, it is anyone's guess what his motivation was for just up and leaving. Perhaps external pressures drove him out of town. After all, this time period coincided with the turbulent Reconstruction era in New Orleans. Maybe Garret, who had fought on the Union side, felt threatened for some reason. Or maybe he was simply fed up with the city's racial and civic turmoil. More likely, though, given what is known about the arc of Garret's life, his primary motivation was internal, with his own restless spirit, adventurous and troubled, beckoning him westward. Like many Americans at the time he may have been inspired by the driving of the Golden Spike in 1869 to make the journey to the Golden State. For the intercontinental railroad had finally opened up the vast vistas of the west to those east of the Mississippi who previously had no easy access to the promised land. But surely Garret's California attraction was not based solely on mere abstract longing. For he did have an actual role model to follow in his quest out west—namely, his uncle-in-law Henry Henke, who had already set up shop in Houston.

Alongside the indeterminate motivations for why Garret ventured out west, a lingering mystery exists about just what he did once he got out there. Assuming the best, Garret spent his time in California scouting out promising business opportunities. Assuming the worst—as is discussed shortly—he spent his time there drinking and gambling his way through a slew of Golden State saloons. Whatever his motives, expectations, and actions, Garret soon found himself out in California with a family in tow and his money running out. There was only one thing to do: Garret, Mary, and the children returned to New Orleans. So what had begun as perhaps an attempt at escape, a bold career move, or simply a flight of fancy ended up being nothing more than an extended family vacation.

Yet it did not end there. Despite an extremely hazy historical record, with few precise dates available to track the subsequent swirl of events, the general picture is fairly clear. After returning to New Orleans from his first trip out west, Garret commenced on a cyclical journey that repeated the same wayward pattern. Every two or three years he would buy a new Bywater corner grocery store, build up its business, then sell it off again and go back out to California. Four of these stores were located at the following intersections: Dauphine and Port; Dauphine and Enghein; Burgundy and Enghein; and Burgundy and Elmire (now Gallier). Amid this period of furious wheeling-and-dealing and gallivanting, he also bought—and sold—the store at Piety and Burgundy. Along with stronger documentation soon to be presented, a stray piece of evidence corroborates his temporary ownership of the legendary corner store. According to military pension records, he occupied a residence at Piety and Burgundy in 1882.[12] Also, his son Garret Jr. (born 1878) remembered living and working there as a boy.

At this point in the timeline, specifically from 1880 to 1882, the alternate version of Garret's story comes fully into play. Yet for just one more moment this version is placed aside, as it is just too odd to incorporate into a smooth narrative. Instead, skip ahead to 1883, when Garret made a deal that is inexplicable except by recourse to pure speculation. Perhaps he hoped that by closing off his options this deal would finally get him out of New Orleans permanently. Or maybe he thought it was just too lucrative to pass up. Then again, the deal might have been done under financial duress. Whatever the reason, Garret sold a grocery store at Dauphine and Engine to a man named F.B. Thriffeley. Written into the contract was a severely restrictive non-compete clause. In it, Schwegmann agreed not to go into the grocery business anywhere within a twelve-block radius of Thriffeley's for five years.

Pause here to consider that had he not kept selling off his stores or signing over his competitive rights in order to finance fruitless junkets out west, by the mid-1880s Garret would have owned a nice-sized chain of Bywater-based grocery stores. This would have placed him in the vanguard of the chain-store phenomenon then just beginning to take shape in American retailing. Garret, however, did not own a blossoming chain-store empire. He had sacrificed this possibility in his reckless gambles on a better future elsewhere.

It is not clear precisely when it happened—probably sometime right after John, her fifth and last child, was born in 1883—but at some point Garret's long-suffering wife, Mary, finally decided that enough was enough. She had had it. She was fed up with his wild-eyed escapades, his mad routine of uprooting the family periodically only to have to return and start all over again from scratch. For her there were to be no more quixotic quests out west. The family would settle permanently in New Orleans—with or without Garret. Likely around the mid-1880s, the couple separated but did not divorce, as Mary was a devout Catholic.

GARRET SCHWEGMANN WAS A COMPLEX MAN. He clearly had a strong personality. Otherwise he never would have separated from his original immigrant family to go it alone down in New Orleans. Nor would he have attracted the sister of a prominent social-climbing merchant family, or had the gumption and ability to buy and sell a string of stores, all profitable, just to fuel his wanderlust. Yet alongside his strong personality, Garret also had a mean weak streak. Put bluntly, he was a drunk, a slave to the bottle. Worse, he was a gambler, reveling in the illicit thrills of poker and dice.[13] This would explain a number of things: especially his bizarre, erratic behavior over the 1870s and 1880s; his worse-than-sloppy recordkeeping; and his wife's growing aversion to him. Yet in Garret's defense, perhaps he was plagued by long-term pain inflicted through his wounds suffered in the Civil War, and he simply sought medicinal relief in alcohol and emotional solace in the conviviality of gambling.

The clash of Garret's strong and weak sides expressed itself in a peripatetic spirit. He was compelled to wander, to search for resolution somewhere outside of himself. Yet in repeatedly venturing out west, he never succeeded in resolving his internal conflicts. Instead he always came back to New Orleans, his demons growing worse each time he returned. Apparently at first Garret's drinking was not so bad, for he was able to support a family of expanding proportions while running a series of successful enterprises. Over time, though, his behavior deteriorated and became more insufferable. In the eyes of his stern and sober in-laws—the solid, stolid, upright, uptight Henkes—Garret grew into an absolute disgrace. "They hated him," according to his grandson John.[14]

*   *   *

It is not known exactly when Garret returned to New Orleans from what proved to be his final California trip. What is known is that the non-compete clause with Thriffeley expired in 1888. And with this factoid, it is finally time to explore the alternate version of Garret Schwegmann's story—presented in these pages for the first time. As documented in the New Orleans Notarial Archive, the widow of a certain Theodore Lederer acquired the property on Piety and Burgundy (with a structure already built on it) in 1866, and she owned it until 1880. Could she have rented the building out to Garret for a store during this interval? Perhaps, but there is no record of this having occurred. Instead, the Notarial Archive shows something different—and slightly disturbing from the viewpoint of official family history.

Specifically, on September 4, 1880, Mrs. Lederer sold the Piety and Burgundy property to a "George" (presumably Garret) Schwegmann. So far, nothing out of the ordinary here, as Garret engages in his usual practice of real estate scheming. But then something weird happens. Six days later, on September 10, 1880, George/Garret sells the property to a family member named August Schwegmann.[15] *August Schwegmann?* Who is this never-before-introduced stranger in the family cast? No Schwegmann interviewed for this book knows anything about any August, and he receives absolutely no mention from John G. Schwegmann on the Cabildo tape, or is acknowledged in any written family record.

After teasing out information from nearly invisible sources, it appears likely that August was Garret's brother. Consider that genealogical records show an August Schwegmann born just a few years before Garret. Moreover, it is known that a branch of the German-American Schwegmann family had settled in Cincinnati, Ohio.[16] So perhaps August was Garret's brother living in Cincinnati. Then again, he might have been a brother or even cousin living in New Orleans all along.

But there is no reason to belabor these speculations. For in the end, the only really insoluble mystery is why Garret so suddenly flipped the Piety and Burgundy property to the unknown August. Did something untoward happen to force the sale? Or was this just Garret's normal way of doing business, tapping family members to front for his surrogate ownership? If the latter, how big of a role did August play in Garret's other kaleidoscopic retail ventures? And finally, why did the New Orleans' branch of the Schwegmann family write August out of its legacy? Unfortunately, the answers to these questions will probably never be known, as August died in the late 1880s. Before he transitioned, though, he sold the store at Piety and Burgundy in 1883 to a man named Dietrich Hustkamp.

And there matters stood until November 2, 1889, when "George" (aka Garret) Schwegmann bought the same store back from Hustkamp for $15,000.[17] Here the timing fits perfectly with the ending of Garret's non-compete agreement with Thriffeley. For after 1888, Garret was free and clear to set up shop once more in the heart of the Bywater. The timing also jibes with what has so far remained inexplicable—namely, the reason for christening Schwegmann's own patented bourbon as "1889." In light of this newly revealed timeline, the liquor's branding can be seen to commemorate the actual establishment of the old corner store in 1889, as opposed to its fabled founding twenty years earlier in 1869.

If true, the alternate timeline—based objectively on records from the New Orleans Notarial Archive—presents two big problems. First, it forces a general historical rewrite to reflect the actual origination date of the old corner store at Piety and Burgundy in 1889, not 1869. Second, it inserts a spanner into the sequence of previously accepted subsequent events. Consider that the family's traditional timeline has Garret Schwegmann buying the old corner store for a third time in 1891 (the two previous times being in 1869 and 1880). According to the family's version of events, Garret Sr. remained the owner of the store from 1891 until 1895, when he sold it to his firstborn son, Garret Jr. The Notarial Archive, by contrast, clearly shows that Senior sold the store to Junior in 1892.

Ultimately the discrepancies between these dates make little difference, although they do tend to snag details in the early historical fabric of the Schwegmann family legacy. What is known in general is that when Garret Sr. bought the old corner store for the last time, whether in 1889 or 1891, the omens were not exactly auspicious. For within three weeks of its opening a gas meter exploded and fire destroyed the store, burning down four surrounding buildings in the process. Fortunately, Garret had insurance and had the store rebuilt. Unfortunately, though, Garret could not rebuild himself. For by now the formerly dashing and daring entrepreneur was deep in his cups, and he proceeded slowly but surely to run his newly renovated store into the ground.

Book-ending his either three- or four-year tenure as owner and operator of the legendary old corner store—either from 1889 to 1892, or 1891 to 1895—two dramatic, and frankly pathetic, family-oriented events took place that will be related later. For now, Garret's story ends on a positive note. After suffering a severe shock and likely hitting proverbial bottom, he ever so gradually (this being New Orleans and all) began cleaning up his act. Garret ceased his futile travels to California and finally settled down into a nice place on the outskirts of the Bywater at the corner of Claiborne and Poland avenues. Now retired, dabbling in and living off real estate investments, he resided there for the next thirty years. Over time in this remote abode he seems to have come to grips with whatever demons had tormented him before. He even quit drinking.

If not exactly happier, the old man seemed more content. No longer getting his kicks on Route 66, as it were, he now found pleasure in more sedentary activities, such as playing checkers with friends, enjoying occasional visits with his grandchildren, or simply sitting on a bench under a china ball tree outside his house. Nevertheless, Garret's old rambunctious spirit reasserted itself at least once a year when he hosted his own annual outdoor birthday parties. These were lively affairs featuring feasts of food, heaps of ice cream, and live German oompah bands playing under arcs of electric lights strung up through the trees, courtesy of his neighbor George Gouguet (who later factors into John's story).

Garret must have had a strong constitution. For despite his excesses, he lived a long life. In his senescence, daughter Mary either moved in or regularly came over to the house to clean up and care for him. Also looking after him were his next-door neighbors, the Ryans. When Garret was in his final days, he developed some sort of stomach rot, which often left him sleepless and in pain. What he did to assuage the agony was knock on the wall of his house and call out to the Ryan boys. Able to hear this signal through the thin walls of their own home, one of the Ryan brothers would come over and play checkers with the old man until his pain subsided and he could sleep. In 1927, at the then-ancient age of 85, Garret finally passed away. He is buried in a family plot at St. Roch Cemetery.

3

UNCLE GARRET AND FATHER JOHN
Two Types of Success

O F GARRET AND MARY'S FIVE CHILDREN, the most remarkable in terms of future accomplishments was their firstborn and eldest son, George. The name was an anglicized version of Gerhardt, which is what his German parents called him.[1] Perhaps in an attempt to reconcile the two extremes of American and German identity, George/ Gerhardt took on his father's name and formally became known as Garret. Throughout this chapter he is referred to as Garret Junior, or simply Garret when the context allows.

Garret Jr. shared many positive traits with Garret Sr. He was handsome, charming, smart, ambitious, and hard working. He was also a chip off the old block in his uncanny knack for making money. For like his father, he was a natural-born businessman. Yet in one crucial respect Junior diverged completely from Senior: namely, he was sober. Except on rare occasions, he was a teetotaler. Certainly as the oldest of the Schwegmann children, he was in the best position to have witnessed the progressively ravaging effects of alcohol on his father. Repulsed by this, he chose instead to follow in the path of his mother's family, the "strong-minded, strong-willed" Henkes.

After graduating from high school, Garret Jr. went to work in the field he knew best—namely, grocery retailing.[2] Over the course of the late 1880s he clerked at two grocery stores: Olstein's, located in central New Orleans at the corner of Baronne and Poydras streets; and Thriffeley's, on Burgundy and Enghein streets. At the same time, determined to improve his business skills, he attended night school at Soule College. Little is known about Garret Jr.'s experience at Thriffeley's beyond that he worked there for about a year beginning in 1888. By contrast, colorful anecdotes about his time at Olstein's have been kept alive through the recollections of his nephew John.

In what was presumably his first job, Garret Jr. worked at Olstein's for a year and a half. When Garret first presented himself as available for employment, the Jewish couple who ran this prominent downtown grocery store were impressed by how serious the young man was, how businesslike. So they took him under their wing, determined to mentor him in merchant skills. As things turned out, though, the relationship was more than one-way, for Garret Jr. brought with him his own boyhood experience working in his father's stores.

Indeed, he ended up helping the couple out as much as they helped him, primarily by demonstrating to the Olsteins how wholesalers and distributors were cheating them. In one instance, Garret attempted to convince the Olsteins that their measuring scale was too small to fully accommodate the bulk products being sold to them by wholesalers. Since the products—sowbellies, salt backs, pickled shoulders—did not quite fit on the store's scale, wholesalers could get away with exaggerating their weight. While Old Man Olstein grumbled and argued over the implications of this observation, Mrs. Olstein came to Garret's defense. "You don't have a big enough scale to weigh 'em," she insisted to her husband. So they bought a larger scale.

In a similar instance, Garret was able to show the couple, using a specially designed measuring gauge, how liquor distributors were making out like bandits by diluting their whiskey with water. He explained how on one hand the distributors profited off the skim and on the other reaped a tax advantage, leaving the retailer to eat the losses flowing from both transactions.

Over the time Garret worked at Olstein's, the young man built up such a reservoir of trust that, according to his nephew John, Garret actually began managing the business. But in 1889, at age 19, Garret Junior suddenly took a swerve, leaving the grocery business for a job as some sort of mechanic. At that point he disappears from the historical record for a couple of years. Meanwhile, Garret Senior was beginning his fall from grace, the tumble commencing after he returned to New Orleans from his last California trip.

Senior's troubles began in earnest when he bought the Piety and Burgundy store in 1889. Try as he might, his old moneymaking mojo was just not working anymore, and the store began sinking. He implored his sons to come help him out. But as Grandson John recounts, Garret Senior was in such bad shape at the time—"He was getting drunk, acting like a fool!"—that nobody in the family wanted to work for him anymore. His estranged wife, who by this time "didn't tolerate anyone who drank," was of course disgusted by her ex-husband's behavior. Yet Mary apparently still had some compassion left for his condition and decided to give him one last chance. She spoke frankly with her oldest son, "Gerhardt," urging him to visit the store and offer to help his father out. When Garret Jr. aggressively balked at this suggestion, Mary remonstrated, promising him that if he found Senior showing signs of persisting in his dipsomania, she would never ask Junior to go back there again. He reluctantly agreed to do it.

The stage was thus set for some sort of dramatic showdown. As the story goes, Garret Junior arrived at the store only to find Garret Senior drunk as a skunk. At first the son pleaded with his father to lay off the bottle: "Can't you see how you are ruining your life, the business, the family!" Obviously getting nowhere, young Garret suddenly snapped. In a fit of rage he violently swept several bottles of booze off the "ballroom" counter, smashing them to pieces in the process. He then lunged around the store, furiously ripping the faucets and bungs (corks) out of all the wine casks and whiskey barrels in the place. As the liquid contents gushed hopelessly onto the floor, he stormed out of the store. After this epic encounter, Garret Jr. once again temporarily vanishes from general historical scrutiny.

*   *   *

By 1892, AFTER THREE YEARS of running the Piety Street store (mostly into the ground), Garret Sr. once more felt the old familiar prurient urge steal down on him: he was itching to go out west. Just as in the past, just like he always did—or so he believed—he would sell the store and soon be back on the glory train clattering out west to his old stomping grounds in the Golden State. But this time events took a more Oedipal turn. As per his usual routine, Garret Sr. put out word on the grapevine that his business was up for sale—this "without even knowing what he was selling for," as John Jr. acidly remarked later about his grandfather's besotten impulsiveness at the time.

What happened next is not exactly clear, although the basic outline of the story is apparent. One source has it that Garret Jr. received word from his mother that his father's grocery store was now on the market. More likely, though, he was tipped off by a Mr. Oemichen, an old friend who worked as a wholesale grocery salesman for H.T. Cottam (a major food distributor in New Orleans at the time).[3] Indeed, Oemichen appears to have provided the spark for two key moves made by Garret. It was he who had earlier recommended that Garret go to work for Olstein's. And now he was probably the one who alerted Junior that Senior was selling the store. One family anecdote has Oemichen excitedly urging Garret, "Come quickly, before he sells it to a stranger." Because he had always wanted to own his own business—although doubtless, with his father's store involved, his motives were overdetermined—young Garret decided then and there to buy the store. In order to do so, he and his mother pooled their savings, which included some properties in which they owned an interest, and came up with enough money for the down payment.

The firstborn son did, in fact, end up buying his father's grocery business. But just how the transaction came about is the subject of two conflicting stories. According to the tamer version, the store was purchased through subterfuge, with a front group representing Garret Junior. Only after the ownership transfer papers were signed was the son's true identity revealed to the father.

Nephew John, however, tells a more memorable and tragic tale.[4] In this version, Garret Jr., his brother Henry, and Mr. Oehmichen all rendezvoused quickly at Garret Sr.'s store with the intention of confronting the old man with an irrefutable offer to buy at the asking price. But then the almost unspeakable occurred. It had been three years since Senior had last gazed upon Junior. In the interim, Garret Jr. had matured and grown a moustache. When Garret Sr. first laid eyes on his estranged eldest son, the old man was so wrecked that he did not recognize him. He then proceeded to ask this apparent stranger—someone who had spent a portion of his childhood there—"Don't you want to see the living quarters upstairs before you buy?" Mr. Oehmichen awkwardly interjected, "Mr. Schwegmann, don't you know this man?" Garret Sr. replied, "No, I've never seen him before in my life." The exasperated salesman quickly retorted, "But Mr. Schwegmann, this is your son Garret!"

According to John Jr., the Schwegmanns are a "very hard, hard people," not prone to showing their emotions. So it was extremely telling when tears suddenly welled up in the old man's eyes as the realization dawned that he was so far gone that he did not even recognize his oldest son. In a feeble, guilt-ridden attempt to make amends for this primal lapse, Garret Senior sought to save face by offering to lease the store to Garret Junior for less than the asking price. But son Garret was having none of it. He stood his ground, responding: "I don't want one thing less than what you were selling it to me before. That's the price." Confronting his son's bold act of self-assertion, and facing the revelation of his own ruination, Garret Sr. threw in the towel. He gave up. He sold his business for the last time and settled into a long and lonely retirement. The former reckless adventurer was never to leave New Orleans again.

WHILE THIS ENCOUNTER BROKE THE FATHER, it liberated the son. Indeed, from that point on, Garret Junior's life was a triumph, his ensuing career presenting a record of unbroken success. According to official family legend, it all began with his purchase of the Piety Street grocery—buying the *business* but not the actual *store*, which he continued to lease from his father—on March 3, 1895. How this particular date was arrived at remains a mystery, as notary records show the ownership transfer occurring in 1892. But leaving aside such historical quibbles, what is known for certain is that Garret Jr.'s first act was to name the business, calling it simply G.A. Schwegmann Grocery Company. Under his direction, with later assistance from his two brothers—first Henry (officially hired 1896) and then John (1898)—the run-down store was renovated, refurbished, and infused with a new energy. Over a few short years it developed a reputation for low prices, honest weight, and high product quality—particularly for cheese, butter, coffee, ham, spareribs, and sauerkraut. By the turn of the century, the store that had by then been rechristened as Schwegmann Brothers Grocery Company was among the leading grocery entities in New Orleans.[5]

Underlying this spectacular turnaround was a new policy Garret Jr. instituted—namely, the elimination of all purchasing on credit. From now on, the only acceptable means of customer payment was cash on the barrelhead. As will be seen, this was a radical departure from the usual practice of the time. Yet young Garret felt that enforcing such a stern, inflexible cash-only policy was absolutely necessary after inheriting a swamp of customer debt from his father.[6] Another change he made was to expand distribution. To accomplish this he bought two mule-drawn wagons, using these to make customer deliveries and street sales. Then, surprisingly—considering his earlier flip-out over his father's alcoholism—Garret Jr. leased additional property located next to the store from Garret Sr. Here, apparently bowing to Bywater cultural realities, this shrewd businessman opened up a thriving saloon called Schwegmann's Bar.

Not long after taking over the helm at the Piety Street store, Garret Jr. fell in love. The object of his affection was a young neighborhood beauty named Anna Emmer, who set his heart aflutter every time she appeared in the store. Their mutual feelings for each other blossomed and ripened, finally culminating in marriage in the late 1890s. The union produced two children: Leo and George. As will be seen, both of these Schwegmann boys played a major, though indirect, role in the formation of their cousin John's aspirations.

Both Leo (who remained in New Orleans) and George (who moved to Washington, D.C.) went on to live long, distinguished lives. Not so their mother, whose end came all too soon. Garret adored Anna, showering her with the finest in life and building her a showcase manse on Pauline Street near Burgundy that was featured in a 1910 *Illustrated Sunday Magazine* as an example of a "Beautiful New Orleans Home." But tragically, Anna suddenly died in 1916 at the young age of forty-one. In his grief, Garret departed the manse, moving into a simple brick home across from Macarty Square.

FROM THE BEGINNING, JAKE EMMER, Anna's father, must have been particularly enthusiastic about his daughter's marriage to Garret, a prosperous grocery store merchant. For Jake was a prominent neighborhood grocery and dry goods distributor.[7]

In the days before motorized vehicles, being a "distributor" of course meant hauling goods by wagon, not truck. Thus Jake could regularly be seen driving a huge "dray" (wagon) pulled by four or more mules through the dusty, unpaved streets of the old Bywater; the "float" (back of the wagon) piled high with cotton bales, casks of molasses, and other bulk commodities. After work, Jake and his fellow draymen would first sequester their mules in a barn on Pauline Street—the barn later converted into the Rutter-Rex Clothing Factory, employer of fictional antihero Ignatius Reilly in *A Confederacy of Dunces*—and then typically went over to Schwegmann's Bar to whet their whistles. So the marriage had been all in the family, cementing relations through business, pleasure, and even home location—for Jake and his family lived on Dauphine Street just a block or two away from Garret and Anna.

For all that, though, the Emmers never strongly established themselves in the extended Schwegmann family network. Likely it was Anna's premature death that served to attenuate attachments. Certainly the Emmers' influence fades in John's later recollections. He recalls, for instance, that Jake went on to own his own trucking company. But he also remembers not knowing until later in life the identity of a strange old lady—it was Jake's wife—who regularly came over to his Grandmother Frey's house to buy her homemade clabber.

USING HIS SUCCESSFUL STORE AS A SPRINGBOARD, Garret Jr. proceeded to dive into the real estate market, buying up numerous properties in the Bywater. From there, Garret's fortunes soared. He invested his profits judiciously, acquiring interests in banks, homesteads (later called savings and loans), utilities, and food and beverage companies. For instance, he owned a major stake in Merchants Coffee Company, which marketed the Union brand of coffee (still sold to this day). He was also on the board of Whitney Bank, a leading New Orleans financial institution. From this position he encouraged commercial development in the Bywater, using his influence to help establish the Third District Bank and Trust Company (later acquired by Whitney Bank) and numerous other businesses in the neighborhood.

Garret Jr. was so successful in his business and financial endeavors that he became quite wealthy. According to the hyperbole of his nephew John, by the early years of the twentieth century Uncle Garret had become a "millionaire" who owned "hundreds and hundreds" of properties. This boast, though, is difficult to reconcile with a more objective claim that in 1916, at the peak of his career, Garret Jr. owned 19 properties in the Ninth Ward worth a total of $38,000.[8] Yet beyond financial reckoning, Garret by this time had achieved an even higher status than merely being a rich man: he was extremely well respected throughout the New Orleans business community. As visible evidence of his personal affluence, he always took care to look his best, with anecdotal accounts suggesting he was considered the best-dressed grocery executive in New Orleans. Along with knowing how to project success, Garret knew how to enjoy it as well. He was an avid angler and traveled extensively around the United States in pursuit of his passion for fishing.

For local leisure, Garret Junior built a lavish fishing camp on the south shore of Lake Pontchartrain. Located at Seabrook near the Industrial Canal, right near Lutchen's Public Bath House (where there was beer, seafood, and dancing), the camp was named Ledora—a blend of the first names of Lillian and Dora McCoy, two longtime, well-loved employees at the old corner store. Costing $2,000 to build, Ledora was huge by fishing-camp standards at 4,000 square feet. It featured a wraparound gallery, numerous bedrooms, and even a ballroom dance floor. Garret generously loaned the luxurious camp to his employees for their family vacations.

Ledora also served as the site for an annual summer weeklong store holiday. The highlight of the holiday was an all-day picnic celebration. Here employees and their families would feast on a forty-pound roast cooked at nearby Fresch's Bakery and engage in such old-fashioned frivolities as greased pole climbing, greased pig chasing, and mixed-shoe and sack races. There were also contests of skill, in which store clerks competed over who could most quickly and perfectly wrap one-pound packages of rice and beans.

At the age of 69, with his health beginning to ebb, Garret Junior decided it was time to retire. So in 1939 he sold the grocery business at Piety and Burgundy (but, like his father, retained ownership of the actual property) to its longtime manager, his brother John. From there the distinguished old gentleman—whose favorite expressions were "By golly," "By Joyce," and "You don't tell me"—went on to live comfortably into his mid-eighties before passing away in 1954.

BY ALL STANDARD MEASURES, Garret Junior clearly stands out as being the most successful offspring of the second generation of New Orleans Schwegmanns. But from a deeper historical perspective, the greater achievement was actually accomplished by his youngest brother. Born in 1883, John William Schwegmann was nowhere near as dynamic as Garret, displaying a fraction of his discipline and none of his drive. Nevertheless, he somehow managed to sire the most ambitious Schwegmann yet, a son whose career far outshone his Uncle Garret's. Since this son was named after his father, the latter is referred to subsequently as John Senior, while the former is called John Junior. Note, however, that from here on out, whenever the appellative context admits of no ambiguity, "Junior" and "Senior" are dropped and the father or son simply becomes "John."

Little is known about the early life of John Senior besides that he was born, raised, and went to school in the Bywater and served piously as an altar boy at Holy Trinity Catholic Church.[9] What is clear, though, is that the youth grew up during a period of considerable emotional turmoil in Schwegmann family life. Right after his birth, John's parents separated on acrimonious terms, his suffering mother repulsed by the wild style of dear old dad—then in the heyday of his wheeling and dealing, dreaming and scheming, and drinking and gambling. This unstable atmosphere did not exactly do wonders for the youngest son's self-esteem, nor did living in the shadow of Garret Jr., his glorious older brother. As a result, John Sr. never developed any grand personal aspirations. A family story is told of how once, as if he had something to prove, John impulsively dove off the dock at Esplanade Avenue and swam across the dangerous Mississippi River. This memory is likely preserved because it stands out as being so uncharacteristic. Certainly over the course of his later life this early form of impetuous self-assertion became submerged. For as he grew older John basically kept his head down, content with being ordinary, not extraordinary.

There is clear evidence that John Sr. was burdened with a sense of at best insecurity and at worst inferiority. For at some unknown point he began to follow his father's example and take solace in the bottle. While he never fell quite so far into the depths of drunkenness as his dad did—nor did he inveterately gamble on risky entrepreneurial ventures or go on wild goose chases out west, preferring instead to stay in New Orleans and placidly keep his nose to the grindstone—John Sr.'s drinking was bad enough to leave a permanent sorrowful impression on his namesake son. Decades later, John Jr. would honestly admit that he had had an unhappy childhood due to the influence of alcohol on his parents. Yes, he lamented, it was not just his father who had a drinking problem but his mother too.

In 1898, at just age fifteen, John Senior quit high school to help his brother Garret run the old corner store. Although he could not have known it at the time, this decision sealed his fate. For from thenceforward, he would never again leave the store. But before projecting onto his later life a future of unmitigated drudgery and boredom, consider that he must have had a lively time of it at least in his late teens and middle twenties. For John Sr. spent this prime time of coming to manhood serving on the front lines of the delightful war between the sexes.

To explain, there grew up around the traditional corner grocery store a cultural custom that revolved around the rites of flirting and courtship. Perfectly acceptable at the time as a legitimate mating ritual, the object of the game was to bring together in holy matrimony a spirited, attractive young lady with a solid, hardworking young man. Everyone played along. Before sending them off on a mission to the store, mothers would, as was said back then, "set their daughter's caps"—roughly the distaff equivalent of a military inspection, followed perhaps by an inspirational pre-battle harangue. Meanwhile back in the trenches, nervous male clerks would practice putting on their best, most charming faces to prepare for possible romantic encounters with favored single female customers. In the end, many a grocery clerk met his future wife in this way.

To give credence to this custom, consider how it played out in the context of the Schwegmann family story: Garret Sr. and Mary Henke met and fell in love at Hank's Grocery; and Garret Jr. and Anna Emmer did the same at Schwegmann's Grocery. This pattern was repeated in the case of John Sr., who also met his spouse at the old corner store. In John's case, he must have been mighty choosy, for he held out for a whole decade in the thick of the flirtation action before finally deciding on a wife.

The "lucky lady" was Marie Frey. John and Marie married in 1910, he aged twenty-seven, she twenty-five. Immediately afterward they began raising a family. Altogether they produced six children: John Gerald (born 1911), Anthony (1913), Paul (1914), Odile (1915), Francis (1919), and Marguerite (1922).

John Senior had chosen well. For Marie Frey was the daughter of an industrious, self-sufficient family that would come to play an extremely influential role in shaping the Schwegmann legacy, particularly through its overwhelmingly positive impact on the formative life of John Junior. This family's history in New Orleans commenced in 1864, when Andreas and Francesca Frey arrived in the city with their children from the Alsace-Lorraine region of France/Germany.[10] Just a few years later, one of their sons, Anton, met and began romancing Apollonia Pauline Morrel. Anton married Apollonia in 1870. Over the next two decades, the loving couple had seven children: Pauline (born 1873), Anthony (1876), Francis (1878), Joseph (1881), Marie (1885), Aloysius (1887), and Helen (1890).

BEFORE PROCEEDING, IT SHOULD BE REMEMBERED that in the second half of the nineteenth century—and even up to as late as the "teen" years of the twentieth century—distinct rural accents still colored the urban landscape. In other words, back before the spread of dense urban agglomerations and strict zoning ordinances, it was not at all uncommon for city folk, especially in working-class neighborhoods such as the Bywater, to grow food and even raise animals at home.[11]

Looking back at this practice of old-fashioned urban agriculture, many modern observers, especially of the "green" variety, make the mistake of considering it in a vacuum, as simply an abstract means employed by preceding generations to provide some semblance of "food security." What they tend to overlook is that the practice also had real sociological ramifications. For wherever geographic clusters of urban farms formed, city and country tended to blend together to create what took on the essential characteristics of small towns existing within the larger metropolis. Naturally within these urban/rural amalgams, some cultural virtues traditionally associated with small towns persisted.

Thus, for example, a high value continued to be placed within these city/country enclaves on tight-knit family structures. Certainly this was the case for the Schwegmann extended family network, which was close, even claustrophobic. Not only did the two Schwegmann brothers, Garret and John, live within a few blocks of each other, their two parental in-law families, the Emmers and the Freys, also resided within this same few-block radius. Indeed, in the in-laws' case, the distance between them was even more constricted, as the Emmers and Freys lived right across the street from each other (on Dauphine and Pauline).

Related to tight-knit family structures, a similar small-town value was placed on self-reliance. In the case of Anton and Apollonia Frey, they perfectly epitomized this late-nineteenth-century ethos of the self-sufficient city family, as after their marriage they went on to establish the very model of what nowadays would be called a "sustainable urban homestead."

The site for this homestead was a Bywater lot encompassing an entire city square bounded by four blocks: Pauline, Dauphine, Alvar, and Royal streets. Fronted on the north side of the square by a large, exceptionally solid house they built at 3802 Dauphine Street, the property extended south to encompass a small-scale farm. This farm included a horse stable, a cow barn, chicken coops, food and herb gardens, and fruit trees. Even more, it incorporated a small abattoir for butchering livestock and a concrete pit for salting and drying animal hides. Anton himself was a butcher by trade, selling his fresh meat from a stall at the French Market. Anton's brother Joseph and his cousin L.A. Frey were also in the business. Joseph made a good living off selling hides, while L.A. Frey and Sons became regionally famous for making fine sausages. Back in the day, the L.A. Frey sausage factory was located on Burgundy between Alvar and Bartholomew streets.

For her part, Apollonia Frey kept two dairy cows, using their fresh milk to make cream cheese and clabber, which she served to the family as well as sold on the market. (Clabber, by the way, is similar to cottage cheese. Her husband loved it, eating a plate of boiled potatoes and clabber every night right before bedtime.) Not to be outdone, Apollonia's youngest daughter, Helen, raised hogs on the property. The four or more hungry hogs Helen always kept were fed with both table scraps and offal (waste products of butchering). She collected the offal from three slaughterhouses: two in the Lower Ninth Ward, one along Caffin Avenue and another in Arabi; and one in central New Orleans called the New Orleans Butcher Abbatoir.

Helen Frey was a consummate agriculturist in the traditional sense. It was not enough that she oversaw a small-scale farm and garden and raised animals. For she also took care to recycle everything. A charming family photo shows Helen and sister Pauline posing together holding a baby lamb. The kicker is that they are both sitting atop a bone box. This was a wooden bin holding the leftover bones from soup meats and rendering. The bones were subsequently sold as raw materials for making various organic products, such as fertilizer.

SOMETIME IN THE FIRST DECADE of the 1900s, after building up Schwegmann Brothers sufficiently, Garret Jr. selected his brother John to manage it while he went off to pursue an ever-widening range of business interests. In exchange for managing the old corner store, John Sr. at first received the princely sum of $65 a month—a salary that after twenty long years positively ballooned to $125 per month. But in the deal he received a major perquisite: he got to live on top of the store in its six-room living quarters—for a rental fee, of course.

It was here, up above the old corner store, that John Sr. and Marie raised a family. Under their straitened circumstances, the family was long on economy and short on luxury. Nonetheless, perennially strapped as he was, at least John had a stable job and income. This he and Marie leveraged to raise a crop of good, decent, hard-working children—one of whom would grow up to be a star in the retail firmament.

As mentioned, in 1939, finally ready to retire, Garret Jr. offered to sell the Schwegmann Brothers grocery business to brother John. Since John Sr. was far from being able to come up with the funds to buy the company, he brought in a willing and eager financier—namely, his eldest son. Yet this is getting ahead of the story. Here suffice to note that, unlike the inauspicious moment half a century earlier when a horrified Garret Senior watched helplessly as the old corner store burnt to a crisp just three weeks after he opened it, the omens were much more propitious when John Senior took over.

In July 1939, a 425-foot Spanish freighter fully loaded with a cargo of fancy imported groceries rammed a tugboat in the Mississippi River, causing the freighter to run aground at the Bienville Street Wharf in New Orleans.[12] Although the wreck was duly towed across the river and sunk at the port of Algiers, it continued to present a navigational hazard, as her bow still poked out of the water. So six months later, in December 1939, the decision was taken to dynamite the half-sunken Spanish ship. Immediately following an immense blast, which cracked the sidewalks in Algiers, a horde of small boats swarmed the area chasing after floating remnants of the cargo. A good portion of the scavengers' surprisingly bountiful haul soon found its way to Schwegmann Brothers Grocery Company—now under new management—where Christmas-time shoppers were delighted to be presented with an abundance of stuffed Spanish olives, Torrido peppers, cooking oil, and whiskey at prices that were basically a steal.

After the changing of the guard in 1939, the old corner store on Piety and Burgundy continued on in operation throughout the difficult years of World War II (a story detailed later). But only three years after the war, in 1948, John Senior sold off the business, this time for good. For at that point his son was calling on the tired old man to help manage a new-fangled type of grocery store. John Senior went on to occupy a figurehead position at John Junior's wildly successful Airline supermarket for a few years of semi-retirement. After decades of merely eking out a living, he was finally rich! But he did not live long enough to really enjoy his new wealth. For in 1955, only seven years removed from his fifty years spent slaving away at the old corner store, John Senior died at the age of seventy-two.

4

REFLECTIONS ON OLD-TIME CORNER GROCERY STORES

Summing up the situation so far, the Schwegmann family and its in-laws had dedicated roughly ninety years in New Orleans—from 1855 to 1945—to building up a solid foundation in that sector of the retail food trade known as grocery stores. Growing up from these deep local roots in the grocery business, John Gerald Schwegmann would go on to flower and crown his family legacy. But before his visionary achievements can be properly appreciated, some idea must be gained, some picture or general impression formed, of what grocery stores looked like back in the "good old days" of his forebears. For only by looking through the prism of what preceded him can the magnitude of John's accomplishments be truly understood.[1]

When in the mid-nineteenth century the Henke family and Garret Senior first went into the grocery business, nothing even remotely resembling a modern supermarket existed. Instead, the world of grocery retailing was still in what could be characterized as a "pre-industrial" state. In other words, by modern standards it was primitive on all levels—from transportation and distribution to quality and quantity and health and safety. There were no cars or trucks for food delivery, no electricity available for store lighting or refrigeration. Food packaging was almost nonexistent. There were no brand-name products lining the shelves; indeed, there were few shelves at all. Worst of all, sanitary conditions at most stores were appalling.

Indeed, the only thing really going for old-time grocery stores was convenient location. They were everywhere. The reason for this was simple. Between 1850 and 1910, U.S. cities exploded in size to accommodate the inflow of millions of new arrivals to America, with the cumulative number of mostly European immigrants skyrocketing sevenfold, from roughly 2 million to 14 million, over the two-generation period. To service this ballooning demand, old-time grocery stores proliferated all over urban America, eventually to be located almost "literally…on every corner."[2]

These ubiquitous old-time corner grocery stores—which at an average size of 600 to 800 square feet would all be dwarfed by even the smallest modern supermarket—offered only an extremely limited selection of food items within their confined space. The number of product types they carried (mostly food, but also a few "dry goods") averaged between 200 and 500 "stock-keeping units," in contrast to the tens of thousands of SKUs carried by contemporary supermarkets.

Yet in the general retail scheme of things at the time, grocery stores did not have to be large or offer thousands of products. This was because they were not primary food destinations for consumers. Indeed, how could they be? Given the primitive state of technology in the mid- to late nineteenth century, old-time grocery stores simply did not have the equipment, labor, or managerial capacity to maintain a comprehensive stock of food items.

This was especially the case in regard to fresh, or "perishable," foods. Aside from a few perishables that could be stored in an "icebox," the old stores rarely carried any fresh meat, fish, milk, or bread at all. Moreover, the fruits and vegetables they stocked were limited to a few of the more easily shipped types, such as potatoes, apples, cabbages, and the occasional local or regional seasonal item.

So in order to acquire fresh foods, consumers at the time did not go to grocery stores. Instead, they obtained them from retailers who specialized in procuring, producing, and preserving fresh stock—butchers, bakers, dairies, produce vendors, and other specialty outlets. Consider also that it was more common in those days for people to grow vegetables and raise animals at home. For this reason, many had at least some access to their own independent supply of fresh foods.

Old-time grocery stores, then, functioned mainly as secondary food destinations. What this means is that their major focus was on selling the essential staples used to *prepare* and *flavor* food. These staples included cooking oil, lard, flour, starch, baking powder, vinegar, molasses, sugar, and salt. They also typically offered a small selection of what could be called "subsistence extras" used to supplement and enhance the diet. These extras consisted of processed forms of fresh foods that could remain edible for extended periods with little to no refrigeration—bacon, cheese, crackers, and pickles, for example. Along with the essential staples and subsistence extras, most grocery stores at the time carried a few general merchandise sundries in common use, such as washing powder (used as both soap and detergent), kerosene and coal oil (used for lighting, heating, and cooking), and mops and brooms. Rounding out their product lineup, most old-time grocery stores offered a small number of "luxury" items appealing on the basis of pleasure or vice. These discretionary types of products included coffee, tea, wine, liquor, candy, and tobacco.

From a contemporary perspective, what is most astonishing about the old-time grocery stores is not so much how limited their selections were but rather their "near-total absence" of branded offerings.[3] Not until the late nineteenth century did grocers begin selling name-brand products to any significant degree—and even then these early brands were far from the trustworthy products featuring fixed weights, specified ingredients, and hygienic packages known today. For before brands, the grocers of yore offered anonymous commodities of unknown quantity and quality sold unpackaged in bulk. Depending on the form of the product, the commodity would either be integrally displayed somehow—a cheese wheel under a glass cover, preserved meat hanging from a hook—or it would be stocked in some sort of bulk container: a barrel, drum, canister, cask, sack, box, basket, can, jar, or drawer.

*   *   *

OLD-TIME GROCERY STORES WERE KNOWN as "full-service" retailers. What this means is self-explanatory, if somewhat unbelievable from a modern perspective. A clerk would directly attend to each individual customer, one at a time. Sometimes assisted by a helper, but more often than not totally alone, the clerk would then gather and assemble each individual customer's order. This process entailed the clerk maneuvering throughout the store between generic product displays and bulk containers where he (it was usually a "he") would variously scoop, pour, pump, spoon, cut, slice, grind, or otherwise extract the products desired by the customer. The clerk might also be sent to retrieve some type of packaged specialty item from up on a rare shelf or in back of the store. The full-service process concluded with measuring and weighing, wrapping each item in brown paper, and, finally, payment—or, more likely, haggling over payment. The customer would then leave with his or her purchases, or in some cases arrange for the purchases to be delivered.

These days it is hard to conceive of how anyone could summon the necessary patience and stamina to endure such a dreadfully long transaction. Consider the sum of the time it took for a customer to walk to the store, the idle half hours spent waiting in line for service, the long-drawn-out process of having a clerk retrieve and package each individual item, the inevitable and occasionally interminable bargaining over prices, and the final trek back home. No wonder grocery stores became social hubs in the old days, as customers must have spent a lot of time there together—whether they liked it or not.

So who were these customers? Granted that they represented an extreme diversity of individuals and character types, it is still safe to say that three generalizations apply to all old-time grocery-store shoppers. First, they tended to be neighbors, as most lived within walking distance of the store. Before the advent of cars and buses, most shoppers had to "hoof it" to the store, although a more fortunate few were able to arrive via wagon or barouche (carriage). Because the stores did not as a rule give out bags—paper bags were rare, and plastic had yet to be invented—the walkers were further burdened with having to bring their own containers in which to carry purchased groceries back home. Thus were shoppers forced to carry baskets, buckets, pitchers, and a variety of other containers to and from the store, which provided another incentive to live close by.

A second generalization applying to shoppers at old-time corner stores is that these customer-neighbors had to be at least minimally sociable. The full-service interaction demanded it. There was simply no opportunity to indulge in any form of the skulking anonymity possible with self-service. On the contrary, grocery clerks knew most shoppers by name and, going further, were often enough privy to their joys and sorrows. In this way, the full-service interaction encouraged an atmosphere of conviviality, perhaps even a faint family feeling, which worked to cement community ties.

In a final generalization, many old-time grocery store customers were immigrants. For this was the epic age of American immigration, with the majority of newcomers moving into cities. Here they invariably found a welcoming local corner grocery store eager for their business. Indeed, often enough these corner stores were themselves run by foreign-speaking immigrants, thus providing the new arrivals with a sympathetic space from which to begin the assimilation process.

When customers arrived at the old-time grocery store, while they might find a neighborly social environment, they rarely found a bright, inviting place where it was a delight to spend time. Instead, they were more likely to encounter a drab space, austere in appearance, with few if any vivid colors or attractive decorations, and little in the way of signage or merchandising. Adding to the drabness was an ambient darkness. Before electricity, only daylight and lamplight were available to brighten the stores. Even after electricity was introduced the lighting was not so great, as typically only a few dim bulbs hanging from the ceiling were used to illuminate the store.

What customers could see in the less-than-stellar light were common features shared by most old-time grocery stores. At the front of the store they encountered the all-important service, or "ballroom," counter. This was the theatrical stage where grocery clerks interacted with customers and took orders. Typically made of wood, the service counter had room on its surface for product display, with some space set aside for use as a cutting surface. Either placed directly on the service counter, or located conveniently around it, would typically be found a wheel of cheese, a coffee mill/grinder, and a hanging scale.

Behind the counter were tall wooden shelves on which were stacked any packaged foods then available. Many stores also had hooks behind the counter holding hanging slabs of meat. Underneath the counter, fronting the customer, were open shelves or glass-covered display cases containing small impulse items, such as candy and cigarettes. Also placed underneath the counter, but on the backside facing the clerk, was the all-important money drawer, or some kind of new-fangled cash register.

Beyond the ballroom counter, in the main space of the store, bulk containers were located that formed the sum and substance of what passed for the store's display. Here were the famous cracker barrels and pickle barrels of legend, the burlap sacks of flour, casks of wine and whiskey, baskets and stacks of produce, and the rest. Underfoot, customers would tread on wooden plank floors covered in sawdust, sprinkled around to help sop up rain, mud, and various foul substances that clung to the shoes and boots of shoppers.

Perhaps the dimly lit appearance of the old-time stores was a blessing in disguise. For the stores tended to be far from clean, with many being downright filthy. All stores had a big problem with pests of various types, both animate and inanimate, ranging from the merely annoying to the totally vile. In the days before screen doors and windows, frequently buzzing through the air would be flies and mosquitoes, along with a constant circulation of dust from the streets. Occasionally skittering around at ground level were mice, rats, and roaches attracted to any exposed bulk foods. Meanwhile, the only forms of pest control available were streamers of flypaper, mousetraps, and cats and dogs.

The primitive conditions of the early stores naturally conspired against food quality: the unclean funk of the stores not helping to guarantee any great degree of sanitary purity. Yet perhaps worse, because old-time grocery stores had no electrical refrigeration, any perishable foods they carried easily spoiled. Even having a meat locker or cold-storage chamber was of little help. Being chilled with hundred-pound blocks of ice, they only lowered temperatures to between forty and fifty degrees Fahrenheit—well above freezing.

Yet beyond any issues of cleanliness or freshness, the very nature of the unregulated bulk commodities on offer militated against any kind of objective quality assurance. Products distributed in bulk were inherently sketchy, as they could easily be diluted or otherwise compromised. At the same time, the extremely limited product selection available at most grocery stores precluded comparison shopping—or the ability to compare between good, better, and best quality; or poor, for that matter. Meanwhile, since producers, vendors, and distributors represented no trusted brand names at the time, they were mostly anonymous to the public. Given their anonymity, along with the ever-shifting ownership structures that came from being under constant laissez-faire economic pressure, all these suppliers were difficult to hold accountable in the quality arena.

Any mitigation of the primitive conditions that were the norm at old-time grocery stores ultimately depended on the character of the storeowner. Exceptional mom-and-pop merchants dealt with cleanliness through constant diligence, and they addressed quality issues through the painstaking acquisition of product knowledge and purchasing expertise. Yet there were plenty of grocery retailers more lackadaisical or even slovenly in their approach to these virtues. But whatever their attitude to cleanliness and quality, all grocery store owners shared one character trait in common: they were all hard workers. They had to be. Being lazy was just not an option.

Owners of grocery stores kept incredible hours. They awoke before dawn, usually around four in the morning. They would then either make a trip to the wholesale or produce markets themselves or get ready to receive deliveries to their stores—all still in the wee hours. Grocery stores typically opened their doors at 7 A.M. On weekdays, Monday through Thursday, closing time was twelve hours later at 7 P.M. On weekends, the hours were even longer, with the store doors not closing till 9 P.M., or in some cases as late as 11 P.M. As if this were not enough, many owners also worked on Sundays, performing maintenance and cleaning chores while their stores were closed. As can be imagined, this was an excruciatingly rough schedule, tending to exhaust all but the most hardy and dedicated. That this schedule led to a high degree of owner burnout is apparent from the large number of family-owned grocery stores that lasted for only three years or less.[4]

So who were these owners of old-time grocery stores? Almost invariably they were a husband and wife raising a family, hence the classic designation "mom-and-pop" stores. While a minority of more profitable old-time stores might have a few employees—with these clerks managing to endure a schedule almost as punishing as that of the owners—the majority of small independent family grocery businesses had no hired help whatsoever. In other words, most stores got by simply on the work of father, mother, and children. (Of course, some enterprising neighborhood boys might perform delivery jobs after school, but they typically worked only for tips.) Throughout the grueling schedule grocery store owners had to endure, they were blessed with one major saving grace—namely, that they and their families did not have to travel to work. Mom, pop, and kids typically lived at the store itself, either in back or on top. That they lived here also meant that the owner and family did not have to eat out for breakfast, lunch or dinner. They simply ate meals in their own kitchen. Indeed, John Jr. recalls that even the employees at his father's store would eat lunch and occasionally dinner in the upstairs kitchen.

For all the hard work involved in running a grocery store, owners typically realized little in the way of compensatory monetary reward. Scratching out a living from a limited demographic base of neighborhood customers, the mom-and-pops could in most cases barely afford to stay afloat, eking out meager annual sales totals of just a few thousand dollars. Consider that out of their minuscule sales, owners had to pay rents or mortgages, taxes, operating expenses, distribution and merchandising costs, and any salaries, among other debits. After deducting these costs and expenses, most grocery store owners were lucky to turn even a few hundred dollars in profits per year.

*   *   *

ONE OF THE MAJOR FINANCIAL DRAINS on old-time full-service grocery stores was the common practice of extending credit to customers. As can be easily imagined, in the days before credit cards it was exceedingly difficult to assiduously manage money between paydays—and extremely easy to run out of money in the interim. Since so many of a store's frequent customers tended to be familiar people from the neighborhood, it was only natural that a policy of credit acceptance developed at the old-time grocery stores. This "policy," more an ad hoc response to unstable economic conditions than a well-developed system, was in many ways an inchoate version of revolving credit.

The practice of extending credit to regular customers was widespread, with an average of one-third of old-time grocery store sales made on loan. Note, though, that this average combines both rich and poor stores. In the most poverty-stricken working-class neighborhoods, credit accounted for upward of 70%-80% of sales. While the policy of extending credit to local customers might be seen as representing an investment in the community, like all investments it was risky—in this case, excessively risky. Lord knows how many grocery store merchants had to take a bath on customer defaults. Of course, customers had both good and bad excuses for stiffing the store. But in the end it made little difference to the owner, who was stuck eating the losses.

Besides credit acceptance, another costly service commonly offered at old-time stores was free delivery. The practice of offering delivery for free came about haphazardly in response to the expansion of cities. For along with geographic growth came longer distances needing to be traveled—either horizontally across expanding urban areas or vertically up into multistory apartment buildings, which had begun proliferating in the early twentieth century. Until cars became affordable, and shoppers no longer had to negotiate these longer distances by foot, some grocery store owners figured that offering free delivery services would be a good way to attract an increasingly far-flung customer base. This put competitive pressures on others to follow suit. The only trouble was that free delivery was terribly uneconomic and wreaked havoc on the bottom line. By one estimate, free delivery devoured up to two-thirds of store profits.[5]

A final factor tending to crush the profitability of old-time grocery stores was their unstructured pricing policies. Many stores had no posted prices on their bulk products at all. The clerk and customer were thus left to haggle over the price of each individual commodity—the final price usually reflecting previous charges set off against perceived quality of the current offering. This type of improvised price realization can be tricky. All shoppers look for bargains. But if the price being offered on a product is too low, its quality automatically becomes suspect.

Most grocers of the time simply avoided any confusion in this regard by trying to charge the highest possible prices in any transaction. This seemingly piratical impulse was actually a practical response to the structural economic inefficiencies then embedded in the prevailing grocery store business model. Their profitability bleeding from credit losses, free delivery, low service productivity, and numerous extra-retail factors, such as inefficiencies in supply and distribution, grocery store owners had almost no choice but to jack up prices to make up for the hemorrhaging in other areas.

MANY OF THE NEGATIVE ASPECTS of old-time grocery stores discussed so far—their tiny size, limited selection, drab appearance, unpredictable product quality, and want of cleanliness, among others—were not writ in stone. As noted, diligent efforts made by zealous storeowners could go a long way toward mitigating some of these problems, especially those regarding product quality, store appearance, and cleanliness. But by and large, amelioration of the generally dismal conditions characterizing old-time grocery stores would have to await advances in technology. With these occurring in the early twentieth century, successful storeowners now found it feasible to introduce such up-to-date improvements as greater selection, better quality, brighter lights, colder refrigerators, and labor-saving methods for cleaning.

Yet ultimately these types of advancements amounted to little more than rearranging deck chairs on a sinking business model. For the fundamental reality was that old-time grocery stores were just not making enough money, their profitability undermined from within by inherent inefficiencies in pricing, credit, and service policies. In the end, the diseconomies plaguing old-time grocery stores were only overcome not with tinkering around the edges but by an evolutionary leap, a sudden metamorphosis into a new form of grocery retailing called the supermarket. As always, this phase change culminated from a series of previous mutations that burst forth seemingly at random, which then coalesced, as if by magic, to bring into being the new phenomenon.

Rapid progress in technology and changing economic conditions are often cited as being the two most important factors favoring the emergence of supermarkets. Certainly from a purely technological standpoint it does seem that the old-school grocery-store model was bound to bite the dust one way or another, as it simply could not withstand the assault on its raison d'être under the relentless battering of revolutions in energy, electricity, transportation, and communications. Moreover, it cannot be denied that the Great Depression was a key force in driving bargain pricing to the forefront of consumer consciousness.

Yet it can also be argued that an even more fundamental factor underlying the superseding of old-time grocery stores was the rise of the corporation.[6] Understanding the term "corporation" not strictly in the legalistic sense but more abstractly as a professionally managed "big business," a relatively new type of economic organization called the corporation arose in the post–Civil War world that proved amazingly adept at capitalizing on rapid advances in science and technology. Indeed, the quickly growing influence of the corporation on all aspects of society at the time is of such towering significance that a case could be made that what is commonly referred to as "modern progress" is actually merely a reflection of the historical process of corporate consolidation of the economy on all levels, from manufacturer and distributor to retailer and consumer.

To put some meat on the bones of this argument, first consider that corporations were far superior to most types of previous business organizations—mostly consisting of family-run companies and loosely defined partnerships—in being able to take maximum advantage of mass-production methods. For it took a tightly run, expertly administered organization operating on a large scale to manage the vast quantities of goods pouring forth from the industrial cornucopia. This principle applied not just to manufacturing but to retailing as well. Its first manifestation in the retail sector came in the form of corporate-owned chain stores. These appeared abruptly over the 1890s, skyrocketing from next to no presence at the beginning of the decade to nearly 5% of all retail business formations by 1900.[7] The rise of the corporate-owned chain store was to have agonizing political repercussions over the next half century, as the stage was set for a battle royale over the nature of competition in a free society. Saving discussion of this then-all-consuming but now all-but-forgotten struggle for later, suffice here to note that it was largely the intrusion of big-business methodology into a retail sector then dominated by independent companies that caused all the trouble—and excited all the promise.

Arguably the most important contribution made to retailing by the newly arising corporations was the "brand." Within the universe of food retailing, branded products began appearing in a big way around the late 1890s into the early 1900s with such processed commodities as crackers (Nabisco), cereal (Kellogg and General Mills), and coffee (Folgers, Maxwell House). What above all distinguished these branded products from the bulk commodities of the past was that corporate reputations were now on the line, as manufacturers took direct responsibility for delivering quality and consistency. When manufacturing corporations seemed to perform this task admirably, aided by the credulity conjured by advertising, consumers embraced brands and even demanded them. The supermarket later proved to be the perfect distribution vehicle to supply this explosive corporate-inspired demand for brands to a rapidly expanding consumer population.

Beyond branding, though, the inroads made by big business structures into the retail domain had three other profound effects. First, corporations played a primary role in developing and channeling innovations in packaging—tin cans, cardboard, aluminum foil, and cellophane film—that proved invaluable in advancing the fortunes of supermarkets.[8] Second, along with the guaranteed product quality offered by their brands, corporations introduced a predictable pricing policy. With no more haggling at the register, a higher volume of sales would be achieved. Finally, corporations were able as never before to harness the psychological power of advertising and promotion. This was made possible by their increased operational efficiencies, which freed up funds to devote to marketing. With the advent of mass advertising, the era of old-time grocery stores—which were typically promoted by little more than annual calendars—was effectively over. A new era of supermarket showmanship was dawning.

5

SCHWEGMANN BROTHERS GROCERY COMPANY
A Superior Corner Store

WHEN GARRET JUNIOR TOOK OVER Garret Senior's business on Piety and Burgundy in the 1890s, it was prime time for the old-style corner grocery store. In many ways, Schwegmann Brothers Grocery typified the classic mom-and-pop retail model so common in post-bellum nineteenth-century urban America. Located on a corner under a bright arc light, the store was full-service, sold bulk commodities, catered to a neighborhood and immigrant clientele, and suffered from many of the intrinsic inefficiencies that plagued all old-style grocery stores. Also characteristic, its owners and employees worked extraordinarily hard, and a mom and pop lived with kids on top. Yet for all its similarities with the average generic old-time corner grocery store, Schwegmann Brothers stood apart from the pack for two reasons. First, it was extremely successful.[1] Second, it was located in the quirky metropolis of New Orleans. In combining these factors, what resulted was a retail formation that would provide the perfect platform for something greater than anything yet seen in U.S. retailing.

In accounting for the store's success, it is not enough simply to attribute it to Garret's magisterial managerial abilities, the seasoned experience of his brother-partners, or the hard work of its employees. For beyond the virtues of ability, competence, and dedication, the Schwegmann family held to an overriding faith that they were better than the rest and could therefore build a better retail mousetrap. To this end, the family expanded the size of the store to 1,200 square feet—one-third to one-half larger than the average corner store at the time—and added an attached warehouse. They leveraged this greater space to feature lower prices and greater selection than their run-of-the-mill competitors. The store was also more inviting than most, being better organized and as clean as could be. Finally, in addressing business fundamentals, Garret instituted a no-credit policy. While in practice this became more of a "stingy" policy rather than an outright refusal to extend credit, the step definitely helped put the store on a more sound financial footing than most.

In a concrete measure of its success, Schwegmann Brothers Grocery employed about a dozen people—this as opposed to the mere one or two employees typical of most old-time grocery stores. There were the three brother-partners, Garret, Henry, and John; at least three clerks, William Mayer, Frank Mayer, and Albert Martin; four female assistants and secretaries, Dora McCoy, Lillian McCoy, Agnes McCoy, and Rose Markey; a warehouseman affectionately nicknamed "Dummy" Bauers; an old wagon driver known as Grandpop "Speedy" Voelker; and an African American cook remembered only as Clara, who was famous among the neighborhood kids for handing out sticks of sugarcane grown in the backyard of her home on Dauphine Street (across from Meyer's Bakery). When Clara died, the Schwegmann family crossed Jim Crow lines to attend her funeral in St. Bernard Parish. But this was not unusual, for the Schwegmanns treated all their employees nearly as family. In return, the employees were extremely loyal, most staying with the store for decades.

Another indicator of the Piety Street store's superiority over its competitors was its comparatively more extensive selection. A quick look around the store gives some idea of this.[2] All the way in the rear were bins of various kinds of animal feed. Moving toward the middle of the store, drums and barrels were displayed containing lard, cooking oil, brown sugar, molasses, pickles, and crackers, the usual large-bulk commodities. But there were also barrels full of syrup, condensed milk, and pig's feet. Closer to the front, covered wooden boxes held not just the typical coffee, tea, flour, and baking powder but also those necessities of New Orleans' culinary couture—namely, grits, rice, and red beans. Nearby, raisins, prunes, and macaroni were displayed in open wooden boxes, while small wooden drawers contained starch, salt, pepper, and a variety of spices, such as filé, unique to the city.

Returning now to the front of the store, appearing on the main service counter was the typical cheese "hoop" (wheel), placed in the Schwegmann store under a wooden cover rather than a glass bell, and the typical slab of bacon, here displayed under cheesecloth rather than suspended from a hook. But another type of "salt meat" was invariably available alongside the bacon.

Also placed on the counter was a daily supply of fresh French bread, which Garret had arranged to be delivered every morning. Arriving early from the bakery, the unwrapped loaves of French bread were unceremoniously dumped into a bin located outside the store. From there they would soon be fished out and displayed on the counter next to a large pan featuring donuts, coffee cake, and other pastries. The bread and breakfast desserts were sold on a first-come, first-serve basis.

As earlier noted, fresh foods were not a strong suit for most old-time corner stores, so the regular availability of French bread and pastries served to distinguish Schwegmann Brothers Grocery. Yet these baked goods were not the only type of perishable products carried by the store. Eggs, butter, and raw milk straight from the cow (unpasteurized) were also routinely offered—with these dairy products, along with a boiled ham, kept semi-fresh by being stored in an ample icebox.

Bread and dairy, however, were just the tip of the iceberg when it came to perishables carried. For over his approximately fifteen years of hands-on running of the store, Garret built up extensive distribution networks that allowed for regular shipments of both live and fresh-killed animals, birds, and fish. Received at the store's warehouse from area farmers were live chickens, turkeys, ducks, and geese. Caught by hunters and fishermen and delivered from distributors were barrels of wild rabbits from Morgan City, Louisiana, drums of wild mallard ducks from Missouri, buckets of fish from regional waterways, and "champagnes" of shrimp from the Gulf of Mexico.

CEMENTING ITS REPUTATION as a destination location, Schwegmann Brothers Grocery carried unique items in key food, beverage, and nonfood categories. For its base of immigrant customers, it offered sauerkraut and German mustard, among other ethnic food products. For its base of non-electrified households seeking light and heat (most of the neighborhood at the time), there was a big tank of kerosene located at the entrance surrounded by a cross-merchandised display of firewood, kindling, charcoal, lamps, chimneys, and furnaces.

For its Bywater base of regular tipplers, the store's selection of cheap booze—including California wine, "city" beer, and whiskey—could not be beat. Most popular here was the store's own Schwegmann 1889 brand, a 90 proof "rectified straight barrel whiskey," which in actuality was one-third whiskey and two-thirds grain alcohol. Humorously referred to as "Schwegmann's Baby Wash," the beverage was said to contain medicinal properties such that if applied to a baby's skin would help keep it from getting sick. A much later ad for the brand spoofed its reputation: "Keep a bottle handy for mosquitoes, rattlesnake bites, or to keep the dog from catching cold."[3]

While it is difficult to get a fix on pricing values in the early years of the twentieth century, it is clear from surveying selected products that Schwegmann Brothers' prices were pretty darn cheap. In basic commodities, for example, twenty-five pounds of sugar sold for just a dollar, while prices for butter and hog lard were twenty-five cents and five cents per pound, respectively. Louisiana-sourced products could also be had at a bargain, with syrup from Union priced at ten cents a quart, Creole eggs from Opelousas at four cents a dozen, and wild mallard ducks from Morgan City at twenty-five cents per pair.[4]

In the all-important alcoholic beverage category, wine could be purchased at ten cents a quart and twenty-five cents a gallon, and city beer was priced at between five and ten cents for a pitcher's worth. As for whiskey, a name brand, Martin's Rye, sold for fifty cents a quart, while Schwegmann's own 1889 brand went for thirty-five cents a quart.

Of course, if the customer just wanted a drink or two, he could buy a shot of liquor next door at Schwegmann's Bar for a picayune, which is what New Orleanians at the time called a nickel. If a gent bought that five-cent shot at night, he might consider tipping the monkey, who clowned around with an organ grinder some evenings at the bar. If the herr preferred instead to drink at night in the comfort of his own home, he would likely join with a crowd of his fellow Bywater compatriots in "rushing the growler"—that is, dashing to the store right before closing time to pick up a pitcher or two of beer. A similar mad scramble occurred among local *hausfrauen*, who clogged the store at closing time to buy kerosene and "insurance oil," which were used to light and heat their homes at night.[5]

Of course, this being New Orleans, heating was needed for only about four, maybe five, months out of the year, and then only sporadically. But this is not meant to minimize the issue. For when the weather does get cold in New Orleans, it tends to be bone chilling, as frigid air mixes with the omnipresent humidity. This atmospheric condition comes into play in regard to a strict policy established by Garret Junior that the front doors of the store were always to remain propped wide open all day long, from early morning until closing time. To Garret's mind, this gesture made it clear that the store was always open for business and welcoming to all.

Throughout most of the year this policy received no complaints. On the contrary, since there was no air conditioning in those days, customers and employees alike were grateful for any wisp of cool air circulation, especially during the sweltering summer months. The problem came in winter. For besides having no air conditioning, the store also had no heat. Nevertheless, Garret continued to rigidly enforce his inflexible open-door policy. Customers accepted this frigid state of affairs, as it was the norm in a time before electricity; and besides they could simply rush back to their warm homes after shopping. Not so the employees, who spent the entire workday freezing their keisters off. Protest as they might, Garret would not budge. He patiently explained to his clerks that heat was bad. It made them drowsy and thus less attentive to the customer. Cold, on the other hand, was good. It not only kept them alert, it helped maintain a fresh bloom on the fruits and vegetables. Thus did the clerks end up shivering their way through many a bitter-cold New Orleans' winter day. Along the way they preserved a story about the time it was so cold in the store that the plagnoil (olive oil) froze on the shelf and had to be chipped off in pieces for any customer requesting it.[6]

That Garret would insist on such a relentless regimen, even to point of bringing suffering to his employees, just goes to show what an intense competitor he was. As he saw it, he had to be. There were just too many rivals out there waiting to put him out of business. And he was right. All American cities at the time were bursting to the seams with mom-and-pop grocery stores, and New Orleans was no different. In the Crescent City, a partial listing of successful names in the grocery store business at the turn of the century would include Charlie Wirth, Clark & Meador, Feeney, Hackendorf, Henke, Herman Eicke, Martin Cull, Olstein, Schwegmann, Thriffeley, and Votage. This is not to mention two gourmet groceries, Smith & Rauch (located in the Garden District) and Solari's (Royal and Iberville), which catered to the silk-stocking set with imported wine, fine pastries, and (believe it or not) canned foods.[7]

SINCE OLD-TIME CORNER GROCERY STORES tended to serve only a captive neighborhood customer base, it might be surmised that little direct competition took place among them. In fact, this is largely true. Against the better interests of a dynamically advancing retail food sector, the old grocery stores dug in, encouraging a stasis by forming protective "customer loyalty" bubbles around their built-in clienteles. That the old-school groceries actually discouraged competition, even to the point of cutting their own throats, comes straight from the horse's mouth in the form of an anecdote told by John Schwegmann himself.

As John tells it, one day a loyal customer of Herman Eicke's grocery store, located just around the corner and down the street from Schwegmann Brothers, slipped into the Piety Street store. The clerk on duty was sharp with him: "You don't belong here. Go buy your groceries where you've been buying them."[8] By modern retail standards this story is incredible: a clerk actually turns down a sale because the customer shops at another store! But there was more to this interaction than meets the eye. For as it turns out, the clerk was right to be harsh—the Eicke's customer had ventured over to Schwegmann's only because he needed a new line of credit. In the end, the renegade customer was allowed to buy from Schwegmann's, but only for cash.

Despite registering some success in using this type of socio-economic pressure to police territory-based competitive boundaries, old-time grocers nevertheless remained under an ever-present threat from a more abstract, but more powerful, force than mere geography—namely, the sheer dynamism of American retailing. Aside from the constant flow of newcomers into the field, there was always another nearby neighborhood store either waiting for a competitor to falter, then rushing in to take them over, or otherwise looking to expand.

In an example of this phenomenon, a grocer named William McKernan once boasted that Garret Junior did not have a clue about how to run a grocery store, and that he, McKernan, was here to school him on how to do it right.[9] So McKernan opened up a store, his second, on Louisa and Burgundy, just a block away from Schwegmann Brothers. As it turned out, the boast proved full of hot air. For soon after the store opened, it folded, unable to make the slightest inroads into Schwegmann's customer base. Forced to eat crow, McKernan sold the store to Garret, who rented it out to the Lazarus family for a crockery shop, which incidentally stayed in business for years afterward. So despite the deceptive appearance of softball competition anchored in a safe neighborhood customer base, it is clear that successful grocers always needed to be prepared to play hardball.

In this spirit, Garret took active measures to stay on top of the heap. In order to carve out a distinctive reputation for product quality—a difficult positioning tactic in a pre-brand age dominated by bulk commodities—he honed his product knowledge and purchasing skills to the highest pitch of perfection. Thus he knew all about red beans (moisture content, best time of year to buy, finest came from New York State, etc.); sugar (all varieties of brown and light-clarified, different sizes of hogshead casks ranging from 63 to 140 gallons, etc.); and a host of other products. Garret's specialties were said to be butter, coffee, flour, rice, and pickled spareribs. Compare this with Votage's, a nearby Bywater competitor, which was known only for ham and "expert slicing."

To further solidify his competitive position at the retail level, Garret formed excellent relations with local suppliers on the distributor level. These suppliers fall into two broad categories: grocery wholesalers; and what are called "jobbers." Grocery wholesalers receive goods directly from producers and processors and then store them in warehouses until delivery to retail stores. Among the top grocery wholesalers operating in New Orleans during the late 1800s and over the early decades of the 1900s were H.T. Cottam, Leon Hirsch, R. Guercio, S. Pfeiffer & Company, the Imperial Trading Company, L. Frank & Company, Kingham & Company, and the Spot Cash Wholesale Grocery.

Meanwhile, jobbers represent a hybrid position combining both sales and distribution functions. Acting on an independent basis both apart and in liaison with wholesalers and retailers, jobbers actually visit stores, take merchandise orders, and occasionally deliver goods to, and even help stock, the stores. Some of the top independent jobbers in New Orleans back in Garret's day included Albert Mackie, Morrison & Company, A. Dumser & Company, Grabenheimer, Schmidt & Ziegler, and Kelly & Zoller.[10]

Among the grocery wholesalers, Tom J. Flanagan (born 1886), the owner of the Spot Cash Wholesale Grocery—a supplier of Schwegmann Brothers Grocery under John Senior's management—left a special impression on young John Junior. For Flanagan had devised two major innovations in distribution. First, he demanded that retailers come to the warehouse to pick up their merchandise, rather than wait to have it delivered. Second, he instituted a strict cash-and-carry policy. To facilitate this policy, he was one of the first wholesalers to publish set-in-stone price lists for retailers. Flanagan's motto, taken to heart by John Jr., was this: "Be cash-wise, not credit-foolish."[11]

ALTHOUGH GARRET JR. TOOK GREAT PAINS to remain competitively superior, he was forced by cultural customs rooted in the unique economic history of New Orleans to follow certain non-competitive practices. One of these was the offering of "lagniappe," a French word derived from the Spanish term "la nape" that generally means giving away something for nothing. In its most common usage, the term lagniappe refers to a little "extra" offered for free by a retail merchant to help secure customer loyalty. Or put more bluntly by a disgruntled pharmacist practicing in New Orleans in 1890, it is "a bribe to secure future patronage."[12] Back in the old days, lagniappe took a variety of forms—a piece of licorice, a cookie, an onion, a sprig of parsley, and the like. What all these free items shared in common was that they were small and cheap. Yet all these seemingly insignificant gifts added up at the margin. The pharmacist quoted above estimated that lagniappe ended up costing the retailer a full one to two percent of gross sales. So by no means was extending lagniappe efficient in generating profit. Indeed, the irrational practice can only be understood in the context of the effluvial carnival atmosphere of New Orleans.

Another non-competitive cultural roadblock that Garret could do nothing but give in to concerned the peculiar currency system that had evolved in the Crescent City. During the period of Spanish ascendance, New Orleans adopted some of Spain's monetary units, particularly its silver doubloon. The doubloon's value was commonly divided by eighths, thus the "pieces of eight" of pirate legend. Each piece of eight eventually came to be called a "bit," worth twelve-and-a-half cents American—with the well known slang term "two bits" referring to a quarter.

Given the somewhat bizarre overlay of previous Spanish currency on American monetary values, it is no wonder that for a long time New Orleans rejected the penny as a legitimate denomination. In its place the city established a slightly higher unit of exchange known as the "quartee."[13] Worth two-and-a-half cents, or half a nickel, the quartee bought small portions of rice, beans, cheese, bread, or similar items—enough to make a quick meal. If by chance the purchaser only had a nickel but wanted just a quartee's-worth of an item, the retailer would complete the transaction by giving change in the form of a metal disc approximately the size of a quarter to use in the customer's next two-and-a-half-cent purchase.

Eccentric customs involving lagniappe and odd currency values, however, ranked as of little consequence when stacked against the overwhelming anti-competitive power of the so-called "public markets." The entire Schwegmann grocery clan had so far been forced to gingerly negotiate its way around this gigantic competitive roadblock unique to New Orleans. It would take John Jr., in a Gordian-knot moment, to once and for all solve this problem. Until then, when it came to fresh-food distribution, the city was firmly in the grip of a government-controlled public-market system.[14]

This system had thick roots in New Orleans tracing back to Spanish rule. For decades after its official founding in 1718, most of the city's food needs were supplied through two markets that sprang up spontaneously: the French Market on the Mississippi waterfront, and the African Market in Congo Square. These two fixed spots were supplemented by roving pushcarts. This informal system worked well enough in the early days, but as the city expanded, distribution problems arose. At newly created markets, widespread allegations surfaced of price gouging on food, accompanied by reports of near-starvation.

In response, the Spanish government took matters in hand—not through passive regulation but by active intervention. In 1779, it set up a government-controlled market area at the waterfront where "general provisions" were sold at a fair price. Three years later, in 1782, it built a second market, which specialized in meat, at Moreau (now Chartres) and Dumaine streets, which was moved a block away to Decatur Street in 1791. Then in 1799, the Spanish rulers erected a third market, this one devoted to fish and seafood. Thus by the time the U.S. government took over the city after the Louisiana Purchase in 1803, the tradition of public markets had been firmly established in New Orleans.

Working within this tradition, the new American metropolitan authorities set up a similar public vegetable market in 1823. Yet fifteen years later, after rethinking the concept, city officials decided to introduce "licensed" public markets instead. What apparently happened in the interim was that they realized that rather than directly operate fresh food markets it would be more lucrative for the city to grant indirect retailing rights to the private sector. Thus under the aegis of the Board of Health, the exclusive right to retail perishable foods was auctioned off by New Orleans to the highest bidder. Theoretically, nobody else within a specified radius was allowed to sell fresh meat, fish, or produce, although apparently there was some leeway in this injunction. The first licensed public market—the Washington Market at Chartres and Louisa (later moved to Faubourg Marigny)—was established in 1838. By 1865, fifteen of these types of licensed "public" markets were in operation. But it did not end there. By 1911, the year John Schwegmann was born, the city boasted thirty-four public markets, far more than have ever been established in any other city in the United States.

In and around the Bywater were seven licensed public markets. The closest one to Schwegmann Brothers was Zengel's Market, located cattycorner to the Piety Street store. (In the 1990s, local legendary art couple Quintron and Miss Pussycat inhabited it for a spell, using the space for performances.) The Zengel public market occupied a focal point in the old Bywater, where it was a center of social activity. John Jr. used to complain about how boring life was on Sundays when Zengel's was closed. The names of the other six licensed public markets in the vicinity included Guillotte (located on Alvar between Burgundy and Rampart), Doulluth (at Dauphine and Poland), Washington and Lautenschlaeger (both in the Marigny), St. Roch (at St. Claude, established 1875), and Behrman (in Holy Cross, established 1908).

The Guillotte public market is particularly interesting in that it was located within spitting distance of Macarty Square, an area spanning four city blocks designed in 1859 as an urban park. Macarty Square has played a singular role in the history of New Orleans. In 1899 it was the first public space to be electrified. During World War I, troops mustered at Macarty, with an impressive arch of triumph erected there in 1919 to commemorate the soldiers' sacrifices. Later, in the 1920s, Macarty Square served as the backdrop for some of Huey Long's first fiery speeches.[15] Here, the Kingfish held huge crowds spellbound with his now-famous populist rhetoric proclaiming "Every man a king!"

Such was the world of Schwegmann Brothers Grocery in New Orleans during the peak decades of the old-time corner grocery store. Within this milieu John Junior was born and came of age, inheriting a legacy based on a deep continuity of roots in the retail food trade.

6

JOHN G. SCHWEGMANN
Born in the Poor Glorious Third

J OHN GERALD SCHWEGMANN WAS BORN in the heart-throttling heat of a New Orleans summer on August 14, 1911. As it turned out, this year also represented summertime for Mayor Martin Behrmann—the longest-serving mayor in the city's history then at the peak of his power. As might be expected under the lengthy reign of such a powerful political boss, New Orleans was wide open at the time, an American Gomorrah infamously symbolized by Storyville, which flourished for two decades, from 1897 until 1917, before the U.S. Navy finally forced its shutdown.

Yet even as the center of the city was engulfed in corruption in 1911—with Storyville in full decadent bloom, the French Quarter grown seedy, and the waterfront exceedingly dangerous—New Orleans as a whole was far from being completely steeped in vice. For in the upriver districts, south and west of the French Quarter, residents had embraced the progressive capitalistic virtues associated with industry and commerce, and they were busy attaining unprecedented heights of opulence as a result. This efflorescence of riches was expressed above all in architecture, in the grand and stately beauty of homes, churches, schools, and parks built in surfeit throughout the Garden District and Uptown. Meanwhile, the downriver "poor" and (sarcastically) "glorious" Third District had become home to burgeoning communities of immigrants.[1] Here the working-class residents could not afford to fend off the nefarious moral influences emanating from the city center through a talismanic display of wealth. So they attempted to ward them off by cleaving to the traditional immigrant values of thrift and hard work—though the city's sinful nature, particularly in its embrace of evil alcohol, still took its toll here.

Generally helping to balance out the attraction of vice—which is rooted, after all, in a devil-may-care sense of fatalism—were advances in technology. At last, the application of scientific knowledge was beginning to tame the nature of this urban swamp, previously so prone to disease and watery catastrophe. Consider, for example, that the final yellow fever epidemic to sweep New Orleans occurred in 1905.[2] Six years before John was born, then, this plague had finally been overcome through advances in medical understanding. Another technological triumph, this one an unprecedented feat of engineering, was achieved during the early twentieth century with the installation of a system of gargantuan pumps. Designed by A. Baldwin Wood, these pumps would at last save the city from permanent flooding. Through these and similar technological advancements, New Orleans for the first time in its history truly had grounds for optimism about its future.

John G. Schwegmann was born into the New Orleans of these conflicted years of notorious vice and industrious virtue, of moral decadence and material progress. The clash of these opposing cultural tendencies might have led a lesser city into some form of urban schizophrenia. In New Orleans, however, it resulted in a creative synthesis that began to manifest around the turn of the twentieth century in an all-new musical art form called "jazz." Jazz places a premium on individuality of vision and expression, technical virtuosity, improvisational flexibility, and adventurousness in exploring new sounds. It also places prime emphasis on maintaining an entertaining and exciting flow of rhythmic vitality known as "swing." Certainly John, born and raised in New Orleans at the dawn of the Jazz Age, was imbued with its essence. This will be seen in his resolute pursuit of a personal vision grounded in sophisticated knowledge, his uniqueness of expression and infectious showmanship, his remarkable ability to improvise, and his constant exploration of new terrain, all the while swinging with the flow.

JOHN'S EARLIEST MEMORY was of the great New Orleans Hurricane of 1915, a fierce windstorm unrivaled in intensity until half a century later.[3] On September 29, 1915, the unnamed hurricane smashed into the coast of Louisiana as an estimated Category Four then barreled through New Orleans, taking 275 lives along the way. Only four years old at the time, John could still vividly recall the chaotic scene decades afterward. From a perch in his family's living quarters above Schwegmann Brothers Grocery, "I could see all the slates flying like feathers from a chicken off the houses on Burgundy Street. We had a big porch swing [on the second-story gallery], and that swing was taken from on the Burgundy side of this building…and moved [to the] Piety Street [side]."[4] The storm's damage to the store was significant, though not devastating. The back end devoted to animal feed was blown down, as were several outbuildings attached to the store's warehouse. Most dramatic of all, huge cisterns holding thousands of gallons of water were whooshed off the roof and shattered against the ground.

Though he grew up in the rough-and-tumble Bywater, populated by German and Irish gangs, young moon-faced, blond-haired John managed for the most part to keep his nose clean. Of course, like all kids he liked to have fun, engaging in the typical boyhood gambols of his time: playing marbles, trading baseball cards, making popguns out of sugarcane reeds and seeds of china ball trees, climbing oak trees in Macarty Square to catch the singing locusts. But even when he occasionally got into trouble—when he was caught playing hooky from school, for example—it was never for anything serious. Indeed, far from being a juvenile delinquent, John was in many ways a model child: responsible, well behaved, and hard working.

Nevertheless, despite all appearances, young John was in trouble—not from the outside but the inside. Physically he had a bad heart, the result of a simple tonsil flare-up that occurred when he was seven years old and ended up inflaming out of control. When he first contracted the infection, John's parents made the unfortunate mistake of taking him to a doctor who did not believe in removing tonsils.[5] The doctor's reasoning—"Whatever God gave you, you keep"—was not uncommon at the time, and many children suffered as a result. In John's case, the doctor prescribed gargling as a remedy and sent him home. Quickly taking a turn for the worse, John developed a case of rheumatic fever that left his body temperature so high and joints so stiff he could barely move. Given his fearful deterioration, John's parents rushed him to the New Orleans Eye, Ear, and Throat Hospital, where he immediately had his tonsils removed. Although the fever soon subsided, he was left with a permanently leaking heart valve. As will be seen, while John managed to cope with this condition throughout his extremely energetic prime, it finally caught up with him when he was just sixty-six years old, at which point he suffered a debilitating stroke.

More than by anything physical, though, young John was troubled psychologically. By all accounts he was introverted throughout his youth.[6] In retrospect, considering that he would eventually transform into an extravagant extrovert, there are strong grounds for believing his initial hesitance to express himself resulted from internal disturbance rather than any intrinsic personality orientation. Indeed, the evidence is straightforward that as a youth he was wrestling with a major unresolved emotional conflict. Consider that John candidly admits on the Cabildo tape that he did not have a happy childhood. The reason? He felt ashamed and inferior. That he ultimately overcame these feelings of shame and inferiority proved to be the key to his success as an adult.

From the beginning, John distinguished himself as exceptionally diligent and enterprising. As a youngster, he would rise each morning at dawn and faithfully perform the chores assigned him at the family store. These tasks involved what was called "getting the show out"—meaning preparing the store for opening.[7] On a typical day he would take eggs out of the cooler, place meats and sauerkraut on display, put a collection of brooms and mops out on the sidewalk, and set up promotional signs. Some mornings, if he still had time before school started, John would trek over to the Frey family homestead at 3802 Dauphine Street. As already described, the Frey clan kept a complement of farm animals, including a cow, a horse, and chickens, and John would help take care of them. "I remember milking the cow for my grandmother and grandfather…then cleaning out the manure, then making the bran and various things we fed the cow with, and feeding the horse, and cleaning out the chicken houses." In learning how to milk the cow, he fondly recalls how Grandfather Anton "taught me how to make the milk pot sing."[8]

After school and during summers, though he spent a fair share of time playing with friends, John tried to keep busy. Sometimes he would help out around the Piety Street store: stocking groceries, making deliveries, and assisting his mother with washing copious amounts of dishes. Other times he would head over to the Frey homestead to do various odd jobs, such as cutting the grass (receiving a nickel for every wheelbarrow load) or helping take care of the animals. Exhibiting an emerging entrepreneurial streak, he would occasionally go down to the French Market to peddle figs and herbs harvested from the Frey women's gardens. He recalls selling bunches of parsley, thyme, and bay leaves, bundled by his Aunt Helen, for 25 cents a dozen, afterward splitting the proceeds with her fifty-fifty.[9]

Any spare time John had away from work, play, or school he tended to spend not at his own place but over at the Frey house. It was his home away from home, a surrogate family dwelling where he clearly preferred to be. And who can blame him? The house was spacious and comfortable, in sharp relief to the cramped confines of John's living quarters above the Piety Street store. It was vibrant, with a bustling urban barnyard out back. And even better, it was located at a discrete distance away from his parents, about both of whom he had ambivalent feelings.

The Frey house fronted an entire square block of Bywater property inherited by Apollonia Pauline Morrel, John's maternal grandmother, when she married Anton Frey. The newlyweds proceeded to expand the original home on the site—a simple two-room structure built before 1850—into a sprawling single-story ten-room manor, with finished dormer rooms in the attic. Though the house itself did not look like much from the outside—just an elongated bulky rectangle—its charms were betrayed by a few external details: an elegant roof made of imported sea-green slates, numerous long French windows, and a capacious porch surrounded by a fancy cast-iron railing. In its interior the house contained an abundance of aesthetic and practical features, such as alabaster rosettes above chandeliers and fireplaces located in every room. Yet what really distinguished the house was the rigorous stolidity of its construction. Raised solidly on a foundation of bricks and pesky cypress footings, the house was built using only the best materials and employing the most superior craftsmanship. Even after a hundred years, as testified by John, the house had not settled one bit, with nary a crack in its plaster walls.

The formidable architecture of the Frey family manor remained with John throughout his life as a potent influence on his approach to construction. He also carried a poignant memory of the manor's destruction. This he witnessed in the 1960s, when it was demolished to make way for a parking lot. He felt righteous anger as a wrecking crew wielding crowbars, axes, and sledgehammers utterly destroyed this perfectly good building in which so many of his emotions and memories were invested. His bitterness could be consoled only by a mournful stoicism, as he contemplated the cold hard truth of the psalm, "From dust thou art, to dust thou shalt return."[10]

As this anecdote obliquely reveals, religion—specifically the Catholic faith—played an important part in molding John's values and character. Not that he ever came completely under its sway. Instead, as is not uncommon among children who are brought up Catholic, after reaching adulthood he jettisoned many of its external rituals. Yet throughout his life, John held tenaciously to its essential core, which in his case meant maintaining a strong grounding in discipline and ethics.

Both the Schwegmann and Frey families were perfectly Catholic. Every Sunday they attended Holy Trinity Catholic Church, on St. Ferdinand Street off Dauphine, where both families maintained private pews. They sent their children to Catholic schools. And to demonstrate their piety, the families participated in annual Catholic devotional rituals, such as Good Friday processions, which involved walking to nine different churches scattered throughout the city. Family members were also encouraged to perform various services for the church. For instance, John, like his father before him, "proudly served" as an altar boy, waking at dawn to assist in the 6 A.M. Sunday mass at Holy Trinity then dashing over to the St. Roch Chapel to perform another mass at 7 A.M.

But the Schwegmann and Frey families were not just Catholics: they were German Catholics. Theoretically this meant they followed liturgical practices slightly different from other forms of Catholic worship. Yet in the end, this type of subtle sectarianism was not so much about theological as sociological distinctions—specifically sectarianism based on ethnicity. Indeed, all across early-twentieth-century urban America, religious affiliations (even within the "universal" church) almost invariably split along ethnic lines. This is seen among Catholic denominations in the old Bywater, where Holy Trinity was considered "German Catholic," St. Vincent De Paul (at Dauphine and Montegut) "French Catholic," and St. Peter and Paul (on Burgundy) "Irish Catholic."

These distinctions, though, were not rigid. There was no strict enforcement of ethnic boundaries among the Catholic laity, and denominational crossover was fairly common. A case in point is Mary Schwegmann, Garret Senior's estranged wife and John's grandmother. Mary favored the Irish church, where she had developed a strong relationship with its pastor, Father Hanrahan. By John's account, Mary suffered from an advancing case of hypochondria, and Father Hanrahan indulged her in it, making himself available to her at all hours of the day and night as she erratically sent frantic messages warning of her imminent demise. When Mary finally did shuffle off the mortal coil, in her late eighties, Father Hanrahan presided over her funeral.[11]

*   *   *

JOHN FIRST ATTENDED SCHOOL at a single-cottage located on Desire Street between Dauphine and Burgundy (about a block and a half away from the family store). This "private school," which offered the equivalent of kindergarten through second grade, was actually the home of Miss Elise Livaudais.[12] It contained three rooms: a front bedroom, a back kitchen, and a middle classroom.

The twelve to fifteen neighborhood children who attended the school (costing their parents somewhere between a dollar-fifty and two dollars a month per child) would enter the cottage through an alleyway side door that led into the middle room, which measured about twelve-by-twelve feet. There the students would sit on "chairs"— actually wooden orange crates and apple boxes—and learn lessons in reading, writing, and arithmetic, all to the tune of the occasional whack of a hickory stick. Miss Livaudais conducted the class sitting in front of it in an oversized rocking chair. During breaks she would go back to the kitchen and stir the pot that perennially simmered on her big oil stove, for she was always cooking something. If she lacked fuel to keep the stove going, Miss Elise would send one of the kids over to the Piety Street store to fetch a gallon of kerosene. If she ran out of bread for the meal she was preparing, a student would be chosen to run over to nearby Meyer's Bakery to pick up a couple of five-cent loaves of French bread.

Miss Livaudais was strict, combining conservative pedagogy with old-fashioned morality. She brooked no nonsense. Students had to improve or else. John remembers his lessons in handwriting: "No matter what you did, it couldn't be sloppy… the last line had to be better than the first." Backsliders received the slap of a ruler across their knuckles. She taught the children to be neat and clean and to respect their teachers and elders. "Everything was, 'Yes ma'am,' 'No ma'am,' 'Thank you,' 'No sir,'" polite locutions that are, according to John "the most powerful words in the English language." Into her students Miss Elise inculcated a sense that her authority was absolute. As John says, "When she told us something, it was like God talking."

She had a lasting influence on him: "She was a very, very conservative woman…a great, great woman…one of the finest teachers a boy could ever go to…. I don't know of anyone that ever made such an impression upon me [in terms of] discipline."[13]

Picturesquely illustrating the small-town character of the Bywater at the time, John recalls waiting on Miss Elise about twenty years after he had left the old school and was working at his father's store. He sold her "a dime of butter, a dime of ham, a nickel bag of cheese, and the best kind of coffee at fifteen cents a pound." By this time, of course, he had come to realize the one flaw his former teacher possessed—namely, that this Voice of God taught grammar half in French and half in English. The result was a permanent garbling of his spoken expression. It got so bad at one point that a later teacher, a Brother at Holy Cross, "asked me if I was studying a foreign language at night." Apparently John addressed the problem, for he eventually became sufficiently proficient in oral communications to run a small retail empire. Yet his syntax remained forever scrambled. As John admitted at age sixty-four, "To this day I haven't mastered the order of the English language."[14]

EVERY ONCE IN A WHILE—after school, on weekends or holidays— John would venture out to the edge of the Bywater, there to pay a visit to his paternal grandfather, Garret Senior. Delighted to see his grandson, Garret always demanded a kiss from him. John recalls the unpleasant sensations accompanying this ritual, in particular the smell of soup unwashed from his grandfather's bushy moustache. But none of this really mattered to John, for he loved his grandfather, and he felt Garret's unconditional love for him in return. Besides, he enjoyed the journey out to grandpa's house at Claiborne and Poland, for it was like an idyllic adventure to the wilderness.

Occasionally, after spending time with his grandfather, John would run down to the nearby Claiborne Canal, where off in the distance he could see a giant cement plant and sprawling paper mill (the magnitudes of which probably appeared absolutely immense to a kid growing up in the claustrophobic confines of the Bywater). Here he would "fish" for crawfish "with a string with a little piece of meat on it." On John's return from the canal with even the most minimal catch of crawfish, his grandfather would excitedly cry out, "Weiskopf! We gotta make a boil!" Indeed, Garret was always so happy to see his grandson that he encouraged him to come over more frequently by building him a special playhouse, one wired for electricity.[15]

Because his father's salary was so meager, John grew up in what today might be considered the lower-middle class. John himself rarely had any money. Whenever he managed to "save a nickel, I thought it was as big as this room!" he later exclaimed in an interview at his spacious Airline store office.

Certainly under these circumstances, where a premium was placed on thrift, there was little money in the family budget for such luxuries as store-bought clothes. So in his early boyhood years, most of his clothes were handmade, sewn by his mother and her sisters, aunts Helen and Pauline. His everyday dress consisted of simple overalls on the outside and underclothes fashioned out of flour and sugar sacks. For church and other special occasions, however, he wore more formal attire—most of it also tailored by the family seamstresses. This formal outfit consisted of a pongee shirt, a Peter Pan collar, fancy pants, and long black stockings. Since he was the oldest male child, he got all the newly made boys' clothes. His brothers got only hand-me-downs. The same was true of the family bicycle, which was merely slapped with a new coat of paint before being passed down the sibling chain at Christmastime.

John's downscale lifestyle might have been less noticeable and certainly more bearable to him had it not contrasted so starkly with that of his two cousins, Leo and George. These two children of Uncle Garret lived high on the hog in the lap of luxury. In John's words, "They had everything and wanted for nothing."[16]

For some reason—blame it on a fierce competitive streak—the vast gulf that lay between his cousins' wealth and his own family's poverty sorely troubled young John. It deeply hurt him to see how Leo and

George had so much while he and his siblings had so little. But this was not the only thing that troubled John. He was also pained by the contrast between Uncle Garret's sobriety and his father's drinking. That he was evidently wrestling mightily at the time with all sorts of negative emotions—envy, self-pity, and probably some measure of shame—can be seen in retrospect in his unnatural youthful introversion (as testified to by others) and his former "inferiority complex" (self-described).

After suffering what must have been a long, difficult period of serious introspection lasting throughout his childhood and into his early teens, John finally experienced an emotional epiphany: he realized that he actually did not feel sorry for himself at all…but rather for his father! And with this revelation he resolved the primal conflict arising from the unfairness of life. Instead of internalizing negative feelings of shame and the rest, allowing these emotions to flow inward where they could be closed off and likely fester into a permanent conviction of inferiority, he was able to deflect the negativity outward onto his father. While this was not the greatest solution for his already beleaguered dad, it did enable his ambitious son to transform the conflict into something positive for himself.

With this emotional acrobatic of outward projection, twisting impressively and landing gracefully in an affirmation of his own self-worth, John's internal torment was over. In place of anxiety and insecurity, a firm conviction now took root out of which a newfound confidence blossomed. As John expressed both this conviction and confidence: "I was determined beyond question or doubt that I was going to amount to something in this world."[17]

In effect, he had cleared the psychological decks for battle against any force that dared block his path to success. For just as in his interior wars he had learned two complementary lessons—never surrender to feelings of inferiority, and victory over victimhood requires an active, spirited struggle—he was now prepared to fight externally for whatever worthwhile vision he brought to the world. In other words, this precocious youngster clearly understood that he had a choice: he could tear out his hair and surrender to despair, or he could come out swinging. John chose the latter, pugilistic path. And with this decision he was able to transmute any obstacles blocking his ambitions into grist for his invincible aspirations.

Indulging in a little psychological analysis here, it appears that John's irascible, combative attitude ultimately sprang from the differing degrees of love he felt for his mother and father. In a surprising, and frankly awkward, admission on the Cabildo tape, John makes no bones about his true parental feelings: namely, that he loved his father more than his mother. This masculine agape orientation likely fueled John's warrior mentality, which played such a crucial role in his future idealistic crusades.

This is not to say, however, that feminine influences were absent in his character development. Indeed, quite the contrary. His aunts on both sides of the family—Mary and Theresa Schwegmann, as well as Pauline and Helen Frey—made deep impressions on him through their emotional nurturing and setting of practical examples. Aunt Mary in particular held him in thrall, for she made it her task to take extra-special care of John—bringing him to the dentist, buying him his first store-bought clothes, taking him to nice restaurants, and the like. In response to Mary's attentions, her nephew was beyond grateful. He absolutely adored her, his heart leaping with delight every time he espied her from the second-story gallery coming over for a visit. As he tells it, Aunt Mary was like his "second mother," and he "loved her more than words can express."[18] Aunt Helen also played a particularly influential role in John's development, specifically in encouraging his entrepreneurial instincts and broadening his cultural horizons. Yet for now enough has been said to illustrate the point: that while John manifestly embraced a martial attitude to life that can be traced to masculine affiliations, this attitude was well tempered by feminine influences. As a result, despite being pugnacious, John never (or hardly ever) descended into chest-thumping belligerence.

Yet underneath the surface of an outward emotional structure balancing his own peculiar blend of masculine assertiveness with feminine flexibility, a deeper conflict resided than the sense of inferiority he had previously conquered through his gymnastic asseveration of self-esteem. This conflict, more Oedipal in nature and thus more difficult to resolve, involved that primary maternal love which John had displaced onto secondary female relatives. Here it must be emphasized that this tilt in familial love away from mother and toward aunts is just plain weird in the context of the matrifocal culture of New Orleans, where mother/son dynamics are considered sacrosanct. What caused this bent is uncertain, though John hints at his mother's drinking as the source of his ambivalence toward her. Whatever the case, circumstantial evidence suggests that John's askew maternal affections later played a role in causing severely troubled marital relations.

AT AGE EIGHT OR THEREABOUTS, having outgrown Miss Elise's tiny classroom, John began attending Catholic grammar school at Holy Trinity. There he encountered a now-lost world resembling something out of a classic Father Flanagan/Bing Crosby movie. There was Sister Theckla, the sweet, saintly nun beloved by all the children. Then there was Sister Boniface, a fearsome disciplinarian who wore a three-inch leather strap on her belt. Presiding over all was another distinctive authority figure, Father John Baptiste Prim. As with Miss Livaudais, the good Father's utterances were "like God talking." Yet unlike her, Father Prim rarely had to speak a word to enforce discipline. Instead, as John recalls, "He only had to look at you…he didn't have to tell you anything." Father Prim maintained a ubiquitous presence at the school, actively patrolling the halls with hands clasped firmly behind his back while chomping on a cigar.[19]

In 1922, eleven-year-old John breathed a sigh of relief when his parents finally moved the family from its cramped confines above the Piety Street store into a real house. Although the place was quite modest—a simple shotgun double located at 834-36 Pauline Street—John was overjoyed that at least it had a backyard, and his outside play space was no longer limited to a second-story porch. Along with the sense of physical relaxation and invigoration that accompanied the move came a corresponding loosening and broadening of what had previously been his mostly provincial mentality. For over the course of living at the new house, John was exposed to a whole new social menagerie he never would have known about otherwise.[20] Tellingly, rather than being put off by the novel characters he encountered, he instead displayed an eager, even adventurous, curiosity toward them, including the most marginal. This openness ultimately paid off for John, yielding up an abundance of insights into human nature.

John was exposed to several colorful characters through sheer economic happenstance. Since his struggling family was perennially strapped for cash, the Schwegmann parents had little choice but to rent out the adjoining half of their new shotgun double. The first of their tenants was a somewhat sinister character remembered by John only as "The Slavonian." As gradually became apparent, the Slavonian turned out to be the neighborhood bootlegger, who procured and even distilled liquor on the premises for the frequent visitors who stopped by briefly to see him in those early days of Prohibition. Following his ouster, a Mr. Miller moved in. Employed as a commercial sign painter, Miller undoubtedly opened John's eyes to the attractive beauties of visual art in the marketplace.

A less-transitory tenant was Clarence Todhunter, who worked in the printing trade as a lithographic pressman. Besides exposing John to the then-rapidly advancing world of print media—which Schwegmann would later go on to exploit mercilessly—Todhunter may have played an even more significant role in the trajectory of John's future career. How this happened was roundabout. By John's recollection, his father bonded with Mr. Todhunter around their mutual enthusiasm for amateur radio. Frequently getting together after dinner, the two hobbyists would disappear into their workshop, there to fiddle around building radios and earpieces and attempting to tune in to various broadcasts.

One radio station they were able to receive was KWKH out of Shreveport, Louisiana. Owned by William Kennon Henderson, a successful businessman and pioneer of political talk radio, KWKH—the call letters embedding its owner's initials—began transmitting on a local level in 1924. Granted two consecutive major boosts in signal by the Federal Radio Commission, the station boomed first into a regional radio powerhouse in 1927 then exploded into a national "clear channel" in 1929. Along the way, Henderson gradually morphed from an old-school huckster hawking his own signature Hello World Coffee into the Rush Limbaugh of his day. In a twist, however, his primary demagogic target was not liberals but the "thieving chain store scoundrels" who were just beginning to spread across small-town America. Sounding more like an Occupy than a Tea Party activist, Henderson colorfully expressed his bile like this: Those "dirty, stinking chain stores are coming into your home town and taking your money and sending it out to a bunch of crooked, no-account loafers on Wall Street."[21]

When Henderson's tirades against retail chain stores commenced in 1929, they were in the vanguard of a then-burgeoning populist anger directed against concentrated wealth—Huey Long, for example, was a guest on KWKH—that would gain vehemence as the paralysis of the Great Depression took hold. This intense animus culminated legislatively in price fixing actions that were dubbed "fair trade" laws. Since these laws figure so prominently in the Schwegmann saga, and because they form such a complicated subject in themselves, the story of fair trade laws and John's primal battle against them is saved for later. For now it is enough to simply imbibe the image of John inhaling his first heady whiffs of big-time retail controversy while listening through static-y earphones to the "dollar-a-pound coffee man" on a primitive audio receiver built by his father and Mister Todhunter, two amateur radio buffs.[22]

But the reader should not get the wrong impression that John's broadening social horizons over his "tween" and teen years were due solely to the influences of his family's tenants. Consider, for instance, that it was around the time of his move to Pauline Street that Aunt Mary initiated a program to acculturate John to a more haute bourgeois milieu than he was accustomed to. Thus she frequently took him downtown to dine at D.H. Holmes Restaurant. There a sweet-jazz orchestra played as patrons indulged in semi-fine dining—a spectacle that certainly reverberated forever with John. In another example serving to exhibit a growing cosmopolitan outlook, after moving to his new digs on Pauline Street, John became fast friends with a kid named Abe Pekovar, son of an Orthodox Jewish family headed by David Pekovar, owner of a shoe store on the block. The two boys eventually grew so close that Abe came to be considered part of the Schwegmann family. But John's openness to social experience certainly did not stop there. A disparate kaleidoscope of eccentric characters fascinated him, ranging from Mr. Wolf, a Russian immigrant photographer whose main subject was City Park, to the "Westerhaus men," neighborhood elders who "held up the corner" in front of the Piety Street store after they got off work.

A particularly revealing episode illustrates John's open-minded curiosity about—or, going further, brave fascination with—the wilder side of human nature. John dwelled on this story in depth in a published collection of anecdotes, so it surely must have left a lasting impression on him.

Occurring around the time of his move to the new house in 1922, it revolved around what was known as the Little Red Church.[23] Located in Destrehan, thirty miles from New Orleans along the so-called "German Coast" in St. Charles Parish, the Little Red Church was among the oldest houses of worship in the entire metropolitan region, having been established in 1723. Although it was destroyed by fire in 1877, it reopened a generation later in 1918 under the pastoral supervision of Father Basty, originally hailing from Alsace-Lorraine.

As it happened, Aunt Pauline occasionally kept house for Father Basty, and John, when on vacation from school, would sometimes accompany her on these trips to Destrehan. While out at the Little Red Church he was far from idle, serving as an altar boy and working as a sexton—a job traditionally involving ringing bells and digging graves. In John's case, he did not actually do any grave-digging but instead merely located empty plots suitable for burial. Back in those days, the grieving family members themselves actually dug the grave!

One morning at the Little Red Church, young John encountered an old hobo by the name of Johnny Behazey, who showed up looking for food in exchange for work. Far from feeling threatened by this unkempt stranger, John immediately made him a sandwich, while the hobo, as promised, eventually set to work sawing firewood. Behazey ended up staying at the church for a few weeks. But rather than working diligently during his time there, the grizzled old man spent much of his time telling tall tales about his travels. For his part, John was completely mesmerized by these stories of adventure on the open road. Indeed, he was so noticeably enchanted by the old hobo that the other boys around at the time kidded him about his obsession, satirically nicknaming John "Johnny Behazey."

From a formative point of view this episode speaks volumes about John's character development. For one thing, he had clearly inherited Garret Senior's sense of adventure and soaring imagination. Moreover, it is plain to see here that John was not bound by conventional expectations. Where the other boys were intimidated, John was intrigued, welcoming the weird character and the odd experience. Also apparent from this incident is that John was animated by a strong democratic impulse—a gut feeling for equality accompanied by compassion for the downtrodden. But above all, it shows that John was awake to the power of storytelling. What remained was only for him to apply the potent universal appeal of stories to a business proposition.

AFTER COMPLETING GRAMMAR SCHOOL at Holy Trinity, John went on to attend seventh grade at Holy Cross, a venerable Catholic high school and college then located in the Lower Ninth Ward of New Orleans. But by this time the natural-born entrepreneur was seriously bored and restless. So much so that after just one year at Holy Cross, against his parents' wishes, John quit school. The year was 1925. He was just fourteen years old.

7

FROM HIGH SCHOOL DROPOUT
TO REAL ESTATE MAGNATE

W ITH NO FORMAL EDUCATION BEYOND A YEAR in what is now called middle school, and only the foggiest notion about what job to do or career to pursue, John took a blind leap into the world of work. His initial impulse was to take the easy route and go for a full-time job at the family grocery store. But to John's dismay, Uncle Garret was having none of it. He had long made a policy out of not hiring relatives beyond his immediate circle of brothers. Thus when nephew John came sniffing around for a position at the store, Uncle Garret turned him down point-blank. To assuage the shock of this summary rejection, Garret explained the reasoning behind his decision. He had nothing against his nephew. On the contrary, he loved him and wished him all success. He simply believed it was in young John's best interest to get a job somewhere else in order to learn different ways of doing business. This would pay off in the long run in greater knowledge and flexibility.[1]

After being rebuffed by his Uncle Garret, John attended Soule Business School for a few months before finally landing his first real job. This was as an assistant to an electrical contractor. No doubt his grandfather had pulled some strings behind the scenes, for John's boss was none other than Garret Senior's best friend and neighbor, George Gouguet. In early 1927, Gouguet snagged a contract to wire the new Station D Post Office, then being erected at the corner of Dauphine and Piety streets. In need of a helper, he hired fifteen-year-old John, paying him either $4.50 or $7.50 per week, depending on which source to believe.[2] Either way, though, it was a pretty meager salary. What was worse, John had to turn most of it over to his parents for rent.

The post office job was a commercial one-off for George Gouguet. Normally his bread and butter came from retrofitting residential properties for electricity. Yes, unbelievable as it seems—considering that electricity had been introduced to New Orleans as far back as 1889—existing residential homes were still in need of being wired as late as the late 1920s. Indeed, it took over a generation to fully connect the city to the grid. As an adult, John liked to reminisce about how things were at the old corner store back before the days of plug-in and switch-on electrical luxury. As he describes the situation, every evening at around fifteen minutes till closing time, a gaggle of local customers would flood into the store to buy coal oil—colloquially referred to at the time as "insurance oil."[3] Because few Bywater residents had electricity back in the 1910s, they would burn this insurance oil for illumination.

Clearly, then, a strong demand existed for a more convenient source of light. Of course, the appeal of electricity extended far beyond offering mere illumination, for electricity could power any household appliance imaginable. So absolutely everyone wanted to be hooked up to the grid, and an abundance of jobs were created to fill this demand.

This is where Mr. Gouguet came in. While in general his jobs involved residential retrofitting, he specialized in shotgun houses that were over fifty years old (built in the 1870s and earlier). A typical job involved the following: replacing gas light fixtures with electric chandeliers, putting in ceiling fans, and installing various types of plug-in outlets throughout the house—base outlets in living rooms and bedrooms, cord drops in the kitchen, and an outlet over the bathroom medicine cabinet. The retrofitting process was extremely laborious. For John it meant performing the repetitive task of boring holes through floor and ceiling joists using nothing but a hand drill. It also involved having to crawl on his stomach through lots of tight, dusty spaces. This type of intensive physical exertion took a toll on John, dangerously aggravating his heart condition. So after about a year as an electrician's assistant, he took his family doctor's advice and quit the job for health reasons.[4]

LEARNING THE HARD WAY that he was not cut out for blue-collar manual labor, John instead sought employment in the white-collar service sector. While he quickly succeeded in finding a job there, he had to start out at the bottom—specifically as a debt collector for the Sonny Boy Margarine Company. To supplement his $27 monthly salary paid for performing this unpleasant task, John worked weekends as a salesman and product demonstrator. In this capacity he would pitch the company's two oleomargarine lines: Good Luck, a premium yellow brand; and Sonny Boy, a budget brand that was actually white but was artificially colored yellow. This experience may have been the source of one of the first merchandising tricks John picked up over the course of an extensive retail career. For, as noted, there were two types of margarine being sold at the time: the more expensive yellow product, which resembled and almost rivaled the taste of real butter; and the cheaper white version, which looked and tasted exactly like the unappetizing butter substitute it was. John noticed how some grocers tried to increase white margarine's retail appeal by inserting a vanilla bean through a small hole made in the container. The bean acted to dye the oleo yellow.

Yet John picked up more than a mere parlor trick during his year at Sonny Boy. In fact, he learned a valuable lesson in management. Even before he began working for Sonny Boy, the company was already struggling, as evidenced by its need to hire a debt collector. John quickly figured out why the business was so shaky: because its almost sole focus was on bolstering the appearance of a healthy bottom line by registering as many sales as possible, meanwhile paying only a sidelong glance at the creditworthiness of its customers. The obvious folly of this approach was too much for John, leading to his first recorded instance of the sort of unshackled muckraking that would later make him famous. As the story goes, it was at the annual Sonny Boy shareholders' banquet that John stood up and delivered an impassioned diatribe against the company's poor debt-management practices. As would be expected, the speech went over like a lead balloon.[5]

Unsurprisingly, after the Great Depression hit in 1929, Sonny Boy lost control over its finances altogether and entered bankruptcy. Though John was once more out of a job, he was undeterred, for he had gained confidence in his aptitude for service-sector work. In this spirit, despite having no secretarial experience to speak of, John responded to a blind ad for a clerical position, figuring he could pick up the necessary skills to handle it along the way. As it turned out, the ad was for employment at the Canal Bank and Trust Company, which had its headquarters in the Central Business District of New Orleans at Common and Baronne streets. John did manage to get the job, but once again he had to start at the bottom, this time as a mailroom clerk. After spending a couple of years here racking up a track record of exceptional reliability, John was promoted to the bank's Transit Department. This plum position paid the vast sum of $55 per month.[6]

WITH HIS LIFE ROLLING OUT on a seemingly steady course—the future promising a secure but bland career marked by incremental rises up the banking ladder—two events occurred to destabilize John's world. First, in 1931 his mother died unexpectedly at the young age of forty-six. No record exists of how John took this blow. What is known is that he barely mentions Marie's death in his various recollections, and when he does it is without elaboration. Likely this reflects his deeply conflicted feelings toward her, feelings he admits bordered on shame.[7]

Though he had lost his mother, at least John still had his budding career at the bank—that is, until disaster struck. On March 9, 1933, President Franklin Delano Roosevelt, in his initial desperate efforts to halt the economic hemorrhaging caused by the Great Depression, declared a bank holiday. All the nation's banks were temporarily closed to assess their solvency. When the holiday ended four days later on March 13, hundreds of banks failed to reopen, having flunked what today are called "stress tests." Among them was Canal Bank and Trust, which was shut down and its assets liquidated. Once again, through no fault of his own, John found himself without employment.

Nevertheless, keeping his chin up, John and his now-best friend, Wilfred Meyer—whom he had met and bonded with during their four-year tenure together in the mail and transit departments at Canal Bank—decided to offer their talents to one of the few New Orleans banks that had survived the purge, Whitney Bank and Trust Company.[8] So they both applied for employment at Whitney, confident that given their previous experience they would be shoo-ins to get hired. Yet in a disappointing blow to John, only Wilfred received a job offer. Likely John's lack of schooling and absence of social polish came to the fore here, with haughty Whitney deciding that homespun John was just not up to snuff. Ironically, Whitney Bank would years later present a similar obstacle in the way of his career advancement. Each time, though, John used Whitney's block as a pivot into a far more promising pathway.

For now, though, the rejection by Whitney floored John. After two consecutive layoffs, he found himself flustered, flummoxed about his next move. At this vulnerable moment, after his hopes for a banking career had been crushed, he made a shaky, even flaky, decision. Taking the advice of his beloved Aunt Mary, he enrolled at the Moler Barber College. Apparently Mary, who sensibly encouraged him to learn a trade, had gone on to recommend becoming a barber because "hair always grows," so he would never be out of work. With his decision to enter Moler, John came uncomfortably close to surrendering his grand ambitions, thinking he just might confine his bursting entrepreneurial spirit to opening up a barbershop.

Fortunately, though, fate intervened to restore his confidence and set him on a new career path. But before this happened, one of those telling incidents occurred that reveals John's character to a tee. At the

Moler Barber School haircuts were free every weekday except Friday, when a shave cost a nickel and a cut cost a dime. On one of the free days a great big shabby hobo with pustulating sores all over his scalp came in for a haircut. John had been told that he could refuse any customer for hygienic reasons, but he took pity on the derelict and consented to do the cut. First, however, he washed the hobo's hair, and on observing the advanced state of his scalp rot decided to take drastic action. So without warning, like players do to the coach after winning the big game, John suddenly doused the tramp, splashing an entire bottle of formaldehyde over his head. Screaming bloody murder, his pate aflame, the giant immediately leaped out of the barber chair, grabbed John, and threatened to kill him. Luckily for posterity he held back. In fact, he even returned a few weeks later—his scalp now healed but his hair a mite thinner—to thank John.[9] Having demonstrated his compassion and egalitarian sympathies, even if a bit recklessly, John became a hero to the hobo.

JOHN'S RESCUE FROM A FUTURE LIFE of barbering came like a bolt out of the blue. In summer 1933, after he had "graduated" from Moler, Aunt Helen Frey—perhaps attempting to counteract Aunt Mary Schwegmann's baleful influence on her nephew's aspirations —swooped over, scooped him up, and took him on a steamship trip to France. All of a sudden the plucky but floundering young man of twenty-two found himself aboard the S.S. San Pedro on a fifteen-day cruise across the Atlantic to Le Havre! Who could have predicted this turn of events? It was as if an angel had saved him, one concerned to rekindle and nurture his ambitions.

Actually operating on a more mundane plane, Aunt Helen hoped to expose John to higher cultural standards and ways of life outside his limited domain of experience. In this she succeeded admirably. For instance, while on the steamship cruise, John "ate the best food he had ever tasted in his life." And in fine-dining style, these gourmet meals were served in "courses," a custom with which he was utterly unfamiliar, as everything he had previously consumed, except for dessert, was served up all at once on a soup plate. John was also wowed by the evening entertainments—featuring music, singing, dancing, and a coterie of lively people. He remembered watching in awe as a Galatoire son (scion of an aristocratic New Orleans family) took turns dancing with each girl from among a bevy of traveling schoolteachers.

Aunt Helen had more up her sleeve, however, than a mere leisure excursion. For she insisted from the beginning that penniless John must pay for his passage. Her destination being Alsace-Lorraine (in 1933 a property of France, but a political football with Germany), John was thus compelled upon landing there to take a job around the town of Rosenwiller. Here he harvested hops for a beer-maker, spending sixty straight days from sunup to sundown cutting ripe yellow-leaved hops from large poles. Perhaps not surprisingly, this hard work turned out to be pure pleasure. Indeed, John later recalled the long days spent toiling outside in the fields of Rosenwiller as being among the happiest of his life. It is easy to see why. The pastoral scenery of the French countryside was obviously gorgeous. And unlike back home, the summer air was fresh, cool, and dry, instead of being damp, hot, and fetid. For the first time in a long time John was breathing deeply, exercising strenuously, and gaining weight. By the end of the two months spent harvesting hops, he was beaming health.[10]

The trip to France must have been enormously cathartic for John. Away, if only for a few months, from the bitter disappointments and polluted atmosphere of New Orleans, sailing in luxury, harvesting the lush Alsatian fields, living amid spectacular landscapes, he finally had the time and space for thought and reflection. When John arrived back in New Orleans in autumn 1933, he was clearly a new man, refreshed, revitalized, and raring to go.

Indeed, to say he was charged up would be an understatement. It was more like he had been supernaturally possessed. For in fact everything he did from this point forward in his business career led from one success to the next. Perhaps while sojourning along the French-German crossroads he had secretly met up with Mephistopheles and diabolically acquired the Midas touch. Of course, a more down-to-earth explanation for the new energy and clarity of vision he possessed might be that he had simply gotten in touch with his maternal Alsacich roots. But whatever the reason, there is no question that when he returned to New Orleans, he was finally fully in command of his forebears' "knack for making money."

AFTER BEING REJECTED by Whitney Bank, flirting with a career as a barber, and returning from France, John switched his career focus from banking to real estate. As it turned out, this was the perfect move, one much more amenable to his nature. For banking did not really suit John's personality. It was too stuffy, too full of pedigree, pretence, and snobbery. John was just the opposite: more like a diamond in the rough than a cultured pearl. Moreover, beyond this basic incompatibility, the world of banking was simply too confining for such an expansive, aspiring spirit as John.

Real estate, on the other hand, offered immense vistas of opportunity to someone blessed with business smarts who was willing to hustle and eager to learn. "Now hold it right there," one could easily object. This portrayal of real estate as a vast field of promise appears extremely at odds with the times being discussed—namely, the mid-1930s, among the worst years of the Great Depression, when the national real estate market had crashed into seeming oblivion. But as the saying goes, in every economic disaster there are always those who end up smelling like a rose. These rare few tend to have a gift for obdurately maintaining optimism in the face of tragedy. They are also likely to be fighters, not necessarily in a mean-spirited way, but in the sense of always struggling to turn every opportunity into some sort of positive advantage. Such was John Schwegmann, an optimist and a fighter.

John spent much of the Great Depression working in the real estate business.[11] The details about exactly how and when he got into it, however, are somewhat murky. One story in circulation suggests that his first foray into the business occurred in late 1933 or early 1934, when he accepted an offer from a real estate firm for employment as a broker. Yet according to John himself, it was actually Uncle Garret—yes, the same Uncle Garret who had originally discouraged John from working for the family—who first employed him in real estate back in 1931.

As John tells it, Garret hired him as a rent collector, a job that either deliberately or coincidentally took advantage of John's previous experience as a debt collector for the oleomargarine company. He recalls performing this thankless task (chasing down money from bankrupt tenants) for Uncle Garret between 1931 and 1933. But it will be remembered that this was during the period he was working full-time at Canal Bank. To give John's recollection the benefit of the doubt, the most likely story is that, just as he had earlier supplemented his income from Sonny Boy by working weekends as a salesman and product demonstrator, he probably augmented his salary at Canal Bank by moonlighting as a rent collector for Uncle Garret.

Whatever the truth about the timing of his original entry into real estate, it is known for certain that John's first official job as a real estate broker was with James F. Turnbull, Realtor, with the Turnbull office located at 413 Carondelet in downtown New Orleans. During his tenure there, spanning the mid-1930s, John made a lot of money.

But this income was earned not simply through the buying and selling of properties. Indeed, John's son, John Francis Schwegmann, tells a colorful tale about the highly unusual nature of his father's first full-time job in real estate.[12] In his somewhat shocking, though mordantly funny, version of the story, there was once a gentleman with a significant amount of clout in the world of New Orleans real estate in need of a sympathetic assistant. This man—perhaps Turnbull himself, or maybe an associate—inhabited the ambiguous nexus between economics and politics. He was not exactly what could be called a political fixer, nor was he merely a commonplace realtor. He was more a facilitator, a go-between, who brought together government officials and wealthy investors for their mutual profit. This gentleman was lively, gregarious, a real backslapper who knew everybody with power, ranging from the rich city elites to Mayor Robert Maestri, who was then trying mightily to hold the city together during the Depression.

The reason this gentleman needed a sympathetic assistant was because he had a problem: namely, he was a regular "Cooter Brown." This is where John came in. On being hired as his assistant it was John's job to wake the man up in the morning, rouse him out of a hung-over stupor, pour him a stiff drink to steady his nerves, and get him dressed and ready for another day of pressing the flesh. Once this character out of W.C. Fields got going, he was purportedly a brilliant performer. He was also extremely knowledgeable about the real estate business, and John was his extremely successful apprentice. Although this is speculative, it is probable that under the tutelage of this flawed master John began developing his extroverted style, which became his eccentric trademark forever after.

Now, just what was going on at the time that would require the services of a specialty liaison between government officials and wealthy investors? The answer is found in a federal entity established in 1933 called the Homeowners Loan Corporation, or HOLC, with which Turnbull Realty undoubtedly had significant dealings. Hastily improvised under the rubric of the New Deal to help combat the effects of the Great Depression, HOLC was instituted as a means to put a brake on home foreclosures, which were running rampant at the time. The basic idea was to replace existing short-term home loans with longer-term loans, which would stretch out the time needed to pay back mortgages, and thus in theory allow for lower and more affordable monthly payments.

This replacement process was supposed to be done through government buying of existing mortgages from their owners—namely, private banks specializing in home mortgages, which were at the time called "homesteads" (referred to today as "savings and loan associations"). Considering that property values were plummeting anyway, the homesteads would naturally have to take a loss on the mortgage principal when they sold to the government. But they nonetheless had an incentive to participate in this voluntary program: they would receive payment for their mortgages in the form of solid government bonds. Certainly this payout beat the risky alternative of ending up with total losses from write-offs.

Whenever a homestead agreed to sell off a mortgage, the new government landlord would issue a significantly lower long-term loan. Or at least that is how the program was supposed to work. Though designed with good intentions, HOLC was seriously flawed from the outset.[13] Two of its biggest problems were the voluntary nature of the program, and its failure to set forth any clear standards for appraising property values. Since there was no requirement at all to participate, banks were reluctant to do so unless they could somehow minimize the haircut they took when selling to the feds. Taking advantage of the lack of appraisal standards, it became common for banks to try to manipulate property values upward, essentially attempting to game the system. For the most part, HOLC administrators acquiesced in these shenanigans. As a result they routinely ended up doling out overly generous payments to the banks in exchange for the mortgages. This, of course, subverted the entire purpose of the program, which was to help ease the burden of mortgage payments on homeowners. Instead, the banks got great deals, while homeowners received only marginal mortgage reductions.

Under HOLC, then, the game was rigged in favor of lenders, with borrowers getting the short end of the stick. That the homeowner received little relief can be seen statistically in the high failure rate of the program. Over its short life span, HOLC bought roughly one million home mortgages. Despite being supposedly more affordable, about one in five (200.000) of these mortgages ended up in default anyway. Unable to make any real dent in the foreclosure crisis, and with its flaws becoming patently obvious, HOLC was phased out in 1935, just two years after its institution.

It is tempting to view the HOLC fiasco simply as a variation on the old familiar theme of the little guy getting shafted by the chiseling banks. But John saw things in a more complex light. Having worked for a bank (Canal Bank and Trust) that had just been forced out of business by the federal government, he knew the tremendous pressure homesteads were under to maintain an acceptable level of liquidity—and that to fall below a certain reserve-capital threshold meant the feds shut you down. John was thus in a position to be sympathetic to both sides: the suffering homeowners pinched painfully between the pincers of deflation and foreclosure; and the misunderstood Snidely Whiplashes, who were themselves struggling to stay in business.

To John, who was now working with investors engaged in HOLC dealings, the whole program was nothing but a desperate attempt to correct what was originally "a very grave mistake" by FDR—namely, establishing a mandatory liquidity requirement for the banks and homesteads. The scramble by financial institutions to get liquid set off a tremendous wave of foreclosures, and by the time HOLC came on the scene most of the worst damage had already been done. As John tells it, the whole situation was nothing short of a tragic disaster.

> Everybody had to be liquid, and when they [the creditors] got liquid, what did that mean? It meant that all these people [the debtors] lost their homes—not just homes, but farms, cattle, everything…. Many a man lost his farm, lost his home, lost his business on account of this immediate action of becoming liquid.

> A homestead or a bank can't have your home, your money, and have it invested, and have it waiting for you at the same time…. [FDR] went from one extreme to another one. [At first] everybody had to be liquid. Then afterwards, he found out what tremendous harm it did to the country. And then he wanted them to go out there and figure out a way he could get these people's homes back. But most of them never got their homes back [because] they had already been bought up by people like myself…. And some of them died and lost confidence, and it was a sad state of affairs.[14]

In brokering the heartbreaking real estate foreclosure circuit in New Orleans, and actively witnessing futile federal attempts to stanch the hemorrhaging of property values, John experienced the full brunt of the onslaught known as the Great Depression. According to John, many of the New Orleanians he was dealing with "were so broke, they didn't even have foreclosures." This is technically correct. For in Louisiana, which conducts its legal affairs according to the Napoleonic

Code, there is a variation on foreclosure called "dation en paiement," a French legal term meaning "to call things square."[15] Here, instead of suffering under a long drawn-out bureaucratic procedure, the mortgage owner and the foreclosed-on homeowner both simply agree to end the relationship, with no lingering strings attached.

As a broker for Turnbull, it was John's job to acquire residential rental properties at distressed prices—double shotguns, for example, were selling at 60%-to-75% discounts for $2,000 to $3,000 apiece, or even less—then sell them into a pool comprised of wealthy investors, in the process receiving commissions. This turned out to be very lucrative for John, as he "sold hundreds and hundreds of these homes." So finally, for the first time in his life, John was making some real money. More importantly, he was meeting and interacting with rich, influential people, "some of the finest people in the world," as he remembers them.[16] This was a valuable experience for at least two reasons. First, it helped John come out of his introverted shell and get comfortable in dealing with the city's elites. Second, he was able to establish a network of contacts that would serve him in future endeavors.

Perhaps taking a cue from Uncle Garret, or simply following his own sharp business instincts, John used the money he made from commissions to begin investing in real estate on his own. In his daily dealings he would occasionally come across spectacular bargains. Instead of selling these off to the wealthy investor pool, he would buy them himself. He then used the rents he collected to acquire even more properties. In this way John ended up accumulating a considerable amount of money—on the order of tens of thousands of dollars. Almost needless to say, this was an amazing feat to pull off during the depths of the Great Depression. Moreover, with the first glimmerings of recovery in the late 1930s, property values on his rental homes began to soar. In one instance, for example, a "double" he owned skyrocketed in value from $1,900 when he bought it in the mid-1930s to $14,000 by the end of the decade.[17]

8

THE SUPERMARKET REVOLUTION

HAVING ACCUMULATED A SMALL FORTUNE by the late 1930s, John faced an enviable dilemma. On one hand he could continue to pursue a career in real estate, a field he admittedly enjoyed and was obviously good at, and where he stood a good chance of becoming a major player on the New Orleans scene. On the other hand, as a well-off young man still only in his late twenties, he now had the time, money, and hence freedom to do what most people only dream of doing—namely, to pursue his own vision.

But here the question arises: Did he even have a vision? This is not mere idle pondering. For possessing a vision differs dramatically from vaguely dreaming about where one wants to go or who one wants to be in life. A vision is an active process. In order to exist it must first be conceived, and then it must be acted on. This process of conception and action calls on all the highest faculties, requiring intelligence, insight, foresight, passion, imagination, devotion, and daring. As a result, it is rare in human affairs to encounter anyone—young, rich, or otherwise—who can even conceive a personal vision, much less one who has the passion, stamina, and courage to pursue its actualization.

So did John have a vision? The answer is an unequivocal yes. Indeed, he had two visions: one general and one specific. In general he wanted to "amount to something." To achieve this grand ambition he determined to become a "merchant," meaning a retailer. Why did he choose this particular career path? As he admits on the Cabildo tape, "I read that the great fortunes were always made by merchants." So despite having achieved success in the real estate business, John made a fateful decision: "I knew where I belonged. I knew I had to be a merchant."[1]

Yet John's general vision was far from being just some foggy reverie about someday becoming a rich businessman in the retail trade. Specifically, he determined to realize his dream by becoming a food store merchant. In this area, John knew with confidence that he could excel. After all, he knew the grocery business backwards and forwards, inside and out, having grown up in the culture of the old corner store. He also had a rich familial reservoir on which to draw: food stores were in his DNA, just as surely as was his uncanny moneymaking ability.

So grocery retailing was to be the future platform from which John would swan dive into the bountiful pool of riches and fame. But before he could even begin to build this enchanted platform he would have to engage in some deep thinking and intensive study. For he knew that the hardest part that lay ahead—way more difficult than performing the yeoman tasks involved in setting up a grocery business—would be in wrestling with the grand conception and devilish details of his specific vision. Certainly as a forward-looking young man of the 1930s, John knew that he could not hope to make his mark as a grocery merchant by following the same old tired food-store formulas of the past. Instead, John could see clearly a new world dawning beyond the Depression, and that this coming modernity would require a radically different business model.

While the vision of a brave new world of food retailing did not originate with John, the promising new approaches to the grocery business then in ascendance obviously resonated deeply with this keen student of economic trends. Specifically, John was enthralled with an all-new food-store retailing phenomenon then just beginning to be called the "supermarket." Clearly he had been studying the principles underlying the basis of supermarkets closely during his real estate years.[2] For when he finally got the opportunity to put these principles into practice, he hit the ground running, full steam ahead.

SUPERMARKETS DID NOT COME INTO EXISTENCE until the early 1930s. Before then, the grocery sector consisted almost solely of tiny family-owned corner grocery stores and a handful of slightly larger chain outlets. So when full-fledged supermarkets made their initial appearance it was as if a surprise new dinosaur species had suddenly burst forth from out of nowhere. And in crucial respects these much bigger stores were indeed a novel retail form without precedent, operating on alien principles that few could grasp at the time.

But they did not emerge in a vacuum. Many of their distinctive features were based on the results of successful experimentation that had gone on previously. Yet as with all cases of punctuated equilibrium, the most important factors leading up to their sudden appearance were external, not internal. In the case of supermarkets, these novel retail entities emerged against a backdrop of larger historical forces that included general expansionist tendencies and epic revolutions in technology, organization, marketing, and culture.

In tracing the transformation of old-time grocery stores into modern supermarkets, the first larger historical force needing to be taken into account is expansion—meaning expansion on all levels. In the early twentieth century, the U.S. population was soaring in numbers and spreading geographically throughout the nation. Cities and even farms were growing exponentially in size. Business and industry were getting bigger, and so was the administrative machinery of government. Also expanding during this time were people's expectations, as they sought to rise in class and status in an attempt to achieve the American Dream. What ultimately made all this expansion possible was the ongoing technological revolution, a science-fueled fiery furnace from whose furiously burning Faustian cauldron emerged seemingly endless advances in energy, machinery, appliances, materials, transportation, and communications. Without these advances, the supermarket would have never appeared.

Breakthroughs in corporate organization also occurred in the early twentieth century. By exploiting modern scientific management and accounting techniques, businesses could grow larger, more efficient, and more productive all at the same time. Without question, running a chain of comparatively humongous supermarkets would not have been possible using the traditional mom-and-pop methods of store management. Nor were old-time grocery stores able to take advantage of the revolution in marketing then taking place. First, they simply did not have enough space to stock and display the cascade of brands that began flooding the stores beginning in the early 1900s.[3] Moreover, most did not have the financial wherewithal to invest in advertising, which was then in the process of becoming an absolutely indispensable competitive weapon.

Finally, all these larger forces came together to give birth to an entirely new cultural phenomenon—namely, the consumer society. Driven by an exploding population and corresponding growing aspirations, and enabled by advances in technology, organization, and marketing, a mass demand began arising for a better quality of life. More comfort, more ease, more leisure and pleasure—these were the watchwords of the consumer society then taking shape. Life for the average Joe and Jane was not just about drudgery anymore. It was now also about entertainment and enjoyment. Yet consumers desired more than just fun and frivolity from the new technological civilization. They also demanded empowerment—more freedom and opportunity, a greater scope for personal and political choices.

In retrospect, given all the larger forces favoring its appearance, the emergence of the supermarket as an economically rational and socially desirable retail phenomenon looks inevitable. So it is somewhat disconcerting to realize what a struggle supermarkets were forced to engage in before they became established as a legitimate retail form. As with all new ideas, they were at first greeted mostly with suspicion, skepticism, or indifference by rival food and even drug

retailers. Even after they had firmly proven themselves, they still had
to fight further to overcome numerous entrenched political, legal, and
psychological obstacles.[4] Here it is appropriate to note that one of the
preeminent champions of this fight, rarely acknowledged in the annals
of supermarket lore, was John G. Schwegmann.

AS A RADICAL DEPARTURE IN FOOD RETAILING, the original supermarkets were distinguished from old-time grocery stores by three
primary characteristics. First, supermarkets were not *full-service* venues
like the old stores. Rather they were *self-service* (or, more accurately,
minimum-service). In practice this meant that supermarket customers
had to gather their own merchandise (clerks no longer did it for them),
they had to pay for their merchandise at the time of purchase (no
buying on credit), and they had to get it home under their own steam
(no delivery). In eliminating these personalized services, the so-called
"cash and carry" supermarkets gambled that any off-putting lack of
convenience suffered by their customers would be more than offset by
the appeal of dramatically lower prices—a bet they won hands-down.

The second characteristic that distinguished supermarkets from
old-time grocery stores was their adoption of a revolutionary business
model forged in response to the then-emerging mass market. This model
is based on the dynamic interaction of three factors: low operating
costs, low merchandise prices, and high sales volume. Its first principle
is simple enough to easily understand: if a store cuts its operational
costs to the bone—if it lowers its labor costs through elimination of
unnecessary services, purchases its merchandise stock in large quantities
(receiving bulk buying discounts in return), exercises strict inventory
controls, and squeezes money out of overhead in any other way it
can—then these cost savings can be passed along to the consumer in
the form of significantly lower prices on merchandise. In other words,
lower operating costs can easily translate into lower prices.

At this point, however, things begin to get more complicated,
as the principles involved in this three-factor dynamic interaction

are essentially based on a whole-systems analysis. Indeed, the few merchants who originally grasped the new principles—among them John Schwegmann—had to hammer them home over and over again before the vast majority of retailers properly understood them.[5]

Here the following explanation is offered. Lower operating costs combine with lower merchandise prices to set up a favorable feedback loop leading to a higher volume of customer purchasing. As the logic goes, ever-greater numbers of customers will flock to a store, and they will buy more than they normally would while there in order to take advantage of its extraordinarily low prices. According to the theory, the increasing store traffic and accelerating turnover more than compensates for any loss in profits that results from charging lower prices. Indeed, the higher traffic and faster turnover together generate far greater profits than could be gained by charging higher prices. John Schwegmann expressed this process in a pithy aphorism: "I'd rather make a fast nickel than a slow dime."[6] Moreover, he claimed that putting these principles into action is like creating "a money-making machine."

Although this elegant theory, a masterstroke of counter-intuition, has since proven to be correct, it took decades for the general grocery trade to accept what seemed to be its pretzel logic. Conventional wisdom had previously been straightforward: if you charge higher prices, you will make more money, simple as that. Yet, as it turns out, this is not true, at least not in a mass-market environment. For higher prices undermine higher volume. Customers no longer flock to the store to take advantage of low prices. So the end result of charging higher prices is actually a static customer base, with corresponding low-to-no growth to show for it. No wonder, then, that when true supermarkets based on sales velocity finally hit the retail scene in a big way in the 1950s, they ground the old-time grocery stores, still wedded to high prices, into the dust. (Note that an accounting aspect to all this is discussed subsequently.)

The third primary characteristic that distinguished supermarkets from mom-and-pop stores was size. Compared with the old-time grocery stores, supermarkets were absolutely gigantic. Even the smallish 1950s' supermarkets, which averaged 13,000 square feet in 1955, positively dwarfed both the earliest mom-and-pop stores (less than 1,000 square feet) and the larger combination grocery stores that began proliferating in the 1920s (between 1,000 and 2,000 square feet).[7] Pursuing the logic of expansive size forward in time, contemporary supermarkets are built on an immense scale—70,000 square feet or more—barely conceivable when the format first appeared.

Of course, the concept of "super" size did not arise from nowhere. For it logically complemented the self-service and high-volume characteristics of supermarkets. Consider that if a store is self-service, then more space is needed for various shopping purposes, including more room for product display and wider aisles for easier customer maneuverability, among others. But most important in justifying store size expansion is the underlying high-volume philosophy. For if it is true that greater sales velocity leads to greater profits, then surely the idea would be to build bigger and bigger stores to accommodate more and more products to facilitate faster and faster turnover.[8]

Along with their radically different approaches to service, size, and velocity, three other characteristics set supermarkets definitively apart from old-time grocery stores. First, supermarkets invariably featured parking lots for their swelling ranks of car-owning customers. Second, they displayed stunning architecture deliberately designed to draw in customers with awe-inspiring dimensions and attention-grabbing exteriors. Third, the original supermarket operators often employed showmanship, as they hosted various types of special events both in-store and outside to create a fun, entertaining atmosphere. All of these attractive features—the parking lot, the unique architecture, and the entertaining atmosphere—served important functions in the early years of supermarkets when, in order to make the low-cost economics work, store operators had to set up shop in marginal urban areas.[9]

THE FIRST BUILDING BLOCK in supermarket evolution was self-service. This novel concept initially emerged in the second decade of the twentieth century. Supermarket historians commonly cite 1916 as the year self-service originated—specifically at Clarence Saunders's Piggly Wiggly store in Memphis, Tennessee. Actually, however, it was Alpha Beta, a chain located in southern California, that in 1914 became the first food store to feature self-service. Be that as it may, the concept was so outré at the time it did not begin to be widely adopted for more than a decade afterward. Even the mightiest grocery chain of the day, A&P, still based its stores on full-service up to the mid-1930s.[10]

A&P did, however, pioneer the second, and arguably the most crucial, innovation in supermarket evolution: the low-cost/low-price/high-volume economic equation (subsequently referred to in shorthand as the "Golden Formula"). A&P first introduced this revolutionary business concept in the mid-1920s. It was considered so outrageous at the time that even many of A&P's own division managers did not believe in it. Indeed, as has been and will be discussed, there was a general reluctance all around to embrace the full ramifications of the Golden Formula.

One reason for the inability to believe in, and thus hesitance to adopt, this new idea is economic in nature, and technically concerns accounting. Specifically, the Golden Formula measures profitability by focusing on return on investment (ROI), calculated on the basis of "markup on costs"—a long-term indicator. Alternatively, profit can also be measured by focusing on return on sales (ROS), calculated on the basis of "margin on prices"—a short-term indicator.[11] Without getting bogged down further in technical details, suffice to say here that the accounting method emphasizing ROI is similar to a strict discipline: difficult to learn and even harder to practice consistently. In contrast, the ROS method is easier to understand and follow, even if it yields false-positive results. Guess which method most retailers embraced?

Beyond the convoluted economic arguments that either favored or opposed the Golden Formula, there was a political dimension to its underlying philosophy. Believe it or not, the retail issues raised by the new principles ignited a populist firestorm against its advocates lasting for much of the first half of the twentieth century. Marc Levinson chronicles in exquisite detail this all-but-forgotten chapter of retail history in his book *The Great A&P and the Struggle for Small Business in America.* Much more will be said later about this subject, as it directly concerns the career of John Schwegmann. Here it is enough to understand that the low-cost/low-price/high-volume philosophy was resisted for a long time for both economic and political reasons—as it went against the grain of conventional wisdom on one hand and was ideologically controversial on the other. On an endnote, consider that the validity of the Golden Formula has by now been firmly established, and contemporary supermarkets routinely operate according to its principles.

After self-service was introduced circa 1915, and the new approach to profitability tentatively established in 1925, larger grocery stores began to appear. Once again, A&P got the ball rolling when in 1926 it debuted its new combination store prototype, which was quickly rolled out to hundreds of units.[12] The "combo" store concept took a big step in the direction of one-stop food shopping by adding a meat department to the old-time grocery store and expanding its produce section—thus saving customers respective trips to the butcher shop and produce vendor. Naturally, given the additional merchandise they carried, combination stores had to be bigger in size than old-time stores. At 1,200 to 1,800 square feet, A&P's combos were double and triple the size of old-time stores. Note, however, that at least one operator at the time, Rockmoor Grocery in Miami, Florida, took the size trend even further, opening a combo store in 1926 sized at 2,800 square feet. But this was considered beyond the pale at the time, with no one else daring to follow the expansionist logic that far.

Except for Ralph's. Located in the trendsetter state of California, Ralph's Grocery Company took the first leap into genuine giant size in 1928, when it opened a 12,000 square-foot grocery store. Prior to this time a few such super-sized outlets existed, yet they were more like "flea market" assemblages of independently owned specialty food retailers—butchers, bakers, dairies, and produce vendors—than vertically integrated coherent wholes. Ralph's innovation was to fuse a collection of such disaggregated departments into a wholly owned unitary format.[13] Ralph's even pioneered the look of the modern supermarket, with its curved roof and frontispiece plate-glass windows.

It also featured wider aisles than usual and a large parking lot, both signatures of contemporary stores. Yet it still lacked the one thing that kept it from true modernity—namely, a low-price policy.

THE REAL BREAKTHROUGH CAME two years later with Michael Cullen, a visionary who paid his dues coming up through the management ranks of A&P and Kroger. Weaving together its three essential elements—self-service, large size, and the Golden Formula—Cullen created the first true supermarket in 1930. Called King Kullen, the store was located on the outskirts of New York City way out in Jamaica, Queens. Compared with other grocery stores at the time (at least those outside the anomalous California market), the original King Kullen was, as described by Cullen himself, of "monstrous" proportions at 6,000 square feet. Its major attraction was a huge selection of national brands featured at rock-bottom prices. Promoting his creation as "The World's Greatest Price Wrecker," Cullen trumpeted the slogan, "Pile It High. Sell It Low." Clearly he had totally embraced the low-cost/low-price/high-volume philosophy.[14]

Despite its spartan appearance and no-frills merchandising style, King Kullen was a tremendous success. Quickly capitalizing on his new hit format, Cullen rolled out seven even larger stores (each roughly 12,000 square feet) over the following two years. By 1932, the chain's eight units were averaging $1 million annually in sales per store.

Cullen's success was so stunning that copycats quickly emerged. Often called after imposing beasts, the imitators adopted such names as Giant Tiger, Great Leopard, and Bull Market, One of them, Big Bear, pushed the King Kullen concept to an extreme. Opening in 1932 in Elizabeth, New Jersey, the Big Bear store was colossal at 50,000 square feet. Moreover, not stopping at groceries, Big Bear also sold an assortment of general merchandise, including hardware, tires, and radios, among other GM products.[15]

These early manifestations of modern supermarkets excited intense interest in the grocery industry at the time. Yet they also invited skepticism, even disdain. Established grocery chains, such as Kroger and A&P, tended to view supermarkets as simply a passing fad of the penny-pinching 1930s, their success merely a transitory phenomenon destined to fade away when good times returned. They also saw the huge size of supermarkets as too unwieldy, and their razor-thin profit margins too tiny to bother with. For these reasons and others, mostly involving politics, the major grocery chains avoided entry into the new supermarket niche when it first emerged in the early 1930s.[16] So by default, the soon-to-be soaring supermarket sector was left initially to independent grocery entrepreneurs and wholesalers.

In 1933, just three years after King Kullen's debut, supermarkets had already risen rapidly to claim nearly 2% of all U.S. grocery sales. Over the next couple of years, as this share continued its relentless rise, the major grocery chains started getting nervous, but they were hamstrung from taking action at the time by unfavorable provisions of New Deal legislation contained in the National Industrial Recovery Act. Fortunately for the chains, the NIRA was repealed in 1935, and they finally had the breathing space to take a second, more objective and less dismissive, look at the new retail model.[17]After much agonized scrutiny, and with a certain amount of kicking-and-screaming reluctance, the big grocery chains finally threw in the towel: they conceded the economic superiority of the large-scale, self-service, low-price supermarkets and acted accordingly. Between 1937 and 1938, for example, leader A&P closed down 4,000 of its older grocery stores and opened 750 new supermarkets, thereby permanently transforming the food store landscape.

ALL THESE DEVELOPMENTS IN THE WORLD of grocery retailing swirled around John as he worked the real estate trade during the 1930s. Evidently this ambitious young man, determined to be a food store merchant, was following them closely. The energetic spectacle of the newly arising supermarkets must have thrilled him, as he sensed great opportunity here. Since the chains, as noted, had at first backed off on supermarkets, this left the field wide open to independents. As long as they stayed away, John would face little resistance to his plans. For the soon-to-be retail entrepreneur, this was his big chance.

There was also something in particular about the Crescent City that appealed to John's business instincts, and even his imagination. Given his intimate acquaintance with the city's interlocking retail and residential scene, John must have known that he would face no real competition, at least not at first. In New Orleans, no one was thinking at the time beyond the traditional model of the old corner store. This model was too deeply entrenched in a city designed for easy neighborhood strolling. Besides, New Orleans' neighborhood stores supplied the quirky food items used in the city's unique cuisine.

Precisely because of these factors—along with consideration of the city's profoundly anti-competitive public markets—the major grocery chains proliferating throughout U.S. cities in the 1910s and 1920s had for the most part avoided New Orleans. The local food store structure was just too hard a nut to crack at the time. Under these circumstances, it must have seemed inconceivable during the 1930s that some new-fangled type of giant-sized grocery store not anchored in a particular neighborhood and carrying mostly national brands appealing to mainstream American tastes could possibly succeed in New Orleans.

John felt otherwise. Swimming against the tide of conventional wisdom—a trait that later became one of his signature personality characteristics—John firmly believed he could make the supermarket concept work here. He knew the grocery business, he knew real estate, and he knew the Crescent City's distinctive culinary customs. As a native independent supermarket operator, he would know how to cater to local tastes with unique specialty products judiciously mixed in with a more expansive selection of the bread-and-butter national brands. No out-of-town chain had the insider savvy to compete. He would have the local supermarket scene to himself.

An entertainment angle also played into John's calculations. From King Kullen onward, supermarkets had cultivated a mystique of celebration surrounding the ecstatic act of wallowing in a spectacular abundance of bargains. Early commentators on supermarkets re-marked on their "circus methods" and "carnival atmosphere" featuring publicity stunts and spectacular events.[18] The illusion of some great entertainment—a festival, a fair—was reinforced by a carnival barker's flair for hyperbole. The new stores were called "King," "Big," "Super," "Great," and "Giant," and they all shamelessly boasted about their rock-bottom prices—each one apparently featuring the lowest prices ever seen on earth. The intrinsic entertainment aspect of supermarkets must have deeply appealed to John, who was, after all, a child of New Orleans. Surely he was convinced that it would also appeal to his fellow citizens. For what better American city than New Orleans to establish a new type of store that featured a carnival atmosphere?

9

A PURE DEVOTEE OF ECONOMY PLANS HIS FIRST STORE

BACK IN HIS BOYHOOD DAYS, when he used to hover over at the Frey family homestead just itching to be of assistance, John developed a reputation as a take-charge kind of guy, someone who seized the bull by the horns and figured out how to get a job done. Whenever in the course of taking on some task or performing some chore he encountered a problem, instead of giving in to frustration he would diligently, even delightedly, set about to solve it, focusing what were clearly becoming formidable powers of concentration on overcoming the difficulty at hand. Anton Frey certainly took notice of his grandson's penchant for management and problem solving and nurtured these valuable qualities, shooing away any pesky offers of advice or help for young John with words to the effect of "Leave it to the weiskopf. He will figure it out," or "The weiskopf will take care of everything."[1]

Allied with John's budding management propensities, problem-solving abilities, and what his earliest chronicler, Warren B. Nation, described as "the unnerving ability to concentrate on the matter at hand to the exclusion of everything else" was what Nation referred to as "a tremendous drive."[2] As has been seen, John did indeed harbor an inner fire, blazing away with a burning ambition to succeed. What fueled this intense drive and fanned it into a bright flame was a deep reservoir of envy, stoked by this born fighter's resolute refusal to capitulate to any feeling of inferiority.

The envy stemmed, it will be recalled, from the circumstances of John's two cousins, Leo and George, whose ostentatious lifestyles contrasted so bitterly with his own. That John was both deeply jealous of them and utterly determined to conquer the status gap is attested in his own words: "[Leo and George] had the finest clothes and went to the finest schools. They had fine cars. They went all over the U.S.... I decided I wanted to do what they did one day. I knew I couldn't do it then, but I was going to work like hell to see that I eventually did."[3] As it turned out, he was as good as his word, maintaining lifelong oversized aspirations that achieved success beyond his wildest dreams.

To a catalog of what eventually blossomed into John's primary positive qualities—his magisterial managerial skills, his gifted practical intellect, and his fiery motivation—two more must surely be added. One is an indefatigable curiosity. As a boy his acutely inquisitive nature manifested in sharp powers of observation (as preserved in his numerous vivid recollections), an openness to oddball social encounters, and a fascination with problem solving. Later on it took various other forms, including frequent travels to foreign destinations and a midlife plunge beyond his comfort zone into the unknown world of politics. The thread running through all these youthful and mature displays of curiosity is that they did not stop at the mere wonderment stage. Instead, John was determined to satisfy his urge to know.

A FINAL MECHANISM IN THE MAINSPRINGS of what made John tick was his near-religious devotion to economy. Yea verily, he was a true believer! His worship of the fundamentals and principles of economy seeped so deeply into the core of his being that it came to animate his physical expressions and dominate his metaphysical intentions, motivating his noblest actions and inspiring his highest ideals.

John's enthusiasm for economy was all embracing, spanning across the spectrum of its three essential aspects: as a thing, an ideal, and an attitude. In its first sense, economy can be thought of as a "thing"—the actual organization of society constructed around the needs of survival. This is the way economy is usually understood, as an actual structure, its building blocks consisting of the physical acts of production, distribution, and consumption.

Yet economy can also be understood more abstractly as an ideal. In this second sense it stands for a belief in, or vision of, the best way to organize an economic system for purposes beyond mere survival. Here, within the contours of an ideological faith in the superiority of one particular system of wealth creation over another, practical decisions are embedded in such lofty notions as freedom, ethics, and even aesthetics. In this way, economy as an ideal represents the realm of values. Economically, values are expressed in the flux of supply, demand, and price. Ideologically, values form the emotional core from which choices are made on all levels, from individual and family to business, government, and institutions.

Along with its meanings as a thing and an ideal, economy also implies an attitude. In this third aspect, economy has both positive and negative connotations. In the positive sense, one who has internalized an economic attitude is considered thrifty and frugal, or otherwise judicious in the use of resources. From this perspective, those lacking a prudent economic attitude are viewed as wasteful spendthrifts who generally make decisions that are impulsive, unwise, and ultimately unproductive. Of course, the tables can be turned, with the thrifty man being seen as a stingy miser. But those who truly embrace the economic attitude shun miserliness as a vice to be avoided, since it impedes the healthy circulation of savings into profitable investment.

Such an enlightened economic attitude takes on ecological, even theological, dimensions. To the true devotee of economy, waste is considered a sin—not so much because it is morally wrong as that it is inefficient, failing to contribute anything worthwhile to the greater good of wealth creation. Indeed, those with an economically devout attitude see increasing the common wealth as the very purpose of life.

In respect to the three aspects of economy as a thing, an ideal, and an attitude, John was alternately fascinated, obsessed, and possessed. Thoroughly imbued with a frugal economic attitude, he hated waste and loved making money—feelings so strong in him they almost seemed instinctive. As for economy as an ideal, John held a bedrock belief in the rightness and superiority of the American free-enterprise system. Without the shadow of a doubt in his mind, capitalist organization based on free-trade principles and laissez-faire competition—with the latter's monopolistic tendencies blunted by antitrust regulation—seemed the only way to go, the only true path to wealth creation for both individuals and society as a whole.

So in terms of attitude and ideal, John was good to go; absolutely sure of himself. Where he fell short in his devotion to economy was in his knowledge of it as a thing—or how its parts work together to create a dynamic whole. Here his lack of formal education, little beyond grammar school, came firmly into play. This shortcoming could have permanently handicapped a lesser man, one whose educational deficiency easily could have left him floundering, way out of his depth, in a twentieth-century business environment of increasingly dazzling complexity. Yet in his own classic fashion, John rose to the challenge, as he marshaled the abundant talents he did possess, and held in spades—his natural problem-solving abilities, uncanny powers of concentration, turbo-charged drive, and unrelenting curiosity—and used them to overcome the educational deficit.

So with all the zeal of a highly motivated autodidact, John poured his passion into learning everything he could about the social science of economics. Since he was far from being a bookish intellectual, this mainly took the lowbrow form of immersing himself in business- and trade-devoted newspapers and magazines, obsessively devouring economic developments in these media with the same greedy avidity a hardcore gambler reserves for the daily racing form.[4] In maintaining an intensive reading regimen, he became a keen student of trends across the economic spectrum—from real estate and finance to industry, technology, modern management theory, and retail dynamics. Thus it came about, undoubtedly under the spell of exciting developments in the universe of grocery retailing, that he began formulating plans for his first store. While the idea for this store must have first begun germinating in the mid- to late 1930s, it would take going through some emotional turmoil before the entrepreneurial flower could burst forth into full profitable blossom.

WHEN JOHN SENIOR TOOK OVER the old corner store in 1939, he inherited a business model that was fast becoming outmoded. The deflation of the Great Depression, now gloomily marking its tenth anniversary, had hit all the classic full-service retailers hard, as their built-in inefficiencies forced them to maintain high prices, which rendered them competitively inert. In the world of food retailing, the only bright spot at the time was in the rapidly growing supermarket sector. Old-time grocery stores, meanwhile, were floundering. Certainly the Piety Street store was suffering. After a promising grand opening, celebrated with deep-discount offers on all the exotic booty salvaged from the aforementioned shipwreck, business quickly slacked off, and the store began sinking into the red.[5]

According to John Junior, his father was at a loss for how to stem the hemorrhaging, preferring to soldier on in the old ways while meekly placing his hopes on the return of a time when, as the popular song had it, "Happy days are here again!" For two tortuous years, 1940 and 1941, John Sr. persisted in his delusion that the store's troubles would magically disappear as soon as the economy improved. For his part, John Jr. was beside himself, so frustrated with his father that many a dinner conversation turned into heated argument. To the trendy twenty-nine-year-old, dad was clearly a clueless old fogey who knew nothing of the exciting innovations then sweeping the food store industry. So young John took it on himself to enlighten not only Senior but his brothers as well. He was only semi-successful.

One major change he was able to convince his father to undertake was to go self-service.[6] This was a radical departure for the old man, but once he accepted the logic he embraced it. And thankfully so, as changing over to self-service was not a simple policy pronouncement that could be decreed with the snap of a finger. Instead it involved some serious preliminary work, including redesigning and restructuring the store. First, all the grocery counters—those defining features of the self-service format—had to be removed. Next, all high shelving was reconfigured into low, customer-accessible shelving, and a series of other low shelves were built from scratch and placed throughout the store. Finally, the store itself was enlarged, its interior walls expanded outward to create more space for customer traffic. Significant to note is that John Senior's sons, John, Paul, and Anthony, did all the redesign and construction work themselves.

A hallowed tale in Schwegmann family lore preserves the story of John Senior's first encounter with a longtime female customer after the switchover from full-service to the new self-service regime. The lady entered the renovated store, looked bewilderingly around, and, completely baffled, asked tenuously, "Where is the counter? How can I get waited on?" Determined to lay down the law on the new policy right from the get-go, John Sr. unflinchingly replied. "Here is a basket. You can shop for yourself." The clearly annoyed customer angrily retorted, "If you think I am going to run around this puzzle garden, you're out of your mind. I will stay right here and get served!" At this, Senior merely shrugged his shoulders, took the basket, and filled her order. He then proceeded to add ten percent extra to her grocery bill…as a service charge. The outraged matron immediately got the picture, announcing to all within earshot: "You aren't charging me ten percent more. I'll go pick up my own groceries!" Thus was inaugurated self-service at the old corner store.[7]

Another major change John Sr. eventually acceded to involved accepting his sons as managing partners in the business. Though it may have hurt his pride to admit he needed help, taking this step was probably a boon relief for the obviously overwhelmed elder. In the new management scheme of things, initiated in 1942, his three sons, now business partners, were assigned specific duties: Anthony in charge of buying and markup; John handling accounting and bill paying; and Paul working with dad on general merchandising. Together, the father and sons adhered to an almost military order of the day, collectively rising at four in the morning and opening at six sharp, serving at their assigned tasks throughout evening business hours, then performing any necessary maintenance and construction work on weekends.

With its transformation to self-service and a new management structure in place, the old corner store flourished once again, reborn into the black for the duration of World War II. Yet John Junior was still far from pleased. In fact, he was fed up.[8] For the final and most crucial innovation he tried to convince his father to institute proved a bridge too far. This refers to the cutting-edge supermarket Golden Formula involving the triadic interplay of low costs, low prices, and high volume. Dad could just not make hide nor hair of his son's cockamamie theory about how slicing prices to the bone could ever possibly be good for the bottom line. Being truly confused by this proposition, he was extremely reluctant to put it into practice.

After what were apparently some hellacious family feuds over this issue, John the Younger threw in the towel. He could no longer work for his father. The year was 1943. Perhaps he was still shaken by the death a year earlier of his beloved Aunt Mary, and this added to the charged emotions building up in frustration over his father. Whatever the case, as had happened earlier, he finally reached a breaking point that somehow resolved into a moment of clarity and conviction. There was only one thing to do: he would open his own store.

John made up his mind. His new store would be New Orleans' first genuine supermarket—a large-scale grocery entity run entirely on low-cost, low-price, high-volume principles. Since he already had the money on hand from his real estate dealings to buy property outright, he could skip the normal first step: that is, raising funds from investors. Thus freed he could proceed directly to the next step—namely, finding a suitable location for the store. This he found fairly quickly, selecting a site right at the intersection of St. Claude and Elysian Fields. Located at a central metropolitan nodal point just northeast of the French Quarter, it would draw not only from Schwegmann's Third District stronghold but also be conveniently accessible to nearby neighborhoods in Downtown, Mid-City, and Gentilly.

Before John was born, this site at St. Claude and Elysian Fields had housed a charcoal-making factory. During his youth, the factory transmogrified into an entertainment venue called the Circle Dance Hall, where popular bands featuring such local luminaries as Louis Prima and Pete Fountain performed. Ironically, after the dance hall folded, this formerly lively joint once devoted to the ecstasies of "jump, jive, and wail" was purchased by the Schoen Funeral Home. But before its new pallbearer owners built a restful sanctuary here, Schoen was approached by John, who had zeroed in on this spot as the perfect location for his supermarket. Conducting negotiations during 1943, the two parties came to agreement. John bought the property for $18,000, raising the money by mortgaging some of his doubles. In proudly taking ownership, he proclaimed the good news: "Instead of the property being used to wake the dead, it will be used to feed the living."[9]

WITH THE TITLE PASSING TO JOHN, he began planning the process of building the store. Yet one formidable obstacle still remained to be overcome—namely, the anti-competitive stranglehold over the New Orleans' food trade held by the city's public markets. Somehow he would have to confront and neutralize this power before his supermarket could succeed. In tackling this herculean task, John for the first time on the public stage nakedly displayed his heroic approach to slaying any monster that stood in the way of achieving his vision.

It is a little-known story that John G. Schwegmann was directly responsible for the demise of public markets in New Orleans.[10] Recall that for nearly two centuries up to the 1940s public markets held a near-monopoly over the retailing of fresh meat, fish, produce, and other perishables in NOLA, and that their presence was way more pervasive than in any other American city. Obviously, a supermarket cannot even begin to function without an unconstrained mandate to sell fresh foods. So if supermarkets were ever to operate in New Orleans, something had to be done. And that something was clear: the chokehold of the public markets had to be broken—and, if necessary, eliminated. Like two gunslingers in the Old West, it was either the free market or protectionism; the town was just not big enough for both of them. One would have to go.

John took the adversary head on. Enlisting the moral support of an old associate from Turnbull's real estate office named Emile Fucich, a "Slavonian" with ties to various city politicos, the two together proceeded impetuously to City Hall, then marched right into the "parlor" of Mayor Robert Maestri. Met there by a female receptionist, Emile asked politely but firmly where the mayor was. Incredibly, by today's security standards, she responded seemingly unfazed, "He's in the back room." So without further ado, the two entered the back room, and sure enough there stood the mayor.

Emile and John immediately introduced themselves. Mayor Maestri, friendly as could be to these strangers who had just barged into his inner sanctum, perked up when he heard the name Schwegmann, saying that, oh yes, he knew the name through Uncle Garret. With the ice broken, John got right down to brass tacks. He had just bought "a nice piece of ground" over on St. Claude and Elysian Fields, and he wanted to sell fresh meat there. He then proceeded to bring the mayor up to speed on the dilemmas facing grocers in the Crescent City. Using his uncle as an example, John explained how the laws on public markets had always hamstrung Garret's business, as he was right across the street from Zengel's Market and thus not allowed legally to sell fresh meat. The same fate awaited John's new store, which fell within the radius of the St. Roch Market.

Then he got right to the point. John told Mayor Maestri point blank that public markets had outlived their usefulness. Going even further, he declared them "a farce." They were no longer needed to protect the public's health for the perfectly good reason that refrigeration was now available and affordable to all grocers. And as far as serving the consumer's welfare, why, there was no question: given their significantly greater selections and lower prices, their superior merchandising abilities and much longer hours (open all day vs. half a day), modern private-sector grocery retailers won hands-down over public markets.

Apparently overwhelmed by this persuasive presentation, but still playing his cards like any good politician, Mayor Maestri at first attempted to dicker, asking John how many feet had to be cut from the radius of the St. Roch Market in order to get his new store up and running. Sensing that he held the upper hand in this negotiation, John pressed his advantage. The mayor's offer was all well and good, he said, "but don't forget my friend Joe Papania, whose store is closer to St. Roch than I am! So you should either take care of him, too, or cut it out [the public market laws] altogether."

At that point John eased up a little, graciously taking the mayor off the hook with the sympathetic observation, "I know you can't give me an answer now." But in a shocking response, Robert Maestri—probably in a combination of admiration for the audacity of this ambitious young entrepreneur and appreciation for the truth of which he spoke—extended his hand and intoned a phrase that exceeded all expectations: "John, it will be done."

And sure enough, shortly thereafter the New Orleans City Council passed an ordinance rescinding the exclusive prerogatives of public markets to sell fresh meat and all other perishables. Thus did John Schwegmann, within the space of a single meeting, followed by the stroke of a pen, slash through the Gordian knot of legislation that had tied the hands of New Orleans' retailers for over a century.

NOT MUCH IS KNOWN ABOUT John's love life—his attractions, romantic dalliances, or any intimate marital details. All these he held close to the vest. But what appears clear is that he had little time for close female relationships, preferring to direct his passions mostly into business endeavors.

There is no doubt he loved women. After all, he married twice and also spent years with a paramour. Moreover, he also got along famously with female staff and employees—particularly valuing his twenty-five-year relationship with Mary E. White, his personal secretary and amanuensis.

What is known is that in 1942—the same year that his beloved Aunt Mary died—John attended a dance class and there fell in love with a German girl named Mary Geisenheimer. Shortly afterward, John and Mary got married. Along with a declaration of transcendental love for his bride, John's marriage signaled his severance from the stick-in-the-mud business limitations of his father. The newly minted family man, bursting with entrepreneurial enthusiasm, now felt emotionally free to follow his own path. What he did not foresee was that single-mindedly chasing his dream would take a severe toll on his new marriage.

WITH HIS PROPERTY PURCHASED and the public markets neutralized, it was finally time to build the first supermarket in New Orleans. For design inspiration John had ample examples to draw from, as he could look to the nearly 6,200 U.S. supermarkets already in existence by the early 1940s.[11] This skyrocketing expansion from exactly zero to thousands of stores over the span of a single decade, from 1930 to 1940, signaled the ultimate triumph of the supermarket revolution.

Yet the revolution's advance was all but halted over the years of World War II. The cause was resource shortages and rationing. In the first case, iron, steel, rubber, timber, fasteners, and other construction inputs were directed to the war effort between 1941 and 1945 and hence in short supply on the home front. Because it was so hard to scare up architectural materials, only the rare supermarket was built during wartime.[12]

Food rationing presented another disincentive to building stores. Shortages of all sorts of foodstuffs, ranging from meat to produce, already wreaked havoc on the supermarkets' ability to fill up their copious shelf space. This forced most to fill gaps in merchandise displays with nonfoods products, such as over-the-counter drugs, personal care items, even hardware—basically whatever they could get their hands on. In the end, though, having to meet this challenge proved beneficial for supermarket operators, as they gained valuable experience in nonfoods and general merchandise categories.

In the midst of shortages and rationing, the war years witnessed a sort of last hurrah for old-time grocery stores. Former neighborhood customers, who prior to the war had gotten into the habit of tooling around in their automobiles looking for grocery bargains, suddenly felt compelled to renew their previous personal relations with mom and pop over on the corner in hopes of being privy to surprise deliveries of hard-to-come-by items. This phenomenon was probably a contributing factor to the success enjoyed at the time by the old corner store on Piety and Burgundy.[13] It must have been tempting for old-timers like John Senior to believe this resurgence would be permanent. His unblinkered son John Junior, however, knew differently. He clearly understood that supermarkets were the wave of the future. So despite shortages of building materials, and in the teeth of rationing, he pressed ahead with his plans.

JOHN MUST HAVE BEEN MIGHTY PROUD in 1945: his first child, a son, was born; his country had won the war; and construction commenced on his new store. Puffed up with great confidence, he seized the day. In order to cut building costs to the bone, John decided that he and his brother Paul would do all the designing, no architect needed. They would also do all the basic construction work themselves—mostly menial tasks, such as carpentry and scaffolding—while subcontracting out specialty work involving skilled labor (to non-union workers, of course).

One of these specialty subcontractors happened to be an African American, Charles Elam.[14] Mr. Elam came from a deep reservoir of skilled black craftsmen that populated New Orleans from the beginning. Once again demonstrating his renegade social tendencies, over the course of their work together John developed a friendly rapport with Charles. While not unheard of at the time, this type of amicable bonding across racial lines was somewhat unusual in the segregated Southland of the 1940s. Indeed, as can be imagined, it was frowned on by more than some and led to some awkward moments.

The depth of their camaraderie was put to the test one day when the two decided that rather than eat on site like they normally did they would go have lunch together at a local restaurant. Unfortunately, they picked the wrong place, as the proprietor of this particular establishment happened to be a supporter of the Jim Crow restrictions then prevailing. On seeing John and Charles enter, the restaurateur decided he was having none of this progressive-style race mixing. Given his proclivities, he allowed Schwegmann to order but refused to serve Elam, going so far as to eject Charles from the joint. John's response was telling. Rather than give in to the bigoted bullying, he ordered food to go for both himself and his skilled contractor, and on receiving it proceeded to join Charles outside. They both ate lunch out on the sidewalk together. In bonding through experiences like this, John and Charles became lifelong friends, keeping up relations even after Mr. Elam moved out to California.

As the store rose on its foundations, John began plotting out its ownership and operational structure. For the whole shebang to work, he would have to select as principals in the organization people who were at once competent, devoted, and, above all, absolutely trustworthy. Naturally, then, he first turned to his immediate family, asking his experienced grocer-brothers to join him in this great enterprise as managing partners. While Paul was enthusiastic, agreeing wholeheartedly to sign on with the project, Anthony balked, feeling it was his place to remain helping out dear old dad at the old corner store. John more than respected Anthony's decision. In fact, this was the first time in the entire process he felt a sense of chagrin, a twinge of guilt about abandoning his father. Later on, in an audio interview reflecting back on this time, a note of remorse creeps into John's voice as he judges Anthony "a better son to his father" than he would ever be.[15] For the time being though, so fired by the project that he could easily shake off any nagging feelings of guilt, John pushed relentlessly forward with his grand business plans. If Anthony would not hop on the train to glory, so be it. John had an inspired alternative in mind.

Perhaps the decision had actually been made long ago, when two bright young eager beavers shared with each other not only the same job but their dreams and aspirations, too. Maybe they even envisioned one day going into business together. Whatever the case, after Anthony declined the partner position, John immediately turned to his closest friend from the old days, Wilfred I. Meyer. John and Wilfred, it may be recalled, became bosom buddies during the four years (1929 to 1933) they worked together at the now-deceased Canal Bank. Being of the same age and similar enthusiasms, the two made a great team, being promoted together from the lowly mailroom, where they were mentored by Sam Tournillon, up to the mid-level Transit Department, then under the direction of Jeff Schonekas.

When the Canal Bank unceremoniously tanked over the infamous New Deal holiday weekend of April 1933, it was like a shipwreck. John and Wilfred suddenly found themselves castaways drifting on nothing but their own motivation and ingenuity. Being the more intellectually driven of the two, Wilfred applied to and was accepted by Tulane University.[16] But after attending less than a year there, he left, unable to afford the $250 annual tuition. At that point, both he and John applied for newly opened positions at Whitney Bank. While John was outright rejected, Wilfred was accepted into the fraternity and went on to establish a niche for himself at this premier New Orleans' financial institution. Over the course of his several-year sojourn there, Wilfred met his future wife, Albertha Screen. In 1941, answering the call of duty, he left the bank to join the U.S. Navy. Four years later, while on leave in 1945, he married his beloved. Wilfred and Albertha subsequently bought a house in the 900 block of Poland Avenue, where they went on to enjoy a longtime residence.

In 1946, John asked Wilfred to join him in his revolutionary supermarket endeavor. In this tapping of his best friend he hoped to gain more than a mere managing partner. For in John's bold scheme of things, Wilfred was slated to be no less than second in command of the enterprise. Thus in agreeing to come on board, Wilfred assumed the cardinal position in Schwegmann Brothers' future fate, becoming a keystone human resource on which success deeply depended.

10

THE ORIGINAL SCHWEGMANN BROTHERS GIANT SUPER MARKET

O N AUGUST 23, 1946, THE ORIGINAL Schwegmann Brothers Giant Super Market, situated strategically at 2222 St. Claude Avenue near the corner of Elysian Fields, opened for business—thus marking the first-ever appearance of a full-blown supermarket in New Orleans. Of course, by this time John had no liquid assets left for such fancy frills as fixtures (there were none) or merchandise (the store's entire inventory was bought on credit). But despite the poor appearance and shaky financing—and despite spending exactly nothing on promoting the not-so-grand opening—the store was an instant hit, attracting shoppers from all over the metropolitan area.

Now an entirely new episode commenced in John's life. Gone forever were his physical ties to the old corner store (though it would later serve as a symbolic prop for a political campaign). Fading into the background were any strong emotional attachments to his roughhewn Bywater origins. In later reminiscences John recalled the sage advice of a mentor who once told him: "Our roots are in the past, but our eyes are set on the future."[1] While taking this admonition to heart, John at the time of the store opening placed much more importance on the "future" side of the equation, as he plunged wholeheartedly into the brave new world of supermarket retailing that would entirely consume him for the next fifteen years.

After the dust finally settled from construction, the store emerged in all its humble glory.[2] Its simple but elegant design—a one-story horizontal block-like structure—featured a shimmering all-glass front framed by dark-green walls made of stucco over hollow tiles. Its base was of slab construction, with a floor made of smooth cement six inches thick. The roof was flat. In its interior the store was laid out in a gridiron pattern to facilitate customer movement through the various departments. By contemporary standards, construction costs ended up to be a miraculous $1.50 per square foot.

The lot on which the store stood measured 40,000 square feet. What may be surprising is that a majority of this site space was devoted to parking, not actual shopping. Out of the 40,000-square-foot total, only 16,000 was allocated to floor space located within the confines of an actual store. Meanwhile, a full 24,000 square feet went to the parking lot—meaning the site was divided 1.25 to 1 in favor of car over store.

In regard to the size of the store, it was big by mid-1940s' supermarket standards, but not extraordinarily so. In a classification system established by the Supermarket Institute in 1955, the first Schwegmann Brothers Giant Super Market only fell into the "extra-large" category (defined as between 15,000 and 20,000 square feet of floor space). Above this size ranking were those rare stores classified as "colossal" (over 20,000 square feet). Below it were the vast majority of supermarkets categorized as either "large" (10,000 to 15,000 square feet) or "medium" (5,000 to 10,000 square feet).[3]

So in casting the original Schwegmann Brothers at 16,000 square feet in 1946, John was clearly champing at the bit, slyly positioning himself slightly ahead of the pack in eager anticipation of swamping the competition in the size battles to come. For he knew in his bones the incredible potential waiting to be unlocked in a full-on inflation of store dimension.

Consider that after the first burst of supermarket flamboyance in the early 1930s—when truly colossal warehouse-palaces emerged spanning numerous tens of thousands of square feet—the supermarket sector as a whole quickly settled down into a more cautious conservatism, focusing not so much anymore on consumers who were down-and-out as those up-and-coming. Thus due to its newfound respectability and upscale demographic biases, even as the sector remained potentially extremely dynamic it was not yet ready to abandon certain outmoded preconceptions, particularly an unexamined meme concerning size and manageability likely inherited from the era of the old corner store.

Indeed, there was even a tendency to look down on the early entrepreneur-pioneers, derogatorily referring to their brilliant inventions as "cheapies," unsightly relics from the Depression era.[4] As a result of the sector's conservative hesitation to embrace the logic of mass retailing, by 1950 supermarkets measured on average a mere 10,000 square feet—an average only slightly upped to 13,000 square feet by 1955. This shrinking violet approach to what could have been explosive expansion came even in the face of statistical evidence demonstrating conclusively that the larger the store, the greater the profitability.

SIMILAR TO A STRIPPED-DOWN STOCK CAR, John designed his first store for speed. Accelerated customer traffic and rapid turnover was the goal. To this end, overhead costs and services were trimmed to a minimum, and discount deals were exploited to the maximum. The idea, as previously elaborated, was to generate high volume through drastically reduced prices. Within this scheme of things, the original Schwegmann Brothers at St. Claude was the first store in New Orleans to extend the self-service concept beyond grocery into a whole other retail department, namely liquor, where it worked so exceptionally well that self-service was eventually rolled out nearly storewide.

Yet despite this seeming radical stripping of services, the store remained by contemporary standards highly service-centric. Though it looked from the perspective of old-time grocery stores like customers had been cast completely adrift, abandoned and left to wander alone in the consumer wilderness, making their choices without help, the reality was otherwise. For in fact, service remained an omnipresent feature in this first Schwegmann store—from the extensive clerk-service provided in the meat, seafood, drug, and sporting goods sections to the virtual army of stock clerks constantly on duty and tasked with being available to assist shoppers with weighing, carrying, and any queries they might have. Further enhancing services, an extremely customer-friendly communications system featured a central telephone switchboard that took messages and placed calls for shoppers. Moreover, a loudspeaker system was installed to announce customer calls and taxi arrivals, along with pitching merchandise specials on a frequent and regular schedule.

As noted, from day one Schwegmann Brothers was a huge hit. No doubt the outrageously low prices represented the primary reason shoppers flocked to the store. But there was another important draw: namely, that the store presented the incredible vista of an amazing abundance that had never been seen before in New Orleans. At the time, this over-the-top merchandising presentation was the equivalent of throwing T-bone steaks to a pack of famished animals. For wartime rationing had entailed much sacrifice, including having to endure shortages of all sorts of foods. By the time the war ended in 1945, the pent-up demand that had built up was enormous and set to explode in the mega-volcano of consumerism that followed.

Yet it took awhile longer for the nitro to blow. Through 1946 and into 1947, periodic shortages still showed up. This factor contributed to the early success of the St. Claude store. For every day during these early postwar years shoppers would line up outside the store even before it opened in hopes of snaring products on the "scarce list," which were sold on a first-come, first-serve basis. Of course, less-frantic shopping protocols quickly emerged after rationing controls were lifted in the late 1940s. But by then consumers were hooked, fully in thrall to bargains and utterly addicted to abundance.

*   *   *

To RUN HIS STREAMLINED BUSINESS built for speed, John assembled a tight-knit management team consisting of three general partners, a handful of department heads, and a small administrative staff.[5] At the top were the three general partners: John himself, brother Paul, and best friend Wilfred Meyer. Despite John being the only one to invest actual cash in the venture, all three split the profits. Although the profit-sharing arrangement is unknown, it is a safe bet that John received the lion's share. For while he did not directly take on the title of chief executive officer, that is the de facto position he held.

John was the leader, mastermind, driving force of the Schwegmann Brothers organization. As first among equals of the three general partners, he was like a general and president rolled into one. As president, he took charge of the big picture, grand strategy, lofty policy, formulating everything in regard to future direction and expansion, overall pricing and merchandising issues, and economic, political, and legal matters. In his more down-to-earth role as general, he tasked himself with creating a grand marketing strategy. Here he would craft the public aura of the store, designing an irresistible image via unique and compelling advertising and promotion that would attract customers like a magnet. John being John, though, he could not simply restrict himself to playing the part of grand poobah. He had to put boots on the ground in order to keep things real. Thus he took on three micromanagement responsibilities involving personnel. These included determining salary scales by position, reserving final say-so on all employee promotions and demotions, and personally handling all employee firings.

With John's signature personality so firmly implanted and prominently stamped on the store, the two other general partners could do little but function as acolytes of the Great Man, believers in his mission and devoted to furthering his cause. Their reward—if he succeeded—would be profits galore. In this spirit, Wilfred Meyer assumed the position of first mate, which for all intents and purposes meant second in command. Revealing his supreme trust in Wilfred, John even elevated him above his brother Paul. Indeed, Wilfred was the only non-relative ever to ascend into the general-partner hierarchy of the Schwegmann organization. Of course, there was a good meritocratic reason for this beyond being a trusted friend, for Wilfred had gained extensive experience and a thorough grounding in banking before the war. Who better to entrust the company's finances to? So the position John essentially created for Wilfred was as commander of all accounting, in charge of all financial transactions flowing through the organization—perhaps best understood today as a chief financial officer.

Yet being of a similar down-to-earth bent as John, Wilfred also had to have a hands-on stake in the operation. Thus he also assumed the position of general manager at the St. Claude store, his duty to establish and maintain smooth operations. Wilfred's direct assistants were Paul Schwegmann and Charles Acquistipace, a brother-in-law of John. All department heads reported directly to Paul, who was designated as floor manager. Always on the prowl patrolling the aisles, Paul relayed the most important information to Wilfred, who then sent it upward in filtered form to John at the top.

Sequestered within this hierarchy was the store's liquor buyer, Charles Acquistipace. Charles was the husband of John's sister Odile Schwegmann. Through family functions John had gotten to know and grown confident in Charles. So much so that he placed him in the tricky position of being head of the liquor department, a position understandably rife with potential for abuse. As liquor head, Charles was granted a great measure of autonomy in overseeing and controlling ordering, purchasing, and payment. Daily remaining in contact with the vice side of life, Charles proved incorruptible, able to withstand major temptation, even acting as an immovable bedrock in John's future battles with the distillery industry. Indeed, Charles's virtues as a sober broker shone so bright that within a couple of years he ascended to become one of four additional general partners in the Schwegmann organization. In this new role, Acquistipace was basically tasked with project-managing construction of John's second store on Airline Highway.

For the moment, though, in 1946, Charles remained just one among nine department heads. The nine departments they managed included the following: grocery, meat/deli, produce, seafood, drug, liquor, hardware/sporting goods, housewares/gifts, and a snack bar. All these departments were owned outright by Schwegmann Brothers— meaning they were not leased to outside vendors, as would become common in later editions of the Schwegmann franchise.

Since the store was designed for speed, responsibility for the departments was bifurcated between buying and administration. This meant that all department heads would be relieved of the mundane and burdensome tasks of stocking, pricing, and accounting, thus freeing them up to focus solely on the buying function. The idea was to achieve maximum efficiency and flexibility in quick purchasing and rapid fulfillment, to be nimble enough to fully exploit, at the drop of a hat, any temporary discount, any fleeting exceptional deal or advertising allowances offered by suppliers on a daily, even hourly, basis. The end result, of course, being a store filled to the brim with the best bargains in the world.

HERE IT IS IMPORTANT TO STEP BACK and recall the nature of the mastermind orchestrating the venture. Impatient, implacable John Schwegmann was exploding with ideas at the time. Though he focused on achieving success at the St. Claude store, he simultaneously looked at the bigger picture, viewing the project as an experimental prototype— something to learn from, with the lessons to be applied sooner rather than later. For now, though, with only 16,000 square feet to work with, he set up the nine aforementioned departments.

Overwhelmingly dominating these nine was the grocery de-partment.[6] This measured 6,000 square feet, or three-eighths of the store's floor space. Here were placed nineteen gondolas (shelving units), each measuring thirty feet, where a total of 4,000 stock-keeping units (including brands and sizes) of packaged food and beverage items were displayed. Nearly all of these grocery SKUs were national brands, with an average of four brands carried in each specific merchandise group— that is, four brands of canned foods (fruits, vegetables, beans, etc.), four brands of condiments, four brands of soft drinks, and so forth. Most of these grocery brands were purchased direct from the manufacturer, a "one-step" distribution process that saved money through the proverbial eliminating of the middleman (wholesalers and jobbers). That said, wholesalers were routinely used to fulfill "short orders," when grocery merchandise was needed in a hurry to fill a temporary gap in supply. While in theory the entire grocery department was self-service, there were still about thirty clerks in charge of stocking the aisles who were also available to assist customers.

After grocery, the second-largest department was produce, which measured 2,500 square feet. The size of this department, however, was all out of proportion to its actual selling space: only a hundred square feet devoted to a refrigerated display of fresh vegetables and fruits, and thirty feet to open bins of "non-perishable" produce types (potatoes, onions, cabbage, and the like). The vast majority of space devoted to produce was taken up by a behind-the-scenes workroom where daily deliveries were received, stored, sorted, chopped, wrapped, and otherwise prepared for display.

Besides the inordinate amount of space these processes necessitated, the produce department also required a great deal of labor, with fifteen people employed in receiving and prepping the fruits and vegetables. Meanwhile, another two clerks—hard to believe these days—were actually stationed at the scales to help shoppers weigh and price the products. For all its bulbous dimensions, the produce department was lucrative. Consider that grocery items registered at best 12% markups, while fresh vegetables received 30% and fresh fruits 20%. Even non-perishable produce featured greater markups at 15% than most of the best-selling grocery items.

In terms of size, two departments followed grocery and produce. These were meat/deli and liquor—each department measuring 1,500 square feet apiece. Like produce, the area occupied by meat/deli was dominated by a "backstage" workspace dedicated to receiving, storing, and preparing products for retail sale. For their part, what customers encountered was a two-hundred-foot self-serve refrigerated display case full of packaged meats and a fifty-foot service counter featuring fresh meats presided over by a team of professional butchers.

Although deliveries were received on a daily basis from nominally local suppliers, these tended to be mere warehouse affiliates of the giant meatpacking syndicates. Thus nearly every meat and delicatessen item sold in the St. Claude store sported a nationally recognized brand name. Notable exceptions included the regional King Cotton brand and locally sourced products from L.A. Frey and Sons—the sausage-making maestros who just happened to be John's in-laws. Like produce, meat/deli consistently earned higher profits than grocery. For fresh meats, markups averaged 25%, twice that of grocery (12%). Even prepackaged deli items received higher markups than grocery, with imported meats and cheeses at 20%, domestic cold cuts at 17%, and domestic cheeses at 15%.

Closely associated with, but distinct from, meat/deli was the seafood department. This was a smallish section of just 400 square feet. Despite its relatively tiny size, seafood remained a solid bastion of clerk-service, with seven experts on hand to prepare the fish and shellfish and assist customers in purchasing. Both fresh and frozen products were sold here, with frozen fish being prepackaged national brands and the fresh originating from local and regional Louisiana sources purchased daily and prepared in a small workroom. Seafood carried extra-high markups: 20%-35% for fresh and 20% for frozen.

Moving now to a merchandise category holding center stage—and every bit justifying its depth and breadth in terms of being a popular draw—the sprawling liquor department measured a full 1,500 square feet. For comparable supermarkets at the time, this amount of space devoted to demon alcohol was unheard of.[7] Consider that as of the mid-1950s fewer than half (46%) of supermarkets even carried beer. But bucking the puritanical tide, John of New Orleans boldly sallied forth with just such a sinfully massive planogram.

The gargantuan liquor section was placed within the grocery department right up front in full view of the checkouts. Occupying three-and-a-half gondolas were 200 brands and varieties of liquor, mostly "fifths," and fifty brands of wine, mostly quarts. There was also a Schwegmann private-label line consisting of whiskey, bourbon, champagne, and beer (premium and bock). This overflowing alcoholic plenitude was naturally accompanied by a wide variety of cocktail mixers, and even bar accessories.

To stock this fabulous assortment, John was forced to buy branded alcohol products exclusively through wholesalers, as no direct dealing with the powerful liquor distillers was then allowed. Nonetheless, despite having to pay the middleman fee, John made every effort to keep a lid on prices, charging at most a 10% markup on liquor and 12% on wine. As fate would have it, John's commitment on principle to keeping liquor prices low paved the way for his rendezvous with destiny. In fact, it was over this signature product representing New Orleans' premier vice that John first entered the big-time competitive lists, jousting on the national stage in hopes of shattering the lance of the dark knight flying the illegitimate banner of Fair Trade.

WITH THREE-QUARTERS OF THE ST. CLAUDE STORE given over to grocery, produce, liquor, meat, and seafood, there was still a little room left over for nonfoods. This was a merchandise classification then in flux. Since supermarkets were still so new at the time, with only about ten years of focused development behind them as of 1946, no standardized boundaries had yet been drawn between supermarkets and drugstores, "five-and-dime" stores, hardware stores, and other specialty-type outlets.

The nonfoods universe seemed ripe for retail experimentation—in short, a tailor-made situation to beckon an innovative entrepreneur such as John. In this his first store, Schwegmann embraced the opportunity by installing four nonfoods departments: drugs/cosmetics, hardware/sporting goods, housewares/gifts, and a snack bar. As can be seen, these are actually a half-dozen departments crowded into three, plus an added novelty, the snack bar—more familiarly associated in those days with the fountain section at drugstores. It was a mish-mash to be sure, but it was a start. And John was eager to learn.

His first attempt at a drug/cosmetics department was particularly ill defined, although this is understandable in light of the tenuous legalities then governing the selling of these types of products. Moving carefully, John initially phased in the department on a limited scale, essentially subdividing it into three sections: "patent" medicines, health and beauty products, and impulse items related to both. For the time being, no prescription drugs were sold; only prepackaged patent medicines—what are today called over-the-counter (OTC) drugs. Most of the latter were available only at a small clerk-serviced counter placed conspicuously near the front of the store.

Meanwhile, 900 SKUs of health and beauty products were integrated into the grocery department, altogether occupying two gondolas. These items included such staples as toothpaste, shampoo, beauty creams, and shaving lotions, along with electric grooming devices and commercial beauty supplies. Finally, a bevy of small-sized drugs and cosmetics—aspirin, razor blades, and the like—were placed on display as impulse items at checkout counters and the snack bar. Clearly, the drugstore component of the St. Claude supermarket was too scattered, not to mention too hobbled by the legal inability to fill prescriptions, to be totally effective. The department would have to be reconceived.

The same went for the other nonfoods departments. Although for administrative purposes hardware/sporting goods was treated as a single department, on the actual store floor they appeared in two entirely different sections. Allotted 150 square feet, hardware occupied a single gondola within the grocery department. Completely separated from it, set off in a corner at the front of the store, was the sporting goods section. This was devoted mostly to hunting and fishing, though it also catered to family recreational activities. Since some sporting goods items were downright dangerous—yes, guns were sold at the supermarket—a clerk was placed in charge of the section.

Not well thought out but deserving points for effort, John also included a housewares and gifts department. With both housewares and gifts integrated within the grocery department yet located in separate areas, the cumulative size of the department was typically just 300 square feet—though the gifts section tended to triple during holiday seasons (especially Christmas and Mardi Gras). Adding to the confusion, housewares—mainly hard goods, such as kitchen, tabletop, and lighting products—were conjoined with a motley assortment of soft goods, such as linens, work clothes, baby clothes, and underwear. What is most noteworthy about the original Schwegmann housewares/ gifts product array is how ephemeral the brand names then featured in these sections turned out to be. Brands such as Blue Willow, Wearever, FireKing, Ransom, Menli, and many others competing in the late 1940s have by now completely vanished.

As a final fillip designed to increase the appeal of his store, John added a snack bar. This novel feature for supermarkets—only 6% had them as of 1955—was located at the front of the store, right next to sporting goods. But to think of this department simply as a "snack bar" would be to underestimate it. For besides offering sandwiches, hot dogs, soft drinks, popcorn, and pretzels, it also served beer—almost unheard of either then or especially now in today's squeaky-clean supermarket environments. Even more, the snack bar sold convenience items, such as cigarettes, chewing gum, and razor blades, thus permitting the casual customer to enter and exit the store without all the fuss associated with full-on shopping. So basically the snack bar also functioned as a proto–convenience store. Yet it had one further dimension: it served as a customer convenience area where packages could be checked before shopping.

When customers finished piling merchandise into one of the store's 250 grocery "buggies," they paid for it at one of fourteen "auto-belt" checkout stands—twelve main checkouts at the front of the store, and one apiece at sporting goods and the snack bar. The inordinate amount of merchandise they purchased at this first Schwegmann supermarket—designed specifically for velocity—was nothing short of phenomenal. The average ring at the St. Claude store cash register in 1955 was a stupendous $13.17—nearly double the national average of $6.83! John also beat the competition in terms of sales per square foot, with his store raking in $5.13 per square foot, versus $4.25 for comparably sized supermarkets.[8] Altogether, by the mid-1950s the St. Claude store was reaping annual sales of approximately $4 million.

An accounting office consisting of one chief and several clerks administered these sales. Responsible directly to John Schwegmann and Wilfred Meyer, the accounting office was tasked not only with processing merchandise vouchers, maintaining records, and handling taxes but also with exploiting to the max all possible cash discounts available from suppliers. Of course, it also handled issuing paychecks for the store's employees. These employees numbered between one hundred seventy-five and two hundred.

The best paid employees were department managers and the accounting office chief, each of which earned the superlative sum of $120 per week. In the middle of the pay scale were checkout people who, depending on experience and reliability, made between $55 and $90. On the bottom of the pay scale were "colored package boys," who earned $15 to $20 a week. Yet despite the fairly stingy pay and gross racial disparity on display, the team somehow came together to outperform the competition. For as of 1955 they were achieving a productivity level of $35,000 per employee, noticeably higher than the Supermarket Institute's contemporaneous recorded national average of just $34,100.

11

MARKETING, MORALITY, AND THE PEOPLE'S GROCER PERSONA

AFTER FIFTEEN YEARS OF DEPRESSION AND WAR, New Orleans was ready to rock. Having been smothered for far too long under a shroud of hard times and sacrifice, the archetypal party city reacted ecstatically when the dark clouds finally lifted in 1946. In a political signal that New Orleanians were now in an upbeat mood, they elected a reform-minded mayor that year, deLesseps "Chep" Morrison, thus inaugurating a fifteen-year reign that brought a sweet taste of prosperity to the previously distressed metropolis. Over this period the oil business boomed and industry flocked to New Orleans. And with city coffers finally full again, public projects proliferated.

Culturally, New Orleans responded to its postwar good fortune with a joyous shout so loud and powerful that it shook America—and indeed the world. This sound took the form of a style of music at once so rich and complex and so poor and simple that it defies easy categorization. Perhaps it can be thought of as some sort of RNA-like precursor before transfiguration into fully formed DNA. But however this infectious sound is classified, there is no doubt that the recordings that began emanating in 1945 from a humble studio located at 840 North Rampart Street were seminal in laying down roots for the most exuberant and popular musical style of the postwar era—namely, rock and roll. The serendipitous genius behind this recording studio, Cosimo Matassa, is known in rock legend as an engineer, not a producer. As such, he rarely receives the serious kudos he deserves for his formative role in forging the foundations of "the music that will never die."

In the present context, however, music maestro Cosimo Matassa is more appropriately cast as one of history's great entrepreneurs, opportunistically exploiting cutting-edge trends with keen ability and daring agility. Thus did his J&M Recording Studio produce what not a few cognoscenti regard as the very first rock and roll record: "The Fat Man" by Fats Domino, recorded in 1949. Other groundbreaking artists Cosimo recorded between the late 1940s and mid-1950s included Little Richard, Ray Charles, Sam Cook, Jerry Lee Lewis, Professor Longhair, and Mac Rebennack (Dr. John), among many other luminaries who shaped the future of music. But Matassa, the instigator sparking this immortal cultural legacy, was not the only great local entrepreneur of the period. Instead, he—along with Fats, for that matter—can be seen as a symbol of the creative vitality and bold confidence then possessing and embodying businesspeople in New Orleans throughout the Morrison period.

Certainly John Schwegmann brimmed with vitality and confidence right after the war. He had a devoted wife and a first-born son. His supermarket was a raging success. And the future looked nothing but bright. But suddenly John's personal life took an unwanted turn. In 1947, he and Mary bore a second son, Guy George, who was born in a disabled condition then known as being "mentally retarded." Try as he might to take this in stride, John harbored secret regrets and disappointment. The situation hit Mary even harder. Already suffering from extreme neglect by her workaholic husband, after Guy was born Mary entered a twilight state of acute psychological distress akin to catatonia. Faced with such a woebegone situation—having to care for two young boys, one developmentally disabled, while his wife went certifiably insane—John took charge of the situation as best he could.

He hired caretakers—Mrs. Mary Weaver and a couple, Mr. and Mrs. Tobias Eberhardt—to look after John Francis and Guy George while their mother was "ill."[1] Meanwhile, John Gerald moved alone into an apartment on St. Claude Court in the Lower Ninth Ward.

No doubt inwardly troubled, John did not appear outwardly upset by the descent of his first family into the abyss, as he plowed full-steam ahead into planning for the future. Nor did it seem to sour him on love and romance. For despite enduring a punishing workday schedule, he still occasionally found time after-hours to wine and dine a select series of ladies. After dinner, he typically escorted his dates to various entertainment venues, such as nightclubs on Bourbon Street featuring the likes of celebrity songstress Sophie Tucker, entertainer Jimmy Durante, and local legend Chris Owens.[2]

After formally divorcing Mary Geisenheimer in 1949, John took a particular fancy to a young lady named Melba Margaret Wolfe. The two lovebirds, egged on by Melba's father—a worldly German with whom John had formed an intimate bond—were married in 1951.[3] It seemed that John had dodged a bullet. He had suffered a family tragedy yet had not allowed it to interfere with his primary goals of becoming rich, famous, and happy.

AT THE LOWEST EBB of his emotional fortunes, John did once again what he had done as a boy: rather than succumb to troubles, he came out swinging. Darned if he would waste time wallowing in grief. He had a world to win! So in true signature style, he projected his internal troubles outward, transforming them from shadowy creatures in a haunted psychological landscape into vivid visible demons out there in the real world that needed to be defeated. Only this time around, instead of using his hapless father as an object on whom to project his scorn, John chose a more worthy target for his contempt—namely, the weaknesses and failings of the business world itself.

By now he had come to perceive these faults as negative forces to be overcome by positive actions. If this meant putting up active resistance to the corrupt doings of business-as-usual, so be it. He would fight for a greater competitive perfection, utterly determined to challenge the unfair ways and win. Better yet, if positive action called for creative thinking and bold performance, John could do that, too, by innovating new business models and setting an example on how to run a successful ethical enterprise. Out of this deeply rooted "white-hat" attitude, John created his public identity—an eccentric yet heroic persona that reached full flower through one of the most remarkable and memorable advertising campaigns in modern American history.

RECALL THAT ALONG WITH BEING the grand visionary and chief executive of Schwegmann Brothers Giant Super Market, John was also head of marketing. In this role John conceived of and oversaw advertising and promotional strategy.[4] Now one might think that for a store whose raison d'être was based on the lowest of all possible low prices, advertising could be conceived of as a fairly pedestrian exercise. After all, what else is there to do other than flog price discounts and come up with a few friendly visuals and catchy slogans? But John did not view the matter so simplistically. Indeed, his take on advertising was downright profound, perceiving in it a polyvalent platform pregnant with possibilities far beyond mere price positioning.

In his mind's eye he saw that, in its attention-grabbing power, advertising possessed an amazing plasticity that conjured up any number of metaphorical resonances: a soapbox for rants, a lectern for lectures, a pulpit for sermonizing, a bell to peal out alarums or celebrations, a man-o'-war fitted out for broadsides, a storyteller's barstool, a ticket to foreign travels and adventure, and a sanctuary for reflection on the goodness and blessings of home. In his multidimensional view, John used advertising as a vehicle to brand simultaneously both his store and himself. And in the process of serving as the receptacle for the voluminous outpouring of his odd ads, New Orleans itself was caught up in the branding—his native city stamped forever by the eccentric signifiers of the Schwegmann mystique.

John's approach to advertising was by no means off-the-cuff, a mere amateur's folly in wishful expectations about how ads are supposed to work. On the contrary, it was rigorously conceived and vigorously executed, always solid, with numerous flashes of brilliance. What most set it apart from standard ad campaigns was not lack of professionalism in presentation but sheer audacity. Few before or since have had the courage to take the branding concept explicitly beyond the bounds of business into whole new realms of social existence. Yet that is precisely what John did, or at least attempted to do. And in a strange but measurable way, he succeeded.

Schwegmann's extremely well-thought-out approach to advertising encompassed both tactical and strategic levels. The tactical level involved considerations of media deployment, budgeting, and scheduling. In addressing these issues, John followed standard practice in some cases and innovated in others. When Schwegmann's supermarket first opened back in 1946, media was pretty much limited to print and radio, with television on the way but not quite there yet. Under the circumstances, John poured nearly all his efforts into newspapers. Working almost exclusively within this particular print medium, he developed a strict schedule. Ads would appear every Monday in the three major New Orleans' newspapers of record at the time: the *Times-Picayune*, the *Item*, and the *States-Times*.

Then, bucking trends, John decided that the discount prices advertised on Monday would continue for the entire week. There would be no weekend specials, which would only encourage shopper logjams. Instead, consumer bargain hunting would be spread more evenly throughout the week, thus resulting in greater efficiency in turnover. When John first introduced this ad-frequency discount policy in the mid-1940s, it was considered heresy. By the mid-1950s, however, it was becoming the supermarket norm.[5]

Among print media other than newspapers, John above all favored circulars. He contended that these were the most effective medium of all, but only if "properly circulated"—meaning delivered door-to-door. John was known to grouse about the arrogance and laziness of young people, who considered this type of awkward direct ad-distribution method as beneath their pay grade.[6] Perhaps in struggling to come up with an alternative to the circular—the potentially most effective but kinetically most hopeless print medium—John experienced a Eureka moment. It is not known for sure when he devised the idea, but sometime in the late 1940s he began utilizing the paper bag into which groceries are packaged at checkout as a print medium for advertising. What was, and still is, unique about John's approach here is that the paper sacks did not just display the store name, along with perhaps a logo and slogan, as was becoming typical at the time. Instead, his bags also delivered bold messages. Yet this is a whole story unto itself, to be told in chapter sixteen.

Turning now to tactical considerations in relation to marketing expenditures, in keeping with his ultra-thrifty spirit John decided against setting up any formal advertising and promotional budget. Instead, rather than follow some arbitrary formula pegging a specific dollar amount to be dedicated to marketing, he would simply be guided by one general rule: namely, get the most bang per buck while spending the least amount possible. The astonishing result: incredibly high-impact advertising achieved at infinitesimal cost!

Certainly what he spent on advertising was far below the national average. In 1954 and 1955, for example, Schwegmann's ad expenditures as a percentage of sales registered a minuscule 0.31% and 0.19%, respectively. Compare this with the national average for supermarket ad spending at the time, which stood at roughly ten times this amount at between 1.0% and 2.0%.[7] This significant disparity was partly accounted for by the Schwegmann practice of exploiting to the gills any advertising allowances offered by manufacturers to retailers. A factor not to be neglected, however, is the pinchpenny nature of John himself, who considered down-to-earth words to be more cost-effective than fancy visuals.

So just what was it about the content of his newspaper advertising that John placed such great faith in to create maximal branding effect with minimal ad spending? Surely it was not the bulk of the ad, devoted in standard supermarket fashion simply to product listings (with many of the products graphically illustrated) trumpeting discount prices.

There was nothing out of the ordinary here…or was there? In fact, even a cursory glance over a typical Schwegmann ad often enough reveals eccentric twists in the discount listings.

These twists mostly take the form of jarring juxtapositions, with weird pairings of products or services scattered seemingly at random among the otherwise normal presentation of touted values. To give just a few of endless examples: Boston butts are listed just above frog legs; rosaries are placed just below double-barreled shotguns; horsemeat dog food is paired visually with toothpaste; ladies' lingerie appears next to meat pies; and Carnival fruitcake comes right before nylon hosiery. From a contemporary perspective, these oddball juxtapositions tend to provoke laughter. They might have back then, too, or at least acted to pique interest. It is possible to say then that, though the effect is subtle, John's quirky discount listings did add readability to the ads, thereby increasing the value of their content.

In this context it should be noted that there was a brief time in the mid-1950s when John self-consciously ventured far beyond subtlety and comedy in employing the standard discount price-listing technique. Indeed, he was dead serious when he committed what almost amounted to civil disobedience by listing prescription drug prices in his advertising.[8] Aside from the epochal consequences that followed on this simple step (to be detailed later), John once again made history. For he was one of the first, and surely the boldest, of the postwar marketers to utilize a form of "head-to-head" competitive pricing in his advertising.

This particular jousting technique, known formally as "comparative advertising," was not only frowned on in the "positive-thinking" atmosphere prevailing in the wake of World War II, but it actually came to be considered illegal in the case of certain products—prescription drugs being a prime example. Indeed, the stigma against comparative-price advertising only began to be lifted twenty-five years later. What is most pathetic about this saga is that a completely legitimate form of competition—first widely acknowledged as such by the mainstream media in the path-breaking "Coke versus Pepsi" ads of the 1970s—had to be encouraged by the federal government. But John Schwegmann, in a direct attack on the genteel conventions that back then actually served to disguise price manipulation, courageously engaged in "head-to-head" comparative advertising entirely on his own volition, and faced great risk in doing so, back in the mid-1950s.

Up to this point a fairly standard bargain-focused supermarket newspaper ad has been described—albeit one interspersed with funny oddities and the occasional breaking of competitive taboos. Left out of the description so far is what set John's ads completely apart from the mainstream model—namely, the content that rendered them totally unique. But in order to grasp the true nature of this novelty it must first be understood that John at once spurned orthodox and embraced heretical approaches to advertising strategy. He had severe doubts about any claims of cost efficacy associated with conventional advertising techniques.

From this agnostic perspective he decided that the solution to achieving optimum readability at the least cost required him to include in his advertising content what are here referred to as "personalized statements."[9] These personalized statements—some short and pithy, others long and involved, with most falling in-between these extremes— were written in a number of genres, appearing variously as editorials, articles, random anecdotes, words of wisdom, collections of reflections, "customer" testimonials, even obituaries. Their tone was invariably folksy, similar to *Reader's Digest* but less anodyne—with significantly more bite. Although much of John's commentary was serious, even the weightiest statements tended to be leavened with at least a bit of humor. A personalized statement that one week exhorted consumers to take political action would often be followed the next by a statement encouraging the epicurean virtues of "eat, drink, and be merry."

On analysis, John's "personalized statements" divide fairly clearly into two thematic types: advocacy statements and human-interest statements. The advocacy statements tend to be heavy and compelling, revolving around the great themes of politics, economics, law, society, and ideology. The sweep of these advocacy statements grew more audacious over time. In his earliest ads, as if testing the waters, he restricted his commentary to relatively innocuous subject matter. For instance, in one statement—inspired perhaps by his first salesman job—John called for the repeal of a tax on oleomargarine, which he considered a tax on the poor. Other early advocacy statements were similarly softball, as he took low-risk stands on such hot-button issues as the sanctity and duties of fatherhood, the value of education, and the moral perils of shoplifting.

Yet after just a couple of years getting his feet wet in advocacy commentary, in 1949 he stopped pulling his punches. Sharper, more controversial personalized statements began appearing as John focused his editorial ire on more substantial targets than obscure taxes, proper fathers, school budgeting formulas, and retail miscreants. Suddenly his enemies were the big boys of the business world, those whose monopolistic machinations, facilitated by corrupt politicians, acted to squelch free competition. John, of course, came down firmly on the side of workers and consumers. Later on, as the years rolled by, John's advocacy statements turned ever more grandiose, as he railed against the communist menace, for instance, or suggested an agenda for Nixon's first term.

In counterpoint to the advocacy statements are those devoted to human-interest themes. Generously decorated with sentimentality, these human-interest statements tell stories, most brief but some episodic, about all manner of topics with popular appeal. They reminisce nostalgically about the good old days, chat earnestly about community affairs, enthusiastically recount travels and adventures, and celebrate holidays and anniversaries. A particular beauty of the human-interest form is that it grants its prime spokesperson, in this case John Schwegmann, wide latitude to indulge in personal whims. Thus John had the flexibility to discuss such subjects as his childhood, the symbolism behind the Schwegmann family coat of arms, and his French poodle's debutante party, all within the broad context of human interest.

*   *   *

UNDERLYING BOTH TYPES OF PERSONALIZED statements, whether of the advocacy or human-interest variety, was a powerful streak of good-old-fashioned morality. Objectively, morality is rooted in a conviction of right and wrong, with right representing the good and virtuous and wrong associated with evil and vice. Of course, in the real world a great deal of subjectivity goes into influencing the contours of morality, with religious, cultural, and psychological biases acting to shape an individual's moral code. Moreover, these types of subjective factors also give rise to differences in the intensity of morality.

Given differences in moral codes and how heartfelt they are, it stands to reason that people's expressions of morality will vary fairly formulaically depending on general character structure. In other words, those with a particularly strong and solid sense of morality who also happen to be extroverted are more likely to openly declare their belief in what is right or wrong than an introvert with a weak and vacillating moral core. Even more, outgoing types possessing a strong moral streak can be expected to take public action in order to influence their fellow humans to follow the path they see as right and good.

In taking action, however, the outspoken moralist automatically confronts danger. For in seeking to influence others, strong moralists must constantly navigate a tightrope between the extremes of persuasion and compulsion. If, on one hand, an excessive reliance is placed on persuasion—if, for example, his preaching is too insistent and hectoring, or her lecturing too incessant and shrill—the moralist risks being branded a self-righteous prig, a sanctimonious scold, or, worst of all, a hypocrite when (inevitably, given the human condition) he or she fails to practice what they preach. In each case, their off-putting behavior tends to diminish and undermine the persuasive appeal of the high-minded ideals they proclaim.

But strong moralists face an even greater danger than a sullied reputation. Given that they are driven to proclaim what is right, moralists must also necessarily set forth the obverse—namely, what is wrong. The risk here is to lose a balanced perspective and plunge into a black-and-white world where whoever believes in the rightness of the moralist is good, while anyone who does not believe so is bad. With this fall the moralist descends to the level of a malevolent demagogue or creepy cult leader, abandoning reasoned exhortation or encouragement by example in favor of a demonizing discourse laced with slander and vitriol. The object here is to trade on fears and insecurities in order to force change in moral beliefs through violence, either physical or psychological.

The purpose of this brief and admittedly simplistic digression into moral philosophy is to lay the groundwork for understanding the persona John Schwegmann constructed for public consumption. Creating a role for himself not out of thin air but digging into his organic inclinations and natural predilections, he in fact cast himself as a full-bore moralist—a self-appointed judge of what is right and wrong. Obviously his advocacy-type personalized statements directly conveyed his beliefs about what is right, proper, and just.

Yet even though the effect is subtler, the human-interest statements also carry moralistic messages. Indeed, John's value system is revealed here even more clearly than in the advocacy ads. For hanging heavy in the human-interest ads, like Crescent City humidity, is an intense nostalgia for the good old days—back when adults were hard-working, families self-sufficient, and children respectful of their elders; and back when local community was valued as a source of almost spiritual sustenance. Not surprisingly, even John's dreams for the future were tied to the past. For he envisioned a nation freed from the nefarious influences of giant corporate and government juggernauts, its people now at liberty to (what was it again?) to work hard, be self-sufficient, respect wisdom, and nurture community.

BUT ALL THIS COMMENTARY BEGS the question: When, and how, did John become such a strong moralist? Up to this point in his biography, there is nothing to suggest that his personal life was dominated by any great moral struggles or ethical dilemmas. With little evidence otherwise, there is a temptation to believe he simply made up the character of "John on his high horse" for public consumption, that his morality had no more substance than a Mardi Gras costume. Yet John put on no disguise, no mask to fool the public. The character he summoned was not disingenuous but genuine—as real as the take-charge attitude and fighting spirit he had developed from an early age. Indeed, these personal qualities combined with an inner rage against feelings of inferiority to fuel a burning sense of purpose that, when called on at the appropriate moment, expressed itself in the role of a strong moralist.

What is difficult about seeing John in this role is that he was by no means a saint, or any sort of spiritual role model for that matter. He was certainly no Bible-thumper. He rarely even attended church in those days. But herein resides the problem: the association of morality strictly with religion. Although it is easy to conflate the two, as each issues from the higher realms of conscience, in fact morality can be intensely felt and passionately expressed in secular as well as sacred ways—as, for example, within the framework of a social, political, or legal morality. In John's case, he embraced what can only be called an *economic morality*. And from this particular matrix of passion, the righteous truths of efficiency in the service of equity gushed forth like a mighty fountain.

Earlier it was discussed how thoroughly imbued John was with the spirit of economics. Here, going further, it appears that economics actually formed the sum and substance of what was essentially a secular religion—the leanest operational costs being his sacraments, the lowest retail prices his holy grail, the greatest efficiency his heaven. This sacerdotal devotion to the values of economics represented no less than a striving for communion with God, a yearning expressed in an earthly quest to realize the divine will. This quest soon manifested in an epic legal battle that not only crowned John's career but also changed the course of American retailing.

Slightly more prosaically, but no less momentously, John's deeply felt economic values also inspired the prophetic conceptions of his second and third stores—both ostensibly supermarkets but more like mega-bazaars—that not only anticipated but arguably surpassed the one-stop-shopping prototypes of the later supercenters that have since come to dominate brick-and-mortar discount retailing. Pause to consider here that if the Nobel Prize for Economics were ever extended to the retail category, John Schwegmann would surely win one for his farsighted discoveries.

Recognizing that John was a regular *Homo economicus*, and that his strong moral convictions issued from this source, it is not too much of a surprise that when the time came to create a public persona he chose to portray himself as a plain-speaking businessman-crusader absolutely devoted to the best interests of his customers. Thus was born "The People's Grocer." The core of this persona is best expressed by Saul Stone, a widely esteemed New Orleans' attorney who was John's primary legal strategist, close friend, and frequent ghostwriter: "[John's] position was clear from the start: he held himself forth as a champion of the consumer, representing pure gut instinct and common sense."[10] The creation of this image represented a stroke of pure genius. For through his crusader character John was able to appeal simultaneously to both the pocketbooks and hearts of his customers, all the while avoiding getting too stuck in the muck of the controversy he continuously courted.

In attempting to understand any process as complex as the conscious formation of a public persona—especially one as seemingly berserk as "businessman with a conscience"—it helps to break down the role into its constituent elements. In the case of the people's grocer, the persona consists of four essential components: two altruistic and two egoistic.

First is the altruistic quality known as chivalry, an elusive form of expression enwrapped in a higher purpose and characterized by military virtues. These virtues include strong moral conduct, disciplined behavior, devotion to duty, and a fearless standing up for principles and ideals. For John, the noble quality of chivalry was not some fairytale

abstraction but a real feeling infusing his soul with the classical veri-
ties of honor, gallantry, bravery, generosity, and courtesy. And along
with the fabled knights of old, he felt duty-bound to defend the weak
from the strong. This chivalrous impulse, on display throughout his
career, can be glimpsed in microcosm in an early battle from the late
1940s, when John published an "advertorial" protesting a tax that
had been imposed on margarine. Seeing the tax as an attack on salt-
of-the-earth working stiffs unable to afford butter, chivalrous John
found himself compelled to take action. As Warren Nation relates,
"Mr. Schwegmann stated that since the poor people did not have the
money to fight for the repeal of such a law, *he felt the urge to fight for
them*" [emphasis added].[11]

An entirely more straightforward statement of John's authentically
held belief in his own chivalric heritage came later. In a newspaper ad
appearing in July 1963, he both displayed and explained his (in reality
fictional) family coat of arms. The top of the ad portrays a graphic
rendering of the coat of arms etched on a bronze plaque that once
hung in John's Airline store office (and was later stolen). This logo-
like graphic depicts a medieval-style battle-axe labeled (cartoon-style)
"Schwegmann's" slicing viciously into a round wooden shield labeled
"prices." At the bottom of the graphic appears the slogan, "We keep
slashing." Below this rather violent visual, the ad switches into text
mode. Here is explicated the etymology of the Schwegmann name.
Apparently, John came from the Teutonic warrior class. For according
to his version of traditional lore, the word "schweg" in the medieval
dialect of the Jutes, a northern Germanic tribe, meant axe. Thus a
schweg-man is an axe-man; in other words, a soldier or knight. At this
point in the text, John transitions from the chivalrous role played by
military men in the middle ages to underscore the continuity of his
defensive and offensive lineage: "We at Schwegmann's are still carrying
out the old tradition—protecting the people's pocketbook, slashing
prices, and waging war on the price fixers."[12]

Another altruistic element constituting John's persona was a deep
fellow feeling, which manifested in a genuine love of community.
This is partly a function of where he was from. For like so many New

Orleanians, John felt a fanatical attachment to the people, places, and culture of his native city. Yet he was also joined in this former era of American history by many other businesspeople around the country possessing similar strong emotional ties to their cities and communities. Accompanying these emotional attachments were, of course, corresponding feelings of responsibility for the community, which meant not only contributing to physical upkeep and improvement but also promoting civic virtues, such as pride of place, tolerant debate, and aesthetic enhancement, among others.

In regard to encouraging civilized discourse, John and his fellow community boosters regarded it as their duty to participate in public affairs. As Warren Nation explains, John "deeply believed that he himself along with his business were citizens of the community and as such had the obligation to take part in civic affairs affecting the general public." In John's case at least, the motive behind this impulse was ultimately to strengthen the community. Again according to Nation, John elucidated his reason for penning an editorial supporting greater investment in education as follows: "Mr. Schwegmann states that he has tried to show his customers and the general public how good educational facilities and teachers help the community."[13]

While higher emotions associated with nobility and responsibility toward community genuinely informed the creation of John's public persona, less lofty elements were also part of the mix. One of these was the sheer power of his ego. Although John was not known as an unbearable egomaniac, he nevertheless possessed a strong sense of his personal worth. This he had acquired, as previously discussed at length, in a long struggle waged to protect and defend his self-esteem against any and all that conspired to injure it. Over the course of these struggles, he naturally developed—like a weightlifter constantly pushing and pulling against gravity—an impressive "ego physique." For no other reason than to keep it in shape, a well-developed ego such as his needs regular exercise. In this light, all the moralistic rhetoric spouted in his personalized statements might be seen as mere exercises in pure self-aggrandizement. That it was more than meaningless posturing, however, is apparent in the constant, strenuous attempts John made to place his powerful ego in the service of purposes greater than himself. In this way he held it somewhat in check, thus helping to free up the flow of his nobler impulses. It also helped that he had a wry sense of humor and a deep reservoir of *joie de vivre*, both of which prevented him from taking himself too seriously.

A final element that went into the making of his public persona—which like ego was not exactly the most sterling of qualities—was pure commercial calculation. Of course, as a businessman to the bone, John could not help but operate on calculating principles. From his perspective he saw two primary benefits arising from performing the role of people's grocer. First, it represented a modus operandi to maintain strong branding by keeping in close touch with customers as his business expanded. He believed that the bigger the business got, the more it needed to exert extra effort to maintain customer and community relations.[14] What better way to do this than to sit down with everyone on a weekly basis and tell stories, discuss local affairs, and express heartfelt opinions.

A second calculation was more byzantine, as it involved a need to cultivate customer loyalty for far more than mere branding purposes. The gist of it is that John realized that if a small-scale independent retailer such as himself were to wage a successful war against the major industrial producers he must of necessity raise a formidable demographic army of enthusiastically loyal consumers and citizens. Now, any type of strategy along these lines instantly opens the door to charges of cynical manipulation, in which a leader exploits people's loyalty simply to increase his riches. And indeed there is some truth to this, as would be the case for any unabashed profit-seeking merchant. Yet the consistency of John's efforts to rally the troops to overthrow counterproductive legislation, the fact that he sustained this effort for not years but decades, testifies beyond doubt that there was something authentic in his messaging, an idealistic quality that, if not entirely trumping, at least balanced out cynical calculation with sincere devotion to customer well-being and love of community.

*   *   *

HAVING EXPLORED THE INGREDIENTS—chivalry and vanity, devotion and calculation—that combined to form John's moralistic public persona, one final puzzle remains: What drove him to risk alienating his customers by actually broadcasting his morality? Surely taking a strong stand on anything will inevitably stir controversy and cause at least some outrage. And by nearly all lights this is supposed to be bad for business, almost a primal violation of an unwritten business commandment: Thou shalt not offend the customer. But John plunged into the fray anyway. Swimming against the tide, he simply refused to keep his mouth shut and play it safe like the rest of his nominally pro-free-market confrères—men who he says were "a-scared" of stoking controversy. Indeed, what is most remarkable about John's bucking of conventional wisdom is how radical a stance he took in the context of early postwar American culture. This was the 1950s, after all, the era of the "organization man" and the "power of positive thinking." Within this "don't rock the boat" milieu, conformity in thought and happiness in disposition were smiled upon, while their opposites tended to be regarded with extreme suspicion.

The whole smiley-face, go-along-to-get-along pose was anathema to John. He would speak his mind. That was all there was to it. Immense cultural pressure to the contrary, he refused to restrain himself. Obviously it took tremendous strength of character to fly in the face of such forceful conformity. The question is, what within him inspired such strength? Here, three sources are proposed. First was his internal character structure, which combined a gregarious nature, a learned pugnacity, a religiously felt attitude toward economy, and a certain homespun simplicity that can easily be misinterpreted as naïveté. The outspoken personality type that emerged from this admixture was already preternaturally on display back when the young whippersnapper dared to criticize the management of Sonny Boy—at its annual company banquet no less! And lest it be forgotten, entering the mayor of New Orleans' office unannounced as a virtual unknown, John also brazenly confronted Robert Maestri over the city's outmoded policy on public markets. Clearly John Schwegmann had a history of bold confrontation when the truth as he saw it needed to be told.

While his inner character structure provided much of the strength allowing him to take forceful stands on controversial issues, John also derived reinforcement for his outspoken urges from an outside source. Specifically, in the political sphere a movement toward "southern progressivism" had been in ascendance for much of his life. This movement tended to downplay traditional racial divisions in favor of a forward-looking emphasis on how everyone can come together to create a common prosperity. What mainly stood in the way of future riches for all was, ironically, the rich themselves, who sought to block progress for the simple reason that they liked the way power was distributed now. Why should the wealthy want to "Share our Wealth" when they viewed the outcome as threatening to their privileges? The southern progressive movement bubbled up from a grassroots populace, both white and black, tired of suffering poverty in the land of plenty. Spearheading it were leaders in touch with these common folk, the most notorious of them being Huey Long. Under Huey's twenty-year insurgency, the former race war was transformed into a class war.

As a young man, John along with his best friend, Wilfred Meyer, attended a Huey Long rally at Macarty Square.[15] It must have been like a rock concert, with a similar charisma and emotional power on display. Later he remembered the giant crowd there, and with what tremendous enthusiasm the mostly working-class people greeted the Kingfish's populist promises—promises essentially based on taxing the rich for the sake of technological and social advancements. From a mainstream perspective, the moralist Huey Long—governor of Louisiana from 1928 to 1932, then U.S. senator from 1933 until assassinated in 1935—fell into demagogue hell. Not so his younger brother, Earl K. Long, who managed to carry on the tradition of southern progressivism without slipping (too far) into power-madness. Nevertheless, his "shame on the rich" discourse and his semi-friendly attitudes toward "colored people" did eventually run him afoul of the Louisiana powers that be—to the point of being involuntarily incarcerated in a state-run mental asylum for some off-the-cuff remarks made while running for a third gubernatorial term in 1959 (just one of the wildly funny yet darkly disturbing tales chronicled in A.J. Liebling's *The Earl of Louisiana*).[16]

In considering southern progressivism, there is no doubt that John Schwegmann embodied its spirit. His battles were directed at class, not race. He represented the common folk striving to better their living standards against resistance by the rich. He stood foursquare for fairness and against cheating, championing a level playing field against a stacked deck. Fortunately for posterity, John's populist sympathies reflected more Earl than Huey, as his views remained in the moderate mainstream of southern progressivism. That said, all class-based politics along these lines were always looked at askance by the status-quo establishment, and they certainly never attained an enduring majority opinion in the South. Nevertheless, during the period of his business ascendance in the 1950s—a time coinciding with Earl Long's tenure as Louisiana's governor—John Schwegmann managed to assert the spirit of southern progress.

A third source of strength for John, a source beyond inner character or outer influence, resided in what can only be understood as his mystical faith in the fusion of business and morality. Sounds crazy, but there it is. He believed that the two pursuits of making money and serving the sacred are not mutually exclusive at all but are actually two sides of the same coin, joined at the hip and working hand in glove. Indeed, John went so far as to believe that the achievement of true success absolutely required the fusing of the two. For only in a state of economic grace, where greed is balanced by need, can truly great deeds be accomplished. Believe it or not, this mystical faith worked wonders for John.

Drawing down power from these three wellsprings, John plowed forward in an offensive posture that refused to buckle under to conventions of propriety and courageously cast aside fear of controversy or confrontation. His stance was fierce and aggressive, a hard-hitting approach to competition resembling a throwback to the old days of professional football, starring the gnarly visages of Knute Rockne and Bronco Nagurski. John would simply tell the truth, over and over again, letting the chips fall where they may. It was not John's way, it did not echo with his sense of responsibility, to back down under pressure. He would stand up for what he thought was right. In his own words: "I always speak the truth. If something is wrong, I feel it in my heart, and I have to say so. There have been times when I alienated many customers because of my views, but I couldn't let that stop me."[17] Such is the voice of a prophet, an archetypal character defined by moral compulsion. In the late 1940s, John was preparing to place this prophetic voice in the service of leading an epochal legal battle. Meanwhile, he had a new store to build.

12

THE WORLD'S FIRST SUPERCENTER ARISES ON AIRLINE HIGHWAY

As with all American cities at the dawn of the 1950s, New Orleans stood poised on the threshold of transcendent changes in its geographic size, economic makeup, and cultural identity. The keynote of these changes can be summed up in one word: expansion. Of course, the "driving force" behind this expansionist trend was the automobile. Mass ownership of cars not only made possible a more spread-out urban space, it demanded it. In attempting to stay abreast of this development, geographers came up with a new mapping concept called the "standard metropolitan statistical area." The SMSA was a fluid thing, flowing steadily and inexorably in various geophysically convenient directions, much like lava flows from an exploding volcano. In the process of spreading outward, the tidy traditional city model—an urban downtown core surrounded by a discrete accretion of related neighborhoods, all bounded by well-defined limits—came to resemble a much more messy blob-like configuration. In other words, the SMSA concept modeled the growth of suburbia.

Although New Orleans has always been unique among American cities in its outright mystical attachment to a cultural mythology interlaced with spirits and animated by frequent festivity—a seemingly flaky attachment that ironically has helped it preserve an uncommonly vibrant downtown vitality—this singular U.S. metropolis still fell under the irresistible spell of postwar suburban expansion. So it is no wonder that most of the major infrastructure projects completed in New Orleans in the 1950s involved transportation, thus encouraging the growth of car culture and its corollary: a streaming away from the city. Examples of these transportation projects include the Mississippi River Bridge (now called the Crescent City Connection), spanning the East and West banks; the Causeway, connecting New Orleans to the North Shore of Lake Pontchartrain; and Airline Highway, linking the city directly to Baton Rouge. Of course, these ambitious local and state transportation efforts were complemented on the federal level by construction of the Interstate system, which in New Orleans originally involved building I-10 through the city.

Back in the late 1940s, back before there existed a massive new vehicle infrastructure of bridges and highways, and back when he was still working out his public persona, John foresaw the future. He intuitively understood the postwar expansion to come. Not one for relaxing, for basking in the glow of his unalloyed success at the St. Claude store, John resolved to strike while the iron was hot. He had already proven to his own satisfaction that the supermarket concept would work within the idiosyncratic peculiarities of New Orleans. So he was more than eager to get a move on, realizing that events would happen rapidly in the techno-accelerated postwar world. Consequently, as soon as he assured himself that his first business was working according to the Golden Formula, he immediately set about designing his next store.

AIRLINE HIGHWAY, FIRST OPENED TO TRAFFIC in 1933, is located at the terminus of a legendary American highway system U.S. Route 61, which originally stretched northward for 1,700 miles—all the way from New Orleans to the Canadian border. Immortalized by Minnesota native Bob Dylan in his album *Highway 61 Revisited*, the long road basically parallels the Mississippi River. As such, in the decades before the Interstate was built it served as the chief conduit linking traffic from the Mississippi Delta of the Deep South to the northern cities of Memphis, St. Louis, and Chicago. Hence it is easy to see why Route 61 has since been dubbed the "Blues Highway."[1]

Certainly its funky aspect was on full display back in Schwegmann's time, as indeed it is to this day. U.S. Route 61 begins in New Orleans at the intersection of Carrollton and Tulane avenues. From there, Airline Highway (Route 61's southernmost spur) travels first to the international airport—previously Moisant, now Louis Armstrong— then on to Baton Rouge. Though improvements have been made to Airline over the decades, it has never managed to shake a reputation for seediness. Even as recently as the 1980s, Airline Highway presented the dismaying spectacle of an "ugly…endless procession of gas stations, parking lots, billboards, striptease joints, sleazy bars, cheap motels, and neon signs."[2] Airline is where Carlos Marcello, New Orleans' notorious godfather, ran his mob operations for twenty-five years, and it is where celebrity televangelist Jimmy Swaggart was busted with a prostitute.

Airline Highway is also where John decided to locate his second store. Granted, the surroundings were derelict, but the land was cheap. Moreover, the site was not too far away from downtown, certainly not by car. The most important consideration of all, though, was that this location perfectly anticipated the suburban boom to come. The site he selected, located about seven miles west-northwest of the city's central business district, was enormous at 350,000 square feet.[3] But it had to be. For flush with the success of his first store, his ambition now aflame, John determined to build right here on Airline Highway the world's largest modern supermarket.

Although he had faith in himself, he knew the big risks involved. So when the day finally arrived to deliver the down payment, it was not without some trepidation that John plunked down the required 10% on the property's $140,000 purchase price. Any residual fears he harbored were stoked later that same day when John received a surprise phone call from a competitor offering to take the property off his hands for a hefty sum—enough to net John a cool $75,000. After a long night spent agonizing, John refused the offer. History, of course, shows he made the right move. Consider that just five years after John purchased it, the property was valued at $750,000.[4]

Despite appearances to the contrary, New Orleans is essentially a conservative city. Reflecting its origins, the place is stubbornly aristocratic, clinging to tradition and resisting innovation. Certainly John felt the sting of the power structure's resistance to new ideas when he petitioned the leading financial institution in the city, Whitney Bank, to fund the building of his visionary store. He should have known better. For "Witless Bank," as local wags sometimes called the lofty depository, could hardly have been expected to anticipate the suburban boom. As it happened, when John asked the bank for a loan, Whitney basically told him he was crazy. One loan officer went so far as to actively discourage him from pursuing the venture, admonishing John by pointing out that there was "nothing out on Airline Highway but rats and rabbits."[5]

While he may have been disappointed, John absorbed the rejection with equanimity. For having already suffered the experience of being rebuffed by Whitney Bank back in the old days, he was prepared with a backup plan. As an alternative to Whitney he approached a recent local startup, the aptly named Progressive Bank and Trust Company. Unlike Whitney, Progressive enthusiastically embraced John's business case. John asked for a $200,000 loan to build the store. Where Whitney said no, Progressive said yes.

Now it was nail-biting time, as the store moved into the building phase.[6] For his part, John was in an unfamiliar and uneasy position. He had self-financed his previous venture from the proceeds of his real estate properties. Now suddenly he was hugely in debt, to the tune of over $300,000. His partners also felt the pressure, as they were being asked to pour their time, labor, and scant financial resources into a project that could well turn out to be a boondoggle. Bending every effort to keep construction costs to a bare minimum, John took the unusual and innovative step of engaging a single contractor to build the entire store—a cheaper alternative than the common practice at the time of assigning the primary building tasks to multiple contractors. (He continued, however, to subcontract out for specialty work, same as at the St. Claude store.)

Despite all efforts to hold down costs, though, finances began running short, and a near panic set in among the partners. Though they somehow managed to keep a hold of their wits until the store was more or less completed, at that point the emotional dam burst. With all the money now gone, the partners turned utterly defeatist, urging the captain to abandon ship. Indeed, the partners were so desperate they even proposed trying to unload this "white elephant" on supermarket archrival A&P. Yet just like that more famous seeker of a new world before him, John stood fast against his mutinous crew, the men of little faith begging him to call it quits. Thank God for John's backbone. No failure of nerve here. Refusing to back down or sell out, he decreed that the project proceed.

When the Schwegmann Brothers Airline store miraculously managed to open its doors on December 5, 1950, just in time for the Christmas season, this opening was quite a few balloons short of grand. No special advertising or promotion accompanied it, no carnivalesque hoopla. Indeed, the store itself was not quite finished yet, with a significant portion of its interior space empty and roped off. Moreover, John could not afford to stock the shelves, having to beg to purchase merchandise on credit. Most humbling of all, though, he had no money for cash registers. Instead, cashiers were forced to make do with old-fashioned adding machines. Cigar boxes served as cash receptacles.[7]

Yet overcoming all this—the shabby appearance, shaky finances, and primitive technology—the inglorious opening of the second Schwegmann Brothers Giant Super Market turned out to be a terrific success, with turnout exceeding all expectations. It was another instant hit! But then again, how could it not be? For despite its somewhat disheveled state, the store still presented an incredible spectacle. It was colossal, absolutely monumental, by the standards of the time. More than that, this palace of consumer plenitude featured a breathtaking cornucopia of bargains galore. The overall effect was to overawe—and by this magic to draw—wave after wave of delighted customers. For his part, once again John had risked all and won all.[8]

THE MAGNIFICENT SUPERMARKET THAT AROSE on Airline Highway measured an astonishing 84,000 square feet—more than triple, almost quadruple, the size considered at the far edge of optimal (25,000 square feet) by conventional retail wisdom in 1950. Though the store itself was a sight to behold, by insider lights even more impressive was the parking lot. Having anticipated the triumph of car culture, John thought long and hard about the role of the parking lot. In the process he came up with two important innovations. First, he positioned the main parking lot in front of the store, placing the actual store building at the back of the property. Interestingly, his rationale for doing so was psychological rather than economic. For John believed deeply in the power of volume. If people see a mass of cars parked in front of a store, this automatically acts to attract them like a magnet. This insight, now taken for granted, was likely a John Schwegmann original. If not, he was definitely in the forefront of the front-facing parking-lot trend.[9]

John's other parking innovation pertained to size of the lot. Here, just as he had bucked conventional wisdom in vastly expanding store size, so he bumped up the dimensions of the reigning rule-of-thumb parking-lot/store-size ratio from two-to-one to three-to-one. Specifically he devoted 200,000 square feet in front of the store to parking and 30,000 square feet on each side, adding up to a total of 260,000 square feet of parking lot space—just a little under John's target of three times store size. Yet even this swollen requirement was not enough. For John actually believed that only a four-to-one ratio was adequate! For this reason he later added 50,000 more square feet of parking space. At its maximum breadth, the Airline store parking lot could accommodate close to 2,000 cars.[10]

The original parking lot featured a pavement of crushed oyster shells, a popular surfacing material then in use throughout New Orleans. Only later in the decade was the lot covered in asphalt. Although traffic on Airline Highway was relatively light at first, with only 26,000 vehicles a day passing by the store in 1950, the giant parking lot had been conceived to accommodate a much heavier flow as suburban expansion increased. To this end, it incorporated four entrances/exits: two directly opening onto Airline and two placed off on adjacent side streets. When after a couple of years traffic flow did indeed significantly increase, the parking lot began filling up on a regular basis. During peak periods of congestion, traffic supervisors—actually just reassigned "package boys" and "buggy pushers"—were deployed to direct the flow.

Of course, impressive as the dimensions and layout of the parking lot may have been to retail insiders, it was the awe-inspiring appearance of the store itself that captured most people's attention. Everyone must have marveled at how it dwarfed the average-sized supermarket of the early 1950s. Beyond sheer size, though, it also captivated through a stunning display of architectural features. The most visible and attractive of these was the store's utterly unique overall design: a structure consisting of three airplane-hangar-type buildings, each 300 feet long and 100 feet wide, all joined together under one roof—a type of construction modeled on the Quonset hut but here realized on a grand scale. As for its façade, within three Quonset-style arches forming the front of the store, giant steel-framed glass windows were embedded that glistened in the semitropical daylight. Meanwhile, the store's sides were made of mundane concrete blocks, and its floor was a simple six-inch-thick uncovered concrete slab. On top there was no formal interior ceiling, only the exposed roof of the building.

To heat and cool this prodigy required creative solutions in the days before centralized air conditioning. Given New Orleans' climate, heating was easier to deal with than cooling. To warm the store during the relatively short-lived cold season, John simply deployed blower-type heating fans placed strategically throughout the store. On those many more frequent days when heat and humidity in the Crescent

City reach oppressive proportions, the problem presented was much tougher. To meet the challenge, John and his team devised an ingenious three-pronged strategy. Providing primary active cooling were numerous large and industrial-sized floor and ceiling fans placed all around the store. But the store's cooling system also incorporated a much more impressive "passive" component. In employing this progressive, even "green," approach, a constant stream of water was sprayed onto the roof of the building; the water supplied from two wells dug on the property—one pumping 400 gallons per minute, the other 200. Through heat transfer, this soaking of the roof helped significantly to lower store temperatures over the long summer season. The final prong of the cooling strategy was simple but rarely deployed. It involved actual air conditioners. These were used in just two areas. One was upstairs, in some offices and in the pharmacy storage space. The other, the only customer area to receive nice, cool, refreshing blasts of air conditioning was—hallelujah!—the bar.

On first entering the Airline store, the original customers must have been dumbstruck by the scene they encountered: a vista of almost shocking immensity. Stretching out before them for tens of thousands of square feet they beheld a cavernous expanse overloaded with a stunning display of merchandise—the overall impression of vastness magnified by a near-vertiginous vertical spaciousness, as the roof sans ceiling soared overhead. After being suitably wowed, customers would then have plunged eagerly into the store, in all likelihood following the implied track of its gridiron pattern, proceeding to stroll through the store's extra-wide aisles—which at eleven feet were about twice the size of the six feet standard at supermarkets of the time.[11] Along the way they would frequently happen upon one of John's unique merchandising innovations. Called "scrambled merchandising," the concept plays on the delights of novelty by randomly placing unexpected products in surprising juxtapositions throughout the store, typically by way of endcaps or freestanding displays. Shoppers would inevitably also come across another John Schwegmann merchandising innovation—namely, "The World's Largest Display," a freestanding presentation of between 50 and 100 cases of a single item piled high and being sold at drastically reduced prices (shades of King Kullen!). Over the years this phantasmagorical display became such a popular feature that John tried to keep at least one going at all times.

Along with an awesome-sized building and a luxuriant merchandise mix, these first Airline store customers also encountered quite a lot of empty space. Though the store contained greatly expanded versions of all the departments familiar from the St. Claude store, these enlarged departments still did not serve to fill up the entire interior area. Indeed, far from it. For out of the 84,000 total square feet available, somewhere between 15,000 and 20,000 were left unutilized. Yet rather than representing an oversight or a mistake in calculation, the empty space was there by design. John correctly guessed that his customers, mesmerized by the dazzling display of what *was* there, would show forbearance for what *was not* there. Meanwhile, he had plans.

So for the time being John proceeded unabashedly to rope off the thousands of extra square feet from the main selling space, not even bothering to hide it. In the immediate aftermath of the opening, however, he got down to the business of occupying the emptiness. His idea had been visionary all along. Now was his time to make it so. The basic concept was simple enough: to create a one-stop-shopping supermarket-based destination outlet. The "$64,000 question," of course, was how to accomplish this. To do so, John hit on a bold and clever solution: he would lease the extra space out to specialty and service retailers. At this point, the Airline store became a work of art.

OVER THE FIRST FOUR YEARS AFTER OPENING, from 1951 to 1954, the Airline store relentlessly expanded its product and service reach by adding one leased department after another. There was no specific playbook followed here. John simply improvised. He had a general idea of what he wanted, the one-stop shopping experience, and a modus operandi, leasing, for achieving it. Yet as far as who or what or how many merchants were to be included in the grand scheme, he was just not sure. The process of selection was ambiguous, uncertain. As John himself said, there was "no magic formula," and no choice but to "figure it out as you go along."[12]

He did, however, have one loose criterion to guide him: if someone could convince him that they knew more about merchandising a particular category than he did, then the most economical move would be to lease out the category to that person. Following this logic, and with an eye to achieving a well-rounded diversity, John ended up leasing out nine departments. Each time a new one opened, the ropes previously sequestering the lessee's area were removed. This process proceeded rapidly apace until all the interior store space was filled—and then it even spilled outside! By 1955, however, all limits, both interior and exterior, had been breached, which effectively ended the leasing program. The store was finally done.

As if expansion through leasing were not enough, John also focused on growing the Schwegmann-owned side of the business. Most notably, in 1952 he introduced an all-new drug department featuring a full-scale pharmacy. Only tentatively phased in on a test basis at first, it proved a resounding success, functioning both as a major profit center and a popular store draw. With this success, Schwegmann's became one of the first modern supermarkets to successfully incorporate a complete drugstore format (including a pharmacy) into a food/drug combination concept—a commonplace feature of today's supercenters.[13]

By 1955, as the expansion phase ended and the consolidation phase began, the Airline store had grown into a humongous enterprise, resembling more of a "shopping center" than a supermarket. Overall there were nineteen departments. Schwegmann Brothers owned ten of these. They included grocery, produce, meat, deli, seafood, drugs, liquor, housewares/gifts, lunch counter, and bar. Combined, these departments took up the lion's share of store floor space at 70,000 square feet (including warehouse and other storage space). Meanwhile, nine leased departments were spread out across an indeterminate 15,000 to 20.000 square feet of interior and exterior space. These leased departments included a bakery, a barbershop, a dry goods store, a flower shop, a jewelry store, a key shop, a radio/television store, a shoe store, and a shoe repair shop.

AT THIS POINT IT SEEMS ONLY APPROPRIATE to take a tour through the Airline store, making note along the way not only of its distinctive features and exciting innovations but also of its mundane continuities with previous operations. Beginning with the massive grocery department, apart from its dazzling size and greater scale of operations, little else about the Airline store grocery department set it apart from its St. Claude counterpart. Product distribution remained mostly direct from producers and manufacturers, national brands were emphasized in the merchandising mix, and high turnover was enforced through a ruthless weeding-out process wherein slow-movers were sold at clearance prices and never bought again.

Much the same pattern seen in grocery prevailed throughout the other Schwegmann-owned food-oriented departments in the Airline store. In other words, though the produce, meat, deli, and seafood departments were all significantly larger than in the St. Claude store, the underlying operational philosophy remained the same, with an unwavering focus placed on self-service, direct distribution, rock-bottom prices, and rapid turnover. The key thing to realize about the Airline store, then, is that it was not so much designed to operate differently than the St. Claude store than to amplify its successful results—that is, to achieve a greater flow rate of profit. The larger space simply enabled and encouraged this greater flow by making available more room for cars, customers, and, of course, products.

In terms of products, the store offered an astonishing variety of merchandise, a cornucopian display meant to whet consumer appetites and thus stimulate buying. Looking just at grocery products, the selection was enormous. Alongside well-known national brands appeared a depth of regional brands, local names, and private labels. To take one microscopically minor example, consider the almost

Patriarch of the New Orleans branch of the Schwegmann family, Garret Schwegmann Sr. (Grandfather Garret) appears distinguished in this photo taken sometime in the late 19th century.

A photo portrait of Garret Jr. (Uncle Garret) Schwegmann. Uncle Garret was owner of the old corner store at Piety and Burgundy, a real estate powerhouse in the old Third District, and well-respected businessman throughout New Orleans.

Anton Frey, John's maternal grandfather. Anton and his wife owned the Frey family homestead, where John spent much of his time as a boy.

John's father, John William Schwegmann (John Sr.), pictured during his dapper days as young manager at the old corner store.

The interior of the old corner store featuring owner and employees behind the central "ballroom" counter. Garrett Schwegmann Jr. is at far right. (Photo taken in 1895.)

Uncle Garrett expanded distribution by adding delivery and street sales via two mule-drawn wagons. Pictured are two members of the distribution team: Grandpop "Speedy" Voelker and "Dummy" Bauers. Photo taken in front of the Piety and Burgundy store in 1898.

Mary Schwegmann, John's most beloved aunt.

John's agriculturalist aunts, Helen and Pauline Frey. They are posing here with a baby lamb sitting atop a bone box in the "backyard" of their Bywater urban farm.

The young John G. Schwegmann in his days as a real estate broker, sometime during the 1930s.

John in a bridal shot with his first wife, Mary Geisenheimer.

John and his second wife, Melba Margaret Wolfe, posing on board the HMS Queen Elizabeth sometime in the 1950s.

John on a steamship cruise circa the late 1960s with his paramour, Mary Ann Blackledge (pictured at right).

John dining in the Blue Room at the Roosevelt Hotel in 1961 with daughter Margie and his personal secretary and amanuensis, Mary E. White.

John G. Schwegmann around the time he had just opened his first supermarket in 1946. Believed to be outside his home on St. Claude Court in the Lower Ninth Ward.

John G. Schwegmann posing in front of his Gentilly store.

John with Wilfred Meyer, his best friend and second-in-command at Schwegmann Brothers.

John pictured here at Dubuque Packing House. Iowa-based Dubuque was owned by Harry Wahlert, one of John's best friends and with whom he formed a strategic alliance to supply his stores with bargain-priced but high-quality meats.

Here is John posing with a British bobby on a trip to London in the 1950s.

John and his admired friend and frequent traveling companion, George Pereira, head cheese buyer for Schwegmann stores. They are pictured on a trip in County Cork, Ireland, during the late 1950s.

John and Harry Wahlert pictured with a Greek Orthodox priest on a European trip in 1965.

Young protégé John Francis Schwegmann, pictured with Harry Wahlert, on an exotic excursion up the Nile River in Egypt to see the newly built Aswan Dam.

A flyer from John's first political campaign (1955-56). He was running for state senator as a single-issue candidate focusing on the repeal of fair trade laws.

A Schwegmann shopping bag from 1975, when John was running for the Louisiana Public Service Commission.

Pictured here, just one year before his death, is John Schwegmann together with his children Margie and John Francis (seated on the right) and caretaker Marlene Taylor (left front). The photo was taken in 1994 while on board the Queen Elizabeth 2.

Depicted above is the layout of a typical ad featuring personalized statement and novelty highlights embedded within discount price presentations. (Appearing February 4, 1958)

A standard banner appearing at the top of Schwegmann's 1950s' ads announcing a proto-version of everyday low pricing, with advertised discounts are good for a whole week, not just one or two days.

This statement regarding chain stores goes to the core of Schwegmann's neo-populist loyalty to the local economy.

GENTILLY AIR-CONDITIONED BAR

You can enjoy any brand of liquor you may choose in your favorite drink. Every drink contains a full ounce of liquor. Expert mixologists on duty at all times to serve you.

Our usual low prices prevail in both our Gentilly and Airline Bars. These are only a few:

SCOTCH or BOURBON

HI-BALLS Made with a Full Ounce of Whiskey .... 25c up

Tom Collins 30c

Gin Rickey 30c

Old-Fashioned 40c

Martini 35c

Manhattan 35c

Cuba Libre . . . . 30c up

Whiskey Sour 35c

Schwegmann Cocktail . . . 50c

Outrageously low drink prices are featured in this ad snippet highlighting the Gentilly store bar.

Here John details the success of his bond offering, all within the context of a standard supermarket ad.

Thank You, Customers   Thank You, Friends
who have demonstrated your
FAITH IN SCHWEGMANN BROS.

OUR BOND ISSUE IS OVER-SUBSCRIBED!

SHORTLY AFTER THE FIRST OF THE YEAR, OUR $1,500,000 ISSUE OF SCHWEGMANN 6% BONDS WAS COMPLETELY SOLD OUT.

TO ALL OUR BOND HOLDERS, (and those on the waiting list), we wish to say THANK YOU. WE APPRECIATE YOUR FAITH IN SCHWEGMANN BROS.

Anyone who has money to invest asks three questions—

(1) Is the investment safe?

(2) Can I get my money back when I need it?

(3) What is the return on my invested dollar?

SCHWEGMANN BONDS MEET ALL THESE REQUIREMENTS

To those who have applications on file, and for those who may wish to buy bonds in the future:

Our policy is that any bondholder who wishes to cash his bonds has only to present them to our office, where his money will be paid to him immediately, plus interest earned to date. With such an arrangement, from time to time we will be glad to have bonds for sale. We will be glad to take your application and notify you when we have bonds turned in.

125

CU

BAYER ASPIRIN
Box
T

3

If it were not for Schweg
against the "fair trade
would be forced to pay

TIDE
GIANT SIZE PKG.

65c

PRICES GOOD ALL WEEK

HENS
Fresh Ice Packed, Young and Tend

Whole
3 to 4
Pounds
Lb. 2

B
St

REPEATED BY DEMA
Because of tremendous demand for
OYSTER SANDWICH
We Will Continue This Special All This
Get yours at Gentilly & Airline Stores

One example of John's endless attempts to standardize his editorial platform. Here it is entitled "Schwegmann Says," and deals with foreign policy.

Here is a ripe example of bizarre and comical product juxtapositions.

As I Saw Spain's National Sport

When we were in Barcelona, the Spanish were behind in their bullfighting because of bad weather. It had rained for several weeks, and the natives and tourists from all over the world were anxiously awaiting a clear day. Our tickets were for Sunday —and luckily for us, it was a beautiful day for a "corrida" or bull fight. Tickets are secured far in advance—in our case over 30 days in advance. Seats on the shady side cost more than seats on the sunny side. There are two arenas in Barcelona. This Sunday the largest one, which holds over 75,000 people, was to be used. Fiesta was in the air—everybody in the hotels, restaurants, and on the street corners where papers are sold were talking excitedly about the famous matadors and the various bulls they were to meet. The very air was alive with tension— everybody who could walk had plans to see the spectacle. Lottery shops and vendors were all over Barcelona hawking their tickets.

As this was my first experience, I wanted to be sure not to miss anything, so early Sunday morning I went to the arena to see if I could take an advance look at the bulls much like dancers' shoes, and their life depends on their being able to keep their footing. The sand was dampened just the exact amount so that no dust would get in their the bull fighter does not fight the bull at this time—the bull is much too capable a fighter and the man would be no match for him.) Then from another end comes another

A truncated example from John's travelogue appearing in 1955. This entry is devoted to recounting his experience at Spain's "corrida."

AS I SAW RUSSIA-- RUSSIAN WOMEN

Almost all women in Russia work, not only in the usual jobs of nursing, clerking, working in offices, etc., but at jobs that in America are not considered women's work. We saw them laying bricks, mixing mortar and carrying it up on scaffolds, digging ditches, asphalting streets, unloading freight cars of heavy lumber. We saw women on ladders painting in the hotel hallways, using blowtorches to take off the old paint, landscaping in parks, driving bull dozers, moving earth, milking cows and doing all sorts of farm work, planting and hoeing by hand, plowing with an oxen or mule, hauling farm products to market, welding, standing twelve in a truck going to and from work. All these women wear a cloth or scarf on their heads, tied under their chins, men's coats, fairly short skirts and knee boots.

Women in Russia drive street cars, operate trains as engineers and conductors, pave streets and dig sewers. We saw three cleaning out man holes in the street, one down in the hole, one dropping a bucket on a rope to pull up the black muck, the third dumping it in the gutter. The streets of the Russian cities we visited are the cleanest I have ever seen anywhere I have traveled. There was not as much as a cigarette butt in the gutter. What a contrast in our New Orleans, where overloaded dump trucks spill mud, dirt and trash all over our streets! To me it appeared that the sanitation department allots the responsibility of keeping the streets clean in various sections of the city to a crew of women, probably women living in that district. Each crew has about 17 blocks to attend, and you will find them

Another example from a travelogue, this one appearing in 1958. Here he is commenting on Russian women during a trip to the Soviet Union. John is confronted for the first time with hardcore feminism. He is bewildered but strives to be objective.

There the worke bers of w tion. Unde some resp machine v votes.

Seven en, as at teachers.

A full-page ad spotlights the unmatched depth, breadth, and low prices at Schwegmann's store liquor departments. Notice the statement at the top left celebrating victory over liquor price fixing, and the radio and movie camera snuck in at the bottom of this welter of liquor bargains.

ridiculous variety of canned peas. Here the shopper was confronted with a bewildering array of brand names: Libby's, Del Monte, Green Giant, Le Sueur, Autocrat, Dubon, Blue Ridge, and Rodgers. The same type of extensive brand offerings held true in produce (Coney, Top Hat, Caro, Lead, TopSail, Rainbow, Royal Red, Happy) and meat/deli (Swift, Armour, Kraft, Borden, Cudahy, Rath, and Dubuque).

The variety factor particularly stood out in the Airline store's seafood department.[14] Here, appealing to a customer base consisting of Mississippi Delta/Gulf Coast residents and a large number of Catholics—all of whom taken together score in the top tier of U.S. seafood consumption—the giant department featured an untold assortment of locally sourced fish (salt and freshwater), crustaceans, and amphibians. These included perch, flounder, cod, catfish, crab, shrimp, oysters, scallops, crawfish, frog, turtle, and alligator, among other water creatures. Meanwhile, lobster was regularly imported from Maine, Florida, and Cuba. Along with these fresh products, the seafood department also carried an extensive selection of frozen national brands, along with a private-label merchandise line consisting of oyster knives, ice picks, and related items.

While operational continuity with the St. Claude store ruled the day in Airline store food departments, a great deal of experimentation took place in the new store's liquor and nonfoods departments. Specifically in terms of liquor, the department had expanded to such a degree that its footprint rivaled most area liquor stores. In size it was over 2,000 square feet. In selection it featured 350 brands and sizes of whiskey and other hard beverages, 50 SKUs of wine just in the larger sizes, and private labels galore—Schwegmann-branded regular bourbon, bonded bourbon, whiskey, gin, vodka, champagne, and beer (premium and bock), along with a full panoply of cocktail mixers and bar accessories. John's experimentation in liquor was not so much in size or selection, though, but in price. For it was the price factor that above all differentiated the Airline store's liquor department, allowing it to become a major player in New Orleans' retail liquor market. Leveraging the store's vast selection, John pushed the envelope on price, submerging markups to just 6% on whiskey and 10% on wine.

For this act of flagrant discounting, John got slapped down big time by the most powerful liquor distillers in the country. The legal battles that ensued would change the course of retail history.[15]

In the meantime, equally auspicious experimentation at the Airline store was being conducted in other departments. Like liquor, the sporting goods section had expanded to such an extent that it could compete with local independent sports stores.[16] A major advantage the Schwegmann store held was to offer a wide variety of products aimed at all ages, incomes, genders, and other demographic groupings. Yet even more significant, it employed the extra space available at the Airline location to focus on hunting and fishing—two extremely popular pursuits in the "Sportsman's Paradise" Louisiana of the 1950s. Thus not only available but frequently featured at discount at the Airline store were rods, reels, and lures for fishing, and guns, ammunition, and other lethal accessories for hunting.

In contrast to the neat store-within-a-store experiments that took place in liquor and sporting goods, the Airline store version of the hardware department looked like a total mess. For within its parameters it threw together everything from tools, housewares, glassware, toys, and gifts to clothing and household textiles (towels, sheets, and so forth). Casting ultimate irony on the hardware department was that its most heavily promoted items were Mardi Gras costumes.

Of all the original St. Claude store departments, the one reproduced in the Airline store that actually evolved into a whole new species, not just a hyperbolic extension of the old model, was the drug department. John's first foray into drugs and cosmetics had ended up fairly scattered with unsatisfying results. On his second go-round he determined to improve matters by refashioning the department in a more coherent manner. To this end, after spending a couple of years in planning—a drawn-out process necessitated by the extreme sensitivity involving anything related to drugs—he opened a drug department at the Airline store in April 1952, but at first only on a trial basis.[17]

In the two years before this, the drug "department" had actually been more of a drug "section" integrated within the grocery department. Here were available over-the-counter (OTC) "medicine cabinet" drugs, health and beauty aids (HBA), and a hodge-podge of grooming-oriented general merchandise products, such as small electrical appliances, cameras, and clocks, with razor blades and a few other small OTC and HBA items located at checkout. With the opening of the new drug department, all of these products were aggregated in a separate 700-square-foot section located at the very front of the store between its two entrances.

The masterstroke, however, was the addition of a full-service pharmacy. Staffed by six registered pharmacists, twelve to fifteen clerks, and a cashier, the pharmacy turned out to be one of John's most inspired moves of all time. It proved beyond popular. By the mid-1950s, annual sales for the pharmacy amounted to over $1 million. Five hundred prescriptions were being filled per day, a volume so great that a number-selection system had to be instituted to regulate customer orders. This enhanced flow of customers also generated shopper traffic for the rest of the store. The cherry on top was that the pharmacy scored goodwill by offering a public health service.

The product selection available at Schwegmann's new drug department was simply outstanding. Altogether, the combined number of pharmaceuticals, OTC drugs, HBA items, and related general merchandise totaled 14,000 SKUs, nearly all those stock-keeping units being national brands. Clearly, given the tremendous selection and high quality of products on offer, combined with the presence of an on-premise pharmacy, the supermarket at this point begins to compete head-to-head with the average independent drugstore. In this sense, Schwegmann presented a viable, functional challenge to the retail industry status quo in his direct threat to the drugstore sector in the pecking order. Although there were likely few drugstore operators shaking in their boots at the time, with most probably not even aware of the experiment on Airline Highway, the monster had arrived. Among the tentative efforts going on in the early 1950s, John Schwegmann was arguably the first to seize the bull by the horns and successfully establish a food/drug combination ("combo") prototype—an entity that ended up absolutely devastating the independent drugstore sector and which is now ubiquitous.

Yet successfully instituting a new retail form was never enough for John in his heyday. For his thinking always returned to the fundamental element of price. And in this he added a new dimension to the food/drug combo concept—specifically, discount pricing. Airline drug department prices on name brands were almost scandalously lower than at local independent drugstores. Even worse, from a drugstore point of view, were rock-bottom bargains on a raft of Schwegmann private-label items, including vitamins, minerals, thermometers, paregoric, and Brown's mixture with ammonia.

John bent every effort to lower drug department prices. Nevertheless, in those early days they never went as low as he wished—and knew he could still profit off. For back in the early 1950s, the U.S. retail drug sector was still under the sway of regulatory mysticisms and legal obscurities unknown to other merchandise categories. While all these complications and obstacles are understandable in light of the apothecary industry's checkered history of hawking snake oil and outright poisons,[18] none of this history, in John's opinion, justified a manipulated and monopolized price structure. But that is exactly what he confronted with the opening of his new drug department—namely being legally forced to charge heavily inflated prices for drugs and HBA products. Indeed, these items carried among the highest markups in the store: up to 20% for simple health and beauty products, 30% for OTC drugs, and 70% for prescription drugs. Nonetheless, despite being forced to charge these outrageous mandatory markups, Schwegmann still managed to sell at the lowest prices in town.

As with liquor, John soon landed in hot water over drug discounting. But flush from his recent victory over the distillers (detailed in chapter fourteen), John simply could not resist challenging the seemingly all-powerful drug companies on their twisted price fixing schemes. Deliberately tweaking the tiger's tail, he shrewdly picked insulin—what he called a "life-saver"—as a cause célèbre.[19] Dramatizing the situation, he slashed his price on insulin to the bone, selling it at the absolute minimum profit, and promoted this gesture as a public service. Sure enough, unimpressed by this display of altruism, the drug companies immediately and ferociously attacked John's gesture.

Eli Lilly was the first to draw blood, followed in short order by a cavalcade of fifteen additional drug majors, all slapping lawsuits left and right on this impudent upstart who messed with their prices, their fierce battle cries echoing with a resounding "How dare he!" And indeed, soon enough the drug magnates cut John down to size in federal court. But not in state court, where he eventually won his second epochal victory in the ongoing war against the scourge of manufacturer-dictated price fixing.

BESIDES DEVELOPING A SUCCESSFUL food/drug combo concept, John innovated in two other areas at the Airline supermarket. One of these was in adding a lunch counter. As with the pharmacy an obvious borrowing from the drugstore model, Schwegmann's lunch counter opened only at the end of the Airline store's expansion phase in 1954.[20] The idea was to capitalize on three favorable tendencies. First, because of the vast size of the store, customers appreciated having a place to eat and relax at some point during the shopping experience. Second, the fast-food eatery would draw in the proliferating number of construction workers then engaged in the mighty task of building up the suburbs in rapidly expanding Jefferson Parish. Finally, like his family before him, John recognized that providing an in-store location for employees to eat—in this case, in the lunch counter kitchen—would save them lost travel time for lunch breaks.

Set apart from the major self-service areas, the lunch counter area encompassed 950 square feet. The lion's share of this footage was devoted to kitchen and preparation space, with the actual service counter only 66 feet long. There were no tables or booths, only stools on which to sit at the counter. Served by a staff of twelve waitresses and six cooks, customers would receive their orders then apply condiments on their own. Meanwhile, in another Schwegmann innovation, six "porters" were assigned to the lunch counter to recycle glass bottle returns—a task typically, and inefficiently, handled at the time by cashiers at checkout.

The innovative idea of placing lunch counters in supermarkets never really took off, with only a rare few supermarket operators following John's lead, and then mostly in a half-hearted or incomplete fashion. But at least the concept had some legs, albeit short. Not so with John's other innovation—namely, adding a bar to the store.[21] This concept has gained no traction whatsoever over the years. Yet there was John back in the day, following in the footsteps of his forebears at Schwegmann's Grocery and Bar on Piety and Burgundy.

Added to the Airline store in 1954, the new barroom was located in a "lean-to" style building set off from, yet still attached to, the supermarket. Open from noon until store closing, it featured a giant-sized wooden bar 54 feet in length, was staffed by three full-time bartenders, and carried a selection of over 200 brands of liquor. As noted, it was also air-conditioned—the only customer area in the store at the time to enjoy such a wonderful luxury. As would be expected, though, what stood out most of all about the bar were its low-priced drinks. Indeed, at 25 cents for a regular drink, 35 cents for an "exotic" drink, and 16 cents for a bottle of beer, Schwegmann's claimed its drinks were the cheapest in the entire United States. Naturally, then, the bar became a popular attraction for locals, who also used the place as an escape from the New Orleans' tourist crowd—a throng with no clue that one of the best lounges in town was located in a suburban supermarket. Given the cheap drinks, local camaraderie, cool atmosphere, and other enticements, patrons obviously would have been tempted to linger, or malinger, here for hours. To discourage such behavior, John came up with an ingenious solution: everybody had to stand! There were no tables, or booths, or even barstools. Under this unsteady condition, no barfly worthy of the name remained here for too long.

SO FAR, ONLY THE SCHWEGMANN-OWNED departments have been described. Considering that from 1951 on these were piled high with torrents of bargain-priced merchandise, the magnitude of which had never been seen before in New Orleans—and rarely elsewhere, for that matter—it must have been like entering the Emerald City of Oz when customers beheld the Airline store after its ultimate expansion in 1955. For by this time, nine leased departments had been added on top of everything else already there. No doubt John would have loved to squeeze in a few more departments if he could have—and in fact did in his next store. But for now, nine had to suffice. There was simply no more space available on the lot for further growth.

The almost unbelievable spectacle presented by the world's biggest supermarket at the time, bristling to the brink with traditional grocery store merchandise and now bursting with a bevy of specialty departments, must have been a dizzying sight. Perhaps it was like encountering some gaudy cultural efflorescence akin to the dazzling extravagance of Las Vegas, only just then beginning as of the mid-1950s to exert its seductive allure over America. Yet in looking back from a contemporary perspective, it is hard not to see a more exotic influence at work. For in its anarchic exuberance, the Airline store turned out to be more like a Turkish souk than an orderly American marketplace, with customers not so much engaging in a boring shopping run as indulging in an almost ecstatic consumer experience.

Of the nine leased departments, five were devoted to general merchandise, three to services, and only one to food.[22] Six of them were located inside the store, while the other three were set up outside. Most paid a fixed monthly rent for their space, while a few paid a percentage of sales. As a rule, each stuck to one narrowly focused specialty format, although a few burst the bounds of their nominal specialty and became something else entirely. In some cases the leased departments either extended into related services or engaged in unrelated side businesses. With minor exceptions, none competed directly with Schwegmann-owned departments. Regarding the service-oriented leased departments, two out of three of them functioned more as customer courtesies than as profit centers.

The most straightforward of the leased departments was the bakery. Located in-store, it specialized in bread and pastries, baking from scratch a hundred types of items daily. While the bakery could be seen as competing with the grocery department, the fact that it offered more expensive fresh as opposed to cheaper pre-packaged baked goods served to differentiate it sufficiently.

The five general merchandise (GM) leased departments nominally specialized in the following product categories: family dry goods, shoes, jewelry, radio and television, and flowers. The family dry goods outlet (in-store) mostly carried work and casual clothes, men's underwear, and ladies' lingerie, along with a smattering of home linens. Naturally, some competitive overlay existed here with the Schwegmann-owned dry goods section. But for some reason, John allowed this redundancy to remain in place despite its inefficiency. As for the other GM leased departments, none competed directly with Schwegmann departments. The shoe department, for example, carried work and athletic footwear, functional-type shoes not available in any Schwegmann department. Similarly, the jewelry department featured upscale-to-expensive earrings, necklaces, bracelets, rings, watches, and fountain pens, among other aesthetic objects not found elsewhere in the Airline store.

The other two GM leased departments—a radio/television outlet and a flower shop—carried unique products that in no way overlapped with any Schwegmann-owned merchandise. As such, these departments took their independence and ran with it, both morphing way beyond their original bounds. When one thinks of a flower shop, for example, what likely comes to mind is an FTD-type boutique specializing in flower arrangements for weddings, funerals, and other joyous and solemn occasions. This image bears absolutely zero resemblance to what was called a "flower shop" at the Airline store. Instead, this leased department took on the full-blown characteristics of what is now known as a garden center.[23]

Located outside the store in two separate areas, the "flower shop" was divided into small and large sections. The small section, about 800 square feet in size and placed under a protective shed, housed numerous "live goods"—plants, shrubs, flowers, seeds, and bulbs—along with a selection of fertilizers, pesticides, and hand tools. Meanwhile, the large section, measuring around 2,000 square feet and located in a roofless fenced-in area in a corner of the parking lot, contained larger plants, shrubs, and trees too far advanced in their growing cycle to house within the confines of the smaller section. This larger section also featured lawn and garden outdoor power equipment—gas-powered push mowers, riding mowers, tillers, chainsaws, and other power tools—just beginning to sweep the burgeoning suburban market. As can be seen here, John is clearly carving out the prototype parameters of future supercenters, with their all-important integration of garden centers into a total retail discount concept. Note that in this envisioning he was helped along by the New Orleans climate, which encourages lawn and garden purchases year-round.

Besides the "flower shop," the other misnamed leased department was called "radio and television." Selling what today would be classified as home electronics, the outlet was right outside the front of the store located between the two entrances within a semi-protective corrugated shed. From this less than ideal location, the department branched out far beyond peddling radios and televisions into heaters, air conditioners, lawn furniture, paint, wheeled toys, and lawn mowers. In this way the department morphed more into some sort of proto–variety store, with its selection of goods varying throughout the seasons. During December, for example, the radio and TV department sold Christmas trees from its outside plot extended into the parking lot.

The three leased departments offering services at the Airline store included a shoe repair outlet, a key shop (key-making and lock repair), and a barbershop. Only the barbershop was expected to make a profit. As such, it was generously equipped with five barber chairs, each with its own basin. Meanwhile, shoe repair and key/lock services were offered primarily to provide customer convenience. Since neither of the latter netted significant sales, both branched out into supplemental services hoping to make some extra pennies. Shoe repair, for example, offered shoe shines, while the key shop began selling snacks, such as popcorn and candy apples.

*   *   *

So there you have it: John's penultimate stab at grocery store immortality. In building the mammoth Schwegmann Brothers Giant Super Market on Airline Highway—the "biggest store in the world" at the time—John did not just anticipate suburban expansion. Much more profoundly, this premier retail innovator actually pioneered the one-stop-shopping supercenter paradigm that only much later came to dominate brick-and-mortar discount retailing, and continues to do so down to the present day.

13

SCHWEGMANN'S CRUSADE
A History of Fair Trade Laws

O N DECEMBER 20, 1949—AT THE PEAK of the holiday season, at the worst possible time—Calvert Distillers Corporation won a lawsuit in federal district court against Schwegmann Brothers for the crime of selling booze too cheap. When the judge slapped a preliminary injunction on John to prevent this dastardly deed from ever occurring again…well, it was off to the races. John immediately appealed this verdict to the appropriately named "Fifth" U.S. Circuit Court, arguing that the law forbidding the sale of Calvert brand whiskey at cut-rate prices was unconstitutional. He lost the appeal in early 1950. Without batting an eye, John proceeded to take his case all the way to the top, filing a strengthened appeal to the U.S. Supreme Court. In May 1951, John won.

Looking back from our current cornucopian retail era epitomized by the likes of Walmart, Costco, and Amazon, it is difficult to believe that a time once existed, and not so long ago at that, when discounting was flat-out illegal. But it is true. For nearly a generation—from the early 1930s to the late 1950s, and even lingering on into the 1960s and early 1970s—a legal and political consensus held sway across almost the entire United States that retailers should not charge consumers less for a branded product than a price decreed from on high by its manufacturer. Amazing! American legislators and judges actually agreed that manufacturers could and should set prices, even though granting them this power cost consumers dearly and undermined the spirit of free-market competition. In retrospect it seems like a bad dream: the inflated retail prices of everything from milk and bread to aspirins and appliances all fixed by fiat from above. Unfortunately, though, the nightmare lived and breathed, enshrined in law and sanctioned by the courts.

The legislation allowing this top-down price fixing was based on a legal conceit known as "fair trade." Not to be confused with the contemporary notion of "good" fair trade—which relies on moral suasion to justify higher prices, with the extra proceeds passed along in higher wages to workers in developing countries—the original "bad" fair trade laws were first passed in 1931 in the trendsetter state of California. From there they spread like wildfire across the country, the flames burning white-hot for twenty years before being checked in 1951, then only gradually petering out. During this peculiar period, retail price competition was effectively outlawed—inanely immunized from the clear intent of the Sherman Antitrust Act of 1890 because it only involved nice "vertical" and not nasty "horizontal" competition.

Today, the thirty-year era of the original fair trade laws is rarely remembered, much less discussed. It is obvious why. For who wants to dwell on an embarrassing past when an almost totalitarian approach was taken to price realization? Or fondly reminisce about what amounts to a shameful blot on the history of the American free-enterprise system? Certainly politicians, who have plenty of ideological skeletons in the closet over the fair trade issue, must believe the era is best left forgotten. Consider that during this period conservatives railed against big business, liberals supported fat cats, and populists were all over the map, gusting whichever way the most powerful wind blew.

One shudders to imagine if the fixed-price regime had been allowed to last. Resembling more of a rigid Soviet-style command economy than a flexible free-market system, a United States wedded to fair trade laws might not have won the Cold War against communism, as a vibrant middle-class consumer society would probably have never developed without the legalization of discounting. Worse still, an economic system permanently chained to fixed prices would have eventually choked to death on the perpetual oversupply created by the potency of modern industry. Indeed, while oversupply continues to persist as a serious problem, it would have been exacerbated beyond belief if inflexible pricing policies had remained the law of the land. As it happened, a few stout, irate souls resisted this state of affairs, managing to punch holes in the legal armor of fair trade, thus rendering the laws vulnerable to ultimate defeat.

Nonetheless, the war against fair trade laws took years to win. In the meantime, things got so bad that the newly emerging discount store retail sector—naturally arising from the imperatives of mass production—was forced to submerge itself initially in the "gray market," employing subterfuge to off-load an otherwise unaffordable abundance of goods at below fair-trade prices. Specifically, in 1943 semi-illicit discount "houses" (literally houses or warehouses) began to appear that featured products at below-legal prices. Basing their purchasing decisions on display models or samples, discount-house customers would order whatever quantity to be delivered soon thereafter— a method similar to the contemporary catalog showroom format. Operating sub-rosa, their whereabouts known solely through word-of-mouth, these proto–discount stores were little better than drug dealers in the eyes of the law at the time.[1]

HERE IT IS NECESSARY TO STEP back a bit, as several questions must be addressed before proceeding. These questions are fairly straightforward: What are fair trade laws? Where did they come from? How were they allowed to take root in the United States? But before dealing with these queries, an even more pertinent question presents itself: What do fair trade laws have to do with John Schwegmann? The answer is that, as a visionary retail merchant first emerging into his own in the years right after World War II, John began his supermarket career in shackles, imprisoned within a dictatorial pricing regime. To a crusader of John's activist bent, this situation was absolutely intolerable. So just as he had successfully challenged the anti-competitive nature of New Orleans' public markets before opening his first store, he now resolved to challenge the legitimacy of fair trade laws before opening his second store. With the details of this battle coming in the next chapter, suffice to say here that John G. Schwegmann shines forth historically in all resplendent glory as the St. George who slew the price fixing dragon. In the wake of his victory, the way stood open for the creation of the greatest consumer society the world has ever seen.

So what exactly are fair trade laws? In technical terms, fair trade laws allow states to set retail prices based on manufacturer-mandated minimum markups. In legal terms, the ability of a manufacturer to stipulate the price at which its brand is "re-sold" down the distribution chain is referred to as "resale price maintenance" (RPM).[2] In layman's terms, fair trade laws can simply be understood as price fixing.

So how in the world did manufacturers ever acquire the right to fix prices at retail? Why, independent retailers themselves granted them this right—in cahoots, of course, with politicians and judges. For in fact the vast majority of American retailers in the early 1930s demanded manufacturer-mandated minimum markups, and were thereby wholly complicit in undermining free-market competition. The whys and wherefores of how this twisted situation came to be are extremely complex, really requiring an entire book to do the subject justice. Here, for simplicity's sake, the factors behind the birth of fair trade laws are distilled into brief profiles of the historical roles played in this absurdist tragedy by the three major actors in the classic distribution chain: manufacturers, retailers, and consumers. To preview how these roles played out: manufacturers strongly favored fair trade, retailers split in their sympathies between independents (favored) and chains (opposed), and consumers strongly opposed fair trade.

*   *   *

IN THEIR NEVER-ENDING QUEST for ever-higher profits, manufacturers have since time immemorial sought to control the distribution chain to the greatest extent possible. Time and again, however, they have been checked in their efforts by government power and rival social and economic interests. The tensions generated in this process never cease, only wax and wane, depending on particular historical and cultural power configurations.

Modern attempts by manufacturers to control prices at retail first reared their ugly head in the 1890s, as brands began their near-universal displacement of commodity products. First appearing in a noticeable way in the 1870s, brands turned out to be such a capital idea that nearly all producers soon hopped on the branding bandwagon. There was a downside, though. For to apply the concept effectively, manufacturers were required to spend relatively enormous amounts on advertising and promotion in order to firmly implant both the name and the virtues of the branded product on the public mind. As marketing expenditures soared in tandem with the ascendance of brands, manufacturers sensed both strength and weakness. On one hand, the general power of brands, so evidently popular among consumers, gave manufacturers great confidence in their ability to throw their weight around. On the other hand, they were investing huge sums of money on positioning their particular branded products without knowing for sure whether they could recoup these investments.

This combination of hubris and uncertainty led to a fundamental miscalculation on the part of manufacturers. In the eternal competitive interplay between producers and countervailing powers, manufacturers at the dawn of the twentieth century thought they saw an opening to gain the upper hand. They would leverage the power of brands to demand legal control of prices all the way down the distribution chain as a means to guarantee a profitable return on their marketing expenditures.

This power play is seen concretely in several prominent court cases brought in the early 1900s.[3] Here manufacturers brazenly argued that their marketing investments in brands (and trademarks) established property rights that merited the holding of unilateral control over all vertical pricing arrangements—through distributors and wholesalers all the way down to retailers.

Way overplaying their hand, manufacturers lost every one of these cases. Terribly misreading public sentiment, they failed to account for the still incredibly potent reverberations of the Sherman Antitrust Act—a capstone of modern American competitive jurisprudence delivered nearly unanimously by Congress in 1890. In Sherman's wake even the tiniest squeak hinting at price fixing was treated as dangerously monopolistic and therefore summarily squashed. The final juridical word during this period came in the case of *Dr. Miles Medical Co. v. John D. Park and Sons Co.* The Miles decision of 1911 established what has since proven to be a nearly impregnable bedrock precedent—at least on the federal level—that a manufacturer's spending on branding does not entitle it to control prices at retail.[4] With the line here clearly drawn, it remained only to be smudged. But for now, over the remainder of the 1910s and through the 1920s, free-market competition, unhindered by compulsory pricing, was allowed to flourish.

Firmly rebuffed by the courts in 1911, manufacturers were bowed but unbroken. After all, there is more than one way to skin a cat. If the law does not allow vertical price fixing, well then the law must be changed. So directly following the Miles decision, manufacturers turned away from a judicial to a legislative strategy, lobbying federal and state lawmakers to allow resale price maintenance to be imposed by contract. Their first effort in this regard appeared on the federal level in 1914 in the form of the Stevens bill. Although supported by both manufacturers and independent retailers, the price fixing aspect here was just too blatant, and the measure failed.[5]

Undaunted, in 1915 the coalition supporting Stevens joined together in what was called the American Fair-Trade League. Boasting a membership of 1,500 manufacturers, 120,000 independent retailers, and 50 women's clubs, the AFTL would continue on for over fifteen years as a pressure group advocating in favor of fair trade.[6] It came closest to succeeding in 1929 when the Capper-Kelly bill, which legalized RPM by contract for the entire United States, triumphed in the House of Representatives but was defeated in the Senate. At this point, having ripened at the federal level, the legislative initiative for fair trade was harvested by the states. There, manufacturers achieved their greatest success.

IN THE 1870S, AROUND THE SAME TIME as brands made their first appearance, so too did the retail phenomenon known as chain stores. Originally, chain stores were collections of stores united under a single ownership and operating on a metro-wide or regional basis. Destined to become the nemesis of independent retailers, the chains did not cause too much trouble at first, as they expanded only slowly through select locales in the Northeast and Midwest, thus limiting their impact. But as the ball got rolling, and chains began to spread both geographically and into new retail classes—from grocery and drugs into general merchandise categories—independent retailers began to get nervous. Since it took awhile, about a generation, for the expansion process to pick up steam, it was not until a decade after the turn of the century, in the 1910s, that the first rumblings against chain stores began to be heard.[7]

Why were independent retailers so fearful of chain stores? Simple. Because they knew that they could never even begin to compete with the chains on price, the most fundamental of retail variables. Leveraging their larger size, chain stores could lower their buying costs and pass along these savings in the form of lower prices. Independent retailers just did not have that kind of clout. Neither could they match the superior operating efficiencies, managerial talent, or logistical capacities characterizing the larger chain organizations.

Independent retailers aware of the power of the chains were probably shaking in their boots right before World War I. Certainly a fear-based rhetoric began taking shape around this time, with the chains essentially being demonized. Of all the chains' sins, their most abominable transgression, the one revealing most starkly their diabolical nature, consisted in discounting. Listen to a circa-1915 independent grocer from Chicago vilify chains, as he lashed out viciously against those "retail octopuses" with their "damnable methods of killing competition through price-cutting." Even future Supreme Court Justice Louis Brandeis got in on the act, chiming in around this time with a tirade against "the evil results of price-cutting."[8]

In such a panic-stricken atmosphere, the first anti-chain legislation was introduced into Congress in 1912. Naturally it centered on price, specifically on restricting the ability of chains to offer discounts. While the impulse appeared noble, to level the price playing field for chain and independent retailers alike—a principle expressed by the National Association of Retail Grocers as "a fair price and the same to everybody"—the concept did not yet fly, its competitive implications still too distant from the anti-monopoly mainstream to be taken seriously. This remained the case in 1914 when the aforementioned Stevens bill was introduced.

Attempting to improve on the idea of simply declaring a prohibition on discounting, the Stevens bill incorporated a specific modus operandi on how to accomplish it. Within its proposed mechanism, the mutual interests of manufacturers and independent retailers first commingled, and it is where anti-chain and fair-trade efforts most strongly intersected. For Stevens attempted to kill two birds with one stone: hurting the chains and helping the manufacturers. It intended to accomplish this through price fixing from above, with the "producer, grower, manufacturer, or owner" given the legal right "to prescribe the sole, uniform price" of a branded product all the way down the distribution chain.[9] This was a startling proposition, one quite off-putting at the time. In the view of a clear majority, while chains may have indeed appeared threatening, the authoritarian solution of the Stevens bill seemed a cure worse than the disease. It was soundly rejected in 1915.

In surviving their first great legal challenge, chain stores scored an impressive victory. As it turned out, though, this was only the opening salvo in a long war. For in the aftermath of their win in 1915, the overconfident chains began to expand like crazy. Consider, for instance, that by the early 1920s the A&P supermarket juggernaut had ballooned to over 9,000 outlets. If it were not bad enough news already for independents that such established chains were multiplying like rabbits, they faced even worse in the mid-1920s on learning that the nation's two great catalog behemoths, Sears, Roebuck and Montgomery Ward, had also decided to throw their fortunes behind building brick-and-mortar chain stores.

By 1925, then, the power of the chains had become truly terrifying. They no longer merely threatened the old corner store anymore. Now the stability of the entire social structure of small towns and urban neighborhoods was in jeopardy. Suddenly under the gun of the chains were all independent merchants—grocers, druggists, hardware stores, apparel stores, notions shops, you name it—along with locally based banks, distributors, light manufacturers, and business-service providers. In other words, the chains threatened to totally tear apart the carefully woven fabric of traditional American society. As Texas Congressman Wright Patman part eloquently and part eccentrically explained the danger: "The huge chain stores [sap] the civic life of local communities with an absentee overlordship, drawing off their earnings to his coffers, and reducing their independent business men to employees or to idleness."[10]

With so much seemingly at stake it was clearly time to fight back. The only question was how. Over the following three decades, several strategies were pursued. The first direct attack on chain stores took the form of slapping stiff taxes on them, explicitly intending by this action to halt them in their tracks. Thus in 1927 four states passed anti-chain taxes. This number grew to seventeen by 1933. At the peak of the anti-chain mania in the late 1930s, twenty-nine states, a majority, imposed stiff taxes on chain stores.[11] Of interest in the current context, the state of Louisiana imposed the most punishing chain tax of all. For Governor then Senator Huey Long absolutely hated chains: "I would rather have thieves and gangsters than chain stores in Louisiana," he fulminated.[12]

As will be seen in the case of fair trade laws, the fiery defensive energy that originally fueled the tax-the-chains movement began running out of steam after World War II. By 1953, about half the states that had passed anti-chain taxes had abolished them, with the rest on the way. What is painfully ironic about this desperate episode is that the taxes collected from the chain stores were spent mostly to fund the very modernization efforts—building roads, bridges, schools, hospitals, and subsidizing a social safety net—that collectively represented the real culprit, namely the advance of industrial civilization, responsible for small-town America's demise.

To BRIEFLY BACKTRACK, if by the mid-1920s the power of chain stores had been terrifying, by the Depression years of the 1930s—when people were losing jobs, homes, farms, and businesses left and right—the chains' impact became truly horrifying. In the fevered imaginations of catastrophically affected independent retailers and diehard defenders of small-town values, chains came to be perceived in the worst possible light—as cutthroat pirates, as merchant buccaneers price-slicing their way through previously peaceful communities, ravaging economic livelihoods and pillaging traditional morals.

At this ripe moment, during the initial depths of the Great Depression, fair trade laws were finally passed in 1931. These laws resurrected that discredited bad old idea from the Stevens bill, the one imposing manufacturer-mandated fixed prices. In 1933, a whole new sadistic twist was added to these misbegotten laws—namely, giving legal credence to a blatantly unconstitutional device called a "non-signer's clause."

But before getting into the specifics of fair trade laws, one other piece of essentially insane anti-chain Depression-era legislation should be mentioned. This is the Robinson-Patman Act of 1936, which prohibited "price discrimination"—that is, forbidding manufacturers from selling at volume discounts.[13] Under this almost unimaginably irrational act, both large and small retailers were to be treated equally in their buying abilities, no matter their enormous disparities in economic power.

Almost needless to say, for many reasons, including impracticality, unenforceability, and basic economic ignorance, none of the stopgap measures adopted during the 1920s and 1930s—chain store taxes, fair trade laws, and idealistic legislation against price discrimination—halted the growth of chain stores more than temporarily. Today, chains reign supreme. The foreseen damage to independent retailers and small-town folkways has been done. Perhaps the lesson to be learned from all the unnecessary flailing about is not to focus anger on will-o-the-wisps like prices, or to scapegoat mere agents of change like chain stores, but to concentrate protest on ill-conceived paradigms of progress.

AT THE BOTTOM OF THE DISTRIBUTION CHAIN, below manufacturers and retailers, is the final player in the fair trade tragicomedy—namely, the consumer. With roots in the feminist movement of the nineteenth century, the consumer movement began to coalesce early in the twentieth century. Until the 1960s, activist consumer groups were mostly identified with female organizations—associations of housewives and women's clubs, for example. These distaff-oriented groups were by no means demure in their demands, frequently employing demonstrations and strikes to press home their outrage against too-high prices, deceptive marketing practices, tainted brands, and similar bread-and-butter issues.[14]

As a general rule, consumers stood firmly against fair trade laws. A classic study published in 1928 by the Federal Trade Commission showed 70% of consumers (and 78% of farmers) opposing the concept of allowing manufacturers to set retail prices.[15] Why? Consumers were not stupid. They knew from everyday experience that fixed prices meant inflated prices. As it happened, though, their voices were drowned out over the ensuing Depression and war years, as all-male anti-chain state legislatures went to bat for their old-boy constituent networks—namely, the independent retailers (91% in favor of fair trade laws) and manufacturers (73% in favor).

Once things settled down after World War II, however, the suppressed consumer voice finally came to be heard. Indeed, consumers, and particularly women shoppers, would go on to form an enthusiastic constituency in support of John Schwegmann's extended campaigns against price fixers.

RIGHT ON CUE, IN OCTOBER 1929, William Kennon Henderson—a successful businessman turned populist radio personality broadcasting a country-and-blues show out of Shreveport, Louisiana, on super-station KWKH—took up the anti-chain cause with a vengeance. Known for his salty language and vicious barbs directed at political opponents, this original Rush Limbaugh went suddenly ballistic in that opening month of the Great Depression, exploding in rage against the hellacious chains: "Those dirty sneaking chain stores are coming into your home town and taking your money and sending it out to a bunch of crooked no-account loafers on Wall Street!"[16] In this shrill manner, "Hello, World" Henderson, the prototype shock jock, continued hammering the chains throughout those early dark years of economic collapse. Soon joined by numerous imitators and fellow neo-populist rabble-rousers, Henderson and his ilk together fanned the flames in favor of taking even greater action than imposing taxes on the hated chains. Their propaganda worked. The first big blaze they sparked broke out in California in 1931. Chain stores across most of the nation, previously burned by taxes, were about to be consumed by fair trade laws.

The goal of all fair trade laws is to equalize the price differential between independent and chain store retailers, the purpose being to protect independents from getting crushed by the chains on price. Protecting this Achilles heel, however, requires violating the bedrock principle of the level competitive playing field established by the Sherman Antitrust Act of 1890. No problem. In 1931, the California legislature simply exempted from the Sherman Act vertical (though not horizontal) price fixing by manufacturers. Facing assorted challenges from wholesalers and retailers who did not agree that prices could legally be dictated from on high, the Golden State doubled down. In 1933, California amended its law authorizing resale price maintenance to include what is called a "non-signer's clause."[17] This unbelievable legal abomination, an obvious violation of the most elementary contract and property law—as if when your neighbor signs a contract then automatically you do too—nevertheless passed judicial muster in those twisted times.

Just to be clear, the meaning of the non-signer's clause is this: if a manufacturer manages to convince even one wholesaler or retailer in an entire state to sign on the dotted line agreeing that the manufacturer has the right to establish a minimum (or in some cases maximum) markup on its brand—easy enough to do, of course—then this single contract can be applied to every other wholesaler and retailer in the entire state selling the same branded product! In this way, the non-signer's clause represents a breathtaking usurpation of any volitional contractual obligation. Yet for desperate reasons, the totalitarian legal principle animating the non-signer's clause possessed broad appeal in those days of grasping at straws. So much so that the California model soon spread speedily across the nation. By 1939, all but three holdout states—Texas, Vermont, and Missouri—had instituted fair trade laws, with most of these laws bolstered by non-signer's provisions.[18]

This madness was compounded by both a U.S. Supreme Court decision and a federal act. In 1936, the Supreme Court ruled in *Old Dearborn Distributing Co. v. Seagram Distillers* that California's upending of antitrust principles was entirely legitimate based on a states' rights interpretation. The next year, 1937, witnessed the passage of the Miller-Tydings Act. This federal statute, which amended the Clayton Act of 1914, declared that all state-sanctioned measures allowing manufacturer price fixing were henceforth legal—all anti-monopoly considerations be damned!

The profoundly anti-competitive implications of the Miller-Tydings Act apparently made its sponsors so nervous that, according to one interpretation, they fumbled the ball.[19] Judging from later legal developments, this is true. For the Miller-Tydings Act as written was excessively weak in two areas: in its ambiguities regarding applications to intrastate versus interstate commerce; and in its failure to directly address the legitimacy of the non-signer's clause. Unfortunately, though, these weaknesses in the Act could not be fully exploited for more than a decade after it was passed. After all, there were more important things to worry about at the time, such as winning World War II. Thus while successful piecemeal skirmishes were fought against Miller-Tydings in 1939, 1942, and 1946, not until 1949 did a sustained opposition to this odious piece of legislation begin to take shape.

WITHOUT REHEARSING ALL THE LEGAL DETAILS involved, it serves the purpose here simply to note that two retail powerhouses emerged at this point to put the kibosh on the legal rationale upholding Miller-Tydings. These two powerhouses were mail-order firms and the person of John Schwegmann. The mail-order firms, beginning with a U.S. Supreme Court victory in 1950 and climaxing in the *G.E. v. Masters Mail Order* case in 1957—wherein Masters sold and delivered goods from Washington, D.C. (with no fair trade laws) to New York State (with strict fair trade laws)—essentially ended up making a mockery of fair trade applications to interstate commerce. Here the distorted logic involved in justifying state-level coercive pricing schemes in the context of a purportedly national free-market system simply fell apart. By this point, most important players knew the jig was up.[20]

Along with the mail-order firms, the other retail powerhouse that spearheaded the defeat of fair trade was John Schwegmann. Acting virtually alone, certainly with a lot more moral than financial support from numerous sympathetic merchants, John launched a direct attack on the constitutional basis of the non-signer's clause—a necessary enforcement feature of fair trade laws that had been curiously glossed over in the writing of the Miller-Tydings Act. When in its Calvert decision (detailed in the following chapter) the U.S. Supreme Court declared John the victor over the shaky constitutional rationale of the non-signer's clause, it looked as if the beast had finally been slain.

As it turned out, however, the fair trade monster had only been grievously injured. In the meantime, while it licked its wounds, a brief nationwide celebration of discounting occurred. Known in obscure retail history as the "Schwegmann Interlude," for fourteen months spanning 1951 and 1952, R.H. Macy and a significant minority of other department and chain stores joyously slashed prices for the first time in a long time below mandatory minimum markups.[21] It must have been an intoxicating breeze that blew through a merchant world previously incarcerated within a system of fixed prices, a zephyr scented with a sweet hint of the discount freedom to come.

But this brief interregnum was not to last. For in 1952, after swiftly bouncing back from the battering they had received in 1951, manufacturers somehow managed to ram through a countermeasure called the McGuire-Keogh Fair-Trade Enabling Act.[22] This ham-handed attempt to breathe new life into the quickly crumbling fair trade laws essentially said: "To hell with the non-signer's clause!" In other words, the McGuire Act simply bypassed any legal skepticism over the non-signer's aspect of fair trade laws in favor of bluntly declaring that all state laws regarding resale price maintenance were to be respected…or else.

In the blink of an eye, then, McGuire had seemingly trumped John's victory in the Calvert decision. The danger of the Schwegmann Interlude appeared to be over. Manufacturers were back in control… or so they foolishly believed. For in fact this ill-conceived piece of legislation turned out to be only an ineffectual bandage placed over a hemorrhaging body of law. For by the mid-1950s it was becoming clear to all but the dead-enders that fair trade was not only impractical, not only legally embarrassing, but actually harmful to growth of the American economy. With this realization, opposition to fair trade laws became bold and gradually overwhelming. So what if McGuire legalized state-authorized vertical price controls? These state laws would simply be repealed or nullified.

Hence commenced a period marked at first by a weakening and then outright elimination of fair trade laws at the state level. This process actually began in 1949, when Florida and New York poked holes in their legal basis. It gathered force over the 1950s culminating in 1959, when Nebraska became the first state to out-and-out repeal its fair trade laws.[23] From there the spool gradually unwound until by 1970 a majority of thirty states had effectively disowned the fair trade concept. The coup de grâce mercifully occurred in 1975, when the Consumer Protection Act explicitly abolished the Miller-Tydings and McGuire-Keogh acts.

The timing of all these happenings is actually quite profound. For it means that, despite appearances to the contrary, America's contemporary consumer discount paradise is legally quite young—born officially only in 1975. Before this it took more than twenty-five years of legal struggle to undo the constitutional damage wrought by laws passed in desperation during the Great Depression. To the degree that modern consumers have been blessed by the freedom of retailers to be able to discount prices, thanks and praise must above all be offered to John Schwegmann, who as an individual fought the primordial battle to make it all possible.

14

JOHN THE CONQUEROR
Making the Free World Safe for Discounting

H ow he managed to conceive, build, then run the world's largest supermarket while simultaneously pursuing an epic legal battle all the way to the Supreme Court is anyone's guess. Yet over the years 1948 to 1951 this is precisely what John Schwegmann did. By his lights, he had no choice. For he knew that his new consumer cathedral stood not a chance to survive unless the shackles of fair trade were removed. To this end, John seized the first opportunity to slip the knot.

This opportunity came in 1948, when the state of Louisiana empowered a newly established Alcoholic Beverage Control (ABC) Board with the ability to fix liquor prices.[1] Specifically, the ABC's Act 360 set minimum markups to be applied at both the wholesale and retail levels in the following amounts: at wholesale, 15% for liquor, 20% for spirits, and 25% for wine; and at retail, a corresponding 33.3%, 45%, and 50%. It should be noted that there were no fair trade niceties involved here, no contracts, no room for ambiguity. This was simply a heavy-handed pricing decree issued from on high by an authoritarian state.

Act 360, so utterly egregious, played right into John's hands. It was clear to him that the state legislature, intoxicated by the insidious power that flowed from fair-trade logic, had dangerously overstepped its bounds. Believing the law to be patently illegitimate on constitutional grounds, John simply refused to follow it. Moreover, he flaunted his civil disobedience by blatantly advertising liquor prices below the mandated markups. For this flagrant violation, the ABC Board ordered a suspension of Schwegmann's liquor permit. John parried the move with an appeal to the Civil District Court of Orleans Parish. Perhaps unsettled by the constitutional issues at stake, the appeals court issued a murky decision on technical grounds that found in favor of John.

Taken aback by the damage inflicted on its authority by this decision, the ABC Board fought back, appealing to the Louisiana Supreme Court. But this august body, showing no appetite for getting mixed up in such a potentially explosive issue as restraint of trade, simply affirmed the appeals court decision, which in effect voided Act 360. In his first battle against fair trade, then, John emerged victorious.

The ABC case, as it came to be known, transpired over 1948, with the state supreme court issuing its decision in December of that year. On January 8, 1949, in celebration of his triumph, John published what today might be considered a snarky justification for his actions. In his ad that day he remarked: "I think that 33-1/3% markup on whiskey, 45% on cordials and 50% on wines is outrageous, and I feel that the buying public is being unfairly treated when these kinds of markups are forced on whiskey retailers. Anyone who cannot operate his whiskey business on a smaller margin than that should try some other business."[2]

OBVIOUSLY OBSERVING THESE LOCAL DEVELOPMENTS with alarm, the big boys now stepped in. Where blundering state bureaucrats had failed, the national distillers would put a stop to this rebellious upstart. Thus in early 1949, two major liquor manufacturers—Calvert Distillers Corporation and Seagram Distillers Corporation—both charged Schwegmann under Louisiana's Fair Trade Act for illegal discounting of their branded liquors. John made no bones about it: yes, he sold at cut-rate; and no, he had no intention of following the law. Just to get a perspective, according to state fair-trade decrees, a fifth of branded liquor should sell for no less than $4.24. John, however, brazenly sold Calvert's whiskey at $3.35 and Seagram's gin at $3.51.[3] He broke the law with a clear conscience. For in his eyes the state's Fair Trade Act was every bit as unconstitutional as ABC's Act 360. His reasoning was based on, among other things, a close reading of the Miller-Tydings Act—the national fair trade "enabling" law that, as discussed, provided a veneer of legitimacy for "intrastate" vertical price fixing.

The crux of the matter revolved around the legality of what was then known as the "non-signer's clause." As previously described, according to this dubious doctrine, if a manufacturer is able to secure just one signature from a wholesaler or retailer agreeing to fixed prices, then all other wholesalers and retailers in that state are bound by this same fixed-price contract. John steadfastly maintained that he had not signed any such contract and was therefore bound by no such provision. Crying foul on this heretical interpretation of the Miller-Tydings Act, both Calvert and Seagram swooped down on John. The Calvert case came first. It was a slam-dunk. In October 1949, Calvert won an injunction against Schwegmann for clearly violating fair trade laws, forcing John to desist in his illegal liquor discounting.

Not cowed in the slightest, John continued the battle. In an ad from 1950 he solemnly promised to "carry this fight on to the highest court, not only for myself but for the benefit of the entire buying public." He was as good as his word. Taking his case to the Fifth U.S. Circuit Court of Appeals, John argued that, as written, Miller-Tydings contained no explicit non-signer's clause. He was correct. It did not. Indeed, this was ultimately its fatal flaw.

Be that as it may, John lost the case by default when the Fifth Circuit refused his petition for a hearing. Having been smacked down twice now in federal court, a lesser man might have given up. Not so John. Instead, in 1951 the crusader, convinced of the righteousness of his cause, dared to take his case straight to the top. Hoping against hope, his bold effort paid off when the U.S. Supreme Court agreed to hear him out.

The case—*Schwegmann Brothers v. Calvert Distillers Corp.* (341 U.S. 384)—was argued on the ninth and tenth of April 1951. Above all, the hearing revealed the Miller-Tydings Act as a flawed and weak piece of legislation. For various reasons, the Act had been controversial from day one. That it was unable to stand on its own and had to be surreptitiously slipped in as a rider to a revenue bill for Washington, D.C., certainly generated suspicion about its original legitimacy. These suspicions were only heightened over the decade after its passage when vertical price fixing began to be perceived by regulatory authorities as covering up conspiracies in restraint of trade. Given these suspicions of the Miller-Tydings Act—of its origins and its consequences—an air of skepticism colored the Supreme Court's deliberations.

On May 21, 1951, U.S. Supreme Court Justice William O. Douglas delivered the court's majority opinion in the Schwegmann case. It pivoted on the illegitimate application of the non-signer's clause. Without doubt, Douglas was correct when he observed that there was no such explicit clause in the Miller-Tydings Act as written. He noted that Miller-Tydings had had every opportunity to include one. After all, Douglas wrote, such non-signer's language could easily have been lifted whole-cloth from any number of state fair trade laws, including Louisiana's, that already contained such a provision. But for whatever reason, Miller-Tydings failed to do so.

Douglas seized on this omission, making the eminently reasonable case that, lacking an explicit non-signer's clause, Miller-Tydings applied only to voluntary, not compulsory, agreements. As written, the letter if not exactly the spirit of the Act was all about cooperation, not coercion. As Justice Douglas explained: "Contracts or agreements convey the idea of a cooperative arrangement, not a program whereby recalcitrants are dragged in by the heels and compelled to submit to price fixing."

The language was blunt, the decision unequivocal. On that fateful day in May 1951, the Supreme Court voted by a convincing six-to-three majority in favor of John Schwegmann. Although the minority tried to make the case that the non-signer's clause was implicit in the Act, their protest was in vain. Writing for the majority, William O. Douglas had the final say:

> The omission of the nonsigner's [sic] provision from the federal
> law is fatal to the respondents' position…. The [Miller-Tydings]
> Act sanctions only "contracts and agreements."… [In seeking] to
> impose price fixing on persons who have not contracted or agreed
> to the scheme, that is not price fixing by contract or agreement;
> that is price fixing by compulsion. That is not following the path
> of consensual agreement; that is resort to coercion.[4]

With this wave of its legal wand, the Supreme Court thus overturned the Fifth Circuit and formally dismissed the Calvert suit—and
by extension the Seagram suit, along with a half dozen other liquor
company lawsuits that had piled up in the meantime. The decision was
a shot heard round the business world, devastating in its implications
for the future of fair trade.[5] For his part, John was ecstatic. He had
fought fiercely and won. And in his naïveté he gloated, boasting that
in the wake of his victory all fair trade laws would henceforth be
declared illegal.

Poor innocent lamb! Little did he know back then of the relentless,
crushing pressures exerted by fair traders. Nor did he realize that he
was not dealing anymore with hometown mayors or state bureaucrats.
Instead, he was now going up against the combined might of American
manufacturing. As it happened, John was quickly disabused of any
such ridiculous notions about winning some final mythical victory.
For within just seven months of the Calvert decision, an even more
ominous obstacle appeared in the form of the McGuire Act.

For fair trade advocates, the Calvert decision struck with the
force of a massive bomb blast, a sudden and unexpected explosion
packing a wallop so violent that it cut the ground out from under
them. Appalled at the devastation, and perhaps even a bit humiliated
by their unforeseen defeat at the hands of an unknown maverick, the
manufacturers and their independent wholesale and retail cats'-paws
proceeded to pick themselves up, dust themselves off, and start all over
again. Rallying their retreating troops, fair-trade proponents quickly
cobbled together a new defensive perimeter, a legislative trench they
believed would be unassailable. This was the McGuire-Keogh Fair-Trade

Enabling Act, passed by Congress in July 1952. In effect, the McGuire Act thumbed its nose at the Calvert decision, seeming to say, "So the non-signer's clause has been declared illegal? Well then, we will just have to legalize it!" To this end, McGuire amended Section 5 of the FTC Act to exempt state non-signer's provisions from federal antitrust laws. Take that, Schwegmann.

But John was nothing if not resilient. As soon as he heard in early 1952 that McGuire-Keogh was in the works, he jettisoned his false optimism over the Calvert decision and cleared the decks for battle. For he now realized that winning a single victory, however decisive, did not mean winning the war. He had to prepare for the long haul. He steeled himself and took stock. If the war were to be won, forces would have to be raised, weapons forged, strategies plotted, and tactics developed—all in the service of sustaining a drawn-out campaign against his well-entrenched price fixing foes.

Thus opened a new chapter in the saga of John the Conqueror versus the nefarious fair traders. Here, a second phase of the war was fought, this one lasting four years, from 1952 to 1956. Epic in scale, it was waged against pretty much the entire drug industry. During this time, John enjoyed no success nearly as clear-cut as before. Nonetheless, he did manage to pull off one more brilliant victory.

WHEN JOHN FIRST LEARNED in early 1952 about a federal law being pushed primarily by the drug industry to legalize the non-signer's clause, he furiously sprang into action. In a profusion of editorials and press releases he pressed home his case against fair trade. In addition, he penned a petition savaging McGuire-Keogh, gathering signatures from store customers and visitors to the New Orleans Home Show. He even made a television appearance rebutting slanderous accusations planted by drug companies that his store's discount-priced medicines were substandard.[6]

When the McGuire bill first came up in the U.S. House of Representatives, John traveled to Washington to testify. He did not hold back. This "tyrannical" bill violated the right to make contracts. It deprived owners of property rights. It called on Congress to abandon its obligation to protect the public by regulating interstate commerce. And its passage would hike the cost of living by between 15% and 25%. These pleas, however, fell on deaf ears. The drug companies had federal support sewn up. The House easily passed the McGuire bill. In response, John published an open letter praising Louisiana Congressman Hale Boggs, who voted against McGuire, for his courage in standing up to the "powerful [drug industry] lobby."[7]

After moving to the Senate, the McGuire bill passed by a wide margin. It seemed John had lost the initial skirmish. But he had not given up yet. President Truman could still veto the bill. So John swung his propaganda machine into action. In one ad, he published the U.S. Senate voting results, noting with encouragement that both Louisiana senators, Russell B. Long and Allen J. Ellender, had voted against the bill. In another ad he called on the people of the state to write their representatives urging them to kill all bills in favor of fair trade. In a final lunge, he directly beseeched Truman to veto McGuire. In a newspaper ad he told the President that if he killed the McGuire-Keogh bill, John would gladly thank him by traveling to each and every state at his own expense to educate Americans on the evils of fair trade. In the end, of course, Harry Truman did not veto the federally popular McGuire-Keogh Act. Yet he did not sign the law enthusiastically either, instead expressing skepticism about its core claims of protecting small retailers.[8]

Remaining defiant after McGuire's passage in July 1952, John mounted a new offensive. This consisted in a well-publicized out-and-out refusal to raise his retail drug prices to meet fair-trade guidelines. It was the classic slap in the face before throwing down the gauntlet. Eli Lilly and Company quickly stepped up to deliver the first blow. In late summer 1952, the drug-maker sued Schwegmann for under-pricing the company's goods, threatening him with fines and even jail time. John did not budge. In fact, he outlandishly wrote the following in a 1952 advertorial:

> We take orders from our customers, not from price-fixers. We
> are being accused of selling some 2,000 "Fair Traded" items too
> cheap…. To that accusation WE PLEAD GUILTY to the "crime"
> of selling every item everyday at the lowest possible price. Our
> contempt for the un-American price fixing "Fair Trade" system
> is only exceeded by our determination to save money for our
> customers.[9]

In effect he was taunting every manufacturer in the drug industry, saying in effect, "Bring it on." Unfortunately, bring it on they did, mercilessly ganging up and piling on. John didn't know what hit him. Collecting himself after the birdies stopped chirping, he found himself being sued by fifteen of the world's leading pharmaceutical firms. It almost became comical, picking up the *Times-Picayune* nearly every day for a while in 1953 and seeing a new injunction rolling in against Schwegmann Brothers from the likes of Hoffmann-LaRoche, Sterling Drug, Colgate-Palmolive-Peet, Johnson & Johnson, Bristol-Myers, and Mennen.

Throughout this barrage John remained nonplussed, convinced of the righteousness of his cause and the strength of his weapons. First things first, he took on Eli Lilly in U.S. District Court for the Eastern Division of the State of Louisiana. He argued along three lines against the constitutionality of both McGuire-Keogh and Louisiana's own fair-trade laws. For one, they illegally delegated legislative authority to private persons (i.e., the manufacturers). For another, the non-signer's clause represented a denial of due process. Finally, John argued that the Supreme Court had already settled the issue in the Calvert case, when it deemed the non-signer's provision a coercive practice in restraint of trade.[10]

John thought he had an airtight case. He thought wrong. The drug companies had the juice. Displaying legal hairsplitting at its finest, in October 1952 the U.S. District Court found in favor of Eli Lilly. Curiously, in doing so it dusted off some of the mustiest, long-discredited arguments going back to the pre-*Miles* days involving permanent ownership of brand names. This almost unbelievable decision caused many a legal ear to prick up. John had made his case, and it was a solid case. In fact, his very arguments soon began to be used to dethrone fair trade laws across the states. For by now it was all too apparent that coercive price fixing did not have a legal leg to stand on, and it was economically deleterious to boot. As Burton M. Harris opined in a 1955 article in the *Harvard Business Review*: "Many economists feel these [fair trade] laws tend to destroy competition, breed inefficiency, raise prices, and cut down efficiency."[11] Yes, the writing was on the wall. Indeed, that the federal court could prop up its decision against John only by relying on the most hoary and flimsiest of legal justifications served to highlight that it was time for a change.

Of course, the federal level did not see it that way, remaining blind to the sea change in legal sentiment beginning to sweep the states. Thus in 1953 when John appealed the Lilly verdict twice—once to the U.S. Fifth Circuit Court of Appeals (which upheld the lower court's decision), and then to the Supreme Court (which refused to hear the appeal)—he lost both times. The Lilly decision stood. John was forced to back down and raise prices. He did not, however, take this setback lying down. In defeat he remained recalcitrant, running a head-to-head ad directly comparing the old low and new high prices and explaining why he was forced to raise them. He vowed to fight on and called on his customers to join him.

EVEN AS HE BATTLED ON in 1953 over the Lilly decision, General John had the gall to open up a new front in the drug wars, this time engaging prescription pharmaceuticals. He sprang this surprise attack after spotting a weakness in his enemy's defenses. All fair trade laws, he noticed, applied only to branded products. But prescription drugs were not branded, carrying only a pharmacy's label, not a manufacturer's. So while he could be forced by court order to increase branded OTC prices, nothing compelled him to do the same with Rx prices.

In a deliberate tweaking of the tiger's tail, John thus unveiled an ad directly comparing his own low pharmaceutical prices with higher mandated fair trade prices. This was the first time a retailer had ever published prescription drug prices in advertising.[12] The move was wildly successful, with new customers immediately flooding the Airline store pharmacy. Other retailers, and even doctors, across the country also took notice, and thus began a slow but steadily rising clamor in favor of lowering prescription drug prices—a chorus that climaxed decades later with the passage of generic drug laws.

Back in 1953, though, publishing prescription drug prices by name breached a major taboo. John's move thus quickly drew down the wrath of pharmaceutical giant Hoffmann-LaRoche, which sued to end the low-balling on prices of its prescription products. Despite presenting an exceptionally sloppy case—understandable considering John's attack had taken them by surprise—Hoffmann managed to win on a technicality in U.S. District Court.[13] As before, John proceeded to appeal but lost again, when in 1955 the Supreme Court declined to hear his case.

Perhaps at this point he began to worry over the trend of events. After all, since his stellar 1951 victory over the liquor industry John had endured only a string of defeats at the hands of the drug industry. Yet if he was nervous or desperate, he did not show it. Instead, John kept his composure and coolly sized up the situation. Despite his recent setbacks, he felt the wind at his back. For he realized that the feds were nothing but fuddy-duddies, still stuck in a Depression-era mentality. The real action was happening on the state level, where the whole fair trade can of worms had opened up in the first place. Much more in tune with the grassroots than remote federal institutions, state governments could see and feel the mass market soaring into overdrive in postwar America—and how their old fair trade laws were now damming up the flow of riches. Understanding this, John and his lawyers devised an extremely skillful and sophisticated strategy.

REALIZING OVER THE COURSE OF 1953 that he was being checked on the federal level, John shrewdly shifted the battlefield over the constitutionality of fair trade to the state level. He did this through subterfuge, essentially suckering in the plaintiff. This unwitting tool just happened to be Dr. G.H. Tichenor Company, an over-the-counter drug firm incorporated in Louisiana. In late 1953, John began blatantly advertising Tichenor's mouthwash at below fair trade prices, thus acting as a matador goading the company into filing a lawsuit in state court. Tichenor took the bait. In January 1954, it entered a suit against Schwegmann Brothers in the Civil District Court for Orleans Parish.[14]

The trap was sprung. Finally facing off with a drug maker on the more congenial playing field of the states, John swooped down on his opponent, attacking with the fury of a banshee. On the legislative front he trumpeted the Curtis bill (introduced May 1954), which outlawed all fair trade laws in Louisiana. In support of this measure, John lambasted fair trade laws in ads and organized a petition drive against them, which gathered thousands of signatures in his stores. But moving way beyond these conventional tactics, he actually mobilized a consumer army—organizing a caravan of his loyal customers, mostly housewives, to attend a subcommittee hearing on the Curtis bill in the state capital of Baton Rouge.[15]

Dramatic as this gesture was, the subcommittee remained unmoved. Schwegmann's army had had but one demand: that open debate on fair trade be allowed to take place in a full legislative session outside the committee's cloistered chamber. This demand was denied. Instead, not long after the disappointed minions straggled home, the subcommittee moved to kill the Curtis bill. Nevertheless, while this stacked deck of fair-trade proponents remained unimpressed, other powers in Baton Rouge certainly took notice of the potency of consumer sentiment on display—and later acting accordingly.

Meanwhile on the judicial front, John fought Tichenor through the lower state courts from early 1954 through late 1955. Echoing the federal trajectory, though, the tendency here was to lose his appeals. Facing defeat on both fronts, legislative and judicial, it looked like John had hit a brick wall. Better to back off than keep bashing your head against it. But John thought otherwise. Now was the time to serve up a screwball. And just so, John suddenly and unexpectedly entered politics. The only way to escape the logjam, he apparently figured, was to run for office and thus gain some legislative clout. So he campaigned for state senator, basing his candidacy on a single issue: repeal of fair trade laws. He lost, of course, though not badly, to a couple of well-oiled Louisiana machine politicians (see chapter seventeen).

Having come up short so far in all his legislative appeals, court cases, and now even an election, by 1956 John can easily be imagined as inhabiting the doldrums of utter defeat. But actually he was happy. His work was done. Through all his extraordinary efforts—his propaganda blitz, his legal and political battles—he had worked to stoke the spark of resistance to fair trade laws. Now this carefully nurtured kindling suddenly burst into flame. His nonpareil publicizing abilities and tireless organizing efforts had paid off after all, as the state finally bent.

Throughout the entire ordeal, fighting furiously from 1952 to 1956, John somehow remained optimistic. Despite all appearances to the contrary, this optimism was justified. For the days of fair trade were numbered. Since 1949, beginning with Florida and New York and gaining steam from there, the trend at the state level was to eviscerate or outright annul fair trade laws. John believed the same breeze would eventually blow through Louisiana. And so it did.

IN 1956, THE TICHENOR CASE finally wended its way via appeal to the Louisiana Supreme Court. There a miracle occurred. No doubt influenced by the superhuman exertions carried out by John, and taking account of consumer pressure and sister-state legal trends, on June 29, 1956, the court issued a unanimous decision: the non-signer's clause of Louisiana's Fair Trade Act was declared unconstitutional.[16] That was that. As Louisiana became the fourteenth state to reject the enforcement mechanism of fair trade laws, all injunctions against John were dismissed.

With this stunning victory, won only after slogging though many a defeat, John exulted in triumph. As he exclaimed in an ad, the decision represented no less than "Louisiana's D-Day...the day that the consumer in our state was delivered from fair trade price fixing."[17] Nonetheless, though John had indeed once again brilliantly prevailed over his fair trade opponents, his triumphal rhetoric was once again premature. Within months after the Tichenor decision, for example, the drug makers successfully lobbied for a legislative loophole that continued to allow for some forms of price fixing. Then just two years later, in 1958, John was at it again, this time staring down the barrel of the powerful dairy industry. So maybe the D-Day analogy was not so far off after all. For as it turned out, an extended effort to finish off the enemy would still be necessary.

Nevertheless, the major damage had been done, and, except for mopping-up operations, the long war against Depression-era fair trade laws had been won. John had landed two decisive blows in this war. The first was his mighty smiting of the non-signer's clause on the national level in 1951. The second was the more cunning knockout punch he delivered against the same clause on the state level in 1956. For his extraordinary efforts in the fair trade war, John Schwegmann absolutely must be recognized as playing a primary role in the creation of the universally charismatic American consumer society—a society blessed with the greatest abundance of affordable goods ever on offer from the horn of plenty of industrial civilization.

How John engaged and prevailed in the long war over fair trade presents a classic case study in the resolution of business conflict. The desired qualities he displayed here were leadership, tenacity, flexibility, and creativity—the standard clichéd virtues common to successful businesspeople. Yet over and above these qualities and virtues stands a certain inexpressible commitment almost (or in fact) religious in nature. For only with some form of rock-solid conviction can the courage come to persevere through crushing defeats when presented with only a slender chance at victory.

What set John Schwegmann apart was just such a commitment to the ineffable—in his case, an overriding faith in the transcendental goodness of common wealth creation. Empowered by this commitment, he was able to activate his superior abilities in its service. Prime among these abilities were his leadership and communications skills. He acted like a general, ordering the firing of volley after volley of propaganda at his fair-trade enemies—taunting, protesting, shaming, ridiculing, and threatening them in endless barrages of ads, public relations releases, and personal public testimony. To boost morale, he would announce battles, rally the troops, provide reports from the battlefront, and objectively announce outcomes. In victory, he jubilantly celebrated for all to see. In defeat he expressed both remorse and defiance: he was down but not out and will still fight for the right no matter what.

This seizing of the helm in the battle against fair trade garnered John a fanatically loyal following. Indeed, a cynic might claim that this was his objective all along. After all, it was clear to John that a lowly independent retailer did not stand a chance against the manufacturing elites unless he had an army behind him. So by keeping up a drumbeat of anti-fair-trade commentary, John was able to assemble such a devoted customer base. Leveraging the force of this base, John successfully checked his fair-trade opponents.

What is most interesting about the formation of John's army is how its voluntary participants ineluctably crossed over from being passive economic spectators to political actors, transforming in the process from consumers into citizens. That the legacy of John Schwegmann has been smothered has helped to bury any memory of this metamorphosis. Consumers nowadays tend to remember nothing of, and see no reason at all to recall, the political struggles that made the modern-day retail utopia possible.

In this light, John's army deserves a second look. The record shows that it was not raised for purely Machiavellian reasons—just so that John could get rich and powerful. Instead, he was motivated above all by a sacred striving for the common good. This idealistic desire is seen in two things. One was his solid allegiance to place: he never, despite what over time became his cosmopolitan worldliness, expanded outside the New Orleans metropolitan area. This demonstrates his fealty to authenticity, his faithfulness to a culture that functions within the limits of his personal understanding. This is a testament to deep feelings beyond any superficial business manipulations for insidious purposes.

John's essentially religious motives are seen most clearly, however, in court testimony delivered during the run-up to his Supreme Court victory in 1951. Here he clearly references God's judgment in an exchange with a prosecuting attorney. According to John's recollection, the fair-trade advocate came down on him like a ton of bricks, accusing him of brazen criminality for daring to discount prices lower than the law allows. "Who does he think he is," this prosecutor asked the court, "violating the government, the legislature, the law…and he's going to sell it for what he wants?" John's response, delivered in a classic "Yat" accent, went deep: "When I die, the Lord's gonna say, Schwegmann, what are you doin' down there overchargin' all those poor people? Do you think that's gonna do any good [to tell Him that I had to follow the law]? I gotta answer for my own conscience!"[18]

15

COLD WAR CHRONICLES
Travels to Europe and Russia in the 1950s

Between the conclusions of his first two major battles against fair trade—in the interim between his quick victory over big liquor in 1951 and the more drawn-out win over big drugs in 1956—John took a well-deserved break from the war. This much-needed period of "rest and relaxation" took the form of a one-and-a-half-month vacation to Europe. It happened between late July and early September 1954.

This trip meant a great deal to John. It was his first journey to Europe in twenty years—offering a chance to recapture the magic he felt there as a younger man. He also took the opportunity to invite along his father. He believed the two, father and son, would finally be able, amid luxurious circumstances and the pleasures of travel, to mend a lifetime of frayed relations. As it happened, the trip turned out to be way too strenuous for an ailing John Senior, who died soon after their return. But for John Junior, the vacation was a revelation, opening his eyes to political possibilities and inspirational business models.

As John demonstrated over and again throughout his career, he was a trendsetter far in advance of his time. In the current instance, this pioneering quality is seen in the treatment he gave his European trip. For right after returning home, he began, for all intents and purposes, to "blog" about it. Of course, he was not able to do so via the Internet. But he did have the next-best public communications platform: a full-page weekly ad in the major New Orleans newspapers. Within the space of this giant ad he proceeded to provide rich and colorful accounts of his travels. Appearing most Mondays between October 1954 and March 1955, the entire series numbered twenty-three installments.

On first encountering this long-forgotten proto-blog, the research-er experiences the thrill of discovering a long-buried treasure: in this case, an astonishing wealth of travel tales told by a precocious American businessman at a seminal moment in postwar European history. In getting down to the brass tacks of actually reading the installments, however, what appears at first glance as a dazzling treasure trove begins to lose its luster. For on somewhat closer inspection, the series seems to dissolve into a mostly mundane collection of typical tourist clichés and jejune musings. In other words, on quick first reading, John's "blog" comes across as a fairly trite travel diary.

Since the twenty-three-part series is so sprawling and the number of details crammed into it so vast, it really takes a couple of in-depth readings before the entirety is grasped. At that point, magical gates open and the true significance of the series stands revealed. For after moving past the first two stages of thrill and letdown, the series can finally be appreciated for what it is: namely, an extended meditation on the titanic battle then taking place between the "East" (representing the Old World) and the "West" (representing the New World)—an epochal clash known as the Cold War.

Of course, a case can be made that John's touristy itinerary was not trite at all within the context of the mid-1950s. Consider that not many Americans traveled to Europe in the nineteen-fifties. Only in the sixties and seventies, after the commercial airline industry took off, did the United Kingdom and Europe become major United States' vacation destinations. Before then, international travel was still mostly the province of the rich. Certainly, few Americans at the time could afford extended vacations lasting over a month. In this light, John appears as a pioneer in postwar European travel: a self-made son of the working class who through business success now asserted the privilege to take the Continental Tour.

John engaged this privilege with a strong sense of social responsibility. So instead of simply traveling abroad, enjoying it, and leaving it at that, he felt it incumbent upon himself to repay his customers and his city by telling everyone all about it—where to go, what to expect, and so forth. Thus the comprehensive collection of what today we would call clichés. Indeed, it could be said that, in the same way John Schwegmann created the template for the modern retail world, he anticipated patterns of future American tourism to Europe. In other words, what appears now to be commonplace commentary on European travel likely came across as rare and exciting adventure stories back then.

John's restless push to hit all the typical tourist hot spots on this first trip to Europe since boyhood can also be explained by his aim to go back there not just this one time but again and again. Indeed, in this he succeeded beyond all expectations, visiting Europe frequently, often annually, thereafter for the rest of his life. So in this sense it is understandable that he covered the prime tourist bases so thoroughly this time around. For it freed up future journeys for more adventurous explorations, deeper enjoyments, and more profitable interactions.

In its surface structure the travelogue follows in chronological order his late-summer 1954 travels to England and Europe, which begin in London and end in Paris, after swinging through Holland, Germany, Switzerland, Italy, the Riviera, and Spain.

In terms of content, five patterns characterize almost every one of his travel-blog entries. First is an attention to transportation. John invariably describes how he arrives at a city or country—by steamship, by boat, by ferry or train, by car or plane. Moreover, while lolling about his destination he is keenly attuned to all the odd types and weird modes of transportation sported at the time by the Euro-locals:

bicycles, motorcycles, motorbike/automobile hybrids, buses, streetcars, wagons, gondolas, even animals.

After noting how he had arrived, John then typically records his first impressions of a place. These can be of a general or specific nature, but they all involve immediate physical sensations—visually striking sights, the taste of food at restaurants, hotel amenities and aesthetics, the quality of service leading to comfort or discomfort. These impressions are often fleshed out with quick comments ranging in attitude from wry to dry, amused to displeased, and awestruck to caustic.

Following the registering of first impressions, the installment then usually proceeds, in no particular order, to describe visits to tourist sites, to provide relevant historical background, and to point out cultural peculiarities. The tourist site descriptions can be short and rote or lengthy and vivid, depending on his level of fascination. Often enough, John is dazzled and humbled by the beauty and splendor of Europe's art, architecture, and majestic landscapes. Yet for all this, he never succumbs to a simple-minded worship of Europe as somehow culturally superior.

With his judgmental faculties fully intact, John is able to both appreciate and critique where appropriate. The same balanced assessment is reflected in John's historical synopses. These brief birds'-eye views of a city or country's history, though often saturated in stereotypes, strive to be objective, presenting the good with the bad. While Venice, for example, had a glorious past, John sees its present as somewhat sad. Similarly, he paints Barcelona as a gorgeous city with a rich historical legacy that has now fallen into a relatively backward state.

In terms of cultural differences, John loves to season his episodic essays with descriptions of peculiarities. Thus sprinkled liberally and randomly throughout the text are observations on anything and everything that strikes him as odd—styles of dress, use of eating utensils, currency systems, legal codes, relations with animals and pets, entertainment preferences, and a myriad of other customs, habits, looks, and quirks markedly different from American culture.

These five patterns—transportation observations, first impressions, tourist site descriptions, historical overviews, and commentary on peculiarities—form the surface content of the series. Taking up roughly three-quarters of the entirety of the story, these patterns serve to knit together the structural skeleton of the piece into a grand literary vehicle good for several months of extended entertainment. Yet there is also a deeper layer to the series, a level involving business and economics— along with their corollaries in politics and war. This deeper dimension will receive close attention, but only later in the chapter. Here it is better to establish context by proceeding directly, without further ado, to the specific installments.

THE TWENTY-THREE PART SERIES opens with four consecutive weekly installments devoted to England. Collectively titled "As I Saw England," the four parts appeared over October and November 1954.[1] The first piece begins with an account of how John arrived into the heart of London via "boat-train," which deposited him near the fancy Mayfair section of the city. After checking into the historic Grosvenor Hotel, he proceeds to register his first impressions. These are mostly negative. The food is awful and the hotel facilities antiquated. In later years, as American overseas tourism blossomed, these types of perceptions about England would be honed into well-worn tourist clichés. For now, John made the best of the situation by rallying his sense of humor. He found his steak served at the Grosvenor "more boiled than broiled," adding that if there is no improvement in the quality of meat and cooking in England, "future generations will be vegetarians." As for the hotel facilities, John's impression of the bathtub was that it was so voluminous and deep that a simple dunk in the tub required wearing a life preserver.

After relating first impressions, the narrative juts off almost randomly into descriptions of tourist site visits, historical highlights and lowlights, and cultural oddities. Thus over the course of the four-part "England" episode he describes visits to Westminster Abbey, Hyde Park, and Madam Toussaud's Wax Museum, among other tourist hot spots; provides commentary on the ancient Romans, the Great London

Fire, and World War II; and chats in a sort of "golly-gee" way about curious divergences between England and America in such areas as spelling, monetary units, and fork-and-knife use. Then there are some cultural differences he understands and appreciates. For example, he applauded wholeheartedly the great patriotism exhibited by the British people, as manifested in a playing of the national anthem at nearly every social event, including movies. He also responded positively to their clear love of flowers, their custom of cultivating kitchen and backyard gardens, and their preference for purebred dogs.

Taken as a whole, the four-part "England" episode represents the purest example in the entire series of a straightforward travel narrative. In a superficial style it breezes along, lightly touching all the main tourist bases without getting bogged down in weightier ideological issues. This may have been the idea: to lure readers into the series with straight-up entertaining tourist talk before conking them over the head with heavier matters, as happens later. But even here, embedded within the mostly breezy travel prose of the England installments are hints of the murky depths to come.

For example, John will here and there slip in some off-hand remark on the British class system, social inequality, and high taxes. That he seems genuinely confused about how to resolve these issues—as a populist he was for greater equality, but as a conservative he was against extreme taxation (such as the 90% British inheritance tax, which John called a "death tax" decades before current conservatives)—is not the point here. Instead, the idea is simply to indicate the direction of his deeper thoughts and passions, which in fact always gravitate to economics. Even his somber commentary on World War II is presented in an economic frame. For in telling the tale of the terrible toll taken on England in World War II, he talks about the suffering of businessmen and homeowners, uninsured against Nazi bombing, still ruined and struggling with poverty ten years after the war. Overall, though, any observations with an economic bent were more like asides within the general context of the lighthearted "As I Saw England" episode. Within the totality of the entire travel series, however, these asides represent a foreshadowing of the more serious approach to come.

From England, John moved on to Holland.[2] Arriving in Amsterdam by ferry and train, John was immediately struck by two "extraordinary sights": the marvelous latticework of seventy canals and four hundred bridges that interlaced the great Dutch city; and the vast swarms of bicyclists. Proceeding to a restaurant, he was delighted to find, after England's dismal fare, that Amsterdam featured fine-quality food, and the beer was "excellent." Of course, while in Amsterdam he also sampled the Indonesian cuisine called *rijsttafel*—an endless dinner of gastronomic delights that can rarely be finished.

Over his stay in Holland John visited castles, churches, museums, and a re-created traditional Dutch village. He took in the local lore, learning about Edam cheese and Holland's dairy cow culture. He also found out that two industries, horticulture and diamonds, were central to Dutch economic life. So far, the "As I Saw Amsterdam" narrative has indulged in the typical tourist banter characteristic of the "England" episode. But then out of nowhere it veers into some seriously dark territory, when John suddenly begins discussing the Nazi occupation of the Netherlands. The invading Germans slaughtered the dairy cows, stole the diamonds, and plundered much of the nation's value. Worse still were the atrocities committed against Amsterdam's vital Jewish community, which was basically wiped out. In reflecting on such heinous crimes, John pronounces a guilty verdict on his ancestral homeland, seeing Germany as now carrying an "ugly stain" that can be erased only though atonement.

In this grave state of mind, John then passed into Germany itself.[3] Traveling by train, he went first to Cologne, followed by Hamburg. In retrospect, it is probably for the best that John was in less than cheerful spirits when he arrived in Germany. For his bad mood helped him reach down and summon a deeper critical awareness when he needed it most: right before meeting with some of the top-dog retailers and business bigwigs in Germany. In this encounter it was imperative that he retain a balanced assessment regarding differences between Europe and America. Ironically, his troubled reflections had allowed him to draw strength from his American heritage at the moment he needed to stand tall among his elite German peers.

Germany, the nation he most identified with but was most appalled by, was where John Schwegmann came most into his own, rising to the occasion of his journey there by articulating his most potent and enduring critique of European economic approaches and positing a positive way forward. He also took inspiration from this mid-twentieth-century encounter with his German compatriots to continue creating and innovating. For he had seen with his own eyes how blinkered most Europeans were with regard to understanding the dynamics of the mass market. And this paradoxically served to strengthen his conviction that he was on the right path. But the encounter also opened up future possibilities that John had barely glimpsed before.

After entering Germany via Cologne, Schwegmann takes his travel series in a decidedly bizarre direction with an installment entitled "Neckermann's Problems in Germany."[4] With this, the reader is put on notice that from here on out the innocent little travelogue will henceforth present serious, contentious, even radical economic perspectives alongside breezy tourist topics. As the series proceeds, John's economic views pop up with increasing frequency, sometimes taking on the character of lengthy diatribes. This tendency climaxes at the end of the series in a final installment titled "Europe As a Whole."

Before getting into all that, however, it should be noted that the remainder of the series mostly retains the basic quality of a travelogue, despite being peppered with economic argument. While in Germany, after interrupting the narrative with the Neckermann interlude, John continues to tell of his visits to tourist sites, his stays in top-notch hotels, his culinary experiences, and historical and cultural observations.[5] Thus, among many other things, he talks about visiting the Cathedral of Cologne, comments on how similarly seasoned German and American foods are, vividly describes the scene at a German beer garden where the people are "jovial without being intoxicated," details educational trips to a champagne factory and fish cannery, and boggles over Hamburg's ultramodern port facilities and shipbuilding capacities.

This same kind of travel discourse continues on for the remainder of the series. After Germany he ventures to Switzerland, where he indulges in typical tourist doings: visiting William Tell country and the Rhone Glacier; and traveling up to the highest railway station in Europe, the Junfrau-Joch. Mostly, though, he dumbly revels in the magnificent vistas of Switzerland: "There are no words to describe its beautiful scenery." His overall positive impression of the Swiss people is stated succinctly, if stereotypically: they are "industrious, honest, efficient, clean, and rich."[6]

And so the travel-blog proceeds through Italy (Venice, Florence, and Rome), the Riviera, Monte Carlo, Barcelona, and Paris. In Italy, his tour itinerary focused on Catholic heritage sites: St. Mark's in Venice, Vatican City, St. Francis' sanctuary, and the Roman Catacombs. In Florence, while he was overawed by its magnificent art and architectural splendor, economical John found himself truly baffled "by how the Medici could afford such grandeur." Meanwhile, he was pleasantly surprised there in "Firenze" when he ran serendipitously into New Orleans' own Archbishop Rummel in the lobby of the Hotel Italia.[7]

After dutifully visiting religious sites in Italy, John was primed for a more secular, fun-filled experience throughout the rest of his trip. While traveling the Mediterranean Riviera (Italian and French), his more sensual instincts were awakened by the taste of delicious food and the sight of beautiful scenery, especially along the beach. Here he enjoyed watching the first bikini-clad women in the postwar world strutting their stuff on the promenade, along with what seemed an endless parade of immaculately groomed pedigreed French poodles.[8]

Enjoying a short stop in Monte Carlo, the gambling mecca of Europe—a place where, as John shrewdly advised, no one should ever visit *first* on a trip to Europe—he traveled to Barcelona, Spain. This destination was dominated by his experience of attending a classic bullfight, or "corrida."[9] Indeed, John devotes a whole installment to this darkly memorable affair, describing in excruciating detail the crowd in attendance, preparations for the battle behind the scenes, the various actors in the tragedy (including the bull), and the blood-curdling, nerve-wracking feeling in witnessing the brutal drama. John ends this very entertaining entry with a pithy enjoinder: "Everyone should go to see the bullfight—ONCE."

The entire trip finally culminates in Paris.[10] Here John shamelessly indulges in quotidian tourism, visiting every cliché site: the Eiffel Tower, Versailles Palace, Montmartre, Maxim's, and the Folies Bergère, among others. Along the way he tours a slaughterhouse ("more humane" than in America) and partakes in a classic Parisian-style dinner ("three hours to eat, three hours to recover with wine"). While on the subject of restaurants, note that John found the world-famous Maxim's to be no better than New Orleans' own Antoine's, Arnaud's, and Galatoire's. On the other hand, he found the Folies Bergère utterly captivating, as he raved about the unequaled beauty of such a high-class burlesque show.[11]

Innumerable other travel details are packed into the four-part span of the "As I Saw Paris" episode. That the city's primary buildings were made of stone and lead, "truly everlasting material," and French law is based on the Napoleonic Code, the same as in the state of Louisiana, are just two instances. Yet at this point the trip is ready to end, and so is the series. All in all it has been an entertaining ride—that is, if you do not count the numerous digressions into the horrors of World War II, historical excursions into the complicity of German industry in Nazism, reflections on Mussolini, and a photograph of the entrance to Auschwitz.

As discussed, when John hit Germany he came fully into his own as an economic evangelist. He had seen enough of Europe by this time to start passing some serious judgment on how business is conducted on the Continent. Things were not looking good. He thought he had it bad in the States, battling the fair traders at every turn. Yet at least back home he had a fighting chance, and the tide appeared to be turning in his favor. Not so in postwar Europe. Here the fair traders ruled nearly absolute, almost unchallenged in their power. John found Germany "dominated by cartels and price fixers." Everything bought by consumers—"from the shoes on their feet to the medicines they take when they are sick"—carried an artificially inflated price. He found the same to be true in Switzerland ("plagued with price fixing") and

France ("fair traders get along fine there"). Meanwhile, in Italy and Spain the economic situation was so beyond the pale that fair trade pricing was not even an issue. Instead, survival itself was at stake in a system severely stratified between rich and poor.

John could have professed puzzlement by it all—the acquiescence to monopoly pricing, the surrender to extreme social inequality—but then he would never have become an economic evangelist. As it was, he believed he knew why, for the most part, Europe was stuck in a rut. What he did not know, and plainly admitted as much, was why the average European accepted a static, lowly social status, unlike his more restless, aspiring American brethren. He did, however, know businessmen, their motives, what made them tick. Here he was sure of himself. Standing on solid ground he pronounced a mean judgment on the men who ran European business: they loved their money and themselves too much. Sounding every bit the southern neo-populist, John thundered against economic royalty, miserly fortunes built up at the expense of investment in the bettering of society.

When John met with the German merchant elite on his first day in Cologne, he came face-to-face with people from the most advanced distribution sector in Europe, the ones most open to modern American mass-retail methods. Overall, he had respect for them but was not overly impressed. He found that while German businessman "have great ability and know-how," they are simply too self-centered to serve the interests of social progress. As folksy John laments, "Their interest in [raising] the standard of living for the people and their country is secondary to their interest in big profits."

Then he goes on to generalize this statement: "This seems to be true all over Europe." In John's view, the epitome of bad business attitude resided in France. The businessmen there were not only egocentric but actually held the consumer society in contempt. As John tells it, there was a general bafflement on their part at the incredible marketing exertions undertaken by American companies to understand and please the consumer. This just does not happen in condescending France. According to John, "It's unbelievable to meet someone who thinks the customer could be right."

Within this skein of generally negative assessment, however, John also found inspiration. Indeed, it is tempting to see two figures John encountered on his European travels as future role models. One was German, the other Swiss. Both bucked the traditional distribution system by embracing discounting. Both also faced fierce opposition but triumphed in the end through daring, creativity, and perseverance. Both inspired John in his later pursuits.

The German businessman was named Josef Carl Neckermann. Having adventitiously acquired a successful Jewish retail business under murky circumstances during the 1930s (a fact unmentioned by Schwegmann), Neckermann resurfaced after the war in 1948, when he established a mail-order catalog firm focused on selling discount ready-to-wear women's clothing. Taking a cue from Sears, Roebuck and other American cataloguers, he soon expanded into the entire galaxy of general merchandise, pitching all these products at radically discounted prices.

Naturally, Neckermann was vilified without mercy by the fair-trade European establishment, with even uttering his name considered taboo among the dominant merchant and manufacturing classes. John presents two examples of how Neckermann overcame such staunch resistance. One involved radios. Around 1950, Neckermann began selling radios at about a third below the prevailing price in Germany. The production side was outraged. Service shops refused to repair the cheap radios. Manufacturers chimed in by cutting supplies of spare parts and blocking deliveries of replacement tubes. Neckermann was forced to improvise. To get around the service boycott he created his own in-house service network. As for obtaining spare parts and tubes, he lobbied for trade liberalization (early efforts to establish the European Common Market), which eventuated a couple of years later in his ability to source parts from manufacturers in France. The discount radios, now firmly established on the market, became a huge hit with consumers. Free trade had trumped fair trade.

The same dynamic applied to low-priced refrigerators, marketed via catalogue by Neckermann in 1954. Panicked manufacturers, used to setting prices themselves in order to achieve predictable profits, immediately ran a smear campaign against the discount refrigerators. Their talking points revolved around the lack of service and technical knowledge involved in catalogue sales. Mr. Neckermann's rebuttal was plain-spoken: first, we do have a service network; and second, appliance products already have a solid record of sales through catalogues, so providing specialized knowledge is nice but not necessary for these big-ticket sales. Of course, German manufacturers refused to produce the cheap refrigerators for Neckermann. So, taking advantage of the emerging Common Market trade loosening, he outsourced their manufacture to Belgium and the United Kingdom.

What was initially done out of swashbuckling competitive improvisation ultimately proved to be immensely profitable. Following on the farming-out production logic he had initially been forced into with radios and refrigerators, Neckermann restructured his original women's clothing business into a pioneering model for global outsourcing. In this case, he set up primary facilities at German headquarters for research, design, and accounting while contracting out with thirty-eight plants around the world for actual manufacturing.

Based on the heresy of discount pricing, Josef Neckermann's company went on to become a highly successful retail enterprise. Some claim it was one of the main business entities responsible for the German "economic miracle" of the 1950s and 1960s, when an utterly devastated nation somehow rebuilt and a burgeoning middle class arose. Be that as it may, by the early 1970s Neckermann had become a major retail force in Germany, employing some 20,000 service-industry personnel. It began fading at that point, though, as its original driving force had lost interest. Specifically, Josef Carl Neckermann had by then begun devoting his passion to horse training. In an almost unbelievable story, he went on to win *six* Olympic medals in the equestrian sport of "dressage"—all this between the ages of forty-eight and sixty! His namesake business finally closed, amidst the usual acrimony, in 2012.

As noted, John devoted an entire installment to this innovative German merchant. Being a budding preacher of the free trade gospel, Schwegmann took away three primary lessons from the Neckermann example. First, he believed it proved discounting and mass-retailing methods are transferable from America to Europe; that they work regardless of culture. Second, the act of adding discount retail channels to the distribution mix, though it generates some uncomfortable levels of competition, is ultimately a plus in terms of creating a vibrant middle class. John's third takeaway, however, is less positive and more brooding. He believes European merchants *must* follow Neckermann in his abandonment of the fixed-price system. Anything less would be flirting with a resurgence of political extremism.

While John duly admired Neckermann as a fellow comrade-in-arms in the fight against fair trade, willing to take on the German business establishment for the sake of cut-rate pricing, he was more truly inspired by another European businessman, a legendary merchant from Switzerland named Gottlieb Duttweiler. Schwegmann felt a great affinity for Duttweiler, who started at the bottom and worked his way to the top on the strength of vision, courage, and indefatigable effort. He especially appreciated that after achieving success Duttweiler took a bold leap into the unknown, transforming his company into one of the most unique business institutions in the world. Whether he was motivated to do so by spiritual or practical considerations is moot. For in the end, Gottlieb's conversion from the standard business model to a cooperative approach served the Swiss people well, its lowest-price focus acting to raise living standards in Switzerland well beyond the European norm.

Like John, Gottlieb came from a solid background in retail distribution. As a teenager, he clerked for a Swiss wholesale firm. After working in India and other foreign locales for international merchant interests, he returned to his native Zurich in the late 1920s. Here he encountered a fairly bleak scene; yes, even in rich Switzerland. Prices were up, the economy was down, and people needed relief. With the $25,000 he had managed to save from his previous work, Duttweiler invested in a Model-T truck and a limited inventory of just five types of staple items: sugar, coffee, rice, macaroni, and soap. He peddled these products at a radical discount: a quarter to a third below prevailing prices. This simplified approach to merchandising, at the root of all great discounter strategies, proved extremely popular among the citizens of Zurich, and Duttweiler grew rich. By 1941, his business, by now expanded to include brick-and-mortar stores, was valued at $4 million.

Whether it was the trauma of World War II or some other factor that caused it, at that point Duttweiler went through an extraordinary transformation. He had tasted riches and found them wanting. He was a nonconformist on a deeper quest for positive fulfillment. As John puts it: "With characteristic disregard for the conventional, he decided he had little use for great wealth or good living."

So what did Gottlieb do? In 1941, at the stroke of a pen, he transformed his private business into a public cooperative. Thus was born the Swiss Federation of Migros Cooperatives, or simply Migros. The word comes from a combination of two Swiss terms: "mi," meaning "semi"; and "gros," connoting wholesale. Thus the sense of Migros is of retail products sold at just a shade over wholesale prices—the classic expression of a discount store business model. What is truly unique about Migros is that the traditional discount model is turned into a cooperative format. Duttweiler essentially sold off his business to the consumer, with each of Migros's 120,000 registered customers receiving one share apiece. The formula worked fantastically, with sales going through the roof, reaching nearly $100 million at the time John visited in the mid-1950s.

In subsequent years, Migros exploded exponentially, as its discount pricing policy cum cooperative ownership approach was extended into everything under the sun—including clothing stores, newspapers, taxi fleets, ships, sewing machines, book clubs, films, and adult education. How successful Migros has been in its infinitely variegated extensions is a question for future history books. Contemporary criticism has it that Migros has sold out, gone corporate. If so, it is just following general trends. Certainly no matter what happens, Migros will always retain something of the renegade, an against-the-grain business committed ultimately to consumer power.

Like John Schwegmann, Gottlieb Duttweiler was a fighter. In the teeth of tremendous pressure, he refused to surrender, and in fact fought back. When manufacturers cut him off for selling their products at discount, he built his won factories. When the Swiss press refused to run his newspaper ads, he started his own newspaper. When even the government started clamping down on the legal basis of his discounting, Duttweiler started his own political party! Placing himself as a candidate for parliament, he won, as John describes it, "by the biggest vote in [Swiss] history."

While traveling in Switzerland in 1954, John bonded with Gottlieb, spending a day with the great man. He came out of their meeting with nothing but the highest of praise. Duttweiler was "the most enterprising of all Swiss." By the nation's people he was "admired, loved, and respected." And in the greatest populist encomium John would ever pen in honor of a fellow retailer: Gottlieb Duttweiler was "truly a champion of the little man." As an aside, John also approvingly comments on Duttweiler's pragmatic approach to Cold War ideological battles. These battles would not be won by airy-fairy politics but by bread-and-butter economics. As John quotes Gottlieb: "There is no point in fighting Communism by pamphlets, leaflets, or speeches. The place to fight is in the kitchen."

IN CHOOSING TO SPOTLIGHT Duttweiler and Neckermann, John is clearly making a statement. For one thing, he is obviously contrasting their innovativeness and courage with the usual European business mainstream, which tended toward the smug and timid. Yet even more than simply contrasting, he is urging the mainstream to follow the rebels' examples. The system needed shaking up; new thinking was required. If these two were ostracized rather than embraced, if fresh approaches to mass-market distribution were discouraged, John foresaw Europe's prospects as looking grim again.

John summed up this negative assessment in the final installment of his travel-blog, called "Europe As a Whole."[12] Here the storytelling portion of this episodic narrative is dropped entirely. It is now time for the moral of the story, which of course is economic in nature. What he finds is a stark difference in attitudes between the United States and Europe. The United States is essentially optimistic: full of faith and confidence in the future, and thus willing to risk now for a better tomorrow. By contrast, Europe is basically pessimistic. Fundamentally it "lacks faith in the future." As a result, it is "ultra-conservative," only wanting to play it safe today rather than risk for the benefit of tomorrow. John is pretty much aghast at that attitude, as it has some seriously negative consequences both psychologically and socially.

For businesspeople, the prevailing pessimism leads to paralyzing attitudes toward self and society. In John's harsh assessment, the average European businessman is "not interested in the welfare of [his] fellow men," and he "will not risk his capital to improve himself, his neighbor, or his country." Of course, this lack of empathy and miserly psychology play out with ill effects on the body economic. "I want to remind readers again," as John says right off the bat in this final piece, "of the material differences between our country and most of Europe. As I have said before, there does not seem to be any great middle class, such as we have in this country. There are only the poor, who are very poor, and the rich, who are very rich." By John's lights, such a system based on extremes of wealth and poverty was not just tragic, because wasteful and unnecessary, but even dangerous. For it would remain continually vulnerable to what he called "ism trouble"—meaning it would be prone to the destructive seductions of communism and fascism.

Call him naive, but "Dr." John Schwegmann thought he had the cure to Europe's problems. It was simple: it needed to adopt free-market competition. This would stimulate the creation of a strong middle class through lower prices and stronger growth. Unfortunately, two formidable obstacles stood in the way of opening up the Continent to a more competitive system. These were big business and big government. On one hand, cartels so dominated manufacturing that they could fix prices almost without challenge. This situation had prevailed for so long that high prices were now considered the norm. Having thus internalized the monopoly pricing regime, business and consumers alike could barely conceive of how a low-price system could lead to higher living standards. As John put it: Europeans in general "do not understand the American philosophy of abundance and more for all."

Besides cartels, the other great obstacle to free enterprise was big government. European governments were notorious at the time for their outrageously high taxes. These acted as a disincentive to get rich. Why bother struggling when in the end there is so little to show for it? According to John, "Europeans are baffled beyond imagination why Americans work so hard to make money when so much of it is taken in the form of taxes." Thus caught in a vise between high taxes on one side and high prices on the other, Europeans generally have "no incentive to grow." As a result, a system built on the risks and rewards of competition had so far failed to take root. As John observes: "Free enterprise, as we know it, is almost non-existent in Europe."

In sizing up the European situation, John can be brutally blunt, but he also takes pains to be objective. He acknowledges, for instance, that Europe has some good reasons for its pervasive pessimism and risk aversion. After all, through economic depression, currency collapses, and hyperinflation, many Europeans found their faith in money destroyed. Moreover, whatever optimism might be left over after these disasters was polished off by the direct experience of total war. Taking these severe traumas into account, John gets a glimpse into the "I'd rather play it safe" mentality. Nevertheless, he cannot help getting the nagging feeling that the violence of Europe's travails could have been mitigated to an extent if some of the legal structures of competitive markets were already in place before the twentieth-century catastrophes happened. Perhaps a greater sum of optimism could have been salvaged from the wreckage.

By John's reckoning, optimism was the essential ingredient—the roux that infused the free-enterprise system with its seductive flavor. America, he believes, is imbued with optimism. It is encoded in the nation's genetics. The forefathers of the United States of America, the signers of the Declaration of Independence, sacrificed themselves in its honor, risking (and mostly losing) their personal fortunes and comforts for the sake of a better world. This faith in the future has been the "great driving power" behind not only America's accumulation of fantastic riches but also its universally appealing ideological belief in equality of opportunity based on hard work and merit.

In answer to European objections to working hard, and their belief that to do so is futile, John offers two responses. One is pure snark: "If our philosophy were the same as the Europeans, there would not have been any Lend-Lease, Marshall Plan, or any other plan." John's second response is more serious. Here he obliquely addresses financial and economic questions. Why do people work so hard in America if taxes are so confiscatory? The reason is because we have constructed a powerful, flexible financial system that is the envy of the world. As a result, whatever profit people do manage to sock away is secure. As John expresses it: "Our after-tax savings are the safest in the world."

In addressing the more general question regarding why work hard, John ends up exasperated. He is not at a loss for words exactly, but at a loss for justification. It is all so self-evident he seems to say. The United States of America towers over the whole world. We are wealthy beyond belief. The source of this miracle is our faith in the future. This optimistic mindset blesses risk-taking and encourages competition. Combined with our hard work, riches result. As John sums it up: "Our free-enterprise system is our strength."

Mostly coherent, but occasionally contradictory, John's tendentious critique of Europe's pessimism in favor of America's hard-earned optimism continues unabated until the end of this final installment. It is obvious that he loves Europe, finding it extremely attractive in a sensual sense. On the ideological level, however, he is basically turned off by the Continent's backward ways. His sincerest wish is for Europe to advance its economy by embracing free-market over rigged-market principles. Until that happens, Europe presents the perfect object lesson in what is wrong with an economic system based on fixed pricing. Moreover, having seen it up close, John was "more determined than ever to fight the fair trade price fixing conspiracy in this country."

BENEATH THE PREACHING, BEYOND THE AGONIZING over Europe's fate and the hectoring defense of American freedom, John completely and thoroughly enjoyed himself on his first trip to Europe since his younger days. Even more deeply, the act of travel got under his skin. He loved its luxuries, its privileges, the boundless opportunities it offered to satisfy his irrepressible curiosity, the simple act of being in motion to a foreign destination. In fact he was hooked, possessed like his grandfather by wanderlust. For from here on out, travel became a major part of John's life. Whenever possible, often on an annual basis, he would return to Europe or venture even farther—to Istanbul and Egypt and Australia, for example. He would also regularly visit New York, Chicago, and other American cities. Indeed, the passion for travel ran so deep in John that he continued his vacationing even after suffering a series of damaging strokes later in life.

None of these future trips, however, would rival for sheer audacity or historical significance his next journey to Europe, undertaken in summer 1958. This time, John followed the northern route. He toured Ireland, Scotland, and Scandinavia before stopping off in Switzerland, where Gottlieb Duttweiler had invited him to address the Seventh International Conference of the Green Meadow Foundation.[13] Then he visited, of all places, Russia.

John's junket to Russia in 1958, with his sojourn there lasting nearly two weeks, truly qualifies as "mondo bizarro" during the Cold War apex of this particular historical period. At the time, almost nobody went to Russia but diplomats, scientists, military people, and spies. A few businessmen also went there, but they tended to be top-level bankers and corporate types. Certainly Russia was far off the beaten path for the common American tourist. Indeed, in the late 1950s only the most intrepid of American adventurers put Russia on their travel itinerary. For who in their right mind wanted to journey into the heart of darkness, into a land ruled by the evil empire of communism?

Predictably, curiosity got the better of John. The more taboo it became, the more determined John was to explore the Soviet Union. He needed to get a first-hand look at the place that had morphed into our "existential" enemy. Second-hand accounts just did not cut the mustard when it came to understanding such serious matters as war and peace. Yet besides gaining a visceral feel for the primal foe America was dealing with, John had an ulterior motive for visiting the forbidding country of Russia. For in fact he was grooming his image for a future role as politician and statesman.

That he even toured Russia at all is notable in being highly unusual. But what puts John's trip over the top is that, once again, he "blogged" it. Thus a remarkable record is preserved of the epic encounter between an archetypal free-market evangelist and his state-controlled nemesis. The account of this encounter is available to all via the online archives of the *Times-Picayune*. The trouble is, almost nobody knows of the series' existence. To learn that there is such a record and then to actually locate it within the semi-obscurity of the newspaper's archive is like winning a scavenger hunt with a big pay-off.

Although it makes for some turgid reading when taken in its entirety, this series is the real deal, a true treasure trove of Cold War literature. Compared with the mid-1950s' "Europe" series, which tends to get bogged down in breezy travel details, the "Russia" series is pretty hardcore, devoted almost entirely to big-picture economics, politics, and society; entertainment taking a backseat. As such, it makes for an even more valuable find than the "Europe" series in that it pulls no punches. It is raw. It is direct and articulate: a literary artifact expressing the pure unfiltered perspective of a self-made American millionaire in his direct encounter with the communist menace when the Cold War conflict was at its apocalyptic peak

Appearing in seventeen segments over fall/winter 1958 into early 1959, the "As I Saw Russia" series chronicles John's twelve-day stay in what was then known as the Soviet Union.[14] His travel companion was George Pereira, the head cheese-buyer at Schwegmann Brothers and one of John's most affable, intelligent, and beloved friends. Together they visited four Russian cities: Leningrad (now St. Petersburg), Kiev and Kharkov (both now in Ukraine), and Moscow. They left Russia through Germany—specifically Berlin (first East, then West)—followed by a quick stop-off in Belgium for the 1958 Brussels Worlds Fair before finally going home.

*   *   *

To ACCLIMATE THE READER, the series begins with a basic overview. Russia, we are reminded, is enormous, its landmass representing "one-sixth of the inhabited world." This leviathan of a nation is governed by a unique system in which there is no private property. Instead, all the land, and indeed everything, is owned by the state. This is the essence of communism, an ideology that most red-blooded American businessmen, certainly John included, considered with nothing but contempt and filled them with utter revulsion. John saw evidence for the system's wrong-headedness and abject failure all around in a pervasively miserable standard of living and a general lack of ambition.

At this point, though, after laying out the basics of the Russian communist system—how wrong it is, and what a failure it has been—John reveals those character qualities that prevented him from ever becoming a rabid zealot: he shows compassion and understanding. He sees directly the pitiful state of Russian consumer society, and yet he realizes that, from a historical perspective, the Russian people are actually better off now than under the czars, who ruled until just fifty years prior. Yes, bad as things are now, they were much worse before.

The same tempering of an absolute judgment can be seen in John's description of Russian newspapers. There are only three, he says: *The Daily Worker, Moscow Times*, and *Pravda*. All are dreadfully dull, containing mostly only party-approved political stories. There are no sports pages, comics, recipes, garden tips, or other typical human-interest fare. And of course there are no ads, only "public notices." With John admitting that he, like other under-schooled people, rely on a free press in all its variety for "a liberal education," he is naturally aghast at the severely limited coverage of Russian newspapers. Yet once again, he sees some positive in what would otherwise be a total negative. Specifically, he appreciates the Russian papers' lack of sensationalism, their refusal to indulge in yellow journalism, what John calls "sex or murder news." This counterpoint pattern of finding praiseworthy aspects of Russian communist culture even in the bleakest of situations and most dysfunctional of institutions plays as a leitmotif repeated throughout the "Russia" series—though choruses of disdain toward the overall system tend to drown it out.

*   *   *

AFTER SETTING FORTH THE GENERAL PARAMETERS of Russian society circa fifteen years after the end of World War II, the series embarks on a free-ranging journey of discovery anchored only loosely in a chronological sequence of events. There are frequent interruptions to discuss such relevant topics of interest as Russian retail stores, Soviet education, and the role of women in society. There are also several extended digressions dedicated to the heart-rending travails undergone by various Russian and German businessmen over the course of WWII. What most of all ruptures the flow of the series, though, are fairly regular diatribes and screeds against the inefficiencies and dangers of the communist system. These seem to erupt out of the blue, and they gather in intensity over the life of the series. It gets so bad near the end that John figuratively begins yelling at American politicians, chastising them for their weakness in the face of a serious challenger—indeed, a mortal enemy.

Beneath these frequent rhetorical diversions, though, a recognizable vacation timeline can still be descried. Arriving via a one-hour plane ride from Helsinki, Finland, John's first stop in Russia was Leningrad. Here he and George stayed for three days. John proceeds to record his usual first impressions, recollects historical highlights, and recounts visits to tourist sites. Leningrad is actually a sprawling island-city connected by four hundred bridges and featuring a major world port. It is located way north, on a latitude shared with Greenland, and so experiences weird days and nights. When John was there in June, the night was more like twilight.

His general impression of Leningrad was of a decaying city that still betrayed the "grand splendor" of former majestic days. In his hotel, for instance, everything was oversized, fit for a king: the bed, desk, chair and lamp, even the ceiling. Decorative ornamentation abounded. When he went on a city tour, an oversized sedan seating seven drove him around. The streets were beyond wide, as were the sidewalks (twenty-five feet wide). A sports stadium they visited accommodated up to 100,000 fans.

The oversized and majestic themes climaxed in Leningrad's world-famous subway system. When John visited it in 1958, the deep and extensive subway system was utterly modern, its "coaches" totally "up-to-date," every station and car air-conditioned, the system's very construction an "engineering marvel." Yet this was not even to mention its surpassing beauty. The stations resembled fancy hotel lobbies. Made mostly of marble, they featured chandeliers, statues, mosaics, and marble benches. They were clean beyond reproach, and best of all they offered low fares. In regarding the Leningrad subway system, John had one of his mixed moments. On one hand, he had already passed off the Russian people as lacking in ambition. But now, on second thought, he was forced to acknowledge their grand aspirations and colossal accomplishments. He never really managed to reconcile these conflicting feelings of total rejection and grudging admiration throughout the rest of the series.

After Leningrad, John went next to Kiev, which in 1958 was Russia's third-largest city. Like Leningrad, it had been on the front lines of World War II and almost totally destroyed. Yet by the time of John's arrival, both cities had been largely restored—a tribute to the incredibly resilient powers then possessed by Russia in the wake of its costly World War II victory.

John relates two tourist-oriented things he did while in Kiev. One was to attend a 3-D movie. This was a straight-out, no-holds-barred propaganda film of the classical Soviet variety. The social-realist extravaganza featured endless homages to modern technology: machinery, weaponry, energy, highways, dams, oil wells, steel mills, tractors, and factory farms. It also showcased cultural advancements in leisure (vacation resorts) and ideology (stadium shows featuring hundreds of synchronized banner-wavers to show off the symbolic strength and graceful beauty of cooperative behavior). John was swayed by this movie, not so much by its message but by its method of presentation. The propaganda was cutting-edge and giant-sized. This approach could be exploited as a major weapon in the Cold War battle for hearts and minds, something not currently being done effectively by the United States.

The next tourist destination John visited in Kiev was a collective farm. The story of his getting there is fairly funny. Since there were no paved roads on the way to the farm at the time, and having been caught in a maelstrom, the bus he was riding in got stuck in the mud for three hours. After giving up on the bus, its passengers were first put on panel trucks then transferred to sedans. They finally arrived at the collective farm only to be greeted by a depressing scene. There were the defeated workers, the dissembling managers, and the overall inefficiency of the operation, along with its implied serfdom.

After Kiev, John then journeyed to Kharkov, an industrial city in Ukraine much "like Pittsburgh." Very little verbiage is spent on this city. The site of a huge World War II battle, Kharkov was apparently still suffering. John describes its "miserable" living conditions and transportation—trains with no dining cars and filthy toilets. On his tour of Kharkov he visits a candy factory. Here the sugar is made of brown beets and the shortening looks like "candle grease." The actual candy produced there has a "terrible taste," according to John. Ironically enough, as he is being chauffeured out of town, he sees billboards on the highway in Cyrillic, which his driver translates as "We must overtake America."

After the mixed messages from Leningrad, after the propaganda blitz of Kiev, and after the depressing spectacle of Kharkov, John finally arrived in Moscow, the capital of the Soviet Empire. Here he found "the most lively and up-to-date city in Russia." Moscow impressed John beyond anything he could have previously imagined. Yet at the same time it reinforced his worst preconceptions about communist rule.

While in Moscow, John was in pure tourist mode. So naturally he had to visit the architecturally fabulous Kremlin and world-renowned Red Square. There he joined the humongous crowds waiting patiently to enter the Lenin and Stalin mausoleum. Describing how the line stretched for five to six blocks full of folks standing three-to-four abreast, he jokes that they are all there to see the embalmed remains of the "gruesome twosome." Also included on the itinerary were visits to Moscow University—a skyscraper nearly as tall as the Eiffel Tower—and the G.U.M. department store.

What gripped John most, however, were Moscow's museums, which housed knockout collections of jewels, gems, and other amazing riches. Trying hard not to be tongue-tied, John admits: "I thought I had seen wonderful museums and art treasures and churches in London, Rome, and Paris, but nothing can compare to the treasures on display in Moscow." Exhibits featured artworks and royal objects lavishly festooned with gold, silver, sapphires, diamonds, rubies, emeralds, and pearls. In a historical footnote, John mentions that he also viewed the huge boots of Peter the Great, which the nearly seven-foot-tall eighteenth-century czar made himself.

When John left Russia it was almost like an escape. He flew to East Berlin, transferred to a car service as fast as he could, and was driven, after traumatic customs delays, across Checkpoint Charlie directly into West Berlin. There, even before checking into their hotel, John Schwegmann and George Pereira hightailed it to the best German restaurant in town and "ordered two highballs, pot roast, hashed-brown potatoes, a glass of German beer, and a dish of real ice cream." They were both absolutely famished after their trip to Russia. As John describes it, after being there for nearly two weeks, his appetite diminished due to the poor quality of the available food—to the point that all he wanted to eat were hard-boiled eggs. He humorously proposes that all those in American desiring to reduce their weight visit Russia as a dietary destination.

In his quick in-and-out through the two halves of Berlin, John is taken aback by the contrast: "so great that one can hardly believe it." The East is a haunted ghost town—"dark," "dreary," "discouraging looking." Meanwhile, West Berlin is a consumer paradise. The streets are brightly lit. The shops are filled with customers and goods. There is a plenitude of fine foods, luxury cars, and fancy women. Yes, no doubt about it. The West was far superior in satisfying material needs and wants. But whether it was better at satisfying deeper desires was still an open and anxiety-ridden question.

One area in which the West was clearly superior was in retail distribution. John grimaced and worse in his critical descriptions of Russian stores of the Soviet era. As a food merchant, he found Russian grocery outlets to be beyond abysmal. There was nothing comparable to supermarkets, only miserable food stores so dismal in appearance that in America "you'd have to be almost starving to go in." Over there, however, these forbidding-looking stores were shopped by hundreds of customers, all waiting hours in line to get in. When they had accomplished this objective, they encountered the barest of inventory and the most mediocre of quality. There was little in the way of fresh, canned, or frozen produce. Instead, most foods in Russian stores were sold in bulk form: "like our markets fifty years ago," says John, though "truthfully, not as advanced." Certainly, Russia's top-down distribution dysfunction during the Soviet era proved to be an absolute nightmare. People would line up at 6:30 in the morning for a store that opened at 10:00. They would be standing there "with a sauerkraut pail, a milk pail, and a basket" to carry their groceries home. The entire process sometimes took so long that the shopper had to come back the next day.

To the extent that John was appalled by Russian retailing, he felt almost the opposite about Russian education. Impressed by its difficult, demanding curriculum and the well-behaved discipline it instilled in its students, he expressed admiration for how the education system had lifted a vast illiterate peasantry out of medieval backwardness into modern scientific enlightenment in just a couple of generations. He explains that the communists had placed a great value on this process of educating the masses, and they had pretty well succeeded.

Just like in American elementary schools, reading, writing, and arithmetic were taught in their Russian counterparts. Where the two systems diverged was in their treatment of science and technology, which Russian schools emphasized. For example, both boys and girls in Russia learned in elementary school about electricity and machinery. John notes sardonically that, while American kids learn how to drive a car, Russian children learn how to take the car motor apart and put it back together again. Language study emphasis also separated the rival educational systems. This is understandable, as dozens of ethnic minorities coexisted in the former Soviet Union, all speaking different tongues. In response, schools were set up for each major ethnic group, with a total of sixty-two languages taught throughout the Russian educational system.

Much more is said about Russian education: about its top-down uniformity; the process it uses to weed out future workers from the intellectuals, its specialized university system, and so forth. All in all, John likes what he sees. So much so that he perceives promise in the great Soviet educational experiment. For he foresees that a population taught to think, and for whom knowledge is valued, will sooner rather than later figure out how to throw off the totalitarian yoke that enslaves their brainwashed communist minds.

AFTER STORES AND SCHOOLS, John's attention was particularly drawn to Russian women, although not for the typical reasons. He does not talk about how attractive or alluring they are. Instead, what amazes him is how ordinary they appear, how utilitarian they look. His tour guide in Leningrad is the most elegantly appointed woman he encounters. Otherwise he sees no stylish clothes, no makeup, or fancy hairdos. As his trip progresses, John soon discovers the reason behind this general female "dressing-down" phenomenon—namely, that most Russian women worked blue-collar jobs requiring hard physical labor. To a middle-aged American white male traveling in the late 1950s, this hardcore feminist scene must have shaken his tree, seeing women working in every traditionally male-dominated occupation: bricklayer, ditch digger, construction worker, road builder, port stevedore, welder, bulldozer driver, railroad engineer, streetcar conductor, and more.

John enthusiastically tells the story of the all-female teams who clean Moscow's streets. Working from early to late, from five in the morning to ten at night, these women clean the city's streets thoroughly throughout every nook and cranny, even crawling in and out of "manholes" to make sure the avenues are immaculate. John exclaims that Russian city streets are "the cleanest streets I have ever seen." He exults that there is "not as much as a cigarette butt in the gutter"—comparing this disgustedly with his hometown of New Orleans, where trash and litter are carelessly tossed about everywhere.

Continuing on in his feminist education, John is exposed to progressive models of maternal benefits. Since Russia encouraged childbirth for demographic reasons, it offered generous government bonuses for every baby born, and it granted extended childcare leave—three months or more, with full pay and job guarantee. Following the same logic, Russia gave a special shout-out to women who had ten children or more. These were awarded a state medal inducting them into the "Soviet Order of Motherhood Glory."

AT THIS POINT, JOHN IS FINISHED with preliminaries. He is done trying to diplomatically deliver politically correct tourist observations. By now he has visited four Russian cities and formed a firm basis for his opinions. It is time to engage the ideological enemy directly. And make no mistake: despite any admirable qualities Russia may possess in terms of education or women's rights, its ideology of communism was absolutely tyrannical, wicked to the core. There was no doubt about it: the Russian communists were evil and needed to be defeated.

Interesting in all this is how, after visiting Russia, John's previous opinions on Europe suddenly shifted into reverse. Furiously backpedaling, he now sees the light. Europe is no longer a hidebound, stagnant continent in thrall to the worst of the price fixers. Rather it is instead a paragon of dynamism, a place "bulging with shops" and bustling with consumer activity. In mean contrast, as John now sees it, evil Russia contains no competition, no innovation, no ambition, no individual initiative. Human progress is thwarted here. "Everybody [is] just another cog in the wheel." Until this changes, Russia is doomed to a meager existence. As John explains: "Under communism, individual free-thinking has no place. Free enterprise, individuals profiting from their own mistakes, is the reason for our high standard of living."

With his mind totally made up in rejecting communism, John still does his best to retain at least some kind of open approach toward the hated ideology. He recounts a couple of friendly back-and-forth arguments he had with his Russian tour guides. These people, of course, were paid propagandists, programmed with built-in criticisms of American capitalism. Thus they occasionally challenge him, and John is objective enough to record their protestations. They ask some genuinely tough questions. For instance, what about unemployment, and its attendant stress and insecurity? They also ask about oversupply: Since there is no central control over production, does the inevitable surplus simply go to waste?

Unexpectedly, Mr. Free Enterprise's answers to these central questions are pretty feeble. Responding to the first query, he answers with an unenthusiastic discussion of unemployment insurance, which he actually has misgivings about as a state-run entitlement program. Regarding oversupply he offers some lame chatter about how prices are reduced on surplus goods, which takes care of overproduction. He does have a snappy comeback, though, for one Russian criticism of America: that the United States sees an excessive number of traffic accidents. John's reply: You would too if your citizens could afford to buy cars. And so continued the thrust and riposte of ideological fencing between Soviet tour guides and patriotic American John.

But in one case, John offered no response. Whether he thought the critique preposterous or contained some merit is not known. The case involved a poll taken of Russian and American children. In America, 70% of girls wanted to grow up to be movie stars, while nearly 100% of boys wanted to be rich businessmen. By contrast, Russian girls were split on wanting to be doctors, nurses, and teachers, while most boys wanted to be scientists. Clearly, said the tour guide, the poll shows how frivolous and selfish are the underlying values of the American capitalist system.

They could hit on him all they wanted, but nothing was going to make John change his mind. Communism was simply irrational and dysfunctional, he thought, plagued to the core by inefficiency and error. In some cases, his purely visceral response to communism left him tied in knots of contradiction. For instance, he had earlier praised to high heaven the battalions of female street sweepers who kept Russia's cities sparkling clean. Later, however, in his denunciation of communist inefficiency, he rails against the human street sweepers, arguing that mechanical sweeping machines should replace them.

Around halfway through the "As I Saw Russia" series, the narrative begins to take on a dark and ominous tone. There are several stories told about businessmen John encountered—a supermarket architect, the head of a cheese conglomerate, a major resin manufacturer, and a leading fish importer—who wound up getting caught up in the meat-grinder of World War II. All suffered unutterable falls from grace: losing their businesses through arbitrary rule changes and confiscations; suffering the horrors of war on the battlefields and in concentration camps; experiencing starvation, torture, and long years of exile after the war. These men were all major business players, achieving the epitome of success before the war. That they lived to tell the horrible tale gives some room for hope, though their stories remain frightening.

By the time John winds up the "Russia" series, he is exhibiting not a little hysteria and paranoia. For he has begun to glimpse a larger truth: that it is not just communism and fascism but all state-controlled extremisms that are to be feared and guarded against. These "isms" dangle the promise of security at the price of freedom, an age-old technique known to every hunter and angler. We must not succumb to them, John implores.

With John's revelation about extremism, the "Russia" series becomes slightly unhinged as he begins flirting with a politics similar to that on offer at the time from the John Birch Society—itself a form of extremism. Following mainstream thought, he saw Russia as out to subvert America and the entire capitalist system. But where John veered into pure paranoia was in perceiving postwar U.S. presidents as borderline treasonous. Roosevelt comes in for the most blistering attacks, accused of selling out U.S. interests at the 1945 Yalta Conference, among other injurious misdeeds. But Truman and Eisenhower also come under the gun. All three presidents displayed weakness, naïveté, and indecision when strength, wisdom, and resolve were called for.

Especially coming under withering criticism was America's flaccid, vacillating response to the Berlin crisis—a hot-button issue in the late 1950s. What made matters worse was that postwar presidents were becoming ever more powerful, successfully asserting and enhancing executive power in the institutional scheme of things. This power grab threatened the traditional balance between the three branches of U.S. government. John worried that the Constitution itself was being abandoned.

Taken as a whole, the entire seventeen-part "As I Saw Russia" series is a remarkable document. What must be remembered is that it all appeared in the context of supermarket advertising—each episode plopped right there on top or in the middle of a full-page ad featuring everything from baby racks of lamb, cans of asparagus spears, women's blouses, and lawnmowers. Yes, right there within the contours of a newspaper supermarket ad the average consumer was treated to mountainous amounts of controversial commentary. Today it would be beyond belief for any respectable businessman to attach his name to such flagrant celebrations of contentious expression. It is just not done.

THE "RUSSIA" SERIES ENDS on a jarring note. John concludes his trip by flying from West Berlin to Brussels, Belgium. There he attends the World's Fair of 1958, where he is considerably frustrated. The Russians have a magnificent display, while America's is way sub-par. For example, where the Russians featured a model of Sputnik and intercontinental missiles, the United States displayed a spinning wheel from the colonial days, along with other inconsequential items. John was beside himself: what a half-baked exhibit! Having just come from Soviet Russia, he realized how high the ideological stakes were. If we could not win the war of ideas, then we might as well kiss goodbye to future victory. As John warns: "I am only a supermarket operator, but in my opinion if the same persons who made the decisions on what we should display [at the 1958 World's Fair] should have to fight our hot and cold wars, we will lose both."

Of course John being John, he goes on to recommend what the ideal U.S. display would be at the Brussels World's Fair of 1958. It would feature "planes, speedboats, automobiles, a supermarket, a department store, a ranch-type house, road-building machinery, farm equipment, trucks, one of the coaches of our streamlined trains, and one of our new Greyhound Buses...moving pictures of the constant activity in America, showing new products, machinery, buildings, hotels, motels, all provided by the free enterprise system." In the very last sentence of the "Russia" series, John justifies why extraordinary efforts are needed in the propaganda wars: "If every tenth Russian knows what our free enterprise system has given us...the chances of war between their country and ours would be greatly lessened."

16

EPITOME IN GENTILLY
"The Biggest Store in the World"

Aᴄᴛᴇʀ ᴡɪɴɴɪɴɢ ʜɪꜱ ꜱᴇᴄᴏɴᴅ ꜰᴀɪʀ ᴛʀᴀᴅᴇ ʙᴀᴛᴛʟᴇ in 1956, John Schwegmann prepared to ascend. For by then, with his two successful stores providing the propulsion, he was able and confident and inspired enough to rocket beyond the known world. With this journey into the vastness of space, John made retail history, and it is only right that he should be immortalized as a result.

Instead, Schwegmann's creation of a climax retail model has been all but booted from the history books. The silence that engulfs John's supreme achievement—building the first-ever colossal-scale hypermarket in a major U.S. city, a full generation ahead of Sam Walton—is bewildering. This is especially so considering that in Schwegmann hands the ascension into elephantine proportion managed to sustain itself on a profitable basis for nearly four decades, from 1957 to 1995.[1] Under Walton's guidance, by contrast, the hypermarket concept fizzled in less than half a dozen years.

The impetus for John's tour-de-force store is said to have come from deLesseps Story "Chep" Morrison, New Orleans' progressive-minded postwar mayor. As the legend goes, during a friendly encounter occurring sometime in the mid-1950s, Chep good-naturedly jibed John about getting too cozy with Jefferson Parish and forgetting his roots. After flattering the great merchant by acknowledging that he had created the greatest supermarket in the world, Schwegmann's Airline store, the mayor went on to lament that this store was sucking the lifeblood out of the Orleans Parish tax base. Having so far finessed the issue, Chep then confronted John point-blank: How about doing something similar for us over here, where you were born and raised?[2]

It is difficult to believe that John did not take this challenge deeply to heart. After all, ever since the Airline store opening in 1950, he had moved both physically and emotionally far beyond his native Bywater stomping grounds. For all intents and purposes, he had now transferred his allegiance from the city to the suburbs. Perhaps he felt guilty over this, as he himself embodied the insidious process of white flight and urban decay. In a less sentimental interpretation, however, he simply perceived in Morrison's plea a unique opportunity to plant another need-to-see-to-believe supermarket on a prime flank of New Orleans' expansionary frontier.

WHATEVER IT WAS THAT INSPIRED HIM, John proceeded to build a store for the ages in the Gentilly neighborhood of New Orleans. It was an oh-my-god type of structure whose hyperbolic size and jaw-dropping spaciousness is best expressed in bursting magnitudes. The mammoth store spanned more than five football fields. Its geographical footprint inhabited an area equaling three square city blocks. It contained nearly a mile of merchandise display shelving. Over 20,000 cubic yards of concrete (not including the parking lot and outside pavement) were used in its construction, along with 50 miles of metal conduit and 200 miles of electrical wiring. Over 6,000 fluorescent tubes lit up the store's interior, while scores of high-luminescence spotlights illuminated the parking lot. Overall, the electricity requirements for the supermarket were enough to power a small town with a population of between 10,000 and 15,000.[3]

In short, John Schwegmann had created a retail wonder of the world. While likely influenced by previous retail prototypes based on big-box thinking and one-stop-shopping conceptions, John's monstrous new emporium was in a class by itself. In its palatial scale, organizational complexity, streamlined efficiency, and ultra-discount operations, it left all predecessors in the dust. Indeed, in retrospect, the Gentilly store stands out as a true singularity: its dimensions rarely ever equaled; its longevity, never. In fact, even to John Schwegmann the store was a complete anomaly—a freakish extravagance he never attempted again.

IN THE MID-1980S, A SURPRISE retail invasion took place when three leading European "hypermarket" operators—Carrefour, Euromarché, and Auchan—suddenly stormed the United States.[4] Their hypermarkets were enormous, with store sizes ranging from 125,000 to over 250,000 square feet. Having forgotten about Schwegmann's Gentilly store—or, more likely, never having heard about it in the first place—the average American retail analyst of the 1980s viewed the European invaders with utter amazement. According to a common refrain found in the trade press at the time, never before had such monumental supermarket-type operations been seen on this side of the Atlantic.

A few more astute analysts, however, recalled that before the mid-1980s' U.S. invasion by Carrefour, Euromarché, and Auchan, a couple of second-tier European hypermarketers had already entered, but had quickly failed, in the mid-1970s. These analysts also pointed out that a scaled-down domestic version of the hypermarket, Meijer's Thrifty Acres (located in Michigan), had been in business since 1962. The most historically minded observers, though, went even further back, locating the roots of hypermarkets in a food/drug/general merchandise amalgam concept first advanced in the 1930s by Fred Meyer in the Pacific Northwest. (Note, though, that the original Fred Meyer stores were well under 40,000 square feet.)

Yet, as noted above, even the most astute and acute of 1980s' retail analysts failed to notice that the complete manifestation of a fully functional colossal-scale hypermarket already existed at the site of the by-then decades-old Gentilly store. It was as if John Schwegmann's living, breathing prototype had somehow dropped into a black hole and could no longer be seen, even by the most discerning of observers—all quite peculiar to say the least.

At any rate, in regard to the 1980s' European intruders, what almost everyone went most gaga over was their sheer size. Yet in the end, it is not size per se that underlies the hypermarket concept. Instead, a hypermarket is fundamentally defined by a retail commitment to combining food and general merchandise (GM). By this logic, it can be seen that the products carried determine the hyper scale of the store, as a fully stocked GM "department" (basically ending up to be a discount store) combined with a fully stocked supermarket takes up a tremendous amount of space. And this is not even to mention the full complement of drugstore products carried, the ubiquitous garden center, or the relatively elaborate services offered by the typical hypermarket.

Because they attempt to combine such a vast breadth of products and services, hypermarkets will necessarily have to be at least a little bit colossal. Consider that back in the 1970s, before the hypermarkets cracked size parameters wide open, the largest supermarkets clocked in at just 70,000 square feet. These "superstores," as they were called at the time, had expanded wholeheartedly into drugs and health/beauty products but only tentatively into general merchandise. What the European retailers of the 1980s demonstrated to their American counterparts was what a thoroughly dedicated commitment to general merchandise would look like—namely, extraordinarily large stores that exploded the limited superstore paradigm.

THE INVASION OF EUROPEAN HYPERMARKETS onto American terrain both unnerved and inspired U.S. retailers. The best-known response came from the best-known retailer—namely, Walmart. Sam Walton appreciated that the Euro interlopers were trying their best to combine a supermarket with a discount store, but he clearly believed he could do a better job at wedding the two concepts. Thus in 1987, in a major departure from his own previous precedents, Walton introduced a gargantuan prototype called Hypermart USA. With stores averaging around 220,000 square feet, Walmart rolled out its new hypermarkets to four locations in the Midwest. The process climaxed in Kansas City, where a 257,000-square-foot behemoth opened in 1990.

Yet the rollout itself was rolled up not long afterward. Hypermart USA lasted in functional form for only five years, from 1987 to 1992.[5] By then Walmart realized—as indeed had the Europeans, who packed up their tents and exited around the same time—that this hyper retail format was simply too huge to work in hyper-competitive, over-stored America. It would have to be scaled back.

Having adequately explored the concept (and eaten enormous losses in the process), Sam Walton clearly perceived the strengths and weaknesses of hypermarkets. In the end he decided on a compromise between 1970s' superstores and 1980s' hypermarkets as the basis for a future dominant retail concept. This compromise would be dubbed the "supercenter."

Walmart's supercenter concept fully incorporated food/drug combo stores with discount stores and garden centers, but it jettisoned much, but not all, of the service-leasing infrastructure associated with hypermarkets. What remained was a still relatively enormous structure that averaged 180,000 square feet. This was considered more or less the ideal size: big enough but still small enough to attract the average one-stop shopper looking for a bargain. Following Walmart's lead, the two other U.S. discount majors at the time, Kmart and Target, mostly converted to the supercenter format as the 1990s progressed. More than fifteen years into the twenty-first century, supercenters continue their reign as the predominant brick-and-mortar retail format for discount chains.

With the ascendance of the supercenter, the idea of giant stores ranging between 100,000 and 200,000 square feet is no longer inconceivable but the norm. These "new normal" extra-large sizes apply not just to supercenters but also to warehouse clubs. Consider that

Sam's Clubs average 134,000 square feet, while Costco stores are typically around 142,000 square feet. These are spatial areas that attract through sheer mass yet are still manageable. The magnetic pull of a store even larger—up into the range of between 200,000 to 300,000 square feet—risks spinning into retail anarchy. Here the hypermarket concept begins to collide with the mall in terms of both dimension and purpose. No matter how large the hypermarket, it will always be smaller than a million-square-foot mall. So in order to justify its existence as a distended outlet type, a hypermarket must possess some sort of super-charisma to pull customers away from the inherently more bountiful mall.

SUCH GIGANTICALLY ENHANCED DIMENSIONAL considerations had likely been on John's mind ever since he finished elaborating the Airline store in 1955. Of course, in those days there were no 70,000-foot superstores or 140,000-foot warehouse clubs to use as guides. The only truly large stores were department stores, but these had nothing to do with food (except for a few gourmet delicacies). Meanwhile, the mall was still in its infancy.

In short, John had almost nothing to go on in the mid-1950s to use as a model for what turned out to be a hypermarket. Certainly his innovative conception of the Gentilly store issued naturally from the logic of the Golden Formula. So far, no limits had been established regarding optimum store size before reaching diminishing returns. Indeed, store size at the time seemed much like a turbine or generator: for more power, just keep building bigger and bigger.

As a keen student of retail history, John was wholly aware of supermarket origins in the early big boxes of the 1930s. He also dropped tantalizing hints to his earliest chronicler, Warren Nation, about receiving inspiration, insights, and reinforcement for his ideas from certain trade-press writers, though no specific analysts or articles ever surfaced.[6] Suffice to say that Schwegmann's crazy notion for an enormous store did not come out of the blue but was based on experience, logic, and self-education. In building the biggest store in the world, he needed to concentrate all the knowledge he had so far accumulated. Beyond that, he also needed to summon the most crucial quality of all—namely, courage. Like an astronaut of the time, he would need bravery in spades. For he was not just wandering a little ways off the reservation but taking a quantum leap into a new galaxy.

In the late 1950s, supermarkets averaged about 15,000 square feet, with any store over 25,000 considered stretching the limits of manageability. Certainly in this atmosphere the Airline store's 84,000 square feet would have been seen as a freak of nature. So imagine the dumbstruck surprise of anyone paying attention to John's real estate maneuvers in 1956. First he purchased a giant parcel of land on Chef Menteur Highway in Gentilly, a rapidly expanding neighborhood in northeastern New Orleans. This particular plot—now housing the Baptist Theological Seminary—was not quite right, though, and a more favorable location was seized on as soon as it opened up. This spot was in the same general area as the other one but was advantaged by being more set-off and self-contained.[7]

Located on Old Gentilly Road just five miles from downtown New Orleans, the lot John bought was gargantuan in scope, measuring 607,500 square feet (450' by 1,350'). This colossal parcel was divided basically in half, with 300,000 square feet (400' by 750') devoted to the store building itself and 300,000 square feet (500' by 600') going for the parking lot. (An old city street no longer in use took up the extra 7,500 square feet.)[8]

Right away, the careful reader will notice that John violated his own rule by dividing up the store-space/parking-lot ratio on a 1:1 basis. (He had previously insisted on 3:1, even 4:1.) Nevertheless, this just goes to show how obsessed he had become about building the retail equivalent of the QE2. In disregarding his own rules, John probably figured the front parking lot—just as at the Airline store, the main Gentilly parking lot was located in front of the store—was adequate, able to accommodate 1,000 cars. Besides, additional space along the sides and rear of the store could hold another 500 cars, making space available for a total of 1,500 automobiles.

Turning to the store itself, its dimensions were initially projected at a staggering 265,000 square feet: a main floor of 200,000 square feet; a mezzanine of 60,000 square feet; and a 5,000 square-foot basement. Though this stupendous projection shook out slightly during the building process, the Gentilly store still ended up at a mind-boggling, almost shocking, 255,000 square feet—over twenty times the size of the average supermarket in the late 1950s, and even three times the size of the already immense Airline store!

Frankly, it almost beggars belief that this leviathan ever actually existed. First, it is hard to believe that the most ginormous supermarket the world had ever seen up to that point was built in the mid-1950s, an era characterized by business conformity. Even more unbelievable is that this behemoth actually lasted for nearly forty years as a viable, profitable retail enterprise. But what most makes the Gentilly store appear as no more than a chimera is its present state of abject ruin. Far from showing any evidence of its former glory, the once-spectacular supermarket is now nothing but a ghostly specter—a haunted hulking hollowed-out husk festering on the edge of a scary part of town. Who would ever believe that this wreck was once a world-famous store?

NEVERTHELESS, FOR THE SAKE OF HISTORICAL ACCURACY, it is best to believe that a fully functioning titan-sized hypermarket once thrived for a few decades on Old Gentilly Road, right off Chef Menteur Highway. Chef Menteur represents the confluence of U.S. Highways 90 and 11, two routes temporarily conjoined here before going their separate ways along the Gulf Coast, with both streaming eastward into Mississippi, Alabama, and Florida. At this location the store was perfectly positioned along a prime tourist route for the entire Gulf South.

Because it fully lived up to its reputation for breathtaking size, merchandising awesomeness, bargains galore, and overall pizzazz, Schwegmann Brothers' Gentilly supermarket did indeed become a full-fledged "destination store"—the kind of retail phenomenon to which people make a special trip to go to. Not just New Orleanians and Gulf Coast residents but regional travelers from all over upstate Louisiana, Mississippi, and Alabama flocked to this store, as did national and even international visitors. In other words, because the store was so standout spectacular, tourists from all over the country and the world came here to shop. After tour buses regularly began stopping at the store, a gift shop was set up to cater to the swarming crowds. Here tourists could pick up free brochures and purchase postcards featuring "The world's largest supermarket and shopping center under one roof."[9]

So how did this prodigious store, this retail sport of nature, actually materialize? Initially, John had surrounded himself with a ring of businessmen friends and supporters, predominantly from the perishable foods industry, who encouraged him in his extraterrestrial venture. These included Harold Salmon (Holsum Bakeries), Dan Rousseve (Dixiana Bakeries), Harry W. Wahlert (Dubuque Packing Company), and William "Bill" Dickey (Dickey's Potato Chip Company), among a few others.[10] It is not known how much financial backing they contributed, but it was probably not much. For as it happened, John had hit on the perfect idea: he would privately issue bonds for the construction of his monster store.

How much did it cost? With spending on store construction estimated at $7 per square foot, the cost of building the Gentilly Godzilla came to nearly $2 million ($1,855,000)—an astronomical sum in 1957. Certainly John Schwegmann had never spent nearly so much on developing a property. In 1946, the St. Claude store had cost just $1.50 per square foot. In 1950, the Airline store had jumped up slightly to $2.50. Now in 1957, costs had skyrocketed to $7 per square foot. Surely inflation played a part here. But much of the rise was in fact attributable to an anomalous splurge by John. Several factors drove him to do so. One involved an elementary question: Why build the world's most epic supermarket and then scrimp on its appearance and furnishings? So to the best of his abilities, within uncharacteristically indulgent budgetary limits, he made it look magnificent.

Yet practical considerations also drove his emphasis on grandiose aesthetics. For in his vision of things to come, John foresaw a rapid expansion of a burgeoning middle class in this northeastern part of town. After all, Gentilly had been soaring in population, up 71% between 1940 and 1955.[11] Its upscale spillover farther east appeared inevitable. With John's new hypermarket located in this prime place poised for spectacular growth, he took it as an article of faith that the newly minted middle classes in this area would demand elegance as a visual correlate to their rising standard of living. So he spent much more money than normal on elaborate design and sophisticated decoration—most of all to appeal to the coming demographic swarm of social climbers. Yet he also hoped to distinguish it from a shopping center being built nearby. In this sense, the extra money and attention lavished on the store's appearance bought protection from future competitive threats.

Thus convinced of the eventual payoff of his retail cathedral, John boldly went where few storeowners had gone before: he issued "Schwegmann Bonds" to pay for construction of the new mega-store.[12] This private placement took the form of ten-year bonds yielding 6% interest. The bonds were issued in four denominations: $10,000, $1,000, $500, and $100. What is most telling is how many bonds were offered in each denomination: only thirty in the highest rung ($10,000); just 150 for the $1,000 bonds; and 600 for the $500 bonds. By far the lion's share of the offering was aimed at smaller investors, with 10,000 bonds issued at $100.

Clearly John had designed the bond offer specifically to appeal to ordinary people—working- and middle-class people with few investment opportunities. This, of course, was a brilliant move. By buying Schwegmann bonds, customers now shared a stake in the success of the store. Shades of Migros! Only this time, the quasi-public cooperative structure remained firmly in the private sector. This was symbolized by the selling of the very first $100 bond, issued in May 1957, to John Francis Schwegmann, John's first son. This signaled that, despite the populist resonance of the bond issue, ownership of the enterprise would remain firmly in control of the founding family.[13]

The bond issue turned out to be a spectacular success. All denominations sold out in just a few months. Best of all, the offering raised

$1.75 million—nearly the entire cost of construction. John regularly reminded readers of his ads to clip their coupons at semi-annual intervals to redeem their interest payouts. The whole process worked like a charm, with the ten-year issue retiring right on schedule in 1967.

John believed he had found a new formula: if he invested in people, people would invest in him. Thus he agreed to undertake the expensive court battles necessary for freeing prices from the icy grip of the price-fixers. In return, demonstrating their full faith and confidence in Schwegmann's business model, and grateful for his fight to lower prices, loyal customers and other supporters eagerly bought up the bonds. Seizing on the natural momentum of this process, John (and later his son) floated a few more bond issues over the next couple of decades, all to help finance further expansion. These offerings were equally successful, although they faced increasing hurdles. As with the 1957 issue, subsequent ten-year bonds carried 6% interest. That is, until 1970, when rampart inflation forced John to petition the Louisiana Commission on Securities to raise rates to 7%, a request that was granted. But this was nothing compared with the early 1980s when, suddenly forced to compete with astronomical rates offered from recently unleashed savings-and-loan banks, Schwegmann Bond yields skyrocketed to 13%. This searing experience marked the end of the by-now-backfiring bond experiment. Nevertheless, by 1989 all outstanding bonds had been successfully retired.

THE HYPER-SIZED STORE THAT AROSE on Old Gentilly Road in 1957 has had no peer before or since. While a handful of later competitors may have rivaled it in size, never has there been a comparison in terms of breadth, depth, and atmosphere. That said, the Gentilly store, tremendous spectacle as it was, can fairly be seen as merely an expanded and gussied-up version of the Airline store. There were the same Schwegmann-owned departments, little changed but for their Brobdingnagian proportions. And there was the same proliferation of leased departments, though now gone berserk in a giant spatial free-for-all. Indeed, so many general similarities connected the Gentilly and Airline stores that there is no need to dwell overmuch on the particulars of the distended new store. Instead, it is enough to point out a few significant singularities to get some insight into the character of the monster.

The 1957 hypermarket was constructed primarily out of concrete and steel. In another of his continually innovative moves, John built its floor and ceiling using "lift slab" construction, whereby both floor and ceiling are poured simultaneously one atop the other, with the roof then being raised up hydraulically with jacks. Perfect proportion on top and bottom is thus achieved.[14] Moreover, this process is considerably cheaper and faster than standard techniques, as it does not require boxing and supports for casting in place. Lift slab construction was first used in 1952.

Much has been made so far about the store's grand aesthetics without mentioning any specifics. So without further ado, the store's exterior was built in pink roman brick, which matched and blended with the color of the interior terrazzo floor. Sea-green skylights set off the alabaster plaster ceiling. Meanwhile, artistic glass and porcelain enamel works were scattered generously throughout the interior of the store for decorative purposes. And the mezzanine featured wrought-iron railings reminiscent of French Quarter balconies.[15]

Speaking of the Quarter, the Gentilly store was divided left to right by five major aisles. These were named after east-west streets that transect the French Quarter, including Rampart, Royal and Dauphine, with the aisles marked off by old-style gas lampposts. Keeping with the cute street theme, aisles running from front to back sported cartoony street names that evoked the type of items appearing there. Thus customers could shop on Bean Street, Pickledilly, Suds and Tin Pan Alley, Bourbon Street Liquors, Burgundy Street Wines, and Arctic Street (frozen foods), among others.[16] These aisles were way spacious, averaging a clearance of thirteen feet. Altogether they housed forty-three gondolas. Up in front at "Checkout Boulevard," speedy exit flows were facilitated by thirty-seven cash registers. The entire shopping experience at Gentilly was made possible by the service of between 400 and 700 employees. Like the Airline store, the new store was open 74 hours a week.

As had become the norm for John, he spared no expense in equipping the new store with all the latest in machinery, fixtures, cash registers, doors, lighting, heating, cooling, and other advanced retail-related technology. As noted, his electrical needs were enormous, the store drawing the power equivalent of a town of over 10,000. His water needs being similarly over-the-top, he had a well dug 800 feet deep, with a 100-horsepower pump discharging a volume of 2,500 gallons of water per minute.[17]

At the mammoth Gentilly store, John finally overcame his age-old inventory problems, at least in regard to perishable foods. Devoting a humongous space, nearly 4,000 square feet, to storage coolers, the hypermarket was able to accommodate ten railroad carloads of produce, ten carloads of fresh meat, five of prepared delicatessen foods, and three of frozen deli. To illustrate how the delivery-to-storage-to-display process worked, consider the ten railroad cars of fresh meat. These would be delivered by truck to the store, where it was then moved via an overhead rail carriage to the storage cooler. From there the meat was prepared for sale in a tiled and air-conditioned area transparently visible to the customer through an oversized thermopane window large enough to display whole sides of beef and veal. This type of hypnotic merchandising worked its magic back in the day. With the Gentilly store running at full speed in the 1960s, it moved an average of 30,000 pounds of Midwest beef per week—the bulk of it sourced from Harry Wahlert, John's great friend and owner of Iowa-based Dubuque Packing Company, a name featured frequently and prominently in Schwegmann ads throughout the glory years.

Yet for all the wonders of the meat department—its almost military behind-the-scenes operations and its spectacular front-end display—the dairy department provided the knockout punch in terms of blowing minds. For here were featured 300 varieties of cheese, 150 imported and 150 domestic, along with almost uncountable types and brands of milk and other dairy products. The display of these multitudinous products was dominated by what John called a "Dairy

Box": a football-field-sized (104-foot-long) area containing thirty-nine refrigerator cases, all featuring auto-close doors. In the vicinity of these cases were even more dairy displays—enough seemingly to entirely submerge human consciousness in a bath of milk and cheese.

An optical design element was added to the enchantment cast by both the meat and dairy departments. Green block tiles rose up behind all refrigerator cases. Superimposed on these tiles were colorful murals both symbolically depicting and literally spelling out four meat/dairy themes: "Round Up Time," "Chuck Wagon," "Dairy Lands," and "Dutch Milkmaid" (all titled much like Mardi Gras floats).

FOLLOWING THE MODEL OF THE AIRLINE STORE, John divided the Gentilly store into Schwegmann-owned and leased areas. The space owned by Schwegmann totaled roughly 150,000 square feet, leaving approximately 100,000 for leased retail property. Within the superior allotment he granted himself, John established the same food/drug/general merchandise format—essentially a supercenter prototype—he followed for the Airline store. It was all just a matter of stuffing the gargantuan space with merchandise and, where appropriate, adding service personnel. The pharmacy, for example, employed eight full-time pharmacists to fill over 1,500 prescriptions per day.

Meanwhile, over in the stadium-sized grocery sector, the endless diversity of food and beverages merchandised along the cutesy-pie "city streets" challenged the limitations of imagination. And lest anyone think this description is exaggerated, consider the baroque splendor of the gourmet food section.[18] Here, exotic delicacies from all over the world were regularly on display and available for purchase. But it was not just a few things to spice up the store's grocery selection. No, the selection of gourmet delights, fancy foods, alien comestibles, and "gastronomical oddities" went on and on seemingly into a never-never land of fantastical extremes.

So what foods were actually in the gourmet section? Starting out with the more familiar, there were whole squabs and whole pheasants, smoked quail, snails cooked with shells (escargot), anchovy paste with butter, jalapeno chilies stuffed with shrimp, yak-yaks (cocktail-type meatballs), brandy cakes, and several types of wine-based jelly (port, burgundy, champagne, and sherry). Entering into more exotic territory, there were Westphalian pumpernickel breads in cans, Greenland tiny shrimps, Bahamian mustard (with horseradish and sweet spices), and buffalo and reindeer steaks in wine. Then finally, one breached into the land of the truly weird. Here were chocolate-covered ants, roasted and fried caterpillars, baby bees in soy sauce, rattlesnake meat, and fancy whole cocktail broiled sparrows. Note that the foods listed here are just a representative sampling. Dozens more gourmet/exotic victuals were available at the Gentilly store. It must have been a gourmand's dream, or nightmare.

John also used private-label merchandise to fill the store space.[19] Yet he did not go overboard here. Schwegmann had offered private labels—meaning products branded with the store name—only since 1954, beginning with evaporated milk. By the time the Gentilly store opened in 1957, private labels had expanded only slowly and carefully to a few select categories. These included beer, whiskey, coffee, canned milk, margarine, and butter, as well as several types of common medications. Over the following years, despite ample opportunity to expand more into this area, Schwegmann private-label penetration remained relatively low, reaching only twenty-five categories by 1970, including bread, facial tissue, detergent, vitamins, and salt, among others.

John took a subtle approach to private labels, believing they should be used with care. They must not undercut brands, the store's bread and butter. Yet they can be used judiciously in certain favorable circumstances. These involve merchandise areas that see the highest-volume repeat sales—the only areas private-label manufacturers are really interested in supplying on reasonable terms. John also believed, somewhat heretically, that store brands should not be used as profit centers. Although they are tailor-made for this purpose, John saw them as just one more opportunity to pass savings along to customers. Indeed, instead of being direct sources of profit, private labels are most valuable as advertising vehicles. According to John, the longest-lasting impact is gained from store logos sitting long-term on pantry shelves and in other visible household nooks and crannies.

Finally, no quick survey of the Schwegmann-owned portion of the Gentilly store would be complete without mentioning the restaurant and bar. The restaurant was basically a giant lunch counter able to accommodate 150 patrons. Meanwhile, the barroom area—air-conditioned, of course, like the one at the Airline store—featured as its centerpiece a 53-foot-long bar. It served beer, wine, and all the popular mixed drinks. And it was dirt-cheap. Highballs were 25¢, while a shot of twelve-year-old Scotch cost 40¢. All that is left to imagine is what it would be like to get totally crocked and then go shopping in a space the size of Grand Central Station!

TURNING FINALLY TO THE LEASED DEPARTMENTS at the Gentilly store, here the entire supermarket idea appears released from mortal gravity, freed from all natural limits, as every entrepreneur-retailer for miles around piled in to set up shop in a beyond-abundant 100,000 square feet of available space.[20] Here the conceptual "shopping center" hybrid that developed at the Gentilly store can best be seen in all its category-busting glory: it is either a first-of-its-kind hypermarket bursting at the seams; or a full-fledged but small-scale mall. It is frankly a challenge to believe the scope and scale of the leased sector as it has come down from historical sources. Yet there it is (or was): a metastasized shopping area every bit as sprawling and crowded as a big-city Chinatown or Turkish souk.

Most of the leased departments occupied the front part of the store, though a few were located up on the mezzanine. Many are familiar from the Airline store. There were small shops devoted to gifts, jewelry, candy, photos, flowers, keys/locks, and shoes/shoe repair. Larger areas were dedicated to retailers of garden/outdoor products, toys, pets, auto parts, appliances, and electronics. Yet this is far from the end. There were several types of home improvement stores, including furniture, hardware, paint, and do-it-yourself flooring, wallpaper, and the like. Then there were the clothing and soft goods vendors: men's, women's, and children's clothing stores; a "remnant" shop; and a millinery shop. As for services, the Gentilly store featured a complete bakery, a ten-chair barbershop, a beauty parlor, a laundry, and a dry cleaner.

In a new wrinkle not previously seen at the Airline store, the Gentilly store featured a full-service bank (John's old backer Progressive Bank and Trust). Even more impressive, a gas station appeared in the parking lot. Think of it: a supermarket shopper could gas up on site, and at the cheapest prices in town! (Was this another retail first for John Schwegmann?) Finally, the Gentilly store housed a range of professional services, including medical (doctor, dentist, optical) and legal (attorney and notary).

LOOKING BACK OVER THE ARC of John's career, the decade of the 1950s appears as a golden age, when past efforts came together just right and the future looked extraordinarily bright. On top of winning two landmark court victories, he had already achieved his original vision of building a successful large-scale grocery/drug combination fully integrated with general merchandise, a garden center, and specialty outlets—essentially creating what came to be known as a "supercenter" decades ahead of its time. Now this creative process had climaxed in the biggest store in the world: the epitome in Gentilly, the world's first hypermarket—a mammoth behemoth of stupendous proportions weighing in at 255,000 square feet.

By 1958, given the unfettered success of his three supermarkets at St. Claude, Airline, and Gentilly, Schwegmann had the grocery market cornered in New Orleans. The three stores attracted 100,000 customers per week. Aggregate revenues were beginning to hit nine figures. In terms of his financial situation, multi-millionaire John Schwegmann was sitting on top of the world. Indeed, he was not so much sitting as striding atop the world, lavishing his hard-earned riches on luxurious trips to Europe and beyond. This indulgence in high-class wanderlust commenced in 1954. John enjoyed his first month-long vacation so much that foreign travel forever thereafter became a regular feature of his life.

John's successes during the late-fifties' golden era were crowned with the birth of his third child, a beloved daughter. Born on April 28, 1957, Melba Margaret was named after her mother, Melba Margaret Wolfe. John and Melba had married in 1951. Yet as had happened to him before, his marriage soon deteriorated into a brittle relationship, with his wife exhibiting some sort of psychiatric disorder. With the birth of his daughter "Margie," as she came to be known, John must have been ecstatic. Yet this precious gift did not save his marriage. Rather, it wrapped it up. John and Melba divorced in 1959, though they remained on good terms afterward until the end.

THE GOLDEN AGE OF SCHWEGMANN produced one of the most inspired marketing artworks ever conceived. This was the Schwegmann shopping bag. This humble brown paper "sack" came to be the prime signifier of everything unique about the Schwegmann name. Not content with simply featuring the store's brand and logo on the bags, as was (and still is) standard practice, John began to perceive them as possessing much more potent promotional properties. The idea was to use the bags to establish a direct link between store and customer, a personal connection that went beyond the mere commercial into social and political realms of interaction.

Specially tagged Schwegmann bags began appearing around the mid-1950s. At first, along with the store name and logo the bags carried a catchy slogan, or words of wisdom, or a holiday greeting, or some such other folksy communication. As time went on, though, they started taking on a distinctly political cast. John had clearly grasped the propaganda value inherent in the simple paper sack, the apparently ephemeral effluvia of a retail transaction. So he began to use them explicitly to endorse specific political candidates. This move was unheard of: a successful businessman directly endorsing political candidates via promotional materials. The gesture went on to gain great power, as it extended beyond candidates to endorsing complete tickets, commenting on constitutional amendments, and addressing burning issues of the day. As the shopping bags evolved over the 1960s into formidable political instruments, office seekers were reduced to beggars for the "brown-bag blessing… coveted more than [the endorsement of] the *Times-Picayune*."[21]

These are the words of John Maginnis, the preeminent political historian of modern New Orleans, in his book *The Last Hayride*. Here Maginnis appropriately refers to John as a "grocer-emperor." Of course, every decent emperor needs a grand vizier. Saul Stone played this role during Schwegmann's Golden Age. The great legal genius behind John's fair-trade court victories, Stone was also a prime architect of John's shopping bag strategy. Along with helping John conceive of the bags as a "soap box in a working-class kitchen," Saul Stone took on the tortuous behind-the-scenes task of translating John's homespun utterances into succinct dramatic rhetoric that packed a punch in the small space allotted by the bags.[22]

Over time, Schwegmann grocery bags evolved from local sensation to regional phenomenon to veritable symbol of the spirit of New Orleans and Louisiana. Of course their messages were oddball, eccentric, humorous, even ridiculous at times. Yet they were also serious, tough, and courageous. As such, each bag took on a cultural significance that transcended mere politics. In a tongue-in-cheek move designed to increase the bags' value, John cleverly downplayed their influence on politics or culture by emphasizing their utilitarian multi-functionality: they can be used, he said, to stuff clothes in destined for the cleaner; to store Christmas ornaments; and, of course, as garbage can liners.[23]

Today, Schwegmann shopping bags are not only legendary but considered rare "ephemera" by collectors who know of their existence. Over modern New Orleans history they played some high-profile roles, both serious and hilarious. In an example of the first, the bags were seen in abundance during downtown drives for victims of Hurricane Betsy (1965) and Hurricane Camille (1969). On the comedic side, a Schwegmann grocery bag was featured prominently in news coverage of

New Orleans' first major marijuana bust in the sixties. Meanwhile, the bags were a common sight on Mardi Gras and Halloween, when they were used to collect beads and treats. They also played an educational role—used by schoolkids to cover their hand-me-down textbooks.

THE GOLDEN AGE OF SCHWEGMANN LEFT a permanent imprint on both John the man and his blossoming supermarket empire. Having thoroughly explored the outer limits of giganticism, he was now able to rein in his Promethean ambitions in the retail realm, steering them along more settled pathways from here on out. This involved a slow and methodical rollout over ensuing years of a small number of strategically located stores of easily managed size—all operated on the tried-and-proven principles John had developed around razor-sharp pricing. In this way, the ecstasy of the Golden Age bequeathed a surefire formula basically guaranteed to make money, with little effort needed beyond competent management.

In essence, John had invented a cash cow, created a goose that laid golden eggs, established a money-printing mint. Providing he exercised appropriate oversight, avoided excess, and maintained a proper leadership stance, his miniature empire at this point could almost auto-generate. This left him with more time on his hands than he had ever had. What a luxury! Yet at the same time, this potential for leisure must have been unnerving for an over-the-top driven man like John. The temptation for businesspeople of similar workaholic ilk would be to throw this sudden freedom from stress right back into the hopper of anxiety, as to be relaxed is ironically outside their comfort zone. The natural inclination in such cases is to move further into the familiar world of high-pressure business, to continue expanding one's economic presence and get ever richer as a result.

Well, John did not do that. Instead, he began backing away from the business world. This move was confounding to say the least, especially considering that Schwegmann's was on track to expand regionally, and possibly nationally. Certainly John's forgoing of ripe expansionary opportunities in favor of slacking off business and limiting his chain's footprint to New Orleans would be considered a species of madness in today's grow-or-die corporate environment.

Yet John fared perfectly well in his choice to embrace limits over the supposed growth imperative. First of all, he was satisfied with his already-substantial level of wealth. Moreover, he was wary of getting too far out of touch with his customers by accumulating even more riches. Most profoundly, though, he loved his idiosyncratic city so much that he had no desire to expand beyond it. This, incidentally, is not an unheard-of reaction by creative natives of New Orleans to the prospect of achieving national celebrity—rejecting both the perks and burdens of greater fame in favor of remaining within the comfortable cocoon of their local "Big Easy" celebratory ecology.

So what did John do in lieu of further pursuing business with a single-minded focus? For one thing he devoted his newly freed-up spare time to international travel. To spend his treasure in this way gave him great pleasure. Nevertheless, John's passion for travel could only absorb so much free time. If he were not going to wholeheartedly follow an expansionary business path, then some other preoccupation would have to take up his "Type-A" energy.

In John's case, he became obsessed with politics. As is discussed in the next chapter, John began fooling around with running for office in the mid-1950s. His efforts thereafter became increasingly serious until by the early 1960s he had landed a seat in the state legislature. For the rest of his active career, through the mid-1970s, John Schwegmann was intimately involved with politics—so much so that his political exploits ended up somewhat overshadowing his brilliant business career. But such are the risks to posterity undertaken by irrepressible individualists.

Taking stock, by the end of the Golden Age of Schwegmann— which lasted roughly throughout the 1950s—John was operating the world's two largest supermarkets, all three of his stores were massively popular and financially successful, he had become independently wealthy, he had begun traveling the world, and he was flirting with political power. But from that point on, the gleaming promise of the golden age began to take on a less lustrous, more piebald appearance. For instead of settling in to a comfortable future, he wrestled with it. As a result, the outcomes of later events became for Schwegmann far more uncertain and their resolution more difficult to achieve.

This can be seen in John's love life. For after divorcing Melba in 1959, he never married again, preferring instead to maintain his future conjugal relationships on an ambiguous basis. In other words, the illusion could no longer be maintained that John was a happily married man. Furthermore, as will be seen in the next chapter, John's political career did not exactly work to make his life any easier. On the contrary, the petty brutalities of politics worked actively to tarnish the golden glow previously emanating from "the people's grocer." Yet what most of all symbolized the transition from an era of shiny certainty to that of a more mottled ambiguity was the fate of a brand-new fair-trade fight.

John fought against the milk/dairy industry for fifteen long years, from 1958 to 1973. He tried everything in his power to skirt, evade, or defeat milk price fixing. Though he finally won a favorable court victory in 1973, in no time at all the original affliction reappeared in a new form. Clearly, John no longer commanded the clout to beat the fair traders decisively, as he was able to do back in the glory days of the liquor and drug battles. Whether internal or external factors or some combination were responsible for his loss of juice, it is hard to say. Certainly scattering his attention all over the place did not help matters. Then again, John now faced a rising constellation of political actors who held an animus against him and tried their best to subvert his efforts. So it was probably a combination of lack of internal focus and active external attacks that worked to diminish John's power of accomplishment.

Through it all, though, John's fighting spirit showed no diminution whatsoever. Kicking and screaming and forever scheming, he did everything in his power to get discount dairy into his stores. He fought in the legislature, in the courts, and on the streets. In the media his propaganda was blistering and relentless. So it was certainly not for lack of trying that he failed to conquer in his final fair-trade battle.

*   *   *

THE STORY OF JOHN'S THIRD AND FINAL battle against fair trade laws
begins in 1958, when a bill appeared in the state legislature authorizing
the Louisiana Orderly Milk Marketing Act.[24] In a total throwback
to thoroughly discredited arguments in favor of price fixing, the 1958
Milk Act empowered the state's Commissioner of Agriculture to set
prices in the dairy industry. It required anyone selling milk/dairy to
add 8% to baseline costs. Any lower pricing would be considered an
anti-competitive "disruptive practice" and open to sanction. It was a
thoroughly disingenuous law that purported to protect public health
and safety, as well as ensure adequate supply. In fact, it was a blatant
kickback to the powerful dairy processors.

Almost needless to say, the Orderly Milk Marketing Act was like
throwing the toreador's red cape in the face of a fierce charging bull
named John Schwegmann. Not only a veteran but a former conqueror
in the retail wars against manufacturers, John had seen it all before
and knew just what to do. He immediately pounced. Before the Act
had even passed John sent his second-in-command, Wilfred Meyer,
to Baton Rouge to register his objections in an open hearing (the
only retailer present, by the way). Wilfred stated that Louisiana had
the highest milk prices in the Southeast, and this dismal situation
was directly caused by current regulation of milk production. If such
regulation were extended to include distributors and retailers, then
prices would go even higher.

Meyer's statement failed to sway, and the Milk Act passed. This
caused John to slap a lawsuit on the measure, charging that the Act
was unconstitutional, violating the Fourteenth Amendment and the
due process clause. Meanwhile he unleashed the dogs of propaganda,
showering the public with arguments, via his ads, against the Milk Act.
It was supposedly set up to protect public health and safety, but the
State Board of Health already does that. Its intention to secure adequate
supply is actually subverted by price fixing, which eliminates low-cost
suppliers. John even wrote an open letter to President Eisenhower
imploring him to look into the matter. Louisiana, he said, did not

produce enough milk, and the state did not allow milk to be imported due to conflicting regulations. As a result, per capita milk consumption fell far below the national average.

The letter to Ike fell on deaf ears. Furthermore, the courts were not buying the constitutional arguments—that the Milk Act was arbitrary, unreasonable, and illegal in its delegation of power. Despite all John's protestations, in 1959 a federal District Court ruled against him, and a quick appeal to the U.S. Supreme Court was denied a hearing. John had thus lost in both the legislature and the courts.

Did these defeats end John's agitations? Of course not! For at this point he began to explore ways to get around the pricing straitjacket. At first he simply urged consumers to buy evaporated milk, which Schwegmann had been selling cheaply under a private label since 1954. Taking this strategy further, John began buying liquid milk from a low-cost producer, Smith Milk Company out of Franklinton, Louisiana, and retailing it under the Schwegmann store brand. This tactic actually worked, and milk prices descended for a while. But for some reason, Smith Milk suddenly went bankrupt in 1960. John went back to scheming.

The next opportunity to challenge milk price fixing arose in 1962, when the 1958 Orderly Milk Act was amended to establish the Louisiana Milk Commission (LMC). This amendment clarified previous law by specifying the power of the LMC to set prices at all levels of the distribution chain—from producer to processor, wholesaler, and retailer. John immediately challenged the law in federal court but lost. Three years later, in 1965, he lost another case against the LMC, this time in state court. Yet this last loss set the stage for an action and a series of further appeals that twisted in the wind of legal limbo for eight full years before finally being resolved in John's favor. Specifically, in the course of his piratical scheming, John had formed an alliance with a low-cost producer of "ice milk," a company called Pure-Vac based in Memphis, Tennessee. To make a long story short, John sold the ice milk at cut-rate prices and thus ran afoul of the Milk Commission, which cracked the whip. Not backing down, John pursued the case and eventually won—but only on a technicality.

Orchestrating and litigating the appeals process was another great legal mind from the Stone, Pigman firm, Michael R. Fontham.[25] Patiently shepherding the case through the courts for eight years, Fontham's primary argument pointed directly at a violation of the Commerce Clause of the U.S. Constitution. A secondary argument made mention of violation of the Supremacy Clause. As it happened, after going through conniption fits of tortuous logic, a three-judge panel specially empowered to oversee resolution of this case found that, yes, the Louisiana Milk Commission did indeed overstep its bounds in attempting to regulate transportation modalities in Memphis, Tennessee. In this way, the LMC violated federal laws pertaining to interstate commerce. A big hole had opened up in its legal mandate. As the three-judge panel put it: "The Milk Commission must be enjoined from requiring Schwegmann Brothers to conform to minimum prices insofar as purchases are made out of state…."

This ruling delivered a severe blow to the state milk industry, so much so that it was forced to abolish the Louisiana Milk Commission right afterward. And for a third time, John Schwegmann had triumphed over fair trade! But this victory was much more tenuous than in the past. Quickly recovering from their setback, Louisiana dairy processors pushed through a new price-regulating instrument with a few tweaks to accommodate objections regarding interstate commerce. This was the Dairy Stabilization Board (DSB), which in 1974 replaced the Milk Commission.

With the authorization of the DSB, a renegade outfit in John's eyes, he was forced to confront it. Pulling a page from past encounters in regulatory defiance, he contracted with Dairy Fresh Corp., a low-cost producer in Hattiesburg, Mississippi, to supply Schwegmann stores with milk, to be sold at fifteen cents below the minimum decreed by the DSB. Faced with this in-your-face insubordination, the DSB's first impulse was to impound the discount milk, but for some reason it backed down. Mysteriously, not long after it began supplying John with discount milk, Dairy Fresh, like Smith Milk before it, went out of business. John was back to square one—with any future possibilities for combat ending abruptly in 1977 with his devastating stroke.

17

THE PEOPLE'S GROCER
TURNS POPULIST POLITICIAN

WHEN OUT OF THE BLUE in the early 1870s Garret Schwegmann Senior just up and sold his successful first store, using the proceeds to venture blindly out to California, no one knew quite what to make of it. Why had he been so overwhelmed by an irresistible urge to seek his fortune out West when he was sitting so pretty down South? Was it ambition or a sense of adventure that drove him? Was he just crazy, or drunk, or both? Not knowing his motivation, friends and other contemporaries viewed Garret's move with surprise, even alarm, as he defied their expectations by risking respectability on a lark.

What at first appears baffling begins to make sense if the same surprise repeats over and over again. Thus did Garret's apparently rash behavior eventually resolve into a recognizable pattern. For with every store he sold and every trip he took out West, Garret increasingly stood revealed as being possessed by "wanderlust," a burning curiosity that can only be quenched by actively engaging in exploration. The most familiar form this exploration takes is, of course, geographical. Here the character possessed by wanderlust is best expressed in the archetype of the "rambling man" who finds fulfillment only when he is "on the road again." Yet the behavior of a perpetual traveler can also take on more abstract forms. In other words, it is possible to slake exploratory curiosity by taking more metaphorical journeys through social, intellectual, or spiritual realms.

In examining John Schwegmann's life as a whole, there is no question that Garret Senior bequeathed the joys and burdens of wanderlust to his famous grandson. This explains John's perennial journeying to Europe and around the world from the mid-1950s onward for the rest of his life. It also may explain his pursuit of politics. Yes, John's entry and repeated forays into politics—also taking place from the mid-1950s onward—can best be seen as a species of wanderlust. Indeed, how else explain such a radical and ultimately irrational career detour: the genius groceryman suddenly veering onto a new professional pathway to which his temperament is wholly ill suited?

This move was clearly a matter of passion rather than calculation. He had not planned on being seized by an intense desire to pursue political power, yet that is what happened. Moreover, when this passion did strike, he was in a good position to indulge it. He had economic clout, a media platform, and, as icing on the cake, a strong moralizing ego, all of which could be placed easily in the service of political pursuits.

The wanderlust explanation for John's turn to politics, however, may be too facile, with the real reason lying deeper. Without going too far out on a psychological limb, it is certainly possible that his ambivalent feelings toward his mother played a role here. In this case, unresolved primal emotions—perhaps a sense of being unloved or abandoned by her—led John to seek the internal acceptance he longed for from an external source. After all, he had failed to find the love he craved from his two marriages, both of which ended in divorce. So he turned instead to the voting public, whose approval might act to fill the void he felt.

Then again, John's unexpected entrance into politics might simply be taken at face value: he sought office in order to better position himself to fight for the people. Whatever his motives, there remains a hint of madness in John's decision to devote the better part of the second half

of his professional life to politics. It must have been similar to the way
Garret Senior dismayed his peers by shifting gears from out of nowhere
and kicking away near-term success for long-term uncertainty. For
John also sabotaged expectations—in his case by deciding to engage
in overwrought and ineffective political dabbling. Certainly this choice
leaves business analysts and retail historians who had hoped for ever-
greater accomplishments from John G. Schwegmann with more than
a twinge of sadness and regret. Yet such are the ways of passion, often
irrational but always revealing. In John's interesting case, his quixotic
pursuit of politics ends up yielding insights into community loyalty
and love of place.

JOHN'S CAREER AS A POLITICIAN is one of the most obscure chapters
in his life. The fact that he ran for political office eight times over
twenty years has been largely forgotten. Likewise that he was actually
pretty successful in politics, winning four elections and serving in three
state offices for fifteen of those years. Usually what is remembered, if
anything, about John's political career are his failures: being trounced in
an ill-fated run for governor in 1971, for example; or being ridiculed over
his cranky opposition to the Superdome. Meanwhile, little is recalled
of his positives—his broad electoral appeal, his multiple endorsements
by elites, and his distinction as being not just a consistent advocate of
good government but a rare practitioner of it as well.

As with most every major career move John made in his professional life—from entering real estate to building the world's largest
stores—the origins of his decision to enter politics are murky. There is
never any explicit declaration that this was his intention. Instead, he
seemed to slip into politics through the back door, as it were. The initial
move came in the mid-1950s at the climax of his fiercely fought Second
Battle of Fair Trade, this against the drug industry. While still neck-deep
in lawsuits, John took his well-chronicled trip to Europe in 1954. There
he met and was profoundly influenced by the two European discount
giants he singled out in his travelogue, namely Josef Neckermann and

Gottlieb Duttweiler. Both had encountered seemingly insuperable obstacles, but both had fought back and ultimately triumphed by engaging in politics.

It is probably no coincidence, then, that shortly after his return to the States, John threw his hat into the ring. In July 1955, while juggling store operations and legal injunctions, he announced his run for Louisiana state senator from the Tenth District (then comprising Jefferson, St. Charles, and St. John the Baptist parishes).[1] That this decision was made spontaneously is evident from Schwegmann's complete lack of any organization or campaign management. Likely inspired by his European confrères, he simply wanted to exert political pressure to resolve the fair trade issue in his favor. This could be done by running for office and using the campaign to highlight the issue. Indeed, in this his first race he embodied the classic single-issue candidacy, hammering home with the force and fury of an Old Testament prophet the evils of fair trade law and the goodness that will come from its repeal: higher production, higher consumption, higher employment, higher standards of living!

John utilized every angle he could think of to villainize fair trade and valorize free trade. He cast dark shadows on the drug-makers, who charge extortionate prices for life-saving medicines. He called out manufacturers for their hypocritical stance on "Right to Work," promoting a pro-competitive position on labor even as they took anti-competitive positions on price.[2] He also trotted out an old argument from the original days of fair trade: that these laws do not help but actually hurt small retailers, depriving them of a vital competitive tool, discounting, to use against the chains. Finally, John played up the modernity angle, pointing out that Louisiana was woefully behind the times on the matter of fair trade even among her southern sister-states, as Florida, Georgia, South Carolina, Alabama, and Texas had all by now declared crucial parts of the laws unconstitutional.

In his concentrated attack on fair trade, John inevitably drew a challenger from the ranks of its defenders. Considering John's current legal battle against drug industry price fixing, it was no surprise that his rival emerged from this sector. The new candidate was Joseph Lucas, former president of the Louisiana State Pharmacology Association. Lucas characterized Schwegmann's run for state senator as nothing more than a publicity stunt to promote his stores. He also belittled John's single-issue campaign, calling fair trade a piddling priority in the greater scheme of things involving industry, labor, education, and "juvenile delinquency."[3]

John hit back, simultaneously defending the importance of the fair trade issue and trying to paint Lucas as nothing more than an industry flack. The six-month campaign ended on January 20, 1956, when the first primary for state senator was held. Out of a field of seven candidates, Alvin T. Stumpf, the incumbent, won with a vote count of 16,303. Basically tied for second place were French Jordan (13,843) and John Schwegmann (13,083). Joseph Lucas, meanwhile, was way down in the pack at around 2,500 votes.[4]

In his opening electoral gambit, then, John can be seen to have pulled off an entirely respectable showing. That he ran pretty much off-the-cuff, with little organization, less preparation, and no strategy beyond the Johnny-one-note hit on fair trade, suggests that he as yet had no serious designs on entering the political sphere. As discussed, the 1955 campaign for state senator, probably inspired by John's European colleagues, looked like nothing more than a pressure tactic. And in this it was eminently successful, as it clearly indicated by his decent showing that public opinion increasingly rejected fair trade laws. Likely taking this trend into account, the Louisiana Supreme Court undercut the legality of the "non-signer's clause" in 1957.

It must have been a sweet victory for John, the state supreme court's abolition decision on price fixing handed down just as he was opening up the most colossal supermarket yet seen on planet earth. But what would he do now? Given his incredible business success, his astounding record of innovation in the retail world, and his achievement of victories in the legal realm that all but legitimated U.S. discounting, it seemed that John could easily coast to some sort of business prominence beyond New Orleans.

Of course, this did not come to pass. John Schwegmann did not follow the path of regional or national expansion. Beyond metro-wide store saturation of New Orleans, John was done. He was no Hartford brother or Harry Cunningham. Schwegmann had no intention of turning his friendly local empire into the type of chain-store juggernaut he, with his deep roots in populism, had always abhorred.

THE DECENT SHOWING of John's first run for office left a satisfying taste in his mouth. So at the first opportunity to do so again, he plunged into a race. This time he would be running for a local, not state, office—namely, Jefferson Parish president.

The year was 1959, a year so portentous in so many areas of human endeavor that a cultural history has been written about it, appropriately titled *1959: The Year Everything Changed*.[5] For John personally, this was an emotionally challenging period. In 1959, he divorced his second wife, Melba. As with his first wife, Mary, mental instability issues were involved on the woman's side of the breakup. Yet it was becoming increasingly clear that workaholic John simply had neither the time nor the inclination to be a loving, attentive husband. As it happened, the damage caused in the first two marriages eventually healed to the extent that both ex-wives and John all had sociable relations with each other throughout their later lives. Nevertheless, the trauma of the second divorce must have been considerable, for John never married again.

With turmoil in his heart and politics increasingly in his blood, John could easily displace at least some of the rancor he felt over his marital failure onto his new campaign. After all, this was 1959, a time when Jefferson Parish was deeply immersed in a vice-versus-virtue schizophrenic episode quite reminiscent of what its metropolitan forebear, New Orleans, had endured earlier. On one hand, "Jeff" Parish exhibited a high-minded progressivism that fully embraced both science and the "humanities"—art, literature, philosophy, and the like. Correspondingly, it placed high value not just on technological development in the form of roads, schools, lighting, drainage, and other physical infrastructure but also on development of the human capital components of modern progress.[6]

But even as a progressive elite attempted to steer Jefferson Parish toward enlightened ideals, a countervailing undertow pulled powerfully downward toward corruption. For the 1950s represented the heyday of organized crime in New Orleans, then under the supremely diabolical leadership of Carlos Marcello. While the extremely twisted history of the Cosa Nostra and its relationship to New Orleans is obviously beyond the scope of this book, there is one relevant connection that is simple to follow. After Mayor Fiorello LaGuardia banished slot machines from New York City in the 1930s, the same machines somehow ended up down in New Orleans in the 1940s. In a similar sleight of hand, by the 1950s they had managed to migrate out to Jefferson Parish—some of them even appearing in the Schwegmann Brothers Airline store![7]

Slot machines, of course, were just a synecdoche for the influence of organized crime. In the Jefferson Parish of 1959, this baleful influence was becoming irresistible, like a community in the throes of a drug epidemic. While it had to be combatted, the poison of corruption had seeped so deep into the body politic that it was getting hard to tell the good guys from the bad. The white hats and black hats kept shifting, with few purists consistently upholding upright ideals. Into this vacuum stepped John Schwegmann (not so pure, but more principled than most). He had bided his time after building the Gentilly store in 1957, waited (probably impatiently) through 1958, then cast his ("white") hat in the ring in summer 1959. He himself would be the good guy, the candidate most unwavering in defense of the people's best interests.

Like the 1959 race for governor of Louisiana, the campaign for Jefferson Parish president the same year presented itself almost as a parody, albeit both elections were unfunny in their outcomes. At the time, loyalties in Jeff Parish were splintered into three rival political factions: the Independent Democratic Association (IDA), the Parish Democratic Organization (PDO), and the Democrats of Jefferson (DOJ). Charles W. Spencer (IDA) was currently parish president, but he was about to be booted out by M. Daniel Hogan (DOJ). Into this involuted tangle, John inserted himself as the PDO candidate.

Following tradition, each candidate for parish president was expected to ally with a candidate for parish sheriff. Thus presidential challenger Dan Hogan partnered with John G. Fitzgerald, while incumbent Charles Spencer joined with none other than Harry "Wop" Glover. For his part, the "good government" candidate himself, John Schwegmann, was stuck allying on the PDO line with the incumbent sheriff, William S. Coci. The irony is that Coci may have been, as claimed by some researchers, under the sway of Carlos Marcello.[8]

As it happened, John was able to effectively distance himself from his allegedly corrupt partner by consistently insisting on his own independence. In doing so he developed a theme that persisted throughout all future campaigns. In paraphrase, it went as follows:

> I am a rich man, having built a successful business from scratch. I do not need any money from any political organization or economic special interest. As such I am above the fray, with no need to indulge in favors or patronage. I owe nothing to anyone, unlike everyone else in the race. I alone stand for honestly and integrity.

In this his first truly political campaign beyond a single-issue candidacy, John sometimes committed stupid rookie mistakes. Perhaps the most egregious was in promising the moon, proclaiming that there will be "unheard of, undreamt of improvements" if I am elected. A much more plausible promise was presented when John vowed to be a watchdog for Jefferson Parish finances. He had already inspected a school site bought by Jeff Parish officials for $200,000. His verdict: It "ain't worth over $4,000."[9]

In attempting to straddle the roles of conservative businessman and the people's best friend, John was in the forefront of a political tendency emerging at the dawn of the 1960s called "conservative progressive." This tendency proved useful for all middle-of-the-road southern politicians who wanted to have their cake (civic improvements) and eat it too (lower taxes). In its extremely flexible meaning, it could provide ideological cover for everyone from left-leaning progressives like Hale Boggs to right-leaning libertarians like John Schwegmann.

As would be expected of such an unwieldy political position, it did not last. Indeed, the conservative-progressive tendency was only a creature of the tortured two-party system then prevailing in the postwar South. Consider that in the 1950s the Democratic Party uneasily housed both liberals and conservatives, while the Republican Party was split along racial lines between the "black and tan" and "lily white" factions. The reconfiguration of the parties into distinct right and left wings took shape only in 1968, following Nixon's "southern strategy." Before that, Republicans were mostly on the fringe in the South, with the consistently respectable candidates tending to be Democrats, including John Schwegmann. As will be seen, though, maverick John was once again in the vanguard when in 1962 he endorsed a Republican for U.S. Congress.

None of this mattered, though, in 1959 when John was running for parish president. At that time the game involved some serious factional infighting within the Democratic Party. While John's portrayal of himself as a man of honesty and integrity played well among the citizens of Jefferson, he never stood a chance in this venomous election dominated by ruthless power cliques. He did, however, gain first-hand experience in down-and-dirty politics. Almost hilariously, rumors swirled like clockwork about candidates dropping out of the race, or rifts developing between partners, or the coercing of campaign funds, or the offering of bribes, or any number of malicious innuendos.[10] This rumor-mongering was mainly directed at incumbents Charles Spencer and William Coci, along with their respective partners, "Wop" Glover and John Schwegmann. Those who mostly escaped the calumniation— namely, Dan Hogan (running for president) and John Fitzgerald (running for sheriff)—handily won the race.

Although he had been a victim of dirty politics, John valiantly fought back against the fog machine and emerged from the race with his good reputation intact. Even more, he was proving to be a popular candidate. Just as in 1955, he ended up in a virtual tie for second place in 1959, polling just a few hundred votes below Charles Spencer.[11] Thus with two campaigns under his belt, John had established himself as a viable candidate. The only thing he lacked at this point—the very thing necessary to put him over the top—was the backing of an effective political organization. He did not have long to wait.

* * *

AFTER LOSING RESPECTABLY in the 1959 primary for Jefferson Parish president, John sat out most of 1960, watching and waiting. He must have been extremely encouraged by how quickly events were unfolding in his favor. Harry Glover had been right all along. The "bosses" with their "bossism" were corrupt. The men who took over Jefferson Parish were quickly engulfed in a squalid scandal involving—*quelle* surprise!—slot machines. Even Wop's main rival, Sheriff Fitzgerald, was implicated. Straining all his formidable political muscles, newly elected parish president Dan Hogan managed to remain above the fray, portraying himself as a tarnished saint betrayed by a cabal of sinners.

Particularly amusing is how Hogan commented on the scandal to the *Times-Picayune*. He did so by phone from Honolulu (of all places), just happening to be in Hawaii on a "business trip" when the story broke.[12] Taking time away from his strenuous schedule, no doubt, the parish president bemoaned his associates' notorious behavior and solemnly promised to clean up the mess. So who better to help him stanch the stench than "Mr. Clean" himself? Yes, Hogan tapped John Schwegmann to run for an important upcoming office.

Jefferson Parish had grown rapidly over the past decade, so much so that the 1960 census showed its population increase merited the addition of two new seats to the Louisiana State House of Representatives. The election season for these seats was short, lasting only from late 1960 into early 1961. Dan Hogan desperately needed to ally with faces of integrity. He chose John Schwegmann and Jules G. Mollere for the two new seats, giving both of them the full backing of the Jefferson Independent Democrats (formerly the Democrats of Jefferson). Having received the JID's imprimatur, John was a shoo-in for victory. He barely needed to try. No complicated platform. Just utter a few boilerplate speeches about running government like a business and standing for civic improvements, and voilà, the doors to political office finally swung open for John.

On February 26, 1961, John cruised to a dominating first-place primary finish, with enough votes (18,963) to avoid a run-off. To emphasize the magnitude of this win, consider that his JID colleague, Jules Mollere, did have to endure a run-off—which he won, by the way, against the oddly named John Mmahat. On April 12, 1961, both Schwegmann and Mollere coasted to general election victories against their Republican opponents.[13]

Although relatively easy, John's 1961 campaign for state representative did involve one nasty fight. And in this tense confrontation what stands revealed is the intersection of John's public political and private business interests. Firmly believing in the beneficence of his business model, John naturally wanted to expand the Schwegmann store base. In 1960, he decided on Harvey, located on the Westbank of New Orleans, as a choice neighborhood to open his next supermarket. The only trouble was that here he encroached on the turf of Beauregard Miller, chief of the Gretna Police Department and one of the most formidable Jefferson Parish politicians of all time.

What followed was a knockdown drag-out fight between the two over zoning issues contrived by Miller. Their struggle spilled into acrimonious public exchanges, with the politicians hurling vicious insults at each other at the height of the campaign. As to who won this "pissing contest," consider that John navigated comfortably into office in April 1961, and the next year he opened his new Harvey supermarket. In a sign of who had the juice, the stony-faced Dan Hogan was pictured in a publicity photo standing in front of John, almost appearing as his protector, congratulating him on bringing progress to West Jefferson Parish.[14]

At last, John's political persistence had paid off. He was now an elected state representative! His four-year tenure would last until 1964. Whatever would he do with this long-sought political power? The short answer is, not much. But before getting into the specifics, consider that John was so quickly disillusioned with the limits of state politics that he immediately sought a way out by running for national office. Here, he presumed, the greater issues, matters more worthy of his attention, would be addressed.

* * *

So less than a year after being elected to the state legislature, John announced his candidacy for the U.S. House of Representatives.[15] His main opponent was none other than Thomas Hale Boggs, the legendary powerhouse of New Orleans' politics who had risen into the upper echelon of national rule. The race was for Louisiana's Second Congressional District, at the time encompassing four parishes and Uptown New Orleans. John announced his candidacy in May 1962, with the primary to be held in July.

If John believed it was folly to go up against Boggs he did not show it. On the contrary, he acted as if Hale were vulnerable. After all, Boggs was a liberal, which through innuendo could be shaded into socialist, or even communist, back at the height of the Cold War. Of course, being a liberal meant expanding the power of big government and engaging in top-down social engineering schemes, such as racial integration, subsidized healthcare, and urban renewal. These were boiling-hot issues in the South in 1962, and Hale Boggs was smack on the wrong side of them, according to conservatives.

Besides being an easy target as a liberal, Boggs was considered vulnerable by John on a number of other scores. For example, in John's view, Hale's "whip" status in the U.S. House leadership, far from being a symbol of power, was instead a liability. For he had become nothing more than a "rubberstamp" for the Kennedy administration, in the process losing touch with the people of Louisiana. Even worse, Boggs had betrayed the Old South itself by enabling a procedural change—Kennedy's "stacking" of the House Rules Committee—that siphoned power away from southern conservatives. As icing on the cake of disreputability, John liked to emphasize Boggs's elitism. Hale was privileged and pampered, went straight from private school into public service, never spent a day as a working man, and thus could not relate to real people. He could, however, relate to his liberal friends, pointy-headed intellectuals and "long-haired Harvard advisers."[16]

Having demonized Boggs for his socialism, his treason, and his subversive snobbery, John proceeded to pump himself up beyond all proportion as the great seer and savior. During the short campaign, he would pronounce on every topic, pass judgment on every issue. In the process he showered the public with endless tributes to his own virtues. He was an independent thinker, an outspoken conservative, a successful businessman, a proven fighter, and a friend of both labor and business. He came up the hard way and was now wealthy. He was worldly, sophisticated. ("I traveled in Europe, Russia, and behind the Iron Curtain at my own expense for the purpose of training myself for public service.") Above all, John was a patriot. Alarmed by America's drift to socialism, John had no choice but to run for U.S. office: "I am not going to sit back and see this country go to the dogs."[17]

Along with shamelessly promoting his virtues as a candidate, Schwegmann also presented a wide-ranging platform of sorts—although much of it resembles more of a random spouting of opinion than a coherent program. Overall, he represented mainstream conservatism. He trumpeted balanced budgets, railed against taxing and spending, and stood foursquare for free enterprise and old-fashioned honesty and integrity on all levels of society.

When he got into specifics, his pronouncements divided into positions on foreign and domestic affairs. On the foreign front, John took a jaundiced view of overseas entanglements. He expressed old-school conservative isolationism, both financial and military. He particularly winced at "foreign aid," considering it a total waste of money, a "giveaway," no better than a bribe. Foreign aid offended his deepest economic sensibilities, especially as he witnessed firsthand on his European trips how America was subsidizing its future competitors, countries that in truth had already recovered from the war and really could care less about returning the favor. Regarding foreign military adventures, John never did seem to warm up to any type of intervention. As with foreign aid, the money spent on colonial war and intrigue was largely wasted, only on an even grander scale. If it could not buy results in Cuba, "only ninety miles from our land," how could we hope to control Southeast Asia half a world away? In this way, he grounded his aversion to intervention on economic pragmatism.[18]

As for domestic issues, John presented his views in an unappetizing stew of undercooked and badly seasoned ingredients. Beyond his convictions on price fixing, John appears to have done little deep thinking on America's social concerns. Consequently he comes across as alternately foolish and superficial. For example, he took a regressive stance on race, backing the separate-but-equal doctrine regarding education. Integration, he believed, brings "chaos" and "endangers our schools." Thus he allied with retrograde forces that ultimately tarnished his pro-consumer halo. John was similarly behind the curve on healthcare. In the early 1960s, Medicare was being forged. As to be expected, this transformative pillar of Great Society legislation drew the ire of conservatives, who denounced it as blatant socialism. For his part, John threw in his lot with the right on this issue, getting behind half-baked private solutions to an overwhelmingly public problem. Once again, he failed to follow the pro-consumer logic here: that lower healthcare costs translate into more overall funds for consumption.

This type of shallow thinking on domestic issues is also on display in John's opinions on taxes and benefits. Here he is content to merely tinker around the edges of the system, offering nothing in the way of systematic critique or alternative approach. He accepted the federal income tax, for example, but would like to tweak it here and there. One area: deductions for dependents should be raised from $600 to $1,000. After all, "You can't even raise a good dog on $600 a year."[19] He also wanted to eliminate the limits on payments to Social Security recipients aged 65 to 72 who make outside income. He highlighted the absurdity of these limits by contrasting them to the millions of dollars the U.S. government lavished annually on the "Three Princes of Laos" to keep them in our camp. Here money is frivolously frittered away on the pleasure of foreign potentates even as our seniors back home are suffering under ridiculous penny-pinching rules.

As can be seen in John's ragtag, scattershot approaches to foreign and domestic issues, though he had assembled a modestly impressive tactical arsenal with which to attack the fortifications of Hale Boggs, his strategic approach was far from up to the task of toppling the powerful incumbent. John was just too all over the place, his facile character assaults, endless self-puffery, and blunderbuss bloviating over the vital issues of the day never melding into the kind of focused, coherent narrative necessary to defeat such a formidable rival. John seemed to think that simply bombarding the Whip with thunderous denunciations, all the while singing his own praises and setting forth random positions, would be enough to dislodge Boggs.

Almost needless to say, this bumbling strategy stood no chance of success. It simply did not hit with sufficient force. What is unsettling is that John does not appear to have perceived this easy-to-see strategic weakness. Put it this way: if John ever seriously entertained the notion that he presented even the ghost of a threat to Hale Boggs in 1962, this locates him in the la-la land of utter delusion. Of course, more likely is that he knew in his heart of hearts he could not win, and his was only a protest run. But even if he knew he would lose, John still believed too close for comfort in the righteousness of his cause—even though the particulars of this cause, on inspection, form an incoherent muddle.

And precisely here John G. Schwegmann veers into Don Quixote territory. The myth has overtaken the man. He is a warrior for truth and justice, vouchsafed with upholding sacred virtue. By definition he is honorable, and so are all the battles he undertakes, no matter how absurd they may appear. Such is the life and legacy of a true crusader: one doomed to be deemed crazy in solemn defense of some ineffable principle.

The full extent of John's quixotic state of mind at the time is expressed in the following quote from a speech he delivered in June 1962: "I don't believe the people are willing to give away their freedom for the promise of roads or canals, or even the missile plant."[20] Here, incredibly, he denies the primal power of the archetypal politician—the one who brings home the bacon—in favor of some fairy tale about an enlightened electorate favoring "freedom" over economic development. Not to be overly cynical, but in this pronouncement John seems almost off his rocker in thinking average people prefer gossamer ideals over practical improvements from a workaday politician.

Yet as the philosopher David Hume once might have said, "You never know." Certainly in 1962, conventional wisdom concerning predictable political outcomes appeared vulnerable to new visions of liberation. John seems to have been inspired by this possibility. After all, he was running for national office at the height of the Cold War, a time of tremendous social and cultural upheaval. The rapidly evolving situation appeared on the verge of a tipping point, when even one bold gesture or dramatic move could favorably tip the balance of power.

In this pensive atmosphere, John orchestrated two unique events—both political, but one more artistic than the other—designed to raise his profile and establish his authenticity as a genuine alternative to the prevailing power structure. The political move took the form of a "demonstration." Occurring in June 1962, it involved organizing a motorcade from New Orleans to Baton Rouge, using numerous buses and cars to transport about a thousand people to the state capitol building to protest Proposition 777, which aimed to create a state-sanctioned Milk Commission. This tactic was lifted straight out of John's classic anti-price-fixing playbook. In this case, though, it sparkled more spectacularly than ever before, as it included many more people and was more professionally stage-managed. One indication of its sophistication was a sign appearing in the crowd proclaiming: "God took Huey P. Long, but gave us John Schwegmann." The pressure of such a well-done protest definitely threatened opposing legislators, with one Milk Commission supporter angrily accusing Schwegmann of playing "naked politics."

Around the same time as the demonstration, John conducted what can only be dubbed a surreal stunt. Resembling more of a transgressive-style "happening" than a political protest, on June 18, 1962, he (along with his daughter) brought a nanny goat to the state capitol building. Herding it into the hallowed halls, John, Margie, the goat, and two young girls dressed as old-fashioned milkmaids entered the elevator and rode up to the House chamber. There he delivered a thunderous denunciation of the state's dairy lobby while the two maids milked the goat beside the podium—symbolizing, of course, what the legislature was doing to consumers.

Both of these events, the political demonstration and the artistic provocation, were designed to reinforce John's image as a credible conservative alternative to liberal Hale Boggs. Instead, they helped cement his lasting reputation as a loose-cannon eccentric. Nevertheless, despite all his miscues in the 1962 U.S. congressional race, John miraculously pulled off a decent showing. Almost needless to say, all three of Hale's challengers were crushed beneath the weight of his power, as Boggs coasted to victory with two-thirds (64%) of the vote, registering an electoral count of 58,708. Yet despite his raggedy campaign—a would-be hotshot taking potshots at an untouchable incumbent—John Schwegmann once again managed to come in second in the 1962 U.S. congressional election, his vote count at 16,249.[21] So despite naïveté, shallowness, and delusion, he still managed a respectable result.

This race for the U.S. House was arguably the culmination of John's political career. For in 1962 Schwegmann let it all hang out— unflinchingly expressing his heartfelt opinions on a wide range of current controversies, pronouncing guilty verdicts on past corruptions, and warning ominously about future trends. During this reckless campaign he basically represented "John unleashed": the frenzied version of a self-righteous man desperate to make his mark on public discourse like nothing seen before or since. John failed so unutterably in reaching this goal that he dropped out of national politics forever after.

Along the way to abandoning the national scene, however, John could just not help himself. He would always be an innovator, no matter the sphere in which he operated. Being now involved in politics, it is thus no surprise that John, after his loss to Boggs, would follow up by doing something entirely unprecedented. Specifically, in 1962, years before Nixon's southern strategy of 1968, Democrat John Schwegmann endorsed a Republican, David Treen, against Boggs in the general election.[22] In this extremely controversial move at the time, it can be seen how John was in the forefront of the conservative southern switchover to the Republican Party.

OVER HIS PROLIFIC CAREER as a honey-throated jongleur, the singer recorded more than forty albums. While serving in high political office, he had a No. 1 hit on the country charts. A good friend of Lawrence Welk, a former head of the Gospel Music Association, and an inductee into the Country Music Hall of Fame, this consummate entertainer once offered the up-and-coming politician Ronald Reagan some humorous political advice: "Sing softly and carry a big guitar."[23]

Best remembered for writing (or perhaps buying from some anonymous hillbilly songwriter) the immortal country classic "You Are My Sunshine," James Houston "Jimmie" Davis, known in legend as the "Singing Governor," served two terms as executive head of the State of Louisiana. His first term, spanning the initial postwar years of 1944 to 1948, was most notable for his absence. He had more important things to do than run a state, such as recording five Top Ten hit songs between 1944 and 1947, and appearing in numerous below-grade-B Hollywood westerns through 1950.

Then from out of nowhere, after twelve years in the political wilderness, Jimmie Davis suddenly reappeared. This time, however, instead of calming state waters after World War II, the normally placid Davis played the rousing cavalry commander come to rescue the state from a fierce assault by the forces of integration. Over an epic, some say tragic, 1959 election season, Davis came from behind to eke out a slim victory over his two major opponents: old-guard Earl Long and avant-garde Chep Morrison.

Once again, Louisiana was placed under the opaque cloud of a Davis gubernatorial administration. This time, though, it was in an infinitely more explosive context characterized by political hysteria and intensifying racial grievance. Under these precariously charged circumstances, and with a state officialdom cloaked in secrecy, it is no wonder that some of the most murky and abysmal events ever recorded in Louisiana history occurred during the second Davis administration, which lasted from 1960 to 1964. Consider Cuban conspiracy (plots directed against Castro), biomedical murder mystery (Dr. Mary Sherman), notorious criminality (Carlos Marcello), and the assassination of John F. Kennedy (Lee Harvey Oswald). All had Louisiana connections under the autocracy of Davis. Also transpiring under his reign was one of the most embarrassing moments of the Civil Rights movement. Here, Hollywood cowboy Jimmie Davis impetuously rode a horse up the steps of the Louisiana capitol building in protest against federally ordered integration of public schools. This melodramatic gesture fell flat.

Clearly the smooth crooner, who originally rose to recognition based on naughty songs he performed with Afro-American musicians— "Red Nightgown Blues," for example—had by middle age repudiated his past transgressions. By now, he wanted you to know, he was thoroughly conservative, to the extent of being openly racist, and even monarchist. He had little use for the legislative voice, ruling instead through a loyalist clique that would routinely sustain his vetoes and rubberstamp his proposals. With the legislature thus bottled up, Davis was free to pursue his own priorities, which were exceedingly petty. Under the circumstances, it is no surprise that one of his only major accomplishments during an era of jet-fueled global progress was building a new governor's mansion—a myopic homage to clueless executive power.

Under the auspices of the early-sixties' Davis administration, John first took a seat at the table of state power. He clearly went in with high hopes, with plans to repeal fair trade once and for all—to sink a stake into the heart of the vampire. But beyond passing token feel-good legislation on peripheral issues, John soon found that he was being stymied by the current alignment of political forces. No wonder, smothered under the petty diktats of the Davis administration, John wished a quick exit via higher office. With this exit blocked in 1962, he settled into a less-than-stellar stint as a first-term state representative.

Schwegmann spent most of this first term voting no. Racking up an impressive list of "against" decisions, he spoke and acted in opposition to every manifestation of what he perceived to be wasteful spending proposed by Davis. John voted against all raises for public officials, including for district attorneys, judges, and assessors; against pension boosts for legislators; against establishment of overlapping bureaucratic agencies (employed, he said, to pad state budgets); and against the empowering of rate-setting regulatory boards (acting as price-fixing wolves in consumer-protective sheep's clothing).

When Davis proposed a $60 million bond issue, much of it aimed at improving the image of Louisiana as a "sportsman's paradise," John

voted no, claiming it was stuffed with pork. It passed. John also voted
no on a bill authorizing funds to build a new governor's mansion. This
also passed. Indeed, John happened to be the only one, the lone voice
in the entire Louisiana House of Representatives, to vote against the
Jimmie Davis state budget for 1964.[24] What a singular act of sticking
up for principle!

For being consistently negatory, John naturally came under fire. It
was one of Hale Boggs's main anti-Schwegmann talking points in the
1962 election, and it came up again in John's 1963 reelection campaign
for state representative. John developed a deft response to the naysayers
about his naysaying. He rationalized his stance by turning negatives
into positives: it is better to oppose change when the change promises
to turn the future for the worse; saying no is actually a courageous act
rather than a cowardly knuckling under to pressure; negative votes can
act to protect and defend against greed and waste; resistance opposes
the wrong and fights for the right.

In such a manner John attempted to inoculate his negative actions
against accusations of serving as an ineffectual legislator during his first
term. For example, responding to Boggs's 1962 charges over his lack of
accomplishment, he replied, "That's true. But how can you win with a
stacked house?" To similar charges in 1963, he again complained about
how "the Davis administration had complete control of the House…."
What he is saying in both cases is that under such powerfully restricted
circumstances it is better to engage in a spirited, morale-boosting
defense than an enervating, ineffectual offense. As John explained,
he "fought a withholding action to prevent the administration from
wasting still more money." While he may have lost most of the battles,
"I came out fighting. And at least I was loyal to the people."[25]

It could be gathered from the discussion so far that John had
no positive impact during his first term in the Louisiana House of
Representatives. While this is largely true, he did manage to author
two bills during this time that actually passed. The first was a feel-good
measure that everyone could get behind: a $1,000 state tax exemption
for various types of disabled dependents—who were crudely called
blind, deaf, lame, and retarded back in those insensitive days. Clearly the

passage of this bill reflected widespread recognition of, and sympathy for, John's son Guy, who was born mentally disabled. John's other victory, the opposite of altruistic, came from a bill he sponsored that funded the Jefferson Downs racetrack. Though both bills had roots in Schwegmann self-interest, the Louisiana legislature could easily see that the two had only innocuous consequences and thus passed them. Not so, however, with more substantial Schwegmann-sponsored efforts, such as banning the creation of a new milk commission and curtailing the power of the liquor control board. These measures were dead on arrival.

The same fate awaited another cause he got behind. For a reason probably involving his own minimal schooling, fiscal fundamentalist John early on developed a soft spot for education generally and teachers specifically. In 1963 he was in the forefront of advocating salary raises for Louisiana's teachers. A bill authorizing the hikes was introduced in that year but then defeated, having been amended to death. All along, John maintained that the solution was simple. First forgo all raises to elected and appointed officials. Then apply business principles to government finances. After that, money will be readily available for teachers. But until then, teachers will forever be "at the end of the road. There's never going to be a time [for them] because there are too many [other] things to play politics with."[26]

The troubling travails of John's first term as state representative can be summed up in a single episode—this involving John's opposition to an increase in legislator pensions. Note that in today's terms the sums involved were trivial: if a lawmaker served twelve years, then that legislator would receive a $7,500 pension per year, up from $6,000 previously. Yet John was adamantly opposed to this modest surrogate pay hike. In full impolitic fury, he fumed against representatives already overpaid at $50 a day. Surely, he harrumphed, teachers and other civil servants deserved first place in consideration before any lawmaker pension boost.

In making his case against upping legislative pensions, John took on a major sponsor of the bill, a Shreveport attorney and state representative with the elegant name of Wellborn Jack. Apparently,

Wellborn had been John's mentor when he first entered office. So it was with sadness that John stood to oppose him. "Though I love him like a father," he told the chamber, Mr. Jack was wrong on pension raises. Of course, Wellborn Jack retaliated. As John's speech ended, Wellborn bum-rushed the podium and began aggressively massaging John's shoulders, appearing friendly but making things perfectly clear: "Now understand, son, this is our money that is coming to us. Do you understand that, or do we have to go to the woodshed?"[27]

Ultimately, this velvet strong-arm tactic backfired, as Schwegmann used a publicity still of Jack's grasp as grist for his indictment of misallocated state power. In a supermarket ad appearing on September 9, 1963 (using the ad to further his reelection campaign), a photo is featured of Wellborn Jack icily gripping John Schwegmann, with a caption underneath quoting the woodshed comment. In true leadership style, John's ensuing comments on this incident attempt to rise above the controversy. As he says, it is not about pensions but priorities. Wellborn Jack is looking out for himself. Meanwhile, people throughout Louisiana are looking for help. As John reflects, "This is the tragedy of our time—there are so many things in the state that need shoring up." He bemoans that policemen, firemen, and teachers are pitifully underpaid, and hospitals are woefully underfunded. And in the midst of it all, lawmakers push for pension raises. John was disgusted.

Despite having accomplished little, and despite having antagonized colleagues with his disdain for playing the game, it is surprising that important constituencies viewed State Representative Schwegmann more than favorably during his first term in office. For instance, the Louisiana State Chamber of Commerce awarded him a perfect score for his voting record. Similarly, according to a newly formed conservative group, the Louisiana Voter Service, Schwegmann ranked highest of all legislators in its "consistency index," with ratings based on such indices as sound fiscal policy and government integrity.

In the biggest kick of all, he was endorsed for reelection by the *Times-Picayune*. This is what New Orleans' paper of record had to say in an editorial appearing November 15, 1963: "Mr. Schwegmann has been an active, aggressive member of the House and has a top-rung voting record. He has stood for the good government bills and against state waste." It goes on to note favorably his opposition to the lawmakers' pension boost and the new governor's mansion.[28] Given such a glowing media tribute, and with approval from business and conservative organizations, John easily waltzed his way into winning reelection to the Louisiana House.

JOHN'S SECOND TERM AS state representative, lasting from 1964 to 1968—one of the most exciting periods in American history—rolled out much like a dreary remake of his first term. Only this time around, "Machiavellian McKeithen" had replaced the "Singing Governor."

An acolyte of the Long family, John Julian McKeithen was never averse to pandering to the crowd with faux-populist appeals and slogans, the most famous being his lazy-tongued signature line: "Won't you hep me?" Beneath his colloquial veneer, however, "Big John" was calculating to the core. He would play the race card when need be but could subtly change his spots to adapt to shifting circumstances. In his first race for governor, for example, he won by only a slim margin (52% to 48%) partly by race-baiting his opponent, Mayor Chep Morrison of New Orleans, stoking fears of Morrison's ties to the NAACP. Later, however, McKeithen acted to ease racial tensions by appointing well-regarded African Americans to positions of influence. The same type of two-step is seen in his demographic appeals to the masses, rallying class resentments against the rich and their enablers, the "professional politicians, power brokers, and big money people fighting me every step of the way." In truth, Big John embodied all of these descriptions. He was a long-time pro pol, a well-seasoned dealmaker, and an avatar in the art of corporate fundraising.[29]

Slick as he was in presenting a Janus-faced image, McKeithen was no mere dilettante, adept only at the superficialities of public relations. In fact, he was the consummate pragmatic politician. Under his two-term tenure, lasting from 1964 to 1972, he successfully attracted business to Louisiana, streamlined government (eliminating unproductive "deadheads"), managed to raise taxes, and expanded public institutions, such as schools and prisons.

He also pulled off a political masterstroke by amending the state constitution to allow governors to serve two consecutive terms. In the eyes of many in the Louisiana political power structure—including Russell Long, Allen Ellender, and Alton Ochsner, along with the major newspapers in New Orleans, Baton Rouge, Alexandria, and Shreveport—McKeithen apparently had done such a bang-up job that suspending the one-term limit seemed a capital idea at the time. Perhaps the careers of subsequent governors have since led to buyer's remorse among some original supporters. Still, this does not take away from McKeithen's impressive skill in extending his own political life.

As in his first term, Schwegmann spent most of his second term as state representative voting no. In a furious attempt to roll back the fearsome momentum of an ever-expanding state budget—"Now over a billion dollars!" he cried out in alarm in a 1967 ad—he voted against all tax increases, all salary and pension raises for elected and appointed state officials, nearly all bond issues, and a sneaky proposal to grant state colleges the power to raise fees ("I think this thing stinks," he commented on the measure, as it would inevitably open the floodgates to higher tuition).[30] Of course, as before, he lost all these fights. In one stark example, a bill to raise the annual salaries of district attorneys statewide from $17,500 to $22,000 passed in an 89 to 7 landslide, with Schwegmann in the lonely opposition.

Despite appearances, however, John did not spend the entire second term hitting his head against the wall. If nothing else, he made progress in deepening his philosophy of government. Above all, he came to realize that government did indeed have at least some affirmative role to play in helping to improve society. It can be a force for good, for example, if it works judiciously in favor of an increase in health and welfare. Thus in his second term John supported a bond issue that increased funding for New Orleans' Charity Hospital, continued his crusade to raise teacher pay, and successfully co-sponsored a pioneering bill on child abuse, which provided immunity to anyone reporting this silent crime.[31] John also came to see that government could help promote safety. Thus he voted in favor of beefing up administrative procedures in such areas as drivers' licenses, car inspections, liability insurance, and parole boards.

Yet the government's most important role, he believed, was in its responsibility to prevent monopoly. In its tolerance and even furtherance of manufacturer price fixing, the Louisiana state legislature had completely shirked this responsibility. The only progress against monopolistic practices had come via the courts through victories won by Schwegmann himself. As would be expected, in his second term as state representative John tried on numerous occasions to introduce bills against price fixing. With his current dairy fixation, a measure he introduced in 1967 spoke of "suspending price fixing by processors, wholesalers, and retailers of milk." As usual, it lost.

When it came to big-picture social issues, however, John's minimal theory of good government failed him. For it afforded no solutions big enough or creative enough to address the scope of the problems. On crime he had nothing to say beyond the standard reactionary bluster: "[We need] the strongest measures possible to curb the ever-increasing crime rate." Speaking against the massive project of U.S. urban renewal, a huge issue in the 1960s, John lamely protested that "slum eradication" could best be accomplished by "private enterprise." But his most ridiculous response to a larger social issue came in opposition to what was called the "Triche amendment," which attempted to soften a classic Cold War ban on the teaching of communism and atheism in the schools. In speaking against the amendment, John sailed off the rails: "The day we teach there is no God in our schools we are going to need ten million policemen."[32]

In summing up his legislative career so far, it is fair to say that John was stronger on economic and weaker on social issues. He possessed a deep understanding of business, but only a superficial appreciation of its interaction with other cultural spheres. Yet his insipid positions and occasional gaffes on social affairs did not really matter at this point. For John had got it right on the bread-and-butter priorities most important for the rising mass of middle-class consumers. For this reason, the voters of Jefferson Parish decided to kick him upstairs.

* * *

WITH POPULATION GAINS and corresponding reapportionment, an extra seat opened up for Jefferson Parish in the state senate. John got the nod. He was the best man for the job. Despite his oppositional image, he remained steadfast in public perception as the good government candidate. His track record in this regard was above reproach. So it happened in 1967 that John Schwegmann was essentially ushered into the Louisiana State Senate. He would represent the Eighteenth Senatorial District, encompassing Jefferson Parish minus its remote first, second, and third wards. His term would span 1968 to 1972.

Who better to anoint as the new senator than a postwar Jefferson Parish pioneer entrepreneur? It was as if John were swept into higher office on a magic carpet. As early as October 1967, the *Times-Picayune* commented favorably on a Schwegmann candidacy to fill the new "senatorship": He is "by no means a diplomat…but has solid support." Four months later, on the eve of the election in February 1968, the *Times-Picayune* offered its formal endorsement: "The outspoken Representative Schwegmann stands high with Jefferson Parish voters for his integrity and concern for the public interest, and we believe he deserves promotion to the Senate."[33]

Buoyed by such a ringing endorsement, John easily sailed to victory in February 1968, his vote count at 13,222—over four times the total of any Republican challenger. Indeed, this 1968 election was notable for a clean sweep by the Democratic Party of the state legislature: absolutely no Republicans were elected that year. Surely, this represented the darkest hour before the southern Republican dawn.[34]

ON FEBRUARY 1, 1971, John telegraphed his next political move. At the very top of Schwegmann's weekly supermarket ad that day, bold-faced copy asked readers to imagine: "Suppose YOU were the newly elected governor of Louisiana. What would be the first thing you would do?" Yes, it was that time again. Another campaign season had begun. But this time John would aim straight for the brass ring. No more dilly-dallying in the state legislature. He had had it with the House and was already fed up with the Senate. If anything, his one term spent in the upper chamber seemed more unpleasant than the two terms he had spent in the lower. The same pettiness, now combined with a higher level of haughtiness, was enough to leave John almost screaming in despair. "I can't stand the Senate anymore," he sputtered, redoubling his disdain by quoting the old saw, "If you lay down with dogs, you come up with fleas."[35]

The 1960s were over, the 1970s just begun. John looked around, surveyed the political scene, and finally decided to cash in his chips. He could see the same nonsense stretching out into the infinite distance. He had no future as a state senator. It was time to get out. But not before pulling off his most audacious stunt yet. As his last act in politics, or so he believed at the time, he would offer himself up for governor of Louisiana.

He and his choice for lieutenant governor, Parey Branton from Shongaloo (located in Northwest Louisiana), picked a tough year to run. The governor field was crowded, with eighteen Democrats in the race. Among the heavyweights vying to win the November 1971 Democratic primary were U.S. Senator J. Bennett Johnston, U.S. Congressman Edwin Edwards, former Governor Jimmie Davis, and ex-Louisiana Congressman Gillis Long. Each had a particular strength: Johnston his gravitas; Edwards his glamour; Davis his folksiness; Long his family name. Against this impressive pack, Schwegmann possessed only his reputation as a champion of the people—a once-glowing image grown ever more rusty by his lack of results over an eleven-year span in office.

Determined to beat the odds, John designed a radically streamlined campaign. Gone was almost all talk about big-picture national issues. The campaign would not discuss foreign aid or military intervention. It would not come down on communism. It would barely even mention racial integration. Instead, John would pound home a blend of three primary character themes: his honesty and ability; his role as courageous fighter; and his success as a businessman. Aside from some standard denunciations of taxes and government waste, and except for his fierce opposition to the Superdome (discussed in detail in chapter eighteen), that was pretty much it.

But how could he do otherwise than focus on abstract character qualities. Certainly he could not pump up his positive political accomplishments. As it was, he spent a lot of wasted campaign time justifying his record of negative votes. One justification went like this: "I vote against everything that is bad and for everything that is good. If I vote more against, that's because they have more laws that are not in your interest." Here, as he had done before, John can be seen spinning his lack of accomplishment as an affirmative manifestation of courageous behavior.

Going further, John insisted that his absence of significant wins actually reveals a true fighter with real backbone: "Opponents brand me as 'anti-everything' because I refused to be a 'jellyfish' and go along." In one instance, he went full throttle, presenting his lack of results as being the best outcome of all. Here, Schwegmann quoted Huey Long, who once purportedly said, "If we do nothing for the whole four years, we will have accomplished more than all the others." Sometimes, John dispensed altogether with fancy justifications. As he put it bluntly in one speech: "They say John Schwegmann votes against everything. Friend, when it's wrong, I got to."[36]

So in positively positioning himself for his monumental battle for governor, John had no choice but to highlight his three best character qualities. The first of these was his honesty and ability. It was a primary plank in his platform: "To promote honesty and competence in government." He would show up at speeches holding a broom, a symbol of the good sweeping out the bad, of integrity over corruption. He could be high-minded on this score: "Friends, honesty is the foundation of everything." Meanwhile, he was not above scurrilous denunciations of his fellow politicians for their lying and thieving ways. In Baton Rouge, for example, there are "more brains than needed…but no honesty." And regarding his opponents for governor: "It's either me or the crooks."[37]

John needed some type of genuine gauntlet to throw down to prove that his declarations of integrity and ability were no mere empty rhetorical gestures. So in July 1971, he did something that probably sent shockwaves through his opponents' camps. He declared that on being elected he would reveal the source of all his campaign contributions.[38] Going further, he would release all of his federal and state income tax filings for every year he was governor. Certainly in offering up these potentially embarrassing personal records, John was in the forefront of what would later become a general trend toward transparency. At the same time, however, John gave his foes ammunition by leveraging this gesture into a grandiose pronouncement: "I'm not a politician. I'm a statesman."[39] Boy, did all the others in the race make hay out of that inflated statement, ridiculing John for being a pompous ass—and drowning his statesman-like show of transparency under a sea of guffaws.

The second broad theme John ran on in 1971 was his long-proven reputation as a fighter, a crusader, and champion of the common people. He had fought for the people on the legal front, on the economic front, and now on the political front. During the current campaign he reminded voters of his past battles and updated them on those ongoing. As of 1971, for example, a fight was still continuing over the legitimacy of advertising prescription drug prices. John had fought tenaciously over this issue for twenty years, but, as he admitted, "to no avail." John did note in an ad, however, that, as of January 1971, Pennsylvania declared that it would no longer ban advertising of prescription drug prices.

Naturally, John also played up his ongoing battle against the milk industry. As of 1971, this fight had spooled out for over a decade. John used the gubernatorial campaign to highlight how this struggle for the people's interest had cost him "thousands of dollars" and lasted "for years and years." Here he had been stymied at every turn, and prices on health-nurturing milk remained unconscionably high, "from the cow to a baby's belly."

One reason, arguably the main one, why John never successfully resolved the milk price fixing issue is, unlike with liquor and drugs, he simply lost concentration. He could no longer keep his eye on the ball—his awareness constantly shifting between business and politics.

In the process, John's political perceptions, never too keen to begin with, seem to have deteriorated even further. Consider that by 1971 his gubernatorial opponents, some more distinguished than others, were all reduced to nothing more than "crooks," "lowly creatures," "slick, slimy, squirming," "double-talking" "two-bit" hypocrites. Selecting among these debased criminals was "like choosing a thief to unlock your safe." Filled with "corruption, extravagance, waste," they cared nothing for the people, only their careers.[40]

In grotesquely reveling in such vicious indictments against his fellow politicians, John lost his way. Thus unhinged, he fell into a kind of paranoia. Darkly he summed up the situation: He was an "unsuccessful politician with many enemies." Indeed, Schwegmann had so many enemies that "believe me, friend, I might even get killed."[41] In the end, John somewhat recovered his equilibrium, falling back on the more measured formula that "a man of strength and stamina is needed to confront and change" such entrenched corruption.

Besides being honest and a perpetual fighter, John declared as his third major strength that he had achieved business success based on his own exemplary efforts. Then, stretching logic, he contended that his hard-earned retail success provided unique abilities to run government. First he established his own bona fides in this regard: "Grocerymen are the solid foundation of America." From there he leaped to a wild conclusion: "Businessmen know best how to run government." By selecting someone who takes a business approach to government finances, "People can get more for their money and pay less taxes." John prided himself on being the perfect example of a businessman-turned-politician who, given sufficient power, could successfully apply rational economic principles to government. John noted how rare this is: "I am the first businessman in Louisiana to run [for governor] in sixty years." In fact, he argued, this is the reason Louisiana politics is so over-the-top corrupt, because businesspeople in the state do not participate in government.

John demonstrated this business-centric economical approach to governing in his campaign style. First off, all advertising was done on the cheap. Speaking in August 1971, Schwegmann said that he had spent a mere $30,000 so far over the first six months of the campaign. The total included seven billboards statewide and a gaggle of newspaper ads. Sam Hanna, editor of the *Concordia Sentinel* (Ferriday, Louisiana), described how John traveled the state with fistfuls of hundred-dollar bills, personally placing ads in local newspapers on the fly as he bounced around on the Louisiana hustings.[42] These print ads he preferred over television advertising. For John hated TV ads, thinking they made everybody appearing in them look like a "cream pie." Actually, though, he just disliked all the glitz surrounding nouveau political campaigns, which emphasize image over substance. His squeamishness in this regard even extended to a 45-inch single—a pretty decent country ditty composed and recorded by New Orleans' country/rockabilly star Curley Langley—that sang Schwegmann's praises as a champion of the people. Unfortunately, uptight John was too embarrassed to promote such musical frivolity.

John's reluctance to indulge in image over substance worked perfectly well—against him, that is. The same went for his much-criticized "grip-and-grin" style. By several accounts, he was not very good at relating to people up close and personal, exhibiting restraint rather than exuberance in encounters with strangers. As reporter Margaret Martin of the *Shreveport Times* observed: "There's something a little boyish and shy and a little bit of an 'unsure of himself' air about the man…." The perceptive Sam Hanna interpreted John's tentative style this way: "Schwegmann is not the politician type. He doesn't meet people easily and he doesn't get your name. For to him it doesn't really matter. He's speaking past you to the masses of people. That's the way he sells groceries, and that's the way he's running for governor."[43]

John's awkwardness in intimately confronting the public is particularly revealed in one homely incident on the 1971 campaign trail. In this instance, he had traveled back to the place it all began—the old corner store on Piety and Burgundy in the Bywater. Apparently not having visited the place in ages, he was hesitantly looking around when two neighborhood ladies walked up to greet the legend. "You're John Schwegmann, aren't you?" After acknowledging his identity, one of the women asked him, "What are you doing now?" "Well, I'm running for governor," he replied, followed by a bashful laugh. The two responded with a cheerful, "We're going to vote for you then."[44]

Looking objectively at this encounter, it is almost painful to witness the squandered opportunities involved here. Why was he so sheepish? Why did he not seize the moment, boldly proclaiming his noble candidacy at the top of his lungs right here in the heart of his old neighborhood? This visit could have served as the centerpiece of his campaign. As it was, John did not even have the presence of mind to urge the nice women to vote for him. No wonder he lost!

Given John's deficiencies as a campaigner and less-than-stellar legislative record, his opponents for governor found it easy to dismiss him as a serious contender. Thus they were in for quite a shock when, as summer turned to fall in 1971, they began to notice polls showing John suddenly surging to the top of the charts. In his editorial cited earlier, Sam Hanna had warned everyone not to underestimate John Schwegmann. And he was right. In mid-September, gubernatorial rival Gillis Long received internal polling results that nearly floored him: John had risen to number one! In stricken response Gillis exclaimed, "It's unbelievable!"[45] Other pollsters, though, corroborated this finding. Louis, Grace, and Bowles (based in Dallas, Texas) found John running first in New Orleans and second statewide, behind only Edwin Edwards.

Confronted with these sobering polls, John's powerful foes decided to lower the boom on this political interloper. John McKeithen had already set up the attack. In late August, Big John commented to the press as follows: "It would be a tragedy if John Schwegmann were elected to governor." Then he went straight for the jugular, aiming his lance directly at John's most sacred symbol—namely, his image of himself as an honest man and noble crusader. He is none of these, charged McKeithen. In fact, Schwegmann "is a fraud, as everyone who knows him knows." In a final thrust, Big John attacked with his most apocalyptic rhetoric yet, bluntly declaring that, as governor, Schwegmann "would be an absolute catastrophe to this state. He is dangerous."[46]

Building on McKeithen's devastating opening salvo, other allies of the sitting governor piled on like picadors to finish off the wounded candidate. In a doom-and-gloom style matching McKeithen's, State Representative Leon Soniat bemoaned the prospect of John reaching high office: "God help the people of Louisiana if John Schwegmann is elected governor. His election would set the state back fifty years." Uttering a similar admonition, Jamar Adcock, in slightly twisted syntax, warned that, "It would be a tragedy unparalleled by the Civil War for John Schwegmann to be elected governor." Finally, Moon Landrieu, the powerful new mayor of New Orleans, chimed in against John. His tactic was not so much to savage John but to belittle him. According to Moon: "John Schwegmann is so poorly informed on the governmental process, you have to excuse him on the basis of ignorance."[47]

Of course, being a true warrior and not a poseur, John fought back against these fierce stabs with feral counterattacks of his own. Squarely targeting the prime instigator of the undermining effort, Schwegmann mercilessly castigated McKeithen, accusing him of criminal involvement in a major financial scandal surrounding the Louisiana Loan and Thrift Corporation. Meanwhile, he minced no words in describing the "puppeteer's" allies. They were "con artists," "graft peddlers," "bagmen," and "bums."[48]

John then moved on to tackle his direct political opponents. Bennett Johnston was pro-tax and had no backbone; Edwin Edwards was a pro-price-fixing political dandy with one of the worst absentee records in U.S. congressional history; and Gillis Long had done nothing more than feed off the political trough all his life. It should be emphasized here that all these strident positions taken by John against his political foes were thoroughly publicized in amazingly detailed ads for Schwegmann Brothers Giant Super Markets. Such a controversial campaign for governor waged via newspaper advertising by a successful grocery store merchant has never been seen before or since.

As the clock ticked down on the November primary, desperation set in on the part of John. Apparently, polling began showing that his opponents' shock tactics had worked, and John's trend-line was seriously declining. At first, not willing to accept this severe downdraft in momentum, John lashed out with threats and pleading. "You can't afford to let John Schwegmann down," he warned the voters (falling into the fatal embrace of third-person self-reference)…"not after all the fighting I've done for you." In his desperation, John exaggerated the stakes involved in his defeat: there would be "far-reaching bad effects on the state [if] people didn't stick with him." For his loss would discourage future champions of good government from fighting.[49]

Near the end John finally became resigned to the fact that when Louisiana's most powerful political forces ignite their afterburners in defense of the status quo, a maverick challenger stands only a snowball's chance in hell of prevailing. By all rights he should have already learned this lesson throughout three extremely frustrating terms in the state legislature. Yet temporarily blinded by the bright light of the fire that perpetually burned within, he had suspended belief in this implacable reality for most of the campaign. When in the last days of the run he came stoically to accept the death of his political career in this final race, he attempted to do so with dignity. As he summed up the experience: "I came in eleven years ago as a rich man, an honest man with a good reputation, and I'm going out that way."[50]

In the final tally for the November 1971 Louisiana Democratic gubernatorial primary, Edwin Edwards placed first, with 24% of the vote count, followed by J. Bennett Johnston, with 18%. Also racking up double-digit (percentage-wise) vote counts were Gillis Long (14%) and the old croaker himself, Jimmie Davis (12%). For his part, John Schwegmann was pretty much crushed, coming in a distant fifth with a lowly 8% of the vote. What a way to go out, suffering such an ignominious defeat. Yet surprisingly, whatever could be salvaged from his positive political reputation would soon be restored.

WITH HIS HUMILIATING DEFEAT in the race for governor, John surely thought his days in politics were over. He thought wrong. For in early 1975, Lawrence Chehardy—an extremely shrewd power-broker just beginning an unprecedented thirty-four-year reign as Jefferson Parish's tax assessor—approached John to fill an important spot just opening up. Specifically, in the wake of the adoption of a new state constitution in

1973, Louisiana created two new seats on its prestigious Public Service Commission (PSC), thus expanding its exclusive membership from three to five. Chehardy wanted John to run for the new seat representing District One, which included all of New Orleans plus the three most populous Eastbank wards in Jefferson Parish.

Likely climbing the walls, with no outlet to discharge his still-potent political energies, John jumped at the chance to get back in the game. Even sweeter, the PSC was right up his alley. After years spent banging his head against the wall in the legislature, he now had the opportunity to settle into an office devoted solely to protecting the public interest. With its roots in the old Louisiana Railroad Commission (established 1888), the Public Service Commission by John's time had evolved into a powerful regulatory body that oversaw electric utilities, telecommunications, and intrastate transportation. What a perfect job, then, for John Schwegmann, who would love nothing more than to spend his dotage bashing any scheming special interests out to screw the consumer. Hence, concealing his joy beneath a veneer of reluctant acceptance—the battered old veteran called out of retirement one last time to take up his "schweg" (axe) in defense of the common good—John entered the race.

The setting for the announcement of his candidacy for public service commissioner could not have been any more perfect, taking place in the dairy department at the Gentilly store.[51] There he stood within its cavernous expanse, speaking from an elevated podium propped up on multiple cardboard cases of Kool-Aid, his speech piped out (probably in garbled form) over the store's public-address system. His declaration contained some classic Schwegmann-esque utterances, variously angry, endearing, and boastful. "I am a fighter, not a pussycat," he reminded his audience. Then, in updating his shtick, "I have been a consumer protector long before Ralph Nader thought about it." Some customers responded to these zingers with bursts of applause. Other shoppers, meanwhile, merely maneuvered around the cardboard-crate podium in their quest to retrieve milk, cheese, and eggs from the coolers. John probably could not have been happier at the motley scene.

The date of the announcement was August 2, 1975. In November of that year, John sailed to an easy victory over Dan Kelly, a candidate backed by Moon Landrieu, with vote totals of roughly 100,000 to 50,000, respectively.[52] As a politician, John Schwegmann, now sixty-four years old, had fully redeemed himself.

He went on to serve on the PSC until 1981, when illness forced him to relinquish the position. But such was the power of the Schwegmann name that his oldest son ran for and won the vacant slot. Subsequently, John Francis Schwegmann served on the Public Service Commission for fifteen years, from 1981 to 1995.

18

THE EX-CHAMPION'S FINAL BOUT
No to the Superdome!

IN LATE OCTOBER AND EARLY NOVEMBER 1966, a full-page ad appeared in the *Times-Picayune* urging readers to vote yes for Amendment Ten, a measure authorizing establishment of the Louisiana Stadium and Exposition District (LSED): an area to be dedicated to a new professional sports arena—specifically, a domed stadium.[1] Way over-hyping the benefits of the stadium while outright denying its costs, the ad bordered on fraud. The domed stadium, it claimed, would generate millions upon millions of dollars in tourist and tax revenues—up to a gargantuan $445 million (in 1966 dollars) annually. With boatloads of money coming in from sports, conventions, and entertainment events, the stadium could operate at a yearly surplus of up to $3 million.

Best of all, according to the ad, the proposed Superdome "will not cost the taxpayer one red cent." Its primary funding stream would be a tax on hotels and motels. Construction bonds would be financed strictly by the private sector. "Neither the state nor the city [will back] these bonds in any way." For average citizens, the deal would be a slam-dunk win-win. The people of New Orleans and Louisiana would not only receive a virtual eighth wonder of the world for absolutely free, but they would also be floating on a geodesic sea of molten tourist gold. Estimates of riches reached stratospheric proportions. The Superdome would have a "greater economic impact on the city and state than 10 industrial plants." And hey, if all the above was not enough to convince you to vote yea on Amendment Ten, consider that no financial projection made so far has included "revenues brought by Major League Baseball, which is sure to come with the Superdome!"

THE FABULIST BEHIND THIS disingenuous piece of public relations hooey was one David F. Dixon, a legendary sports entrepreneur and scion of the New Orleans elite. Yes, Dave Dixon possessed the vision to imagine the Superdome. He also had the passion, drive, savoir-faire, and sangfroid to see his vision through to completion. Unfortunately, what he did not have was any easy understanding of why John Schwegmann, a mere "eccentric multimillionaire grocer," would dare oppose his master plan: an architectonic vision of pure splendor and civic virtue.[2] Little did Dave know he was pressing every button that buzzed beneath John's thin economic skin. Nor did he realize that he had raised the wrath of the fiercest foe of fiscal waste in the state. It did not take long for Dixon to figure out that he had indeed offended New Orleans' own version of Braveheart. For Schwegmann could just not endure it—all the puffery and hot air promising nothing but ballooning payments as far as the eye could see, with the financial burden inevitably to be placed squarely on the backs of the taxpayer.

So it would be war, as two implacable rivals clashed. One offered a sparkling vision crafted by the powers above to be handed down on a silver platter to a grateful public. The other presented the more prosaic concept of a people's project, financed, designed, and administered in a transparent process, with each major step approved directly from below by the voters. Of course, as is typically the case, top-down glitz and glamour triumphed over the bottom-up struggles inherent in a consensus approach, as Dixon and his formidable allies achieved a smashing victory in the battle over the Superdome. Meanwhile, left stunned and wandering on the battlefield, Schwegmann resembled nothing if not a crazy knight-errant struck senseless in defense of a silly dream against impossible odds.

The story of how the Superdome came to be is not easy to tell. Although the tale has its colorful moments, most of it is dull, involving reams of petty details, rafts of arcane legal and bureaucratic procedures, a mundane assortment of tawdry scandals, and, worst of all, an enormous cast of forgettable characters. Regarding the last, what makes the story so difficult to follow is that few of these characters were well-known public figures. Instead, most were behind-the-scenes power brokers who only came out into the open because they were either put on the spot and asked to perform public service or were forced to enter the limelight as the only way to seize the available spoils.

Consequently, the Superdome saga is populated by an endless series of names few but friends, family, and social/professional acquaintances could ever hope to recall. Nevertheless, this list of names is of more than passing interest. For when compiled and collated in all its complicated and, some would say, sordid glory—as it was by an alternative newspaper, the *New Orleans Courier*, in August 1973—the record presented in the Superdome story illustrates a near-picture-perfect portrait of the New Orleans' power structure as it existed during the decade from 1965 to 1975.[3]

Because the Superdome story is so complex and involves so many little-known actors, it is not told here in depth. Instead, the focus of this chapter is on John Schwegmann and his increasingly frenzied attempts to halt what he perceived to be a financially destructive juggernaut being rammed down the throats of New Orleans' citizens by elitist powers. Yet the reasons for John's fierce opposition can only truly be fathomed if the general outlines of the story are known. Following, therefore, is an abridged, admittedly biased, account of the Superdome saga, featuring John Schwegmann in the mock-heroic role of chief dome opponent.

*   *   *

DAVE DIXON HAD A DREAM. John McKeithen made it real. These two men—supported at crucial moments by Dave's beautiful and insightful wife, Mary—were the guiding lights behind the building of the Superdome. Dixon came first. As heir to the fortune of the Great Southern Box Company, which thrived even during the Great Depression, Dave Dixon had followed in his father's footsteps by becoming a great sports enthusiast.[4] Having attended Tulane University, he was a huge Green Wave fan who was absolutely aghast when Tulane, which in the 1950s fielded a dominating football team, cut back on its sports programs later in the decade. Nevertheless, perennial cheerleader Dixon was determined to make lemonade out of lemons. With championship college football now off the table, this would open the way to professional football!

After all, New Orleans and Louisiana had always been a great city and state for football. Moreover, the times were ripe for change. The stolid old National Football League now faced a nimble challenger, the American Football League, formed in 1960. Their rivalry quickly heated up, as competition between the NFL and AFL for players, fans, money, and media grew ever more intense. As the two leagues feuded, the sparks that flew only worked to stoke the popularity of pro football to new heights. By mid-decade, expansion fever was in the air—along with rumors of secret talks about a merger between the leagues. Clearly, then, Dave Dixon was in the right place at the right time to capitalize on these rapidly evolving developments.

As Dixon tells the story, his quest to pursue a pro football franchise for New Orleans first took shape in 1961.[5] At that point he set about to woo the movers and shakers in the upper echelons of professional football, doing his best to convince them of the desirability of placing a team in the Big Easy. Simultaneous with this pursuit, Dixon dreamed of building a brand-new stadium. While Tulane University already provided the city with a capacious stadium (83,000 seats), this facility would not do over the long haul. New Orleans needed—and indeed deserved—its own dedicated sports arena if it wanted to play with the big boys. The only real questions concerned what form this stadium would take and where would it be built.

Along the way on his parallel pursuits for a pro team and a new stadium, Dave Dixon pulled off a coup de théâtre, managing to arrange for a rare preseason pro football "doubleheader" to be played at Tulane Stadium in August 1963. The two games would feature the Dallas Cowboys, Detroit Lions, Chicago Bears, and Baltimore Colts: a veritable mythological array of football talent. While giving a huge boost to New Orleans' profile as a place where football magic happens, the doubleheader was marred by one incident: a wicked cloudburst flooded the field, causing the first game to be suspended for two hours. This setback at first horrified Dixon. But soon none other than the legendary George Halas himself showed up at Dixon's box to reassure Dave that the delay was no big deal. No need to worry, growled a jocular "Papa Bear." Everyone was having a great time, fans and players alike. Indeed, in retrospect, the flooding was the best thing that could have happened. For as Dave Dixon admits, "[T]he idea for the Superdome was born on that stormy evening."[6]

Yes, he thought, weather proof was the way to go. So naturally his stadium musings turned to some sort of covered structure. At first he entertained a retractable-roof concept, quite novel at the time. But his views soon veered toward a dome-type solution. This was only to be expected, as Houston had just recently completed (in 1963) its Astrodome. Why not take this concept—based originally on the visionary geodesic ideas of futuristic designer Buckminster Fuller—and go to town with it, make it even more splendiferous and fabulous? By 1964, then, a structure had crystallized in the mind's-eye of Dave Dixon that would soon become known as the Superdome. (He toyed with calling it the "Ultradome" but decided "Super" had a better ring to it.)

By late 1964, Dixon had refined his plans enough to take them to the next level. It was high time to bring in the politicians. Little did he know, though, that he himself would soon be ensnared in an entirely new political role, far divorced from the back-slapping old-boys' milieu to which he had grown accustomed. His first approach was to Victor Schiro, then-mayor of New Orleans, who in late 1964 was engaged in a heated reelection campaign with Jimmie Fitzmorris, the ever-popular city councilman. As it turned out, Dixon helped sway the excruciatingly tight mayoral election by throwing the Superdome bone to Schiro, who used it in a last-minute ploy to energize voters. Specifically, in his final speech on the very eve of the election, delivered sympathetically from a hospital room following an emergency appendectomy, the comfortably berobed Schiro described his fantastical plan to build a domed stadium in New Orleans to house a professional football team. The wildly enthusiastic response pushed him over the top in a "squeaker," won by just 800 votes.[7]

Seeing how successful the idea had been on a metro level, Dixon's next stop was to the office of Louisiana governor John McKeithen. Sometime in 1965 he pitched the concept directly to Big John. The domed stadium, he said, would be larger-than-life, "light years ahead of Houston." It would be infinitely more versatile than the Astrodome, a multipurpose facility able to accommodate "conventions, trade shows, and meeting rooms." It would spike the tourist industry higher than ever before.

After about twenty minutes Dixon's pitch began petering out. McKeithen asked him if he was through. While slightly different versions record what happened next, all amount to the same thing: McKeithen's reaction was overwhelmingly, almost embarrassingly, enthusiastic. In his own book, Dave describes how Big John slowly raised his big feet previously propped up on his big desk, stood straight up, raised a big clenched fist, then "slammed it down on his desk, proclaiming, 'My God, that would be the greatest building in the history of mankind! We'll build that sucker.'"[8]

THERE ARE DIFFERENT SCHOOLS OF THOUGHT about what motivated McKeithen's over-the-top embrace of the Superdome. One school views it as a clever political maneuver to garner greater popularity. Another sees it as evidence of statesman-like civic virtue. There is also a more nefarious interpretation: that Big John saw in the Superdome an almost unlimited opportunity for patronage and graft. Perhaps it was a mixture of these or other motives that drove McKeithen to cling tenaciously to the Superdome project as a signature political issue throughout much of his unprecedented eight-year tenure as governor. Certainly he played the project with the finesse of a grand master. Having become acquainted with the Superdome concept in 1965, he waited patiently until just the precise moment—just minutes after Louisiana State University's Cotton Bowl victory on New Year's Day 1966—to announce to the uproarious, joyous, and thoroughly sloshed Tiger fans that he, McKeithen, intended to "build the greatest dome in history." The crowd, of course, went ape.

From this jubilant starting point, dome supporters hit the ground running. In February 1966, the governor set up a Site and Finance Committee to determine where to locate the dome and, most important of all, how to pay for it. On a parallel track, the state legislature jumped on board, passing a yet-to-be-ratified constitutional amendment creating the Louisiana Stadium and Exposition District (LSED)—authorizing the establishment of a stadium location and an overseeing authority—to be submitted for voter approval in November 1966.

On the surface, everything seemed fine and dandy. But looking closer at the amendment, a loophole had been embedded that effectively nullified what were then strict state limits on the amount of money that could be raised on bond issues. Obviously, the lawmakers knew beforehand that the paltry sums being tossed around as cost estimates for the dome—roughly $35 million to $40 million—were pure fiction, and the real costs would be much, much higher. But supporters had no problem foisting this duplicity on the public. Indeed, Dave Dixon went on to barnstorm the state drumming up support for Amendment Ten, disingenuously proclaiming about the dome: "It's all free. Hotel taxes will pay!" And herein lies the initial deception that led to what critics at the time referred to variously as the Superdome "scandal" or "fiasco." Certainly this is what originally poisoned the chalice for the dome's arch-opponent, John Schwegmann.

It all unfurled so perfectly. By October 1966, the domed stadium campaign had been all but wrapped up and tied in a neat bow when the McKeithen-appointed Superdome Commission gave its solemn word of honor that no government backing would ever be needed to build the stadium. Then on November 1, 1966—on All Saints Day, of course—came the blockbuster announcement that the New Orleans Saints had been born as an official franchise of the National Football League! In the tumultuous ecstasy that followed, the LSED amendment passed a week later by an overwhelming 76% of state voters.[9] The Superdome looked to be a done deal, and from here on out it would be full steam ahead, with a completion date set for 1969, just three years later.

But it was not to be. For beginning the very next year, in 1967, the Superdome project submerged into a sea of troubles. As a result, 1969 as a target completion date came and went, as did 1970, 1971, 1972, 1973, and 1974—and still no Superdome. In fact, it took nine long, controversy-encrusted years before the Superdome was finally christened in August 1975. By then, predictably, all the original promises lay shredded in tatters. Instead of being a free gift to taxpayers, the domed stadium was now a ward of the state. Even worse, the Superdome had devolved into a "cash-gulping monster," as colorfully characterized by its most cogent critic, Allan Katz of the New Orleans *States-Item*.[10]

At this juncture in the narrative, it is tempting to step back and consider if and how the monetary costs of building, operating, and maintaining a professional sports stadium are balanced out or even surpassed by their financial, cultural, and even spiritual benefits. But this would be too much of a distraction. For anyone familiar with the perennial debate topic "Are Professional Sports Stadiums Worth It?" realizes that skilled arguments can be marshaled on both sides. Certainly, the Superdome itself can be considered both glorious and notorious in regard to any debate.

So no, the argument over sport stadium costs and benefits is not indulged here, as it digresses too far from the focus of this chapter: namely, John Schwegmann's iron opposition to the New Orleans Superdome project—or, more specifically, its anti-democratic process. For the record, John came down squarely on the side of those who believe that, in general, the costs of professional sports stadiums far outweigh their benefits. In a multifaceted critique, he enunciated much of what is wrong with these stadiums: they are public money sinks, playthings of the elites, and silly misallocations of taxpayer resources away from such serious social concerns as education and health. Moreover, boosters over-hype the tourist industry multiplier effect—with the bulk of benefits actually flowing only to well-connected stakeholders.

Indeed, at one point in his critique John goes to an extreme, suggesting that government should not support professional sports in any way at all, financially or otherwise. Unlike Dave Dixon, John Schwegmann was by no stretch of the imagination a sports fan. Thus he saw clearly the economic waste, social favoritism, and taxpayer burden involved in government sponsorship of professional sports. While he never went so far as to go against the strong civic desire for a new football team and professional stadium, he did forever refuse to acknowledge any transcendental value associated with these frivolities.

JOHN'S BATTLE AGAINST THE SUPERDOME did not begin immediately. This can be seen in a thoughtful editorial he penned in April 1967—six months after the LSED authorization passed in November 1966— about various location options for the stadium.[11] By all indications, the Dixon-headed Superdome Commission had previously decided on downtown. Contrarily, Schwegmann proposed three alternative metropolitan locations: New Orleans East, Lakeview, or somewhere in Jefferson Parish.

Regarding the first option, perhaps John was not privy to the foreknowledge that a New York developer, Marvin Kratter, had already offered a free 155-acre parcel in New Orleans East for the stadium, but the Superdome Commission had rejected it for reasons of expense, as a whole new infrastructure would have to be built there from scratch to accommodate it.[12] Infrastructure considerations went double for a Lakeview site. Nevertheless, John was clearly right that the most viable alternative to a downtown location for the Superdome would have been somewhere in Jefferson Parish. As it happened, a sore spot soon formed in the metro tug-of-war between Orleans and Jeff parishes over where to locate the dome—a battle that dragged on for four years until finally ended by court action.

Perhaps acting to focus the mind of the Dome Commission on selecting a site for the stadium, a bizarre offer was floated in early 1967 by Carlos Marcello. Apparently the Mafia Kingfish had from out of nowhere thrown his property into the pot, offering the city a free Superdome site at his infamous duchy called Churchill Farms, located in the swamps of Barataria.[13] Of course, the red-faced commissioners quickly swept this generous offer under the rug.

Forthwith, in June 1967 the Dome Commission settled on Poydras Street in downtown New Orleans as the future home of the dome. At the same time it also selected an architectural firm, Curtis and Davis, to design the new stadium—appointing its head, Nathaniel C. "Butch" Curtis, as project manager. Both the site and design decisions were somewhat tainted at the time by allegations of corruption involving the Dome Commission and the McKeithen administration. Yet any such pesky rumors were swiftly swatted away, and Superdome planning took a great leap forward. But so did the opposition. As discussed, Jefferson Parish already nursed a grudge against the Orleans-centric Dome Commission and its high-handed decision-making tactics. Now joining the ranks of the disgruntled were two railroads—the Kansas City Southern and the Illinois Central—whose downtown warehouse properties were both on the block to be confiscated and condemned.

It had been a whirlwind. Just six short months after the LSED amendment passed, the Superdome site had been selected and the architect chosen. Meanwhile, proponents and opponents alike paused slack-jawed awaiting word on the most important decision of all: how to pay for the damn thing. Yes, as of mid-1967 there was still no funding mechanism in place to finance the project. Worse still, estimated costs had begun soaring enormously. Remember, supporters had staked much of their persuasive case on how the people of Louisiana would get the dome for nothing. It would be cost-free! How to tell them now that that selling point had been but a bait-and-switch?

* * *

JOHN SCHWEGMANN HAD HAD ENOUGH. The perennial protector of the people was utterly disgusted. So far the whole Superdome project had proceeded in a wham-bam fashion, running roughshod over public opinion with a host of false promises. John was a canny businessman who had by this time seen it all in politics. He could spot a fraud a mile away. In so blatant a case, he had no filters. He must call a spade a spade. As usual, his response would not be popular. Yet he felt compelled to speak out. So John took up the cudgel of opposition to the Superdome with a vengeance, forever afterward nursing a grievance against its origins in elite deceit.[14]

At this point it must be emphasized that John did not stand firmly and irrationally against building a domed stadium. It is true that he displayed ambivalence, leaning to aversion, toward government support of professional sports. Yet he seemed perfectly content to get behind a new stadium—provided it was only as grandiose or modest as the people wish to pay for. In 1967, in his last year as state representative, before he was bumped up to state senator in 1968, Schwegmann introduced a couple of bills calling for transparency and democracy in all matters involving the Superdome. These early bills, along with later legislative and judicial efforts, were all fairly easily shot down.

With any attempts at inserting transparency and community involvement into the stadium decision-making process having been quashed in the legislature, the Dome Commission went freely on its merry, arbitrary way. By the end of 1967, word on the grapevine had it that cost estimates had tripled. Since no way in heck could the hotel/motel tax cover that bill, a mad scramble commenced to find a funding scheme. When rumors began circulating that the state would backtrack on its commitment not to back a dome bond issue, John blew a fuse. He accused McKeithen of using "grab tactics" in forcing a downtown location decision. He charged dome supporters with flat-out lying about costs and who would pay for them. Indeed, by the end of 1967, Schwegmann was predicting that the Superdome would be a super-boondoggle.

All throughout 1968, the mad financial scramble to find funds for the dome continued. Nothing was resolved. In February, Moon

Landrieu, future mayor of New Orleans, denied speculation that cost estimates for constructing the Superdome had skyrocketed from $35 million to $100 million. Technically he was correct: estimated costs had ballooned to only $95 million. To disguise who had to pay the tripled price—supposedly never to have been an issue in the first place—in May 1968 the Dome Commission devised a circuitous "lease" arrangement, whereby it granted itself authority to lease the Superdome to the State of Louisiana. Through this financial trickery, most costs would be passed on ultimately to taxpayers.

Schwegmann was beyond furious. As a new state senator, he immediately entered a bill prohibiting any future lease arrangement to finance the Superdome. In June 1968, this bill failed. Nevertheless, the Dome Commission took the hint and began exploring an alternative plan that involved receiving federal funding through urban renewal channels. This scheme, of course, also drove John ballistic. In anger he protested that if the mostly misled feds were to get involved in anything at all, they should stick to funding do-gooder projects, like improving Charity Hospital.[15]

As 1969 DAWNED, THE DIE was finally cast. The Superdome would be leased to the state after all, thereby receiving Louisiana's sovereign backing for dome bond offerings. A several-month series of rugby-style matches ensued—altogether a knockdown drag-out spectacular where supporters and opponents repeatedly piled on in the courts of legal and public opinion. Moon Landrieu initiated play by filing a "friendly lawsuit" intended to legitimate the lease arrangement. Then John jumped in, joined by luminary J. Bennett Johnston and others, to challenge the lawsuit on unfriendly terms: in other words, to block the leasing arrangement.

In March 1969, to the surprise and consternation of many in the "Comus class," Judge Oliver "Ike" Carriere sided with Schwegmann and his allies in opposing the constitutionality of the Superdome leasing scheme. With this judgment, the gates of hell opened, as dome supporters furiously filed over twenty appeals against the anti-leasing decision. The series of rugby matches finally concluded in June 1969, when the Louisiana Supreme Court overturned Judge Carriere's decision and voted in favor of authorizing the leasing arrangement.

Rather than be deterred by this setback, perpetual battler John Schwegmann actually upped the ante. In July 1969, he formed a watchdog group called HONEST, INC., that filed an injunction against holding any future bond sales to finance the dome. In effect he was telling the elites that although they succeeded in legalizing leasing, they would still face problems in actually selling the construction bonds. Proponents of the dome were incensed by this petty pushback against their grand plans. So they decided to retaliate, and over the last half of 1969 a harassment campaign against Schwegmann ensued.

This campaign employed both softball and hardball tactics. The softer approach borrowed from John's own arsenal. A year earlier, Schwegmann had published a page full of letters from those who supported him in his fight against the dome. For all intents and purposes, they look to have been issued straight from Schwegmann headquarters, but who knows? They certainly echoed all his talking points. One letter says: "I guess it is the poor people's lot again to have another sales tax on the food we eat to pay for this stadium." Another insists, "We need this 'gouging' made known and stopped by public pressure." Several letters feature ripe name-calling, as the dome is referred to as a "financial fiasco," a "white elephant like the Houston Astrodome," and a "$100 million monument to stupidity." Of course, there is also a congratulatory slap on the back for John: "You are to be heartily commended on your forthright statement in opposition [to the dome]."[16]

Turning the tables on this technique, in September of 1969 a Superdome advocate sent John a fiery open letter publicly berating him for his backward and cowardly position on the dome. To his credit, John published the letter in full, along with his own response. The two letters encapsulate much of the rhetoric that fueled the Superdome debate. The letter to Senator Schwegmann begins by establishing the (anonymous) writer's bona fides. Though not a native, he had lived in

New Orleans for so long that he had gone to grammar school at Saint
Aloysius before it became a college. He goes on to recall the opening
of the St. Claude supermarket as a visionary achievement, hailing
its founder's foresight and courage. But then he dispenses with the
mask and laces into John, essentially accusing him of having grown
soft, spoiled by success, and now too afraid to take risks. The original
John Schwegmann was not "faint-hearted and near-sighted." He had
"GUTS" and "CONFIDENCE" in New Orleans. After these slaps
in the face, the writer ended by smugly admonishing John: "Drop
your fight against the stadium…. Be the great man that people know
you are."

John did not take the bait. Rather than join the writer in a mud-
slinging contest, he took the high road. First he thanked the writer
for his initial "laudatory comments." John then took issue with an
accusation about being "near-sighted," insisting that his legendary
foresight was still quite intact, and he could foresee that the monetary
investment in the dome would eventually be dumped on the public—
which it was. At that point, though, he quit with any aspersions
concerning vision, courage, or confidence. Instead, John laid out quite
nicely the essence of his stance against the Superdome. It was not so
much the outrageous amounts of construction money or the horrific
cost overruns that fueled his opposition. As he clearly stated: "I am
against the Domed Stadium for more than just the cost…." Instead,
his ire was primarily fired by the primal violation of honesty and
trust exhibited by dome proponents. The only proper solution to this
violation is a new election. Here in streamlined form is what he said:

> The principal reason [I am against the Superdome] is that the
> people have been deceived…. Misrepresentation was used to get
> the stadium approved by the people…. The sanctity of their vote
> has been assailed, and their decision made null and void…. I am
> convinced that the only honorable thing to do is to re-submit the
> Domed Stadium proposal to the people for their vote. Then if they
> wish to subsidize it … it will be their own decision, not something
> foisted upon them through trickery and deceit.[17]

The anonymous writer's open letter is an example of a softball tactic used against John, trying to shame him publicly on a rhetorical level into dropping his opposition. When this did not work, bigger guns were called in. Rumors suddenly flew in late 1969 that Schwegmann Brothers Giant Super Markets were seriously shortchanging their customers by selling short weights—basically leaning on the scales. This was said to be the judgment of John Pearce, head of the Department of Weights and Measures in Louisiana and a reliable ally of John McKeithen.

When John Schwegmann got wind of this skulduggery, his anger hit the boiling point. He immediately penned an editorial charging the governor with "character assassination." In his commentary, John recalls how in 1968 McKeithen called him into his office for a hardcore tête-à-tête. This is actually a famous moment in Schwegmann lore. For to the question by McKeithen, "John, what can I do for you?" Schwegmann notoriously replied, "Governor, there isn't a thing you can do for me." From that moment on they were wary political opponents.

Aware that McKeithen had it out for him, John thought he was prepared for some sort of retaliation for his anti-dome stance. Little did he know that Big John would stoop so low as to try to destroy his business. This he did by spreading rumors through confederates that Schwegmann was "cheating the poor people of Jefferson of about 30 to 40 cents out of every dollar and a half purchase made in our stores." John pulled no punches in response to these "trumped-up accusations." In total defiance, he coldly intoned (in all capital letters at the end of his editorial): "If our stores have done anything wrong, I suggest that the governor have some of his controlled stooges bring charges against me."[18]

John fended off his attackers through late 1969. But by the end of the year, the formidable powers in favor of the Superdome finally managed to steamroll him. In December 1969, the HONEST lawsuit aimed at preventing dome bond sales was rejected in federal court. A follow-up appeal to the U.S. Supreme Court was summarily dismissed shortly thereafter in January 1970.

From this point on, John's opposition to the Superdome takes on a surreal dimension. By 1970 even the blind could see that the powers that be had decreed that the Superdome—come hell or high water—would be built. Nevertheless, Don Juan quixotically continued to battle on, refusing to cry uncle. It was almost like some terrible sequel to "Rocky"—a former champion being pulverized but refusing to back down. In the same Hollywood vein, it is amazing that he actually managed to eke out a limited victory, a technical knockout, in 1970.

THE 1970S BEGAN IN LOUISIANA with pregnant political pauses across the board. In New Orleans, Mayor Moon Landrieu took over from Victor Schiro, a move that portended an economically and racially uncertain future. Meanwhile, no one yet knew who would fill the shoes of Big John McKeithen. Somehow the new governor would have to guide the state into a brave new world split big-time by tensions between liberals and conservatives.

John Schwegmann was basically oblivious to this transition. He had long stuck to his guns, his guiding economic principles remaining firmly in place throughout a lifetime of rapid transformation. He knew what he had to do: namely, block the dome. Though he knew it was on the fast track to being built, he also realized that one final obstacle remained: the construction bonds actually needed to be sold to financiers. Yes, four years had passed and so far not one dollar for construction funds had yet been secured. For his part, John bent every effort to prevent these bonds from ever being sold.

His most heroic attempt to halt the bond-selling process involved barnstorming throughout Louisiana to defeat an obscure amendment up for vote in November 1970. This measure, Amendment Number 29, was but one of dozens of changes being proposed that year for the Louisiana State Constitution. The legislature had gone crazy, trying to push through an incoherent mish-mash of fifty-three constitutional amendments—a morass of legalistic measures with contradictory consequences and colliding effects that no one could possibly predict.

The chief objector to this mockery of an attempt at a constitutional rewrite was (no surprise) John Schwegmann. Drawing down whatever political capital remained to him as a state senator and consumer champion, John came out vehemently against that one particular measure, Amendment 29. This battle took the form of an extended campaign, not a one-off assault. Lasting from September through November 1970, his anti-29 assault took the state by storm.

John thoroughly explained his position and strategy in a two-part editorial appearing in the *Times-Picayune* on September 28 and October 7, 1970. He begins by emphasizing his lifelong fight against "deceptive methods." Then he cuts straight to the chase, focusing like a laser beam on Amendment 29, "a real sleeper." Talk about deceptive! Number 29 blandly stated that it allowed the state "to set uniform maximum interests rates on bonds…." Well, what was not to like? "Uniform" sounded good…until John unwrapped the slippery package. What it meant in effect was that the state would now have the ability to raise offered interest rates on bonds beyond the previous 6% ceiling to at least 8%. And wouldn't you know it: potential dome investors were asking for 8% returns. John made sure to highlight how in the amendment's fine print it mentions bonds for all the necessary stuff—roads, bridges, sewerage, etc.—but not for financing the domed stadium. In this way, Number 29's authors disguised their true intent: to sneak dome financing through the back door.

John was livid. He called Amendment 29 a "fraud," "complete misrepresentation," and "outright lies." Then he went further, crying foul over the whole amendment-jamming process. In this contrarian stance he rose to the peak of his persuasive power, warning the citizenry of disastrous consequences for wrong choices. Everyone should well consider that if the shameless deception of Amendment 29 is typical of all the other amendments, then it is in the people's best interest to vote against *every single one* of the fifty-three amendments being proposed in the upcoming election. In this acrid recommendation, John was every bit as stoic as the most determined field commander: "If there are any good ones [amendments], the good will have to go with the bad."

The finale of the two-part tirade begins on a regretful note, as John expresses bitterness that he had once again been called to fight.

It should have never been an issue in the first place. "The whole Domed Stadium transaction should have been completely above board—like Caesar's wife, above reproach." The fact that it was not has far-reaching deleterious consequences. "The hypocrisy, fraud, deception, and subterfuge demonstrated by the proponents of the Domed Stadium is one of the big reasons that today the people have no faith in their elected officials." But in the end he strikes a positive chord. By defeating Amendment 29, "People can again show who is Boss." This will be a victory for the ages, "Like David and Goliath, when Little John Q. Public goes against Big John McKeithen."[19]

Unbelievably enough, John actually triumphed in this fight. After two months of stumping the state railing against his pet deceptive amendment, John's message caught fire among core voters. Even more, his general indictment resonated far and wide. In the end, to most pundits' stunned astonishment, not only did Amendment 29 go down to defeat, so did every single one of the other fifty-three proposed amendments![20]

While this wholesale defeat was a disaster for city and state power brokers, it was also a blessing in disguise. For it forced the power structure to pursue the more difficult but more legitimate path forward, which led to a constitutional convention. Indeed, a constitutional convention was held in Louisiana in 1973, which resulted in a generally more positive representative political process. As for John, his big win in 1970 emboldened him. He realized that he had a lot more clout than he thought. He decided to use it to run for governor.

BY ANY NORMAL POLITICAL CALCULUS, John's decision to run for governor in 1971 would surely count as a major mistake. After all, as would be expected, John was basically trounced in the primary. Yet from John's unique perspective, his decision to run could be justified. First, consider that he was sick of being a legislator by then. A run for governor would at least allow him, no matter how it turned out, to go down in a blaze of shining principle. He would represent the best in public service, agitating for more openness and honesty in government, and advocating for more rational and compassionate approaches to taxing and spending. It was a long shot to be sure to stand a winning chance against the charisma, qualifications, and connections of his opponents. But who knew? Maybe his message would ring out to the crowd, appealing to their better instincts and capturing their sympathies. Certainly he had grounds to believe the race could be a replay of 1970, when he so perfectly performed the role of the spoiler.

But the fact that John continued to pursue Superdome opposition in the context of his governor run reveals a certain delusional element in his assessment of the political situation in 1971. First of all, despite his best efforts to stick a spoke in the bond-offering process, dome backers finally managed to sell their first construction bonds in August 1971. To commemorate this moment, the New Orleans *States-Item* (August 12, 1971) ran a hilarious cartoon on its editorial page depicting a Boh Brothers pile driver pounding the head of John Schwegmann, impaled on a pike, into the firmament beneath Poydras Street.[21]

Still, like a pit bull that just won't let go, John fought irascibly on. Prior to the bond sales in August, John had sent out a two-page press release in July burning with purple-faced rage. In it he called out "the Governor, the Dome Commission members, Dave Dixon, and their financial advisors, Blyth and Gillis Long's firm, Kohlmeyer & Co." as being no better than snake-oil salesmen in "an old-time medicine show...." He accuses all of them of playing "Russian roulette" with the state's finances. He even compares their deceptions to "bureaucrats in Washington who fool us into ruinous foreign policy commitments such as Vietnam...." He finally signs off with a threat and a pledge: "I again assert, as firmly as possible, that unless this Dome financing matter is resubmitted to the voters for their approval... if elected governor, I will refuse to appropriate any state funds to pay off the Dome Stadium's financial obligations until all the priorities of the State of Louisiana, such as hospitals, improved educational facilities, highways and bridges sorely needed, are first met."[22]

A primary factor fueling his anger at this time was the skyrocketing cost of the dome. In the beginning, supporters low-balled the estimate at between $35 million and $40 million. As noted, costs then tripled to $95 million. But as it turned out, this was nothing. The third stop up the elevator involved an estimate of $113 million. This amount was floated around the time of the bond sales in late summer 1971. But the upward journey did not end there. By fall, costs had risen to $129.5 million. A year and a half later they were up to $153 million. Finally, everybody basically stopped counting by end 1973, when cost estimates arrived at $163 million: nearly five times the original price.

With costs first starting to inflate when he was in the thick of his race for governor, John could barely contain himself. "The lyin' politicians are attracted to money like a hog to slop," he remarked in a nasty commentary, which went on to attribute soaring Superdome costs to graft, kickbacks, and every kind of corruption. The dome is a "boondoggle" that has been "railroaded and ramrodded down [the people's] throats." It represents "a moral, if not a legal, crime against every taxpayer in the state." Of course, in spewing this feast of imprecations, John did not forget to rub it in with an "I told you so": "When I predicted over three years ago [in 1967] that the domed stadium would cost over $100 million, I was called an irresponsible obstructionist and a kill-joy."[23]

In the wake of the August 1971 bond sale, John got desperate. As such, he performed a rather bizarre maneuver in October. Here he inserted himself directly into the bond-selling process, like a protester lying down in the street to stop a steamroller. Specifically, he began a letter-writing campaign to one of the head honchos of the New York investment community, the one and only David Rockefeller. But he did not stop at letter writing. John actually flew to New York City to meet with the great man, hoping to convince Rockefeller that the dome bonds were issued fraudulently.[24] Remarkably, this weird, almost unseemly, effort actually worked, as John succeeded in rattling the nerves of the New York power investors. Yet the victory was only temporary, as cooler heads soon prevailed, and all the bonds were eventually placed.

John had done absolutely everything in his power to stop the dome. But finally, still kicking and screaming, he had gone down to defeat. On the other side of the street, from the winner's perspective, victory was sweet. Dave Dixon reveled in his accomplishment. Out of thin air he had achieved his vision, the Superdome, a signature symbol of New Orleans and a true wonder of the world.

From this purely positive point of view, John's opposition was seen as inexplicable. Surely every resident of a big city wants a world-class stadium. So what if it goes somewhat over budget? A few tens of millions of dollars beyond projections is not the end of the world. Besides, over time the Superdome will surely easily recoup its original investment and be able to keep up with ongoing upkeep and interest costs—this by profiting off lucrative sports and entertainment events and trading on the mystical radiance of tourist currency. So from the eyes of a Dave Dixon, the obvious question to ask a rabid opponent of the Superdome like Schwegmann is, "What is your problem, sir?"

IN HIS 2008 MEMOIR, *The Saints, the Superdome and the Scandal*, Dave Dixon devotes a four-page-plus section specifically to John Schwegmann.[25] Within this section Dixon is by turns angry, bewildered, wary, bemused, and generous in his assessment of John's character. In the end, his telling of the story of Schwegmann's opposition is magnanimous, though it betrays a thick upper-crust bias that is overly suspicious of John's motives.

Dixon begins by recognizing Schwegmann as a "formidable adversary" and a "national pioneer in supermarkets." He goes on almost in awe of how John carved out his role as "a political force" by sustaining a campaign of presenting "his personal views on various political and social matters, always written clearly, powerfully, and forcefully." Then suddenly Dixon's tone shifts into an accusatory mode. He claims John initially supported the dome (in early 1967) but subsequently denied doing so. Essentially he implies that John lied, and thus could not be trusted.

Dixon continues by heaping praise on John's longtime lawyers representing the legendary New Orleans legal firm of Wisdom and

Stone—later morphing into the equally renowned Stone, Pigman, Walther, Wittman. Not only did this firm provide the brains and brawn behind John's fair trade victories, it was the only practice to win an anti-Superdome judgment (when Judge Carriere agreed that the state leasing arrangement was illegal). After noting that this lonely decision was quickly buried under an avalanche of successful appeals, Dixon goes on to express bewilderment over why Schwegmann would continue to attack the Superdome even after losing a key battle against it. Apparently, Dave could just not fathom John's outrage at the deception involved in pushing this project. Instead, he resorted to two-bit psychological analysis: "[N]o one, including the governor, could figure out what was motivating [Schwegmann]. He seemed confused and erratic."

In this way, Dixon could only cast aspersions on John's sanity. But then Dave realized—via the insight of his perspicacious wife—that John was crazy like a fox: that he was only using the Superdome as a hot-button issue to spring a surprise race for governor. After all, if the campaign were played right, Schwegmann could turn Baton Rouge, Alexandria, Lafayette, Monroe, and the rest of the state against the Superdome. And in the process he might enlist these alienated northern and cross-state minions into his camp.

With this (faulty) realization sinking in, Dixon was suddenly horrified. His emergency response: call the governor! John McKeithen, of course, saw the light. Both he and Dave together cynically concluded that Schwegmann had no real passion for the Superdome issue. Instead he merely used it functionally to attract votes for his governor run. Indeed, the two powerbrokers, Cheerleader Dixon and Machiavellian McKeithen, agreed to destroy the threat, with Big John doing the honors. Like a boss, he would "take care" of John Schwegmann.

Thus it was that McKeithen did his level best to decimate any Schwegmann support in North Louisiana. Speaking to a convention of Southern Baptists in Shreveport, Big John larded his critique on thick, spreading the mud on that remorseless old sinner John Schwegmann—and how he made his original fortune off liquor and gambling. "For many years, until U.S. Senator Estes Kefauver shut him down about ten years ago, he had huge revenues from those ninety-eight slot machines in that big old Giant Supermarket of his down there in N'awlins. And since he won that big anti-trust lawsuit…I understand that he has become the largest liquor dealer in the world. He has such tremendous cash reserves from those old slot machines and those huge wine, whiskey, and beer profits…that he can finance his own campaign."

According to Dixon's account, the classic smear tactics worked, and John discreetly bowed out of the governor's race at an early stage. Yet as has been thoroughly documented, this is simply not true. John fought furiously on in the governor's race to the bitter end. No way would a single speech by the loathed McKeithen intimidate Schwegmann into dropping out of the race. In this way, Dave Dixon's account is either wishful thinking or just plain wrong.

What Dave gets entirely right is how he pays somewhat reluctant but nonetheless respectful homage to a worthy opponent. He is initially puzzled by why, "for some reason, he and I never had cross words for each other." After all, Dixon looked down on Schwegmann for harboring nothing but a puny vision of New Orleans' future. He could have easily rendered every encounter with John unpleasant by scorning the unschooled upstart. But he did not. For Dave Dixon explicitly admired John Schwegmann's impressive warrior legacy—the way "he clawed, bit, kicked, chewed, and fought his way to the top of an impressive empire."

Too bad that Dave Dixon will remain forever distrustful of John's honesty and suspicious of his motives. Maybe he is right to be. Yet the evidence presented so far in this biography suggests Dixon is dealing more with an idealistic Don Quixote on some sort of dream quest than an insidious Lady Macbeth out for nothing but power. Anyway, Dixon actually "ended up liking John Schwegmann" after they finally spent a pleasant visit together. At that point it began to dawn on Dave that John was a true retail genius, "the Walmart of his day. I would not doubt that Sam Walton observed John Schwegmann in action…. In fact, I'd bet on it."

19

SUCKER PUNCH

Unexpected Collapse of the Schwegmann Empire

IN 1977, JOHN GERALD SCHWEGMANN SUFFERED a massive stroke. After being informed of this dread event and rushing to the hospital, his son John Francis encountered there the awful spectacle of a once-formidable man now thoroughly undone and shockingly near death. John F. remembers wondering whether his father would ever recover from this devastating blow. As it happened, John G., summoning his indomitable spirit, did in fact manage to pull through and put himself back together again. Amazingly, he lived another eighteen years after this terrible trauma. Yet the damage had been done, and he would never again burn with the same bright fire as before.

So John lived on, but his career came to a crashing halt. Just like that; from one day to the next, over. While it is certainly sad that John's professional life ended so abruptly, the more powerful emotion this tragedy evokes is an anguished regret. The strong temptation is to bemoan his indulgence in politics, to cast judgment on it as a big mistake, a useless waste of his precious time, a stress-and-frustration-packed fast track to a shorter lifespan. John had spent fifteen good years in the snake pit of state politics, and for what? He had made no noticeable dent for the better in public policy, and he failed to elevate the state's ethics. Meanwhile, he had dropped the ball on significantly expanding his retail empire. If only he had not taken such a disastrous detour into politics, John could have been a much richer, more famous, healthier, and far happier man.

Or so goes the storied formula, the one that sees happiness only as a function of ever-increasing riches and material success. But in an alternative take on this equation, a case can be made that John was actually having the time of his life during the seemingly self-destructive years he spent in politics. For over these years he lived like a virtual baron, an elegant bon vivant touring the world, dining in fine style, being chauffeured around in his Rolls-Royce, participating meaningfully in public affairs. John loved it all. He had an absolute ball traveling to the Continent nearly every year, luxuriating on fancy steamship passages to and from Europe, often accompanied by intimate family or treasured friends (sometimes by his favorite dog). When he arrived he would drive through the cinematic European countryside. On occasion, this pleasurable touring about would take a commercial turn, as he visited a vineyard, bought out the whole vintage, and had it shipped to his stores back home.

Living "la dolce vita" also extended to his love life. After two failed marriages, John decided simply to live in sin and take on a young paramour. This informality suited him perfectly, although it almost got him in big trouble when the arrangement ended after his stroke. It was great while it lasted, though, allowing him both satisfaction and an uncommon degree of freedom to maintain longstanding friendships and other relations without the usual jealousies taking center stage.

As appears clear, John enjoyed himself immensely throughout the political years, even as he exposed himself to high levels of life-threatening stress. So who can really say he made the wrong choice? Certainly it all depends on the value system employed to determine right from wrong. If one believes it better to accumulate ever-greater riches rather than fulfill deeper desires, then the outcome of a massive stroke induced by the futile pursuit of politics will be seen as at best a tragedy, at worst a stupid mistake. On the other hand, if desire fulfillment is placed foremost in the value hierarchy, then the animating idea will be to follow one's heart, wherever it leads, and damn the torpedoes. In this case, the pursuit of passion, whether heroically motivated or simply satisfying, justifies any outcome.

As WILL BE SEEN, during the political years of Schwegmann's career, everything—every decision, every action, and every relation—takes on a double-edged meaning that can be interpreted either positively or negatively, depending on the value system being applied. This double-edged interpretive process is most clearly on display in John's decisions concerning the expansion of the Schwegmann Brothers Giant Super Market chain. From a conventional retail viewpoint, rolling out a mere ten stores over thirty years is surely a glaring sign of failure. Successful chains, once they are up and running, normally grow by threes, fives, dozens, or even scores annually. John was pushing it when he opened two stores a year.

Before proceeding with any assessment of the motives behind Schwegmann's slow-as-molasses approach to chain expansion, store-opening specifics are here presented. As already discussed, John's first three supermarkets appeared roughly over the ten years following World War II: the St. Claude store opening in 1946; Airline in 1950; and Gentilly in 1957.

For the next decade afterward, a total of only four more stores were built. These included a store on Veterans Boulevard at Roosevelt Street, which opened in 1960; a store in Harvey on the Westbank (at 1615 Westside Expressway) in 1962; one on Annunciation and Melpomene streets, also in 1962; and another on Broad and Bienville streets in 1965. John's final spate of store building occurred over the late 1960s and early 1970s. It included three store openings: on West Airline Highway (1969); in Chalmette on Judge Perez Drive (1970); and in Algiers on the Westbank (1973).[1]

At this point, the skein was all but complete, as each of the ten stores occupied a strategic location within the expanding nexus of metropolitan New Orleans. Four stores held down the fort in New Orleans proper, with sites serving Marigny/Bywater, Gentilly/New Orleans East, Mid-City/Lakeview, and Downtown/Lower Garden District. Meanwhile, the Jefferson Parish Schwegmann footprint had grown to three sites: two stores on Airline Highway and one on Veterans Boulevard, which was supplanting ever-seedy Airline as Jefferson Parish's prime commercial thoroughfare. Finally, three supermarkets had been opened in more far-flung outposts, with two on the Westbank and one in Chalmette, which served St. Bernard Parish.

Compared with John's previous monumental approach, what is most striking about his 1960s' store-building efforts is how dramatically scaled back they were. Four of the stores built in the 1960s were sized at an average of only 50,000 square feet (48,000 to 53,000)—or roughly two-thirds the size of the Airline store. Meanwhile, the Annunciation store (1962) was smaller still, at 36,000 square feet. A fairly fanciful explanation for this relatively drastic reduction in scale might point to a guilty conscience. Considering that John's moral core was informed by economy, perhaps he felt somewhat disconnected from this root principle after going way out on a limb to finance the Gentilly monstrosity. Almost by instinct, then, he would have pulled in his horns to regain economic composure. More realistically, though, he simply built smaller-scale stores to better fit into the more compressed areas of urban (rather than suburban) environments. But for whatever reason, during the 1960s, John dramatically dialed down the intensity level of his stores.

That they were smaller stores, however, does not mean that they were stripped down in terms of merchandise or service offerings. On the contrary, all were ingeniously designed by John's chosen architect at the time, Edward Mung-Yok Tsoi—a native of China who emigrated to Louisiana in his late teens and went on to enjoy a distinguished architectural career in New Orleans[2]—to maximize interior and exterior space in order to accommodate a variety of departments in addition to food. Consequently, all the stores designed by Tsoi incorporated drug/pharmacy departments, and most featured gas stations outside. For its part, the moderately sized Broad Street store had space for a laundry/dry cleaner, a barbershop, jewelry and shoe repair departments, a sandwich shop, and an oyster bar, along with food and drugs. Even the tiny Annunciation Street store had room for drugs/pharmacy, hardware, and small appliances.

The pendulum swung back to the large scale, however, with the coming of the 1970s. Of the two new outlier stores, the Chalmette supermarket weighed in at a hefty 76,300 square feet, while the Algiers store—the anchor of a shopping development called Tall Timbers—bulked back up to mega-size at 92,800 square feet. Moreover, during this same early-seventies' period, John pulled out all the stops on his Veterans store (originally built in 1960), more than doubling its size from 48,000 to 114,000 square feet. The old grandiosity was back! And make no mistake. These giant structures were bold for their time, measuring from 5,000 to 45,000 square feet over the largest superstores of the 1970s.

This anticipatory return to oversized stores (supercenters would not appear en masse until the 1990s) was not the only indication that John still had a trend-setting flair, even during his political years. Consider that the Harvey store of 1962 was at the forefront of retail development, as it accommodated both Schwegmann's and a Kmart discount store on the same lot—an early strip-mall concept. Another innovation, this one exuding a certain romantic appeal, was the rooftop parking lot. Designed by Edward Tsoi, three of these were built—one atop the Broad Street store, one at Annunciation, and another at the expanded Veterans store. (Note that the rooftop parking lot on Broad Street served as the pop-up site for a drive-in movie theater in summer 2013, right before the store was made over into a Whole Foods.)

If installing state-of-the-art retail technology also counts as being innovative, then John can be credited for this in his giant new stores of the early 1970s. Nevertheless, it must be conceded that his innovations of the political years were but pale shadows of the magisterial achievements and landmark accomplishments of Schwegmann's Golden Age. But there was a good reason for this—namely, that John had reached the limits of his interest in business success. As a consequence, innovation was just not that important to him anymore.

Consider that in 1961 John was fifty years old. He had already made retail history with his prototype supercenter and hypermarket concepts. Likewise, he held a prominent place in legal history with his resounding victories in the battle against fair trade. Having done so much and come so far, having already reached his goals and seen his dreams come true, is it any wonder that the ever-curious John would not want to spend the rest of his career simply recapitulating his winning business formula over an ever-larger geographical expanse?

Of course, if he had done so, he would have faced some interesting challenges—like how to magnify his New Orleans' persona to project onto other cities; or how to move beyond local loyalties to delegate regional responsibilities. Yet these types of business challenges no longer interested him. Facing the half-century mark and conscious of his heart condition, John realized that the time he had left was limited. If he wanted to get into politics, now was the time to do so, as it would take a few years to establish his reputation as a trusted public servant. Of course, this would mean dividing his attention between business and politics—with the risk that he would lose focus on both. But John fearlessly took this risk. According to his son John Francis, a fire burned in his father's belly. Consumed by righteousness, John had developed a distinct appetite for politics; the direct confrontation, the rough and tumble. So he followed his deeper desires and plunged wholeheartedly into the game he had come to love.

As could have been predicted, this move proved troublesome for John's business interests, as any inclination toward significant retail expansion ended up squelched beneath more passionate political concerns. Then again, a more positive interpretation of his turn away from business could be entertained, a view that sees his failure to indulge in growth as a good thing. In this sense it affirms John's life-long aversion to ever-expanding chain stores. It was a moral meme he had picked up in his populist youth, and a conviction he honored throughout his business life. He would never stoop so low as to own an invasive chain store.

In this way John's value system proved detrimental to further wealth accumulation. But to this consideration John displayed an adiaphorous attitude. Basically he was indifferent to further riches, being already as wealthy as he ever wanted to be (similar to his Swiss mentor, Gottlieb Duttweiler, of Migros fame). By 1975, when his local empire extended to ten stores located strategically throughout the greater New Orleans metro area, the Schwegmann miniature empire accounted for fully one-third of all grocery sales in the Crescent City. This full-bore market share dominance translated into annual revenues approaching $250 million. CEO John was now a multimillionaire. He was swimming in money; way more, it seemed, than he even knew what to do with.[3]

To sum up the situation, paradoxes abound. He was wrong to enter politics from a business and health standpoint, but he did the right thing within his own passion/value matrix. This decision rendered him less wealthy than he could have been, but he was still rich beyond his wildest dreams. Perhaps in the ultimate irony, by failing to expand his local empire, he may have been once again pioneering a strategy ahead of his time. In other words, by *not* breaking new ground he was actually breaking new ground. He was content with having established a homeostatic business model based on efficiency, manageability, hands-on financial control, and fierce local loyalty. Given John's prophetic proclivities, it is certainly possible that this local model could become the paradigm for future retail enterprises in the upcoming age of resource constraints.

THAT EVERYTHING ABOUT JOHN'S LIFE during his political years can be interpreted in a double sense is apparent not just in his business dealings but also in his personal actions. First, consider the contradiction between his reputation as the people's champion and his luxury living. Daughter Margie reports that he felt somewhat guilty about purchasing a discounted Rolls-Royce, but he bought it anyway to satisfy a personal urge for just such an indulgence. This fits John to a tee: not getting overly vexed about the wealth gap that had opened up between him and his average customer, but not wanting the gap to get any bigger either.

A similar double-edged perspective can be applied to his re-lationship with Guy George, his mentally disabled son. After living out his earliest years at St. Vincent's "asylum," Guy had later grown up under the care of his mother. But when he reached high-school age, Guy needed services she could no longer provide. So in 1962 he was moved, with the financial help of John, to the Magnolia School, an institution devoted to special education located at the former Whitehall Plantation on River Road. Throughout the 1960s, John would visit Guy when his schedule permitted. On occasion during this time he treated Guy and his friends to lunch at a nice restaurant. Later on, as Guy aged, John underwrote an expansion of the Magnolia School to accommodate adults. To this end, he arranged a land swap, engaged an architect, and funded the building of "Schwegmann Cottage." Guy moved in there at age twenty-nine when it opened in 1977.

By the way, this was not the only support John offered for special education. For years he had quietly helped to fund not only the Magnolia School but also the Louise Davis Developmental Center, located on Magazine Street in uptown New Orleans. In 1979, the Davis Center faced a crisis, as its building had deteriorated to the point of nearly being condemned. Despite facing his own health crisis, John stepped in to help Louise Davis buy a new building out in New Orleans East. Soon, son John Francis took on oversight of this philanthropic project.[4]

As is evident, John paid more than lip service to support Guy and the developmentally disabled community in general. He made it a point to visit Guy, he provided funding to special education institutions, and he even supported this community in the legislature. As noted previously, in his first term as a state representative, John sponsored a tax credit for children with mental and other disabilities; one of his only bills to pass. Yet despite all his honorable efforts—the visits, the money, the tax breaks—there was something wooden, not quite genuine, about John's relationship with Guy. At least this is how Guy's brother, John Francis, perceived his father's gestures.[5] It was as if he were outwardly going through the motions but inwardly wracked by wounded feelings akin to shame or regret. Whatever the truth of the matter—that he was acting out of saintly or guilty motives—the end result is entirely consistent with the typical conflicting interpretations of John's actions during his political years.

THE DOUBLE-EDGED CHARACTER of his life during the political years reached a crescendo of confusion in regard to his familial relations. In one way, John can be viewed as a happy man basking in the fruits of personal fulfillment. He had three good children, comfortable relations with his two ex-wives, and a deeply knit extended family of longtime friends and business associates. Meanwhile, he had an enthusiastic and experienced son willing to take over the family enterprise. What could be better than all that? Well, obviously John was missing a love interest. He endured this state of affairs for eight long years after his second divorce until finally, in 1967, he met a young beauty working at one of his stores named Mary Ann Blackledge. At the time he was 56, while she was just 24. Their lopsided affair began in earnest at this point, with delighted John happy to play the sugar daddy to his alluring young lover. Now John could say that he truly had it all, his personal life complete.

On the Cabildo tape, which originally inspired this biography, John speaks hauntingly of wonderful dreams suddenly turned to nightmares: "There you are asleep, dreaming you're in heaven, then you wake up and the house is burning down." Whatever the specific context this quote refers to, it acts as an apt metaphor for what happened next in his love life. For there he was, cruising at altitude, enjoying the scenery and the thrill of the ride, when all of a sudden the engine started sputtering, threatening disaster.

This trouble was entirely foreseeable, its probability baked into the cake. For John had never married Mary Ann Blackledge, and there is no evidence that Mary Ann had ever insisted on a formal marriage. So when the time came for the inevitable breakup between the rich old man and the kept young lady, no clear pathway existed for splitting John's wealth with his live-in girlfriend of ten years.

Predictably, the trouble started in 1978, when John broke up with Mary Ann right after his stroke. Retaliating, Mary Ann sued John, demanding half his estate. Now cue John's formidable legal team. Coming to his defense, the lawyers basically steamrolled poor Mary Ann, leaving her all but powerless. Specifically, they managed to relegate her status to a legal limbo that American law calls a "concubine" and Louisiana refers to as a "paramour." To anyone placed in the paramour role, no legal rights flow as they do from a sanctioned marriage contract. While Ms. Blackledge ended up sidelined from any but a minor settlement, the unfairness of hers and similar cases in the loosening moral world of the late 1970s helped pave the way for a novel legal concept known as "palimony." So once again, though this time unintentionally, John was in the forefront of something new, this time in the realm of marital (or divorce) relations.

Backing up a bit, there was John in the late 1960s basking in success, blessed with good family, good friends, and a good-looking paramour, even as his coffers continued to swell. But in the early 1970s, this happy equilibrium began to splinter, as his home life became increasingly chaotic. In an ambiguous temporal sequence, John invited his fourth-grade daughter, Margie, to move in with him while she attended St. Martin's Episcopal school, located pretty much across the street from his home.[6] This was a generous, fatherly thing to do, and she readily accepted. But then John also invited Margie's mother, his ex-wife Melba, to move in. Just to spice things up further, Mary Ann Blackledge soon invited *her* mother to move in. So now there were four women, two pairs of mothers and daughters, inhabiting the house at the same time, with all the soap-opera overtones this implies. Complicating matters even further, there were the dogs—up to seven at a time—running or lazing about the house. To top it all off, John maintained somewhat of an active social life, occasionally receiving friends, relatives, and associates at the house. These visits climaxed on Sundays when he would host a brunch, the entertainment provided from his extensive LP record collection of German oompah and marching bands. So yes, John had it all, all right—including all the joys and miseries associated with an unfettered household.

* * *

TURNING FROM PERSONAL TO SOCIETAL relations, during the 1960s John expressed what could be called extreme ambivalence toward the burning issues of the day—namely, war and race. Concerning war, he was all for it, except when he had to pay for it. He possessed impeccable anti-communist credentials and desired by all means to rid the world of this ideological menace. Yet he just could not see the sense of fighting a full-scale war in Southeast Asia when the real threat was omnipresent. Indeed, not only did it exist ninety miles from U.S. shores, in Cuba, but it also lived on in the cartel-inclined dark hearts of fair traders throughout the West, in both America and Europe. On the Cabildo tape, John definitely expresses unease about the out-of-control costs and misguided policies being pursued in the Vietnam War.

John's positions on the issue of race were similarly ambivalent. On one hand, he had a personal history of humanistic acceptance of, even friendships with, African Americans that extended back to when Jim Crow was in full force. Nevertheless, in his political incarnation John expressed a sort of segregation-lite. As has been seen, he was all gung-ho for education. Yet he was against *integrated* education. From this illogic stemmed regressive attitudes toward law and order—attitudes that tended to criminalize black poverty rather than seek to ameliorate it.

Flowing down from its owner's expression of "soft segregationism" during his early political years (late 1950s to early 1960s), at least some of the Schwegmann organization adopted an insidious tolerance of separate-but-equal ways. Now pause here to consider that, according to historian Kent Germany, New Orleans' civil rights struggles fell fairly evenly into two phases, the early 1960s and the late 1960s, with the fiercest battles happening between 1960 and 1964.[7] Not coincidentally, these were the years when ugly incidents involving racial exclusion in Schwegmann stores peaked in intensity, leaving bitter memories and permanent resentments in some quarters of New Orleans' African-American community.

Fortunately, racial separatism lost some momentum as the sixties progressed. As Germany explains, a combination of liberal local and federal forces coalesced to create conditions conducive to a semi-peaceful transition to racial integration in New Orleans. This optimistic situation began to manifest around 1965: the same year the Louisiana governorship switched over from avowed segregationist Jimmie Davis to nominal integrationist John McKeithen. Fortunately for his enduring reputation, John Schwegmann went with the flow. As of the mid-1960s, his previous soft intolerance was transformed into a squishy acceptance. He was now all for promoting "equal opportunity" in hiring. Nevertheless, John accepted the new integration paradigm mostly by omission—meaning he rarely, if ever, mentioned race from 1965 onward in his endless barrage of opinionated commentary.

FINALLY, ALONG WITH THE BUSINESS decisions, personal actions, and social attitudes of his political years, the by-now-familiar double-edged perspective can also be applied to John's cultural behavior. The term "cultural behavior" presents two aspects: on one hand referring to how people relate to art and entertainment; and on the other how they express themselves creatively. In the first case, it is passive, reflected in tastes, preferences, and relative degrees of sophistication. In the second case, cultural behavior is active, manifested in two forms: in the actual manufacture of art or artifacts; and, more broadly, in the pursuit of particular interests or activities—be it cooking, fishing, collecting, or any expression of extraordinary passion. In John's case, in terms of cultural behavior he stands revealed in all his contradictory glory as both a genuine creative eccentric and an utterly mainstream personality.

John was no outdoorsman like his Uncle Garret, but he did love animals, particularly dogs. As mentioned, he housed up to seven dogs at a time during the political years. His all-time favorite, though, was Gigi, a black French poodle named after the lead character in a hit Broadway musical.[8] Acquired sometime in the mid-1960s, Gigi was a sophisticated traveler, having toured Europe with her owner. She also attended the state legislature—even giving a speech! As the story goes, on a point of personal privilege John delivered a scathing indictment of the Baton Rouge political establishment, rhetorically building up to the zinger, "This state is going to the dogs." At that moment John held Gigi up to the microphone and, right on cue, she barked.

On September 19, 1969, John celebrated Gigi's coming of age with what amounted essentially to a debutante party. In publicizing the event, John called her "Queen of the Schwegmann home," christening Gigi the "Marquise Mignon de la Maison." As it happened, seventy-five poodles attended the party in hopes of receiving her paw in marriage. The lucky winner was Pierre. After Pierre had his way with Gigi, the lovely couple produced four French poodle puppies: Toute de Suite, Anastasia, Francois, and Jobert. When Gigi died in 1973, John sadly published an obituary in his weekly grocery ad recalling her virtues as a "good mother, excellent watchdog, and faithful friend." Commenting on the odd spectacle of a dog "in memoriam" column running within the context of a supermarket ad, the *New York Times* noted ironically that it was placed adjacent to a meat department promotion.

When it came to what might be called "creative eccentricity," John expressed this behavior in spades, from his outrageous stores, to his audacious ads, to his championing of lost causes. But as seen with Gigi, it was in his emotional love of dogs that this character quality was most nakedly on display. Consider another obituary he composed for a dog, a tear-jerking memorial dedicated to Peppy, a stray collie/chow who joined the family in 1957 and lived until 1977: "Peppy's last wish was that all animals would be treated with as much love and kindness as he was."

Though in its active phase John's cultural behavior manifested in an exuberant individuality, its passive expression was firmly rooted in the mass-culture mainstream. In terms of artistic appreciation he showed little sophistication, preferring popular entertainments rather than anything challenging or avant-garde. In other words, he was pretty much a square, a cornball. He loved Broadway musicals like "Fanny" and "Gigi" and movies like "My Fair Lady" and "Going My Way." He was a great fan of big band jazz and cabaret-style acts, frequently attending Bourbon Street performances by local celebrity Chris Owens and her husband during their 1960s' heyday.[9]

With this brief recounting of John's cultural tastes it is easy to see that, once again, a paradox appears: John is both a nonconformist and a conformist. This contradictory state of affairs, along with all the others, lasted until the tension snapped in 1977. After his stroke, the heavenly delights and hellish conflicts of his political years were over. From then on out, complicated relations involving decisions, actions, attitudes, and behaviors dissolved into a single-minded struggle to survive.

FOLLOWING JOHN'S STROKE, the Schwegmann storyline shifts focus from father to son—from John Gerald to John Francis. Tasked with filling the shoes of John G., the charismatic creator of one of New Orleans' most legendary institutions, John F. had inherited quite a burden. Would he be up to the challenge? All indicators pointed to the affirmative. He was, after all, of the Schwegmann lineage, a man with food retailing in his blood. More substantially, he had been thoroughly groomed to take over the top spot. Indeed, he had been "attending class" at Schwegmann stores since the age of three, dragged there by his father every weekend, and even on Christmas, when the recently divorced dad had custody of his son.[10] Although for years John F. resented being deprived of a normal childhood—while his friends were all out playing he was stuck with his father at the store—he gradually learned to appreciate the advantageous hand he had been dealt.

John Francis suffered a fairly traumatic childhood, first residing with two aunts while his distressed mother sojourned at DePaul Sanitarium and later, after she recovered, taking up residence with Mary and his brother Guy in a cinderblock home in Algiers. While living on the Westbank he attended Adolph Meyer grade school. Here he remembers at first feeling almost paralyzed by a sense of inferiority.[11] At age ten, John F. formally commenced apprenticeship at his father's stores. Working summers and over school vacations, he began at the bottom, only slowly moving up. Along the way he worked pretty much every job in the store, from bag boy to butcher to cashier.

He tells a few rich anecdotes about these times. For example, when he first started apprenticing in the mid-1950s, the stores still sold live chickens, turtles, and bullfrogs, all to be rendered on site after purchase. Regarding the frogs, "You could hear them croaking all over the store." Later on, John remembers being baffled by the introduction of disposable paper products, such as paper towels and disposable diapers. These wasteful products will never catch on, he thought to himself as he stocked the convenience advancements. He also tells a story revealing the little-known trickster side of his father. Here John F. describes how he was tasked to use a tiny scoop to hollow out holes in regular cheese to make it look like more-expensive Swiss cheese. Shades of John Gerald's early oleomargarine days! (Note that this unethical practice was soon discovered and the minor scam discontinued.)[12]

FOR JOHN FRANCIS IN HIS EARLY TWENTIES, things went swimmingly. In 1967, he married Melinda Burge, his college sweetheart. In 1968, he graduated from Loyola University and became a manager for the Schwegmann organization. What followed was a frothy decade spent raising a family of three children, building a home in Mississippi, learning to fly, serving in the Coast Guard Reserve, and climbing the Schwegmann corporate ladder. By the time of his father's stroke, John Francis had risen to director of operations.

In 1978, after three decades of being unofficially and officially groomed for the job, thirty-three-year-old John Francis ascended to leadership of the ten-store Schwegmann chain. (He formally purchased the business from his father in 1979.) What he inherited was a successful but somewhat neglected empire. After all, his father had not opened a new store in five years. Moreover, the older stores had seen little in the way of upgrading or modernization. Consequently, though the stores continued to capture significant supermarket share, the spark that originally rendered the enterprise unique definitely needed rekindling.

John Francis thus assumed the leadership under less-than-ideal circumstances. While dear old dad had been out traveling the world and raising heck in the legislature, his business had basically stagnated. It was up to the son to bring it back to life. Yet by no means would this be an easy task. For his father's miniature empire was so idiosyncratic, so rooted in a particular historical moment, so thoroughly stamped with his personal handprint that any revival might seem to require some sort of self-assertive flamboyance on the part of his son. Instead, what John Francis brought to the table, along with abundant reserves of energy, was a more academic, by-the-book approach to business than his father ever possessed.

As a result, one of the first things John Francis did after taking over was to repudiate his father's "limits to growth" philosophy. "A company that is to stay viable must grow," declared John F. in one of his earliest pronouncements.[13] What he meant, of course, was that the Schwegmann operation would be expanded outside New Orleans. This was certainly a reasonable position: indeed, it was long overdue by most lights. And yet there was a hint of foreboding in this decision, a hovering apprehension that to move beyond the city violated some taboo, some invisible principle.

Consider that in an alternative universe John F. could have decided to stay true to New Orleans. Thus, rather than committing to regional growth, he would have devoted himself to refurbishing the existing store base, equipping the supermarkets with state-of-the-art technology, and splurging on a superlatively creative marketing team tasked with maintaining the chain's unique image. What is ironic is that though he did not pursue this parochial, local-economy approach, in the end John Francis was unable to sustain expansion beyond the Crescent City—as if the very attempt itself were mysteriously cursed.

IN SMOOTHING THE PATH TO GROWTH, John Francis took the preliminary step of changing the name of the chain. Since no more relatives were involved in the partnership after a mid-1970s' ownership shakeup, son John dropped the word "Brothers" from the corporate title. So as of 1980, the stores were simply called "Schwegmann Giant Super

Markets." This streamlining of identity was followed in the same year by the construction of a warehouse facility to accommodate future chain expansion.

Thereafter, seven new supermarkets would be opened. These included stores in Kenner (1983), Baton Rouge (1984), Slidell (1986), Hammond (1986), New Orleans East (1987), Lakeview (1993), and Marrero (1993).[14] As can be seen, the major growth spurt happened during the heyday of the Reagan Revolution (1982 to 1987), with a reigniting of the expansionist impulse occurring at the beginning of the Clinton years. Clearly by the early 1990s, after John Francis had been at the helm for over a decade, he was gearing up once again for a period of glorious growth.

This is especially evident considering the gargantuan size of the Marrero store at 121,000 square feet. Opening in 1993, this latest (and, as it turned out, last) Schwegmann store signaled the intention of John Francis to move henceforth into the competitive league of big-time retailing. Note that John's earlier efforts were also large sized, with his 1984 Baton Rouge store, for example, measuring 109,000 square feet. But in a noticeable departure, what particularly marked the Marrero store was its progressive mall-like conception. Specifically, it incorporated a food court featuring pizza, Asian, fried seafood, chicken (barbecue, fried), and a diversity of other fast food cuisines—all this within the confines of a supermarket.

Beyond his building of out-of-town and oversized stores, son John's expansionist impulse took the form of a passion for real estate development.[15] This mostly involved incorporating Schwegmann supermarkets into shopping centers and malls. One example of this occurred in New Orleans East, with John locating a store across from the Lake Forest mall, a forty-two-acre site that featured six anchors and over a hundred retail tenants. Similar but smaller projects could be found in Chalmette and on the Westbank. In a slightly different development mode, in 1985 John erected an office building behind the Schwegmann store on Veterans Boulevard. The swanky two-story office space featured a ground-floor atrium complete with interior garden and large fountain.

To round out the picture of John's activities after taking over leadership of the Schwegmann chain, besides expansion he also devoted efforts to internal chain improvements. To this end, older stores were given a makeover with brighter colors, more contemporary signage, and redecoration. Then there was the issue of marketing. To son John, this area was most in need of change but most impervious to updating. For father John's indelibly quirky signature was inscribed on every marketing expression from the past. How could this individuality possibly be updated to fit a more contemporary setting? In short, John F. decided it could not be. And who can blame him? After all, who nowadays has the chutzpah to pursue such outrageous marketing practices as John G. Schwegmann?

Certainly his son did not. Instead, as if embarrassed by his father's naked display of a passionate public persona, John F. completely overhauled the former marketing department, replacing it with digital graphic designers, computer programmers, and a market research team.[16] As a result, he pretty much dumped the personalized approach to advertising and promotion. Gone were any idiosyncrasies. Banished were any controversies. Welcomed were anodyne expressions typical of mainstream marketing. Perfectly illustrating this transition was the shift in tone of messages appearing on Schwegmann bags. Under John Francis, controversial political statements were discontinued in favor of sentiments promoting civic, charitable, and other do-gooder causes.

THE EARLY 1990S PROMISED great things for John Francis, his wife Melinda, and the Schwegmann legacy. In 1992, Melinda Schwegmann, proving her own mettle as a politician, broke through the female-denying glass ceiling into the upper echelon of state politics—something her famous father-in-law had never accomplished—when she won the race for Louisiana lieutenant governor. Then in 1993, as the Clinton economic recovery took hold, John Francis was able to resume chain expansion after a several-year hiatus. At that moment, the power couple had good reason to think big. If all went well, Melinda would go on to become Louisiana's first female governor. In John's case, in 1993 he was presented with a golden opportunity to increase his fortune by tens of millions.

What happened next is a difficult story to tell: not because it is so heartbreaking, which it is, or so complicated, which it is as well. The story is hard to tell because it is difficult to understand the logic of it, the whys behind the fatal mistakes made. Perhaps the only way to fully explain the collapse of the Schwegmann chain is to put matters into historical perspective.

THIS WILL REQUIRE A TREK back to the 1980s, when U.S. business competition was dominated by privateering enterprises commonly referred to as leveraged buyout (LBO) firms. Their brutal tactics most gruesomely on display in the violent practices of Al "Chainsaw" Dunlap—the archetypal financial buccaneer of his day whose rapacious ways led to the ruin of several great American companies, including Scott Paper and Sunbeam—the piratical LBO firms would swoop down on decent but somewhat underperforming companies and buy them out, financing the buyout with borrowed millions that took the form of high-yield "junk bonds." In more cases than not, what followed was a sorry sight, as the LBO firms proceeded to ravage and pillage the poor company, firing longtime management, slashing good-paying jobs, cutting pipeline investment, looting pensions, and finally selling the hapless business off in dismembered pieces. Meanwhile, the LBO firms made money every step of the way, grabbing a hefty percentage of every transaction involving buying, selling, and slashing, even devising lavish management perks for their insidious efforts, including the infamous "golden parachute."

Of course, a positive case can be made for LBO firms: that most boast not a wicked but a benevolent takeover team; that many of their portfolio companies are happy to be acquired; and that LBO firms serve a useful competitive function within the creative/destructive calculus of classical capitalism. But when all the justifications fall silent, the weeping wreckage left behind after the inglorious years of LBO plunder—years that basically witnessed the decimation of the independent U.S. business sector—speaks for itself.

The LBO frenzy of the 1980s hit the U.S. retail sector hard. Famous department stores came under the gun, many driven to liquidation, others merging. The former dominance of the Big Three catalog giants—Sears, Penney, and Ward—collapsed beneath the discount juggernauts of Walmart, Kmart, and Target. For their part, supermarkets also bore the brunt of major blows from the "corporate raiders." Independent supermarkets surviving the onslaught were rare. Then there was the whole ignominious casino aspect of the process, as long-established local and regional merchants with their loyal followings were traded like chips on a poker table.

BLAME IT ON THE CELEBRATORY ATMOSPHERE of New Orleans, which tends to render the city oblivious to outside trends. Or blame it on a failure to appreciate the magnitude of danger. But for whatever reason, John F. Schwegmann appears to have been unaware of the destructive processes that had already wreaked havoc on independent U.S. supermarkets. In his defense, though, he was wide-awake to the increasingly perilous nature of local competition. To paraphrase, John Francis compared competing with encroaching national chains to arising every morning and having to slug it out with King Kong and Godzilla.[17] So by no means was he naive about mounting pressures. Nevertheless, in 1995 John Francis fell into a trap—a tried-and-true debt trap that the LBO firms had exploited so well since the 1980s. That John fell for the lure of a rescue even after large swaths of the U.S. retail industry had already been hooked by such confidence tricks in the 1980s, well, many a man in his shoes would have done the same. The prospect of easy riches was just that irresistible.

The Schwegmann legacy began to unravel in 1995. The first ominous stroke of bad luck struck with John Gerald's death in March of that year. Then in June, John Francis consummated what proved to be a disastrous deal. Finally, in November, honest government candidate Melinda Schwegmann lost her gubernatorial bid to notorious huckster Edwin Edwards. The actual end of the family-owned Schwegmann chain, however, did not occur until early 1997. This is when John Francis basically threw in the towel, surrendering his family's miniature empire to an invading force.

TORONTO, ONTARIO, IS THE HEADQUARTERS location of Loblaw Companies, Ltd., the leading supermarket chain in Canada.[18] Loblaw is known particularly for its outstanding selection of private-label products, including an extensive line of private-label gourmet food items. Loblaw also pioneered in generic, no-name products—a trend that, despite saving significant amounts in marketing dollars, failed to catch on in the ultra-competitive United States. Indeed, the Canadian retailer was having a rough time of it in the overheated atmosphere of its neighbor down south, where extreme shakeout-and-consolidation pressures had been roiling the retail scene since the 1980s. By 1995, Loblaw decided it was time to vamoose the U.S. market and concentrate on maintaining its top position back home.

For several decades prior to its exit, Loblaw had a presence in the U.S. retail market through a subsidiary, National Holdings, Inc. National Holdings held four retail companies in its portfolio. Of those four, its primary unit was the National Tea Company, originally based in Chicago but acquired by Loblaw back in the late 1950s. National Tea was at one time a regional powerhouse, with 750 supermarkets in twelve states. Over the years, however, Loblaw whittled down the U.S. chain, selling it off piecemeal until by 1995 only about one in ten of the original National Tea stores remained. As for the other three retail companies within Loblaw's National Holdings portfolio, these included Canal Villere, The Real Superstore (the U.S. version of a successful Loblaw concept in Canada), and That Stanley!

As of 1995, Loblaw had 89 stores left in the United States. Of these, 60 were located in St. Louis and 29 in the Gulf South. The

St. Louis stores were all old National Tea supermarkets (by then simply branded as National stores). The Gulf South stores, on the other hand, represented all four companies in the National Holdings portfolio—namely, National, Canal Villere, The Real Superstore, and That Stanley! Just to complicate matters further, the 29 stores bearing these four names were scattered throughout three states: Louisiana, Mississippi, and Alabama. Most, though, were located in metro New Orleans. Here, unfortunately, the word "most" is about as close as it is possible to get in the kaleidoscopic whirlwind of conflicting reporting that followed their sale. But this is getting ahead of the story. For now, it is enough to know two things: first, Loblaw put 89 stores up for sale in 1995; and second, all four retail companies originally in the National Holdings portfolio have since gone kaput.

RETURNING NOW TO JOHN FRANCIS, there he was in the early 1990s nurturing his expansion plans. But he faced one major obstacle: so many out-of-town supermarket and discount chains had entered New Orleans in recent years that expansion opportunities were becoming difficult to find. Surely his ears pricked up, then, when in 1993 a labor strike hobbled operations at metro area supermarkets controlled by National Holdings. Clearly, he realized, parent company Loblaw had an unwanted problem—a problem that presented John with a once-in-a-lifetime opportunity.

Loblaw has a long history of retail-style arbitrage—the buying and selling of stores, using them as tradable collateral and semi-liquid assets. So when it came time to exit the U.S. market, it devised a complex scheme to sell off its stores that few but Loblaw fully understood. This involved a two-pronged swap. First, National Holdings would sell all of its 89 stores to Schnucks Markets, a leading supermarket chain in St. Louis, Missouri. Schnucks would keep the 60 stores already located in the St. Louis area and then pivot, selling the remaining 29 stores located in the Gulf South to Schwegmann's down in New Orleans.[19] The secret negotiations that occurred in late 1994 and early 1995 to pull off this stunt must have been fun. It was a logical, clever deal that would enrich them all—a win-win-win, if you will.

Well, it did not turn out that way, far from it. For its part, Loblaw came out fine and dandy, relieved of its U.S. burden with cash in hand. Meanwhile, its two American partners, Schnucks and Schwegmann's, both ended up looking like schnooks. Neither had fully taken into account that the deal as it stood would not pass muster under U.S. antitrust statutes. To do so, the deal would have to be significantly pared down. As it happened, Schnucks had its fair share of post-acquisition troubles (having to divest twenty-four stores), but Schwegmann's fared far worse. Schnucks was large enough to absorb the blow, but Schwegmann's was not.

Approaching the fatal moment, before he signed off on the deal, John Francis faced what seemed a simple choice: he could reach for the stars, or he could continue on the path of business-as-usual. On one hand, if the deal succeeded, he would be immensely wealthy. If he did not do the deal, however, he was looking at a future of ongoing hard work yielding only modest profits. Which path would anyone choose? Besides, it all seemed so easy, the deal a blessing from heaven fallen into his lap, his decision almost a no-brainer. John would indeed seize this unparalleled opportunity to leap beyond the competition, to acquire tens of millions in revenue, all at the stroke of a pen!

At that point, though, the walls began to tumble down, with the Federal Trade Commission intervening. According to the FTC, John could not just leapfrog over his rivals like that. It violated both the letter and spirit of the Sherman Antitrust Act, which prohibited monopoly practices—ironically, the bête noire of his father. According to the trade journal *Supermarket News* (February 25, 1996), the Federal Trade Commission demanded that, of the twenty-nine stores Schwegmann bought from Loblaw, it had to get rid of eighteen of them: eleven through divestiture (selling off) and six through closing down.[20] Nevertheless, almost inexplicably, John Francis went ahead with the deal—an acquisition that indebted him to the tune of $150 million.

The sour repercussions of the ill-fated acquisition were too much for John Francis. After selling off a couple of units he had acquired, the

Schwegmann chain in 1996 included just 26 stores—a far cry from the nearly double that number he had originally planned for. As a result, the giant debt he had taken on to finance the deal was proving to be an insupportable burden. After a few half-hearted attempts to fold the new stores he had taken on—a couple of Canal Villeres and Real Superstores, and a few National supermarkets—into the Schwegmann organizational structure, John Francis threw in the towel. He simply did not have enough cash on hand to remake the new stores, or even stock his old stores! Indeed, vendors began shutting off inventory flows to Schwegmann's, leaving shelves half-empty and holding inferior products. The end was nigh. John sought rescue.

Lo and behold, a flag appeared on the horizon, a ship offering help. Unfortunately, this ship flew the Jolly Roger. It was a corporate raider: a spin-off of the fearsome LBO firm Kohlberg, Kravis and Roberts called Kohlberg and Company (K&C). This firm promised relief—but for a pirate's price. Have a debt of $150 million? No problem. K&C will pay it off, providing of course that you surrender your business developed over generations. All John needed to do was to figuratively walk the plank and give up ownership and management. If he survived, he could keep the buildings and real estate and lease them back to Kohlberg, which is exactly what John did.

In February 1997, John Francis sold his 125-year-old family business to Kohlberg and Company. What followed was a three-year travesty during which Kohlberg and Company pretended to resuscitate the Schwegmann chain even while demolishing its management team. This teasing cruelty finally concluded in 1999, when K&C ended its benevolent pretense by selling off six of Schwegmann's most choice stores. When John Francis protested against any more selling off of the chain, Kohlberg retaliated by simply liquidating the company under Chapter 11. Like Loblaw before it with the labor strike, K&C just did not tolerate such impudent silliness from a provincial account. As of April 1999, Schwegmann Giant Super Markets was no more.[21]

*   *   *

It is time to return to the father, John G. Schwegmann, who undoubtedly would have been appalled by all this debt mongering. John G. had spent a lifetime playing his economic cards close to the vest. It is inconceivable that he would so wildly gamble such immense sums on a confidence man's promise of a sure thing. But then again, John G. was not able, either mentally or physically, to intervene in any decision-making capacity in the mid-1990s. Instead, his final years were spent mostly in inward struggles to stay alive and remain responsive. This is not to say that John neglected the external world. He continued to travel throughout his declining years, taking great joy in touring the by-now familiar European landscapes bursting with beauty. In a notable departure from past practice, however, he started regularly attending church. Yes, not unexpectedly, in his waning days John got religion—Catholic, of course.[22]

As the harmful effects of his strokes deepened, he was no longer able to read, a fanatical obsession with him. Aware of his deep distress over this, daughter Margie hired him a reader. As he gradually became more incapacitated, his care was entrusted to Marlene Taylor, an African American woman whose assistance allowed him to soldier on in his luxury lifestyle, traveling, dining out, and making the rounds in his limousine until his final demise.

On March 13, 1995, John breathed his last. The legend was dead. Having become increasingly disengaged from his business over the years of decline, John Gerald had little idea what John Francis was up to. As it happened, he mercifully died before his life's work splintered into oblivion.

Mayhem broke out in the wake of the Schwegmann chain's demise in 1999. Bitter family feuds that had festered beneath the surface suddenly burst forth, with Margie suing her half-brother for mismanagement. Meanwhile, John Francis also faced the wrath of long-time employees, who pursued a class-action suit against him for reneging on a food-voucher program after his ownership ended.[23] The employees won, much to the financial chagrin of John Francis, who was only trying to do good in the first place.

And the carnage continued. Sharks circled for remains of the chain; hulks of stores were abandoned in ghostly ruin; the old corner store on Piety and Burgundy, where the legend began, continued to fester in an ugly dysfunctional state ten years after Hurricane Katrina; and the very memory of John G. Schwegmann, retail genius and prophet of the modern retail world, was in danger of being forgotten forever.

20

SCHWEGMANN AS FOLK HERO

IN THE YEARS FOLLOWING JOHN'S DEATH in 1995, memories of his trailblazing supermarket empire have receded quickly. To be sure, every now and then some newspaper article or blog post will appear talking about Schwegmann Brothers Giant Super Markets, the writer fondly reminiscing about treasured moments spent shopping the stores, or wistfully reflecting on the vital role the supermarkets once played in the economic and cultural life of New Orleans. Yet when all is said and done, it is probably safe to say that the only thing, if anything, most anyone now remembers about Schwegmann's is the store logo—presently featured on tee-shirts and other touristy merchandise appealing to hipster sensibilities and the nostalgically inclined. Certainly only a few old-timers are able to recall the original stores in all their transcendent splendor—their mammoth proportions, multidimensional sprawl, and fantastic atmospherics—or how they significantly enriched the quality of life of the average New Orleanian. Yet at least a residual memory remains of the stores. Not so regarding the life of the master: the visionary, marketing wizard, and consumer crusader who put it all together. Almost no one knows his story.

This is tragic. For having extensively surveyed the impressive trajectory of his biography, it is now abundantly clear that John G. Schwegmann during his lifetime was nothing short of a folk hero —an extraordinary individual who rose above his time and place to both envision and bring about a heaven on earth for the common people. True enough, his version of heaven tended to be both quirky and funky. But so is New Orleans itself! In appealing to all masses and classes of the city—the poor and rich, the struggling and thriving, slackers and hard workers alike—John distilled the essence of the Crescent City. In reflecting both the celebratory and resilient spirit of his native hometown, he brought forth a weirdly imaginative consumer paradise. But this was his job. After all, John Schwegmann was the people's grocer.

In *Continuing the Tradition*, a coffee-table-style book published in 1994 commemorating the 125-year history of the Schwegmann family enterprise, John G. Schwegmann's legacy is summed up as follows: He was "an innovator, successful businessman, concerned citizen, and always a warrior for the people."[1] While all true, surely this summation is understated…by an order of magnitude. Yes, John was an "innovator." Yet way beyond that he was a creator, a visionary, even a prophet who conceived and modeled much of the modern retail world way ahead of his time. As far as being a "successful businessman," John left this descriptor in the dust. Much more than being a mere success in business, he achieved the status of major economic force, a powerhouse in his hometown of New Orleans, where he employed thousands and his stores accounted for one-third of all supermarket sales throughout the duration of his ownership (not counting his complete control during the early postwar years).

In further deconstructing the above summary of John's legacy, applying the term "concerned citizen" to him seems weak tea indeed. Rather, he was more like a radical activist, one who constantly placed his reputation on the line for the sake of controversial but heartfelt causes, who was readily willing to sacrifice riches in the service of righteous economics. Finally, the phrase "always a warrior for the people" too smoothly underplays his loftier role as a champion. John was no mere "warrior" but a leader, a commander, a Braveheart with the spirit and fortitude to assemble and lead troops into battle against the oppressor. But he was also Don Quixote, the crazy-quilt knight-errant "willing to march into hell for a heavenly cause." Yes, John believed deeply in the impossible dream.

IF TODAY JOHN'S STORY IS LITTLE KNOWN, how can it begin to be remembered and properly appreciated? A reasonable method employed here is to divide his legacy into two spheres: a legacy of accomplishment; and a legacy of values and meaning. Included in the first sphere are all his achievements in the realms of retailing, marketing, and politics. Prime examples include his prophetic big-box prototypes, which prefigured the supercenter and hypermarket decades in advance of their mass appearance; his institution of "everyday low prices" in the 1950s, way before Walmart even existed; and his never-matched personalized approach to advertising and promotion, sustained over decades. Prodigious and numerous as his achievements are, however, they are not enumerated here. This book is already bursting with examples of John's inventions and trendsetting innovations in every area of business and society he touched. Indeed, this biography is itself a testament to his legacy of accomplishment.

What remains to be explored is the deeper dimension of his legacy—namely, the realm of values and meaning. Paradoxically, the Schwegmann story actually stands out in sharper relief in this metaphysical realm than in his record of physical accomplishments, as it is less focused on passing facts than on enduring truths. From this perspective, it is clear that John's legacy contains qualities that can outlast the collapse of his retail empire.

First and foremost, the people's grocer will live on forever in the timeless pantheon of New Orleans merchants such as D. H. Holmes,

McKenzie's, K&B, Maison Blanche, and select others who through spirited business practices have permanently colored the character of the Crescent City. Here the meaning of John's life—his soul-bending desire to marry the supposedly opposing principles of self-enrichment and serving the public interest—finds fulfillment in his elevation to the metropolitan equivalent of "sainthood." Of course, the meaning of his life could be fulfilled to an even greater degree if he were to be rightfully recognized as a prime moving force in the making of the modern retail world. But that is a matter for business historians to evaluate in light of newly uncovered evidence.

Besides possessing enduring *meaning*—a meaning enshrined in local mythology and hopefully eventually honored in business history—John's legacy also has lasting *value*. This is seen most clearly in his inspiring personal example. For fans of the American Dream, John's life trajectory perfectly mirrors the Horatio Alger story: a classic rags-to-riches tale of hard work and courage leading to success. On the surface, then, John provides a positive role model for young people.

Yet even for those older and wiser, his story contains an uplifting dimension. For within himself he cultivated tremendous stores of self-discipline, drive, and confidence. Regarding confidence—without which discipline and drive would not have mattered so much—John's self-esteem can be seen as an acquired trait gained in a hard-won internal battle over an earlier sense of inferiority. What is so notable about John's example is that he replaced inferiority not with a sense of superiority but with a tough-minded apprehension of a rough human equality. Thus in his mind he stood on a level playing field with everyone, no matter how rich or smart, privileged or powerful. In one particularly pithy expression of this attitude, John once boasted: "The only way to beat me is to cheat me."

IN TERMS OF SOCIAL VALUES, John's enduring legacy resonates on several levels. First, he represents the by-now almost-lost conception of the retailer as personal interface between producer and consumer. According to John, inhabiting this crucial position within the distribution chain grants great privileges to the merchant but also comes with weighty responsibilities. Accordingly, a major retailer reaping abundant riches from a community must also bend every effort to retain a direct personal connection with that community and not disappear into the mists of corporate identity. The alternative is complete alienation of the distribution chain, in which personal human interaction is at best an afterthought—pretty much the situation that exists today. As for John, his old-fashioned values are expressed firmly and directly: "I am the last link in the chain between the producer and customer. My relationship should be a personal one."[2]

Beyond the value inherent in striving to maintain a personal retail relationship with customers—a stance that takes responsibility seriously—his social legacy extends even deeper into the value he placed on commitment to community. Providing a stark alternative to the expansionist ethos of conventional corporate philosophy, the "stay local" movement of recent years trumpets the benefits of community allegiance. There are, of course, economic advantages to be gained from following the local ideal—primarily that wealth and employment remain at home. But cultural advantages also accrue to the community-hugging matrix, such as the promotion of self-reliance and resilience. Less talked about for obvious reasons, the stay local movement also helps set the stage for coping with the coming age of resource limits, now on the horizon.

In John's case, his "act local, think global" mindset allowed him to import food from all over the world even while remaining focused on New Orleans. His business stayed here, his financial resources remained here, and he communicated to the citizenry in a thick native accent. Clearly, John Schwegmann loved New Orleans so much that he had no desire to set up shop anywhere else. He also felt a need to protect and nurture the city "so that we may all prosper together."[3]

Perhaps in his uncommon devotion to the "common good" of New Orleans, John simply acted out an inflated view of himself as some updated version of the Kingfish, Huey Long, who stuck up for regular people against "royalist" interests. Then again, maybe John was a would-be royalist himself, perceiving his role as a perpetual incarnation of Rex, the King of Carnival, whose motto is *Pro Bono Publico* ("for the public good"). While these suppositions may seem fanciful, they might not be so far-fetched after all. Consider John's strong identification with his German heritage, along with his deep Europhilia. A recessive aristocratic impulse could conceivably have been activated as John grew in wealth and power. In Peter H. Wilson's massive tome, *The Thirty Years War*, he describes the roles of the typical princeling in sixteenth-century Germany under the Austrian empire.

> A lord exercising jurisdiction over a village would expect the deference of its inhabitants, a share of their produce and some of their time and labor for certain tasks. In return, he or she was expected to protect their interests against malevolent outsiders, uphold their communal distinctiveness within the wider imperial framework, and to intervene in the management of their internal affairs to resolve serious problems.[4]

In transposing this feudal description into its democratic-era equivalent, it is easy to see the former German prince as a successful merchant utilizing the modern tools of marketing to instill customer loyalty in the local populace. As a result, the citizens provide tribute to the merchant in the form of their patronage and income. And in John's case, they even occasionally volunteer time and money on behalf of his crusades. But according to the old ways, John also owes much to the people in return for their loyalty. He is obligated to protect the local community from malevolent predators (price fixers and spendthrift politicians), to preserve his city's distinctive culture (against American homogenizing tendencies), and to shoulder the burden of conflict resolution (by serving in elective office). On the face of it, then, John's actions certainly look like a cultural survival of older patterns of "German freedom."

Besides the more uplifting personal and social aspects of his legacy, John's story also carries a more somber value. In this it serves as a memento mori, a reminder of death. For his career reveals in all its triumph and tragedy the paradoxically fragile nature of power. Consider that a leading institution built up over more than a century out of inspired leadership, tremendous effort, and dauntless courage can collapse in an instant, leaving nary a trace. To those of a literary bent, what surely comes to mind is "Ozymandias," Percy Shelley's immortal poem reflecting on the utter impermanence of a once-powerful ruler and his long-forgotten empire.

Fortunately in this regard, John left a final legacy concerning the meaning and value of posterity. Posterity does not consist so much in building everlasting edifices, he seems to say, but in remaining passionately loyal to the continuity of shared life. Yes, his stores are all gone now—repurposed, rotting, or torn down; their very name, once symbolizing brilliance now reduced to a dull logo. Yet despite all the destruction, an intensely emotional record remains: an immense outpouring of anecdotes, opinions, observations, recollections, rants and raves, proverbs and jokes, and heartfelt sentiments, all preserving an overwhelmingly vivid memory of a distant time and place. He clearly intended for these memories to live on. Consider how John ended one of his numerous remembrances of life in old New Orleans (appearing, of course, in a weekly ad): "If you find this history of interest, you might want to cut it out and save it for your grandchildren."[5]

In summing up John's legacy, consider the praise bestowed on him by John Maginnis: "At his retirement in 1981 from the Public Service Commission, John Schwegmann was honored as one whose tangible, undeniable contribution to the quality of life of the average Orleanian ranked next to Jean Lafitte's of two centuries past."[6] Wow! One of the city's premier modern political analysts actually compared John Schwegmann to Jean Lafitte, the "good" pirate, who through renegade beneficence and daring defense of New Orleans became a folk hero.

In doing justice to this equivalence, perhaps it is time to formally recognize John's fundamental role in contributing to the past greatness of New Orleans and consider how his example could be a positive influence in furthering the city's future. For starters, the city could erect some sort of monument dedicated to the business genius of its "Born in the Bywater" native son. This recognition could go even further with the declaration of a John Schwegmann Day, a celebration of food discounting complete with a forum devoted to his life and times. As for American business history, it is time to acknowledge how John G. Schwegmann pioneered modern retailing, and how he fought with every fiber of his being to lay the foundation for the world's first great consumer society.

Notes

ABBREVIATIONS USED

AP	Marc Levinson, *The Great A&P and the Struggle for Small Business in America*. New York: Hill and Wang, 2011.
BC	Joan B. Garvey and Mary Lou Widmer, *Beautiful Crescent: A History of New Orleans*. Covington (La.): Garmer Press, 2009.
Cabildo tape	John Gerald Schwegmann, interview by Dorothy Schlesinger, August 12, 1975, audiocassette. Friends of the Cabildo Oral History Program: New Orleans Public Library, Louisiana Division.
CT	Richard A. Reso, *Continuing the Tradition: A History of the Schwegmann Company, 1869-1994*. New Orleans: n.p., 1994.
FT	Anthony J. Greco, "John Schwegmann and Fair Trade Laws." Master's thesis, University of New Orleans, 1971.
JFSI	John Francis Schwegmann, interview by author. New Orleans, May 24, 2011. Several subsequent follow-up interviews.
MSBI	Margie Schwegmann-Brown, interview by author. New Orleans, July 9, 2012. Several subsequent follow-up interviews.
OF	"Just Like Meeting an Old Friend." Fourteen-installment series on New Orleans and Schwegmann family history ran weekly (Wednesdays) in the *New Orleans Times-Picayune* between June and September 1978. Each installment delineated here by number: OF 1 (June 28, sec. 3, p. 14); OF 2 (July 5, p. 16); OF 3 (July 12, p. 13); OF 4 (July 19, p. 17); OF 5 (July 26, sec. 2, p. 8); OF 6 (August 2, p.9); OF 7 (August 9, p. 13); OF 8 (August 16, sec. 2, p. 20); OF 9 (August 23, sec. 2, p.8); OF 10 (August 30, p. 13); OF 11 (September 6, p. 24); OF 12 (September 13, sec. 5, p. 8); OF 13 (September 20, p. 13); OF 14 (September 27, sec. 2, p. 14).
SG	Warren B. Nation, "A Study of Supermarket Growth and Its Economic Significance." Ph.D. diss., University of Alabama, 1957.
TP	*New Orleans Times-Picayune*.

Note: All newspaper page number citations used in abbreviations and subsequently in endnotes refer to section one of the paper unless otherwise indicated.

CHAPTER 1. VANISHING LEGACY: THE RETAIL GENIUS FROM NEW ORLEANS

1 Corroborative evidence for most retail innovations is presented in chapters 12 and 16, which focus on Schwegmann's Airline and Gentilly stores, respectively.

2 Richard Campanella, "Long Before Hurricane Katrina, There Was Sauvé's Crevasse, One of the Worst Floods in New Orleans History," TP, June 11, 2014.

3 In the extensive literature on New Orleans, surprisingly little attention is paid to the downriver areas east of the city—and certainly not to the neighborhood known today as the Bywater. A particularly rich storehouse of historical description about the old "Ninth Ward of the Third District" is found in Schwegmann's fourteen-installment "Just Like Meeting an Old Friend" series. Less expansive, though still valuable, information on the Bywater is derived mainly from four sources: BC; Richard Campanella's *Geographies of New Orleans*; the Preservation Resource Center of New Orleans, at prcno.org/ programs/preservationprint/piparchives/2009 PIP/October 2009/26; and wikipedia.org/wiki/Bywater_New_Orleans.

4 Richard Campanella, *Geographies of New Orleans* (Lafayette: Center for Louisiana Studies, 2006), p. 254.

5 For an invaluable source in helping to untangle the confusion regarding the origins and overlapping of the Third District and Ninth Ward, see Campanella, "The Turbulent History Behind the Seven New Orleans Municipal Districts," TP, October 9, 2013.

6 Mapping of Bywater boundaries is inconsistent from source to source. Here boundaries are distilled into their simplest form.

7 BC, p. 55; James Haskins, *The Creoles of Color of New Orleans* (New York: Thomas Crowell Co., 1975).

8 The portrait presented of the Bywater in its "Golden Age" is a composite drawn from OF 1, OF 2, OF 3, OF 4, and OF 5.

CHAPTER 2. GRANDFATHER GARRET: RECKLESS ADVENTURER AS RETAIL ENTREPRENEUR

1 Grandfather Garret Schwegmann's story has been pieced together from several, sometimes conflicting, sources. These include chapter 1, "Prologue," in CT, pp. 3-24; chapter 3, "History of the Schwegmann Enterprise," in SG, pp. 48-57; OF 1; and the Cabildo tape.

2 Cabildo tape.

3 BC, p. 115.

4 CT, p. 5.

5 Henke family history is documented in some detail in OF 1. Other sources include CT, p. 5; SG, pp. 49-51; and the Cabildo tape.

6 SG, p. 49: "The daily chore of buying groceries [at the original French Market] became a conglomeration of higgling and haggling over prices...."

7 On the Cabildo tape, John erroneously (or perhaps with tongue-in-cheek) refers to his grandmother Mary as "the boss's daughter."

8 AP, p. 58: "Given the industry's high turnover, many [old-time grocery] stores were in business for only a year or two...."

9 The New Orleans Notarial Archives is the depository for "Conveyance Office Books" (COBs) and other materials relating to land purchases made throughout the city's history. Officially known as the Orleans Parish Clerk of Court: Land Records Division, the Notarial Archives cited here contain references to both COB numbers and page (folio) numbers. Thus the reference to Mrs. Theodore Lederer's purchase of a two-lot property from Mrs. Charles F. Daunoy, finalized on Nov. 1, 1866, is cited as follows: Notarial Archive 1866, COB 91, p. 528.

10 The entire issue of when Garret's original store opened and where it was located seems to have been almost deliberately obscured. In CT, for example, a passage on p. 7 clearly calls into question the official family story that Garret's first store opened in 1869 on Piety and Burgundy: "While recorded history does not offer us much during these early years, we do find a listing in 1871 of his business operating on Dauphine Street near Port in the City Directory." Meanwhile, CT accepts the official family version on p. 1. For his part, Warren Nation (in SG, p., 51) explicitly states: "Garret Schwegmann opened the first Schwegmann store in New Orleans on the corner of Engine and Dauphine streets."

11 SG, p. 56.

12 For the various locations of Garret's stores, see CT, pp. 7-9; SG, p. 56; and "How Time Does Fly," Schwegmann ad, TP, August 27, 1956, p. 27.

13 Cabildo tape.

14 Ibid.

15 Notarial Archive 1880, COB 113, pp. 456-7, 463.

16 On the Cabildo tape, John mentions in passing that an uncle in Cincinnati once gave him a piggy bank as a gift.

17 Notarial Archive 1883, COB 120, pp. 121-2; Notarial Archive 1889, COB 132, p. 162.

CHAPTER 3. UNCLE GARRET AND FATHER JOHN: TWO TYPES OF SUCCESS

1 Cabildo tape.

2 Garret Jr.'s story is chronicled in CT, pp. 8-19; SG, pp. 57-8; and OF 1 and OF 2. More emotionally charged remembrances are heard on the Cabildo tape.

3 Mr. Oemichen's role in Garret Jr.'s career development is discussed in CT, p. 11; OF 1.

4 The tame version appears in SG, p. 56. The tragic version is told on the Cabildo tape.

5 See CT, p. 17, where the Piety Street store is described as "the largest retail grocery in the city."

6 SG, p. 57.

7 Details about Jake Emmer and his family appear in OF 2.

8 The "millionaire" quote comes from the Cabildo tape; the more tempered assessment from CT, p. 19.

9 The most potent memories available of John Senior's life come from John Junior, who writes about his father in OF 2 and OF 3 and speaks about him, often with anger and remorse, on the Cabildo tape. Nation offers a spare but more objective view of John Sr. in SG, pp. 57-8.

10 Frey family history is presented in vivid detail in OF 2.

11 AP, p. 40.

12 OF 2.

CHAPTER 4. REFLECTIONS ON OLD-TIME CORNER GROCERY STORES

1 This chapter owes its construction to the deep scholarship and superb portraiture of old-time grocery stores provided by Marc Levinson in AP. See especially pp. 7-8, 40-2, 49-50, 58, and 76-81.

2 AP, p. 7.

3 Ibid., p. 40.

4 Ibid., pp. 80-1:"The average food store…had a very short life expectancy…. In Pittsburgh, nearly half of new grocery stores ceased business within a year, and two-thirds were gone within three years. In Buffalo, the rate of exit was even higher…."

5 Ibid., p. 78. "The average cost of providing home delivery in 1923 came to 1.2 percent of a store's total sales, an amount equal to two-thirds of a typical store's profit."

6 Alan Trachtenberg, *The Incorporation of America: Culture and Society in the Gilded Age* (New York: Hill and Wang, 1982).

7 AP, p. 51.

8 Ibid., pp. 41-42, 126.

CHAPTER 5. SCHWEGMANN BROTHERS GROCERY COMPANY: A SUPERIOR CORNER STORE

1 SG, p. 57.

2 The tour around the Piety Street store is based on descriptions provided in SG, pp. 52-6; OF 3; and the Cabildo tape.

3 CT, p. 17; OF 2.

4 OF 11.

5 OF 1.

6 Ibid.

7 OF 2.

8 Ibid.

9 Ibid.

10 Prominent New Orleans food wholesalers and jobbers from the old days are listed in OF 2.

11 OF 3.

12 Harry Vin Arny, "Pharmacy in the South," *American Journal of Pharmacy*, vol. LXII, Fourth Series, vol. XX (Philadelphia, 1890), pp. 628-30.

13 On quartees, see Vin Arny, cited in note 12 above; SG, p. 52; and OF 3.

14 On the history of New Orleans public markets: Nicole Taylor, "The Public Market System of New Orleans" (Master's thesis, University of New Orleans, 2005), pp. 11-29.

15 OF 6.

Chapter 6. John G. Schwegmann: Born in the Poor Glorious Third

1 Richard Campanella tells of slang terms—"Dirty Third," "Poor Third," and (in a mocking fashion) "Glorious Third"—used in the old days to describe the least affluent district of the city. See Campanella, *Geographies of New Orleans* (Lafayette: Center for Louisiana Studies, 2006), p. 254.

2 Pbs.org/wbgh/amex/fever/timeline/timeline2.

3 Wikipedia.org/wiki/1915_New_Orleans_hurricane.

4 Cabildo tape; OF 3.

5 OF 4.

6 Cabildo tape.

7 CT, p. 28.

8 Cabildo tape.

9 CT, p. 28; OF 3.

10 For John's relations with the Freys and a description of their home and its fate, see OF 2.

11 References to religion in the Schwegmann family and the Old Bywater are scattered throughout OF 3, OF 4, and OF 6.

12 OF 3.

13 Cabildo tape.

14 Ibid.

15 OF 2.

16 CT, p. 27; Cabildo tape.

17 Cabildo tape.

18 Ibid.

19 On characters at Holy Trinity school: OF 3.

20 For the story of John's move to the new house and the people he encountered there, see OF 3.

21 AP, p. 119.

22 OF 3.
23 John's experiences at the Little Red Church are related in OF 4.

Chapter 7. From High School Dropout to Real Estate Magnate

1 Cabildo tape; JFSI.
2 OF 2; OF 4; SG, p. 59.
3 Cabildo tape; OF 3.
4 On John's first job as an electrician's assistant, and the electrifying of New Orleans in general: OF 2; OF 4; SG, p. 59.
5 OF 2; SG, p. 60.
6 SG, p. 60; CT, p. 28.
7 John mentions, but only barely, his feelings about his mother on the Cabildo tape.
8 SG, p. 61.
9 On John's tentative career as a barber: OF 4; CT, p. 29.
10 The story of cosmopolitan Aunt Helen's rescue of nephew John from the clutches of parochial Aunt Mary by taking him on a steamship voyage to Alsace-Lorraine is mentioned in CT (p. 29) but elaborated on in OF 4.
11 On John's career in the real estate business: OF 2; CT, pp. 29-31; Cabildo tape.
12 JFSI.
13 Jonathan D. Rose, "The Incredible HOLC? Mortgage Relief During the Great Depression," January 15, 2010 (iga.ucdavis.edu).
14 Cabildo tape.
15 Ibid.
16 Ibid.
17 SG, p. 62.

Chapter 8. The Supermarket Revolution

1 Cabildo tape.
2 A voracious reader of the business and trade press, John was no doubt familiar with the well-known retail analyst Max M. Zimmerman, who authored a series of seminal articles on supermarkets in the mid-1930s. See, for example, "Super Markets" (article no. 3), *Printers' Ink*, July 23, 1936.
3 AP, p. 56.
4 SG, pp. 7-10.
5 AP, p. 131.
6 OF 12. Compare John Schwegmann's pithy aphorism with a similar, though more lumbering, formulation expressed by A&P's John Hartford: "We would rather sell 200 pounds of butter at 1 cent profit than 100 pounds at 2 cents profit" (AP, p. 4).
7 SG, p. 42.
8 Ibid., p. 44.

9 Ibid., pp. 24, 30-2.

10 AP, p. 77.

11 On the accounting differences between return on investment vs. return on sales: ibid., pp. 102-3, 107.

12 Ibid., p. 127.

13 On pre-supermarket prototypes in general, and Ralph's in particular: SG, pp. 19-23; AP, p. 128.

14 On King Kullen: SG, pp. 24-26; AP, p. 129.

15 On Big Bear and other early "cheapie" supermarket manifestations: SG. pp. 24-6; AP, p. 130.

16 SG, p. 27.

17 AP, p. 149.

18 On the circus/carnival atmosphere associated with original supermarkets: SG, pp. 8, 30; AP, p. 132.

Chapter 9. A Pure Devotee of Economy Plans His First Store

1 Cabildo tape; OF 2.

2 SG, p. 72.

3 CT, p. 27.

4 John's daughter, Margie, verifies his zealous devotion to reading the business and trade press in MSBI.

5 SG, p. 63.

6 SG, p. 64; Cabildo tape. John's original chronicler and John himself state explicitly that it was his idea to go self-service. Note, however, that some accounts claim self-service was his father's idea.

7 OF 2; CT, pp. 21-3.

8 Cabildo tape.

9 CT, p. 29; OF 12.

10 The little-known and perhaps embroidered story of John's confrontation over the public markets with Mayor Maestri is told in skeletal form in CT, pp. 29-31, and elaborated on in OF 11.

11 SG, p. 37.

12 On wartime materials scarcities: SG, pp. 37-9; AP, pp. 238-9.

13 SG, p. 64.

14 OF 12.

15 Cabildo tape.

16 A brief biography of John's right-hand man, Wilfred I. Meyer, appears in OF 4.

Chapter 10. The Original Schwegmann Brothers Giant Super Market

1 Cabildo tape.

2 This chapter is primarily based on an extraordinarily detailed account of

Schwegmann's St. Claude store contained in chapter 5, "The First Super-market," in SG, pp. 96-134.

3 SG, pp. 42-3.
4 Ibid, p. 24.
5 Ibid, pp. 73-80.
6 Ibid, pp. 110-14.
7 Ibid, pp. 125-28.
8 Ibid., pp. 109-10. The "Foodtown Study," conducted in second quarter 1954 by *Progressive Grocer*, analyzed five Foodtown Supermarkets located in Cleveland, Ohio, chosen because they were considered the most successful supermarkets of their time.

CHAPTER 11. MARKETING, MORALITY, AND THE PEOPLE'S GROCER PERSONA

1 OF 11.
2 JFSI.
3 MSBI.
4 SG, p. 82.
5 SG, pp. 82-83. Nation underscores the innovativeness of John's weekly promotional discounting approach, noting that other retailers soon copied him.
6 SG, p. 85. On distributing circulars, John complained: "The young people of the recent generation simply will not work at such a menial task."
7 SG, p. 91.
8 CT, p. 41.
9 SG, pp. 85-86. John's print advertising philosophy was straightforward: "Ads must be personalized if they are going to enjoy the greatest amount of readability."
10 CT, pp. 59-61.
11 SG, p. 87.
12 The faux coat-of-arms is depicted and its legend elaborated on in OF 13. The ad is also reproduced in CT, p. 63.
13 On John's deep sense of responsibility to community: SG, pp. 85-7.
14 Ibid, p. 86.
15 OF 6.
16 A.J. Liebling, *The Earl of Louisiana* (New York: Simon & Schuster, 1961).
17 CT, p. 55.

CHAPTER 12. THE WORLD'S FIRST SUPERCENTER ARISES ON AIRLINE HIGHWAY

1 Msbluestrail.org/blues-trail-markers/highway-61-north.
2 John Davis, *Mafia Kingfish* (New York: New American Library, 1989), p. 74.
3 SG, p. 136.

4 Ibid.

5 JFSI.

6 SG, pp. 69-70.

7 CT, p. 41.

8 Nation's description and analysis of Schwegmann's monumental Airline store in SG forms the backbone of his dissertation. He devotes two chapters to the store: chapter 6, "The Second Store: Statistics" (pp. 135-62); and chapter 7, "The Second Store: Departmental Data" (pp. 163-226).

9 Ibid., p. 140. As Nation states: "There is reason to believe Mr. Schwegmann was one of the first independent store operators to use this principle [front-lot parking] in a single store layout."

10 On standard vs. expanded car/parking lot ratios: ibid., p. 135.

11 On standard supermarket vs. Schwegmann's extra-wide aisles: ibid., p. 142.

12 Ibid., pp. 163-4. Nation here discusses John's improvisatory leasing strategy.

13 Ibid., p. 178. Nation documents how as of the early 1950s only the most tentative steps had yet been taken by supermarkets to incorporate the drugstore format, clearly indicating that Schwegmann was in the forefront of a successful combination of the two previously separate retail concepts.

14 For cultural background and departmental details on the Airline store seafood section: ibid., pp. 185-7.

15 On the vast magnitude of the Airline store's liquor department and Schwegmann's "illegal" liquor discounting: ibid., pp. 191-4.

16 On the Airline store's locally competitive sporting goods section: ibid., pp. 195-7.

17 For an extended discussion of the development of Airline's drug department, including the addition of pharmaceuticals, see ibid., pp. 170-8.

18 Consider, for example, the controversy that raged in Louisiana over the sale of Hadacol: Ford M. Clay, *Coozan Dudley LeBlanc: From Huey Long to Hadacol* (Gretna [La.]: Pelican Publishing, 1973).

19 On John's insulin gambit: SG, p 171; FT, pp. 19-20.

20 On the lunch counter: SG, pp. 203-4.

21 On the bar: ibid., pp. 205-7.

22 Ibid., pp. 210-25. Includes detailed discussion of all leased departments.

23 See ibid., pp. 220-2, for a clear description of the forerunner of a garden center.

CHAPTER 13. SCHWEGMANN'S CRUSADE: A HISTORY OF FAIR TRADE LAWS

1 SG, pp. 272-3. For his account of early discount stores, Nation relies on F.M. Lehman, "The Discount House," *Journal of Retailing*, vol. 19, February 1943, pp. 19-26.

2 A technical definition of resale price maintenance is presented in FT, p. 2

3 On the fate of early court cases (1901-22) addressing the legality of RPM: FT, pp. 4-9; SG, pp. 247-8; AP, p. 64.

4 The ramifications of the *Miles* decision are discussed in FT, pp. 5-7.

5 On the Stevens bill: SG, pp. 249-50.
6 Ibid., p. 250.
7 AP, p. 66.
8 Ibid.
9 SG, pp. 250-1.
10 AP, p. 158.
11 Ibid., p. 171.
12 Ibid., p. 146.
13 Ibid. For a full picture of the congressman's populist backlash against chain stores, see chapter 14, "Wright Patman," pp. 151-66.
14 Ibid., pp. 137-9.
15 For a detailed presentation of the 1928 FTC study, see SG, pp. 252-63.
16 AP, p. 118.
17 The non-signer's clause is explained in SG, p. 265; FT, p.11.
18 SG, p. 273; FT, p. 28.
19 FT, pp. 13-14.
20 See ibid., pp. 21-6, for an extended discussion of how and why several major manufacturers, including Westinghouse, Eastman Kodak, and even General Electric, began abandoning their former adherence to fair trade principles from the mid-1950s onward.
21 On the "Schwegmann Interlude": SG, p. 276; FT. p. 52.
22 On McGuire-Keogh: SG, p. 277; FT, p. 19. On John's energetic response to McGuire-Keogh: FT, pp. 82-5.
23 FT, pp. 28, 112-13.

Chapter 14. John the Conqueror: Making the Free World Safe for Discounting

1 FT, pp. 47-9.
2 CT, p. 33.
3 FT, pp. 49-53.
4 Supreme.justia.com/cases/federal/us/341/384/case.
5 FT, p. 18; AP, p. 246. Greco states that the Schwegmann Supreme Court victory in 1951 "dealt the truly crippling blow to resale price maintenance," while in a similar vein Levinson notes that it "dealt a devastating blow" to fair trade.
6 FT, pp. 83-4.
7 CT, p. 39; FT p. 85.
8 FT, p. 85.
9 CT, p. 41.
10 John's constitutional arguments against McGuire are detailed in FT, pp. 53-8.
11 Burton M. Harris, 33 *Harvard Business Review*, 1955, pp. 53-61.
12 On John's battles in favor of prescription drug advertising: FT, pp. 86, 91-4.
13 FT, pp. 65-8; SG, pp. 280-1.
14 FT, pp. 58-65; SG, pp. 281-3.

15 FT, pp. 88-9; SG, pp. 282-3.
16 SG, pp. 283-4.
17 "Louisiana's 'D' Day," Schwegmann ad, TP, July 9, 1956, p. 29; "We Have Been Freed," Schwegmann ad, TP, July 23, 1956, p. 17.
18 Cabildo tape.

CHAPTER 15. COLD WAR CHRONICLES: TRAVELS TO EUROPE AND RUSSIA IN THE 1950S

1   "As I Saw England," TP, October 4, 1954, p. 32; October 18, 1954, p. 28; October 25, 1954, p. 26; November 1, 1954, p. 36.
2   "As I Saw Amsterdam," TP, November 8, 1954, p. 32.
3   "From Amsterdam to Germany," TP, November 15, 1954, p. 27.
4   "Neckermann's Problems in Germany," TP, November 22, 1954, p. 36.
5   "As I Saw Germany," TP, November 29, 1954, p. 40; December 6, 1954, p. 19.
6   "As I Saw Germany and Switzerland," TP, December 13, 1954, p. 36. Also, "As I Saw Switzerland," TP, December 19, 1954, p. 12; January 10, 1955, p. 13.
7   "As I Saw Venice," TP, January 17, 1955, p. 30. Also, "As I Saw Italy," TP, January 24, 1955, p. 24; January 31, 1955, p. 26; February 7, 1955, p. 36.
8   "As I Saw Nice, Monte Carlo, and Barcelona," TP, February 14, 1955, p. 11.
9   "As I Saw Spain's National Sport," TP, February 21, 1955, p. 11.
10 "As I Saw Paris," TP, February 28, 1955, p. 24; March 7, 1955, p. 29; March 14, 1955, p. 36.
11 "As I Saw Versailles, Maxims, and the Folies Bergere," TP, March 21, 1955, p. 21.
12 "Europe As a Whole," TP, March 28, 1955, p. 30.
13 Schwegmann's speech to the Green Meadow Foundation is reproduced in two consecutive ads in TP (appearing July 21 and July 28, 1958) under the title "An Anti-Fair Trade Speech in Zurich, Switzerland."
14 The seventeen-installment series entitled "As I Saw Russia" begins in October 1958 and ends in February 1959. Though it roughly follows an itinerary proceeding from Leningrad through Ukraine to Moscow, the series splinters into a thousand pieces along the way, rendering any detailed citing of specific installments overly complex. For this reason, only the dates and page numbers of the seventeen installments as they appeared in Schwegmann ads in TP are here provided. In 1958: October 6, p. 19; October 13, p. 13; October 20, p. 19; October 27, p. 23; November 3 (n.p.); November 10, p. 25; November 17, p. 27; December 1, p. 27; December 8, p. 27. In 1959: January 5, p. 15; January 12, p. 21; January 19, p. 15; January 19, p. 15; January 26, p. 23; February 2, p. 19; February 11, p. 17; and February 16, p. 25.

CHAPTER 16. EPITOME IN GENTILLY: "THE BIGGEST STORE IN THE WORLD"

1   JFSI.
2   CT, p. 43; OF 12.

3 On the sprawling dimensions of the Gentilly store: "View of the Gentilly Store from the Lobby," TP, September 23, 1957, p. 27; SG, pp. 233-5; CT, pp. 45-7.
4 Material on hypermarkets, superstores, and supercenters is taken from the author's own "Retailing in the 1990s," a syndicated market research study published by Packaged Facts, Inc. (New York, 1989).
5 Although Hypermart USA was not officially discontinued until 2000, Walmart had abandoned its plans for any further expansion of the hypermarket concept by 1992.
6 SG, p. 228, pp. 240-1.
7 OF 7; CT, p. 43.
8 On the size of the Gentilly store and parking lot: SG, pp. 233-5.
9 CT, p. 49; SG, p. 227.
10 CT, p. 43.
11 SG, pp. 228-9.
12 On Schwegmann bonds: SG, pp. 229-33; CT, p. 51; OF 12.
13 SG, p. 233.
14 Ibid., p. 235.
15 "View of the Gentilly Store from the Concourse," TP, September 23, 1957.
16 CT, p. 47.
17 Ibid.
18 Schwegmann ad, TP, February 3, 1958, p. 19.
19 SG, pp. 88-91.
20 On leased departments: ibid., p. 238.
21 John Maginnis, *The Last Hayride* (Baton Rouge: Gris Gris Press, 1984), p. 230.
22 CT, p. 59.
23 OF 12.
24 Greco provides an in-depth discussion of John's extended battles with the Louisiana milk industry in FT, pp. 94-111.
25 Wikipedia.org/wiki/John_G._Schwegmann.

CHAPTER 17. THE PEOPLE'S GROCER TURNS POPULIST POLITICIAN

1 "Fair Trade Foe in Race," TP, July 17, 1955, p. 15.
2 "Right to Work," Schwegmann ad, TP, January 1, 1956, sec. 3, p. 6.
3 "Lucas to Enter Senatorial Race," TP, September 19, 1955, p. 23.
4 Election results, TP, January 20, 1956, p. 4.
5 Fred Kaplan, 1959: *The Year Everything Changed* (Hoboken: John Wiley & Sons, 2009).
6 For evidence of Jefferson Parish's progressivism in the 1950s, see JeffersonHistoricalSociety.com/virtualarchives/1950sJYR.
7 JFSI.
8 Michael L. Kurtz and Morgan D. Peoples, *Earl K. Long: The Saga of Uncle Earl and Louisiana Politics* (Baton Rouge: LSU Press, 1991).
9 "Aims Stressed by Schwegmann," TP, September 26, 1959, sec. 3, p. 11.

10 See, for example, "Rift with Schwegmann in Race Denied by Coci," TP, August 19, 1959, p. 11; "Glover Asserts in Race to Stay," TP, October 18, 1959, p. 1.

11 Election results, TP, December 7, 1959, p. 1.

12 For a mention of the slot machine scandal and Hogan's response from Hawaii: "JID Supports Three in Jeff," TP, February 6, 1961, p. 20. See also "Jeff Crime Held Industrial Curb," TP, February 25, 1961, sec. 3, p. 5.

13 For election results: "Schwegmann Victor in Jeff," TP, February 26, 1961, p. 1; "Demos Swamp GOP Opponents," TP, April 12, 1961, p. 2.

14 See, for example, "$30,000 Worth of Animosity," Schwegmann ad, TP, February 20, 1961, p. 27. For the photo of Dan Hogan: TP, May 11, 1962, sec. 4, p. 11.

15 "Schwegmann Opposes Boggs," TP, May 6, 1962, p. 4.

16 Ibid. Note, though, that Schwegmann spewed this type of invective in speeches and ads throughout the brief 1962 campaign. See, for example: "John Schwegmann for Congress," campaign ad accusing Boggs of socialism, TP, July 26, 1962, sec. 6, p. 9; "Spite Charged by Schwegmann," TP, July 12, 1962, sec. 2, p. 5.

17 "Schwegmann Hits Aid, Taxes," TP, July 24, 1962, sec. 2, p. 8.

18 "US Policy Hit by Schwegmann," TP, July 7, 1962, sec. 2, p. 6..

19 "Won't Promise Job: Candidate," TP, July 3, 1962, p. 3.

20 "Opponent Raps Boggs Position," TP, June 17, 1962.

21 Election results, TP, July 30, 1962, sec. 3, p. 7.

22 Schwegmann endorsed Treen in an ad appearing in TP, November 5, 1962, p. 14

23 Wikipedia.org/wiki/Jimmie_Davis.

24 Schwegmann's positions and first-term voting record is laid out in "Background on Jefferson Candidates," TP, October 29, 1963, sec. 3, p. 2.

25 "US Policy Hit by Schwegmann," TP, July 26, 1962, sec. 2, p. 6.

26 "Bill Providing for Teacher Pay Boost Withdrawn," TP, June 4, 1963, sec. 3 p. 3.

27 John reprises the Wellborn Jack story, featuring a photo of the incident, in a Schwegmann ad, TP, September 9, 1963, p. 19.

28 "Voting Record Index Drafted," TP, March 11, 1963, p. 18; "Solons Voting Record Given," TP, September 8, 1963, p. 15. For TP endorsement, see November 15, 1963, p. 12.

29 Wikipedia.org/wiki/John_McKeithen.

30 "Bill Allowing La. Colleges to Charge Fees Approved," TP, June 1, 1967, sec. 3, p. 4.

31 John lays out his second-term record in an ad titled "Message to the People of Jefferson Parish," TP, October 8, 1967, sec. 3, p. 8.

32 "Atheist/Communist Ban OK'd," TP, June 2, 1967, p. 5.

33 For TP endorsements: October 27, 1967, p. 10; February 2, 1968.

34 Election results, TP, February 7, 1968, pp. 1, 3.

35 "Blasts Leveled by Schwegmann," TP, August 9, 1971, sec. 3, p. 19.

36 Ibid.

37 Ibid.

38 "Candidate Vows to List Sources," TP, July 31, 1971, p. 6.

39 "Governor's Link to LL&T Alleged," TP, October 15, 1971, p. 9.

40 "Chandler Good Guy, Rival Says," TP, September 21, 1971, sec. 2, p. 23.

41 Ibid.

42 Sam Hanna, "Schwegmann Like Earl," *Concordia (La.) Sentinel*, September 8, 1971, reprinted in a Schwegmann ad, TP, September 20, 1971; Margaret Martin, "Schwegmann: Run the State Like a Business," *Shreveport Times*, reproduced in Schwegmann ad, TP, November 3, 1971.

43 Hanna, cited in note 42 above.

44 CT, p. 71.

45 Schwegmann ad, TP, September 24, 1971, p. 23.

46 "Mayor Still Not Backing Candidates for Governor," TP, August 6, 1971, p. 4; "Suit Possible, McKeithen Says," TP, August 25, 1971, p. 4.

47 "Alliance Is Hit by Legislator," TP, August 31, 1971, p. 10; "Adcock Assails Schwegmann," TP, October 20, 1971, p. 16. For Moon Landrieu's quote, see wikipedia.org/wiki/John_G._Schwegmann.

48 "Treen Pledges Auditor Help," TP, October 22, 1971, p. 3.

49 "Bridge Proposal Causes Candidates' Lively Talk," TP, September 22, 1971, p. 20.

50 Martin, cited in note 42 above.

51 "Grocer Pledges Aid for Consumer," TP, August 2, 1975, p. 4.

52 Election results, TP, November 2, 1975, p. 1. On Lawrence Chehardy's influence: "Schwegmann Vows Honesty," TP, November 2, 1975, p. 10.

CHAPTER 18. THE EX-CHAMPION'S FINAL BOUT: NO TO THE SUPERDOME!

1   Pro-Superdome ad, TP, November 2, 1966, p. 19. This ad appears in a collection of correspondence and clippings contained in Special Collections at the University of New Orleans, Earl K. Long Library, under the heading: John Schwegmann, Jr. collection, Papers, 1966-1978, Archives 225. Much of the material in this chapter has been gleaned from this file.

2   Dave Dixon, *The Saints, the Superdome, and the Scandal: An Insider's Perspective* (Gretna [La.]: Pelican Publishing, 2008), p. 108.

3   "The Making of a Super Syndicate: How the Whole Scandal Works," *New Orleans Courier*, August 31-September 6, 1973.

4   Dixon, pp. 15-36. Discussion of Dixon's background and early adulthood.

5   Ibid., pp. 37-8.

6   Ibid., pp. 48-9.

7   Ibid., pp. 84-8.

8   Ibid., pp. 88-91.

9   Ibid., p. 98.

10 Allan Katz, "Reflections on a Diet of Dollars: I Told You So, I Toldyouso," *New Orleans States-Item*, May 18, 1973, p. 31.

11 "Off the Cuff: About the Domed Stadium," Schwegmann ad, TP, April 3, 1967.

12 Dixon, pp. 85-7.

13 "Domed Stadium Site Chosen on Recommendation—Graham," TP, January 8, 1967.

14 "Millionaire Grocer Schwegmann Refuses to Enter Dome," *Baton Rouge Morning Advocate*, February 23, 1978.

15 "Schwegmann Says," Schwegmann ad, TP, November 8, 1968. p. 29.

16 "More on the Domed Stadium," Schwegmann ad, TP, April 1, 1968.

17 "More on the Dome!" Schwegmann ad, TP, October 6, 1969, p. 17.

18 "John Schwegmann Answers Governor McKeithen's Attempted Character Assassination," Schwegmann ad, undated (appearing in John Schwegmann papers, Archives 225).

19 "Dome Stadium Interest Rate Amendment," Schwegmann ad (two parts), TP, September 28, 1970, and October 2, 1970. See also "Equal Time," Schwegmann ad, TP, October 12, 1970, p. 23.

20 "The Real Hero of the La. Election," *Lake Charles (La.) American Press*, November 7, 1970.

21 "Credit Where Due," editorial, *New Orleans States-Item*, August 12, 1971, p. 8.

22 Schwegmann press release, July 11, 1971. A two-page anti-dome rant against his opponents.

23 "Fool Me Once, Shame on You...Fool Me Twice, Shame on Me," Schwegmann ad, TP, April 5, 1971.

24 "Schwegmann Plans Trip for Anti-Dome Campaign," *New Orleans States-Item*, July 27, 1971. See also a mock-letter written in Cajun dialect to Mr. Rockefeller titled "Et, La Bas!" Schwegmann ad, TP, October 1, 1971, p. 27.

25 Dixon, pp. 107-11.

CHAPTER 19. SUCKER PUNCH: UNEXPECTED COLLAPSE OF THE SCHWEGMANN EMPIRE

1 CT, pp. 49-51. Details provided on locations, sizes, and features of new Schwegmann stores built in the 1960s and 1970s.

2 Southeastern architecture.blogspot.com/2013/04/Schwegmann_brothers_stores.

3 MSBI. Margie mentioned that her father used to buy houses for relatives and friends seemingly on a whim, "the way some people buy shoes."

4 On Guy, the Magnolia School, and the Louise Davis Center, see CT, pp. 71-5

5 JFSI.

6 MSBI.

7 Kent B. Germany, *New Orleans After the Promises: Poverty, Citizenship, and the Search for the Great Society* (Athens and London: University of Georgia Press, 2007), pp. 14-17.

8 On Gigi, Peppy, and John's love for dogs in general: OF 10.

9 John's cultural tastes are discussed at length in OF 11.

10 John Francis Schwegmann's youth and early adulthood are chronicled in CT, pp, 79-83.

11 JFSI.

12 Ibid.

13 CT, p. 87.

14 Ibid., pp. 85-91. Explains John Francis's decision to drop "Brothers" from the corporate name and details the locations and dimensions of his new Schwegmann stores of the 1980s and early 1990s.

15 On John Francis's passion for and accomplishments in real estate development: ibid., pp. 103-7.

16 On his modernized approach to marketing and advertising: ibid, pp. 95-7.

17 JFSI.

18 Wikipedia.org/wiki/Loblaw_Companies. Note that a certain familiarity with Loblaw's post-1985 competitive moves in the U.S. retail market comes from the author's own market study, "Retailing in the 1990s," cited in note 4, chapter 16.

19 "Schnucks Was Able to Keep a Secret, but Canadian Law Forced Disclosure," *St. Louis Post-Dispatch*, January 17, 1995.

20 "Schwegmann's Is Reportedly in Agreement to Be Acquired," *Supermarket News*, November 25, 1996; "Schwegmann's Is Acquired by Kohlberg; "CEO Retires," *Supermarket News*, February 24, 1997.

21 "Schwegmann in Chapter 11; Plans to Sell All 24 Units," *Supermarket News*, April 5, 1999.

22 MSBI.

23 Findlaw.com/us-5th-circuit/1158712.

CHAPTER 20. SCHWEGMANN AS FOLK HERO

1 CT, p. 77.

2 SG, p. 314.

3 Ibid., p. 315.

4 Peter H. Wilson, *The Thirty Years War: Europe's Tragedy* (Cambridge: Harvard University Press, 2009), p. 16.

5 This humble appeal to posterity was expressed in John's original "Just Like Meeting an Old Friend" series of just three parts, with the quote appearing in TP on May 21, 1967, sec. 3, p. 22. The series later morphed into the magnificent fourteen-installment OF opus published in 1978, as detailed.

6 Maginnis, *The Last Hayride*, p. 230.

Acknowledgments

As an independent researcher and author unattached to any university, I was wonderfully surprised in writing this book to encounter such a uniformity of helpful librarians. No matter their institutional affiliation—be it government, academic, or museum—librarians across the board could not have been more gracious in their assistance. Here I offer a special salute to librarians at the New Orleans Public Library, the University of New Orleans, the University of Alabama at Tuscaloosa, and various New Orleans and Louisiana public and private archives. I would especially like to thank Sally K. Reeves, Consulting Archivist at the New Orleans Notarial Archives; Miriam Childs, Director of the Law Library of Louisiana; and Connie L. Phelps, Chair, Services Department at UNO, Earl K. Long Library. Professor Phelps, in particular, went above and beyond the call of duty in her labyrinthine efforts to track down the family of the photographer who took the picture that now graces the cover of *The People's Grocer*.

This project could not have sustained itself without the active encouragement of two individuals. From day one, Jessica Dorman, the Director of Publications at The Historic New Orleans Collection, has open-heartedly offered her precious time and acute thoughts on this project, thereby inspiring me to continue. I could not have wrapped up this book, though, without the enthusiastic encouragement of James D. Wilson, Associate Director for the University of Louisiana at Lafayette Press. James has been more than generous in helping to get this book published.

Playing a less direct, but no less influential, role in providing encouragement to pursue this project have been several friends. These include Dar Wolnick, a community activist, public market consultant, and acerbic humorist with a keen insight into retail processes; Bill Milkowski, an internationally renowned music writer and the best kind of friend, who originally persuaded me to move down to New Orleans and encouraged this publishing effort; Frier McCollister, a theater manager and producer who has always supported my creative endeavors; and Beth Leuchten, who is smart, insightful, and the fastest reader in the west. And speaking of encouragement, I would be remiss not to mention Mitchell Vaillant, my adventurous former runnin' pardner from New York City who accompanied me on my first trip to a Schwegmann's supermarket.

In terms of the content of this biography, I owe a tremendous debt of gratitude to both Margie Schwegmann-Brown and John Francis Schwegmann. Each in their own individual ways offered honest and copious insights into their family legacy. Without their sincere sharing of memories and feelings, this book could never have been written.

Ultimately, all the inspiration, encouragement, and actual capacity to be able to write this epic biography has come from John Schackai III and Lynne Schackai. It was John's idea to write this book in the first place, and Lynne has been preternaturally supportive every step of the way. I cannot thank them enough for having faith in me. Finally, I would like to thank you know who you are. My deepest love and unfathomable respect forever.

For its part, Neutral Ground Press would also like to thank John and Lynne Schackai for being steadfast pillars in holding up this endeavor. Kim Rainey, Tana Coman, and John Schackai IV must also be thanked for sharing their technical wizardry. A special acknowledgment goes out to Keli Rylance for pointing the way through the tall grass. Regarding the photos that appear in this book, we would like to thank Rebecca Smith at THNOC, Judy Held, and especially Margie Schwegmann-Brown and John F. Schwegmann, who shared their personal photos through this book with the general public.

Index

388   INDEX